DRAMA AND THEATRE IN NIGERIA:

A CRITICAL SOURCE BOOK

Other Nigeria Magazine Special Publications

DRAMA AND THEATRE IN NIGERIA:

A CRITICAL SOURCE BOOK

by

YEMI OGUNBIYI

© Nigeria Magazine 1981

ISBN 978–173–008–0

Text set in 11/12 pt Linotron 202 Times, printed and bound
in Great Britain at The Pitman Press, Bath for
Nigeria Magazine,
Department of Culture,
Federal Ministry of Social Development,
Youth, Sports and Culture, Lagos

CONTENTS

v

ACKNOWLEDGEMENTS

During the course of putting this anthology together, I have acquired debts of gratitude to various persons and institutions:

To Ulli Beier for permission to reprint "E. K. Ogunmola: A personal Memoir," from *Neo-African Literature and Culture: Essays in Memory of Janheinz John* ed. by Bernth Lindfors and Ulla Schild, Wiesbaden, Heymann, 1976;

To Professor M. J. C. Echeruo, for permission to reprint "The Dramatic Limits of Igbo Ritual", from *Research in African Literatures*;

Dapo Adelugba, for permission to reprint "Trance and Theatre: The Nigerian Experience", from *Ufhamu*;

Professor J. A. Adedeji and the University of Ibadan Press for permission to reprint "Alarinjo: The Traditional Yoruba Travelling Theatre", from *Theatre in Africa*, edited by Ogunba and Irele;

The Nigerian Field for permission to reprint R. T. E. Ellison's "A Bornu Puppet Show";

African Language Studies and C. G. B. Gidley for permission to reprint "Yankamanci: The Craft of the Hausa Comedians"; and Demas Nwoko and *Presence Africaine* for permission to reprint extracts of "Search for a New African Theatre".

I am also immensely grateful to all the authors whose essays are presented in this volume. Their beliefs in this collective endeavour made the task of editing an easier one. Special mention ought to be made of those whose essays were specially written for the volume. They are, Dr. Ossie Enekwe, Mr. Kofoworola, Mr. Segun Olusola, Mr. Femi Euba, Dr. Akinwunmi Isola, Mr. Olu Akomolafe, Dr. Meki Nzewi and Mr. G. G. Darah.

The project itself, from the very beginning, was made possible by a subsidy from the Federal Ministry of Social Development,

Youth, Sports and Culture. And in this regard, I wish to express my deep appreciation to the Federal Director of Culture, Dr. Garba Ashiwaju for his unflinching support for the project. I also wish to express my appreciation to Ms. Edith Enem, Principal Cultural Officer in the Federal Ministry of Social Development, Youth, Sports and Culture whose first suggestion and subsequent encouragement and support made the work possible. Several other officers of the Ministry were also very kind, Mr. A. O. Olusesi, Mr. U. N. Abalogu and Mr. O. Soyombo.

I also must thank my good friends Dr. Femi Osofisan, Dr. John Ohiorenuan, Dr. Kole Omotoso and Dr. Biodun Jeyifo for urging me on and for reading through some of the manuscripts. I learnt a lot from them. In particular, Dr. Omotoso read through my introductory essay and made very useful suggestions on those areas that needed clarification, while Dr. Jeyifo extensively discussed the conclusions of the essay with me. Needless to add, of course, that any errors to be found in that essay are mine, not his.

I am also indebted to Professor Wole Soyinka and Professor Adedeji who took time off to speak with me at different times on various aspects of the project. Professor Soyinka most willingly spoke with me about the "1960 Masks" and Orisun years. And the sight of Professor Soyinka literally struggling with himself to recall details of those crowded years was something else!

I am also immensely grateful to Mr. Uko Atai, who painstakingly proof-read the manuscripts. I must also thank Messrs Francis Akhabue, Kehinde Ayegbe, Bukola Ogedengbe and Tunde Ibikunle for their secretarial assistance in the typing of these manuscripts; in particular Mr. Tunde Ibikunle who took time off from a busy schedule to type the final manuscripts.

Finally, of course, I thank Sade, my wife, for being so understanding, even in spite of myself—for being so beautiful a human being, for being so infinitely my best friend—and thereby making this project a reality.

FOREWORD

Theatre and Drama have always existed in one form or the other in Nigerian Societies, having their foundation in festivals and religious rituals. This is why it offers a fascinating field of study.

Unfortunately no effort had been made in the past to co-ordinate all the isolated scholarly essays on the subject into a book easily accessible to teachers and students of Nigerian Drama and Theatre. *Drama and Theatre in Nigeria* has therefore gone a long way in trying to meet this expectation.

It offers a critical look at the Nigerian Theatre from its inception to the present, while correcting omissions and erroneous impressions made in past studies. In short, it gives a perspective to Nigerian Drama and foreign ones alike including those actually involved in Nigerian Drama and Theatre. The study therefore presents a description and criticism of the major aspects of Nigerian Drama and Theatre, bringing forward new data and fresh insights concerning the subject.

It is hoped that this book will enrich Theatre and Drama in Nigeria or failing this, that it will stimulate more extensive enquiry than has been possible here, thus leading to its deeper understanding.

I heartily recommend '*Drama and Theatre in Nigeria*' to all those who seek an authentic and deeper insight into Drama and Theatre in Nigeria.

Dr. Garba Ashiwaju
Federal Director of Culture

PREFACE

Sometime in early 1979, Ms. Edith Enem, then an editor of *Nigeria Magazine* came down to Ife on some kind of official visit. The visit was most timely. I was teaching a course at the time on African theatre history at the University of Ife and had difficulty obtaining past numbers of *Nigeria Magazine*, particularly those numbers which had carried some of the most illuminating essays on Nigerian drama and theatre. Ms. Enem kindly offered to provide me with the missing back numbers I needed for my course, including one in which her essay on Kwagh-hir Tiv theatre had appeared. And then, in the ensuing discussion after her promise, we both agreed that a collection of essays on Nigerian theatre and drama was long overdue and that the essays in the back numbers of *Nigeria Magazine* could form the basis of such an anthology.

Such a collection would immediately do two things, we felt. It would readily make available those essays which are not quite accessible to students and teachers of African theatre history in our universities and colleges. It would also provide a serious starting-point for the much-needed revaluation of Nigerian drama and theatre. Generally, Nigerian drama and literature have suffered from the glib generalizations and facile critiques of particularly foreign critics whose only claim to authority on the subject is based on short vacation stints in Nigeria. Consider, for instance, that James Booth, who spent only one full term in the Department of Literature in English at Ife, published in 1981, a work, *Writers and Politics in Nigeria*. In almost the same vein, it can also be argued that Graham-White's book, *The Drama of Black Africa*, would have benefited more from a mere visit to Africa by the author.

The point, of course, is not that foreigners cannot do insightful critiques of Nigerian drama and theatre. If anything, this anthology stands as a refutation of such narrow, nationalist chauvinism. Some of the finer essays in this anthology have been written by non-Nigerians. And some of the works I mentioned above are useful works which unfortunately contain serious errors of ignorance and omission which, in the end, affect the overall value of the works themselves. The time is long overdue when those who have helped make the history of Nigerian theatre must tell their own stories themselves.

Therefore, my task as editor of this volume was not a very easy one, compounded, as it were, by the fact that this is the first attempt ever to publish a collection of scholarly essays on Nigerian drama and theatre. The task was two-fold. First, I had to go through virtually all the past numbers of *Nigeria Magazine* from the inception of the magazine in the 1930's to the present and to determine what can be reproduced in the more compact format of a book. Secondly, I had to find out what other works had been done on Nigerian theatre and drama—dissertations, essays in other journals and even books.

My find was most illuminating. There was ready evidence of scholarly work which had been done in the past ten years and serious efforts on the part of scholars to redefine Nigerian drama and what constitutes traditional theatre. Since Ogunba's pioneering work on Agemo and traditional theatre, Joel Adedeji, James Amankulor, Zulu Sofala, Victoria Ezeokoli, Oyekan Owomoyela and Nnabuenyi Ugonna have completed different doctoral dissertations on the subject of Nigerian drama—to say nothing of the several M.A. theses which also exist. Unfortunately, most of these works are locked away in the archives and libraries of universities abroad. And except for Mrs. Clark's recent and most welcome book on Ogunde (which was originally a Master's thesis), these works have not been published and therefore remain out of the reach of many.

In the archives of *Nigeria Magazine* I found a wide range of essays on Nigerian art and culture generally, most obviously dated and badly in need of updating and re-writing, a few others still relevant and contemporary in tone, and still a few others not relevant to our immediate purpose. It immediately became clear that we would have to solicit for fresh articles and essays if a balanced picture of Nigerian drama and theatre is to be presented. By mid-1979, letters went out to some thirty-five prospective contributors, taking cognizance of their special interests and requesting that they send in their articles, with no rigid guidelines other than that it be between fifteen to twenty-five pages of typewritten, quarto size material. And although some of the solicited essays are still arriving, even as we go to press (that is, nearly two years after!) a third of the essays reproduced in this anthology were specially solicited. Six other essays were reproduced, with permission, from other journals, while the rest were reproduced from *Nigeria Magazine.*

Following conventional, though modified criteria of classification of Nigerian drama and theatre, the anthology was broken into seven sections. After my own introductory essay, there is J. P. Clark's seminal and popular essay which is also general and introductory in tone. The third part, which has two sub-sections, covers the area of traditional theatre. A conscious effort was made to cover, as broadly as possible, the various examples of ethnic drama in Nigeria. Thus, traditional Hausa drama, about which, unfortunately, very little is known, is adequately presented. Some of the most burning issues around traditional Igbo theatre are also given prominence. Partly because of its uniqueness and partly because it looms large in the history of Nigerian theatre and drama, Yoruba travelling theatre has been separately dealt with in Part Four. The literary tradition covers the fifth part. Conscious of the paucity of material on concrete techniques of theatre practice, a sixth part dealing with theatre organization, management and production is included. The seventh and final part of the volume is an appendix of three recreated traditional dramas, *Ikaki, Ezeigboezue* and *Udje.*

It is important to add that this is not a study of individual Nigerian artists and their works—although extensive references have inevitably been made to them in this volume. While such a volume is also badly needed, it is certainly work for another time. Basically, this is a critical look at Nigerian theatre from its earliest beginnings to now, a look at the theatre as a movement and the nature of the growth of such a movement. And while this volume cannot possibly address all the problems and various aspects of

our study of Nigerian theatre, its achievement of bringing forward some new data and fresh insights concerning Nigerian
theatre is, I believe, one of considerable importance. It is hoped
that it will open the way for new lines of investigation by artists,
critics and scholars alike.

YEMI OGUNBIYI
Ile-Ife, June, 1981

PART I
INTRODUCTION

NIGERIAN THEATRE AND DRAMA:
A CRITICAL PROFILE
Yemi Ogunbiyi

The specific origins of Nigerian theatre and drama are speculative.[1] What is, however, not speculative, as will be seen in the chapters which follow, is the existence, in many Nigerian societies, of a robust theatrical tradition. The primitive root of that tradition must be sought in the numerous religious rituals and festivals that exist in many Nigerian communities. For, as an expression of the relationship between man, society and nature, drama arose out of fundamental human needs in the dawn of human civilization and has continued to express those needs ever since. Which is to say, that Nigerian theatre and drama originated with the Nigerian himself, embodying his first preoccupations, his first struggles, successes, set-backs and all.

In the course of history, man learnt to make nature work according to his needs. Invariably, this meant learning to court nature, to coax it and not to suppose for a moment that an arbitrary will can be imposed on it to make it render its wealth. This unity with the rest of nature, constantly rediscovered and developed in struggle and through productive labour, is the essence of human fulfilment. In the area of food gathering, for instance, the need to meet the requirements of all, motivated efficiency, it motivated a certain degree of planning, a strategy, a methodology. Thus, man played at fighting, in preparation for victory in real battle over anticipated adversaries. Similarly, hunt dances were initiated to imitate the movements and the pacing of the game hunted. The ritual of this expiatory dance for a slaughtered enemy, became, it has been argued, the archetypal African and consequently, Nigerian drama.

With time, man's acquired knowledge of his environment sharpened his awareness about nature, even if his means remained limited to what was an implacably hostile environment, a

3

fact which prevented his penetration of the major secrets of nature. However, in his desire to ensure the steady flow of food as a permanent victory over his numerous adversaries, he soon learnt that he could achieve his desires by dancing and acting them out in the form of rites. And there was reason to believe that these rites, hitherto unformalized, were efficacious since the results which man strove for magically were promoted, possibly by inspiration and autosuggestion, induced by the rites themselves in the 'actors'. Magic thus became a conjuration with its attendant rites producing the different gestures acquired from experience. Illusionary as this was, it yielded results. George Thomson put it more succinctly:

> By a supreme effort of will, they endeavour to impose illusion on reality. In this they fail, but the effort is not wasted. Thereby the physical conflict between them and their environment is resolved. Equilibrium is restored. And so, when they return to reality, they are actually more fit to grapple with it than they were before.[2]

Beyond this, man gradually introduced some "scientific" thinking into these rites. He perceived a relationship between the seasonal cycles and his food supply, believing that his domination of that relationship (through its dramatization in rites) ensured some form of control over the forces that determine his existence. These rites were subsequently idealized by the myths, stories, tales, songs, proverbs which further expressed the wish for a bountiful production and the experience of man's mastery over nature. With the regularity of performance dictated by need, these rites, over time, became ritualized. And with greater awareness these rites (now rituals), were modified and altered, such that it became possible with time to isolate the myths which have developed around the rituals and to act them out as traditional drama of some sort.

Applied to the context of Nigeria, the widely accepted view stated above would indicate, as I stated earlier on, that the origins of Nigerian theatre and drama lie in the numerous traditional, religious and functional rituals to be found in practically every Nigerian society. What is, however, not clear and therefore remains speculative, is the question of the precise evolutionary growth of drama from rituals, that is if at all it did. The problem is compounded by the fact that the distinction often made between ritual and drama in a society where the sacred is so inextricably linked with the profane, the popular so interwoven with the religious, could well be a tenuous one. To be sure, broad distinctions can be made between ritual and drama, for while ritual is essentially functional, drama is not, at least not in the sense of immediate results and consequences beyond itself. The real problem arises from the fact that the most important criterion for distinguishing drama from ritual in a traditional Nigerian society, that of the total context of the performance, including the responses and reactions of the participants and spectators—is not easily verifiable in the absence of records of such performances. If we proceed from the premise that context is a crucial determining factor, it would seem that ritual can quite easily be transformed into entertainment (theatre), and entertainment into ritual. And as Dr. Ossie Enekwe argues in his summary of Richard Schechner in an essay which is reproduced in this anthology, "a ritual becomes entertainment once it is outside its original context or when the belief that sustains it has lost its potency".[3]

But there is even another reason why in Nigeria, the effort to distinguish ritual from drama can be frustrating and self-defeating. Even if we were to accept in its entirety the evolutionist approach that drama evolved from rituals, problems do persist, because sometimes the evolutionary line is not as straight as is presumed. There is, for example, a situation where a robust dramatic tradition has developed *alongside* ritual without cutting itself off from its origin. In his important study of traditional Yoruba theatre, Professor J. A. Adedeji argues that as masque theatre—that is, as a courtly form of entertainment characterized by song, dance, lavish costume and extraordinary spectacle—Yoruba traditional theatre emerged from three developmental phases, ritual, festival and theatre. "The process shows," he writes, "the treatment and use of the masquerade for both ritual and secular occasions."[4] Here it does seem that there was a straight development from ritual to theatre. Subsequently, the drama was taken outside the court and became known, first as

Egun Alare and eventually *Alarinjo*, the first professional Travelling theatre among the Yorubas. But while the Alarinjo performers have not supplanted the ritual ceremonies of the Egungun society from which they initially transpired, they have developed an almost independent entertainment-oriented style, different in emphasis from the essentialist art of the original *egungun* performance, even as they remain adjoined to it. To the extent that the Alarinjos (who are members of the theatre guild, and considered plain entertainers by the people) are bound to the *egungun* cult by ancestor worship and participate at *egungun* festivals, to that extent Alarinjo has remained an integral part of ritual. This is therefore not so much a case of theatre developing *from*, but rather *alongside*, ritual.

Adedeji's studies are important for other reasons. There is, for instance, his leading attempt to identify the specific period of transition of traditional theatre from ritual into entertainment, that is, with reference to Yoruba theatre. Drawing extensively from historical evidence, Adedeji demonstrates how Sango, who reigned as Alafin of Oyo, "probably about the fourteenth century, is thought to have introduced the phenomenon of the ancestor-worship called *baba* (father) or later, *egungun* (masquerade)".[5] By the middle of the 16th century the institution had become formalized into a kind of festival of "All souls" in which lineage groups presented a dance-display during the highlights of the lineage's history. Invariably, each group became more adept at particular aspects of the dance-displays of each lineage masquerade. The refinement and perfection of those aspects, ostensibly for purely entertainment purposes, marked, by 1700, the birth of professional Yoruba theatre.

This conclusion helps throw some light on the controversy surrounding attempts to distinguish ritual from drama, and by extension, identify what really constitutes drama in the Nigerian context. Dr. Enekwe's position, the so-called relativist school, maintains that drama and ritual "are not anti-podal", but rather, "reciprocal in function and similar in structure", since one can easily lead to the other, depending on the context. In so far as it relates to the example of the Alarinjo, Adedeji's evidence seems to support, in broad terms, Enekwe's point of view. The most often quoted spokesman for the other school, the evolutionary school, is Professor M. J. C. Echeruo. Taking Ruth Finnegan as a theoretical starting point,[6] he contends that there are considerable limitations to be encountered in any attempts to classify Igbo festival as drama. Echeruo argues that until the ritual content of Igbo festival (for example, *Mbom-Ama* and *Odo* festivals) is forced "to yield its story," the dramatic content of these festivals will remain subsumed in their "ritual purity". Since ritual is a dead-end, "what is needed is to . . . expand ritual into life and give that life a secular base".[7]

For the record, it is important to add that Professor Echeruo's call for caution and a more precise nomenclature in our discussion of the origins of our drama and what in fact constitutes drama is one that is shared by many scholars on the subject, with some others holding much stronger views. Kalu Uka is unsparing: "What is usually called traditional drama, . . . is not yet drama. It is the huge legacy upon which drama may draw and draw with ever increasing returns. . . . What some usually and glibly call traditional drama is properly and essentially elements of drama. In short, traditional drama is the sum total of the doings of peoples before written records were kept."[8] And although Andrew Horn's piece in this anthology deals principally with Bori as spirit mediumship, he is also concerned with the generic distinction between the several genres and melange of forms which constitute the theatre in the broadest sense. Such argument is clearly implied in Ola Rotimi's short but important essay, except that here, his distinguishing criterion is straight-forwardly Aristotelian. In partial consonance with the "content-argument" of Echeruo, Ola Rotimi maintains that any ritual display which contains "mimetic impulse" ought to be classified as drama, not ritual.

Properly considered, therefore, the Echeruo–Enekwe controversy as presented above, touches on the whole question of elements of "medium" and "context" versus those of content. The question of whether or not ritual has enough "mimetic impulse" or enough "force of action," as Echeruo puts it, are valid enough. Obviously with some traditional festivals and rituals, certain "dramatic phenomena" (to use Finnegan's phrase) or "peri-theatrical modes" (the expression is Andrew Horn's) are present. Festivals may be dramatic in themselves without being drama. Our task is to distinguish between spectacle and drama. The Fulani *Soro* dance, for instance, which is a manhood-endurance test may be spectacular as an event in itself, but it is not drama. It is pure spectacle, a show. Similarly, it can be argued without prejudice to the laudable work which Dr. Meki Nzewi has been doing on Igbo traditional theatre, that his inclusion of the sympathetic wailing by Igbo women at a funeral ceremony as an example of "spontaneous" Igbo traditional theatre, is perhaps over-stretched.[9]

However, it would be dangerous to generalize on the basis of the examples mentioned above or any single example for that matter and to that extent the "content-centered" criterion is inadequate. The crucial point that needs to be emphasised is that examples are peculiar to specific events. For instance, while *Soro* may not be drama, the flogging sequence that precedes most Yoruba masquerade festivals is drama when considered as part of the larger masquerade festival to which it belongs. Examples also abound in Nigeria of traditional festivals where the dramatic re-enactment of a story or stories is central to the event. Ulli Beier's seminal study of traditional Yoruba festivals which he carried out in Ede in 1959 stands to dispel any doubts about this.[10] No one could argue with any conviction that ritual drama does not form the basis of the annual Obatala festival as celebrated in Ede, given its structure, the dramatic enactment, the tension generated by the mock fight between the protagonist and the antagonist.[11]

What recommends the Enekwe position, to my mind, is the relativist argument, the view that "theatre is first and foremost an experience", and that what can pass for ritual, drama or plain entertainment would vary from a given context to another, a given time to another and one place to another. Mr. Kofoworola's recent studies of traditional forms of Hausa drama, which is reproduced in this anthology, indicates that traditional Hausa drama is classified, almost entirely by the context of performance, hence the existence of "occupational" forms, "social" forms, "ceremonial", "dramatic" and "Royal Court" forms. In the end, therefore, we must admit that until more work is done in the area of our traditional theatre and drama, each ritual, each festival, each dramatic event must be taken on its own merit and adjudged not merely from whether it fulfils the "content-criteria", but more importantly from the context-criteria; from the dimension of how it is experienced by the actor/participants, itself a difficult task in a predominantly oral society such as ours. The entire exercise in effect, becomes a sterile one, and in our present circumstances, counterproductive.

This controversy notwithstanding, attempts have been made to classify Nigerian drama. J. P. Clark's classification, one which has influenced, in part, my own sectional breakdown in this collection, seems to have crystallized. His classification falls into two broad groups—traditional and the literary.[12] Faced with a myriad of varied traditional forms, J. P. Clark further breaks the group into the religious and secular form. And "within the sacred species, there are again two types", the myth and ancestral plays on one hand and the masquerade plays of different cult and age groups on the other. Under the secular forms of traditional Nigerian drama, he identifies five different types—magic or trick plays, pastoral or puppet plays, civic drama, dance or song dramas, narrative or epic drama. Starting with Yoruba travelling theatre as his first example of modern theatre, Professor Clark concludes his classification with the addition of contemporary literary works under that section.

The classification is, without doubt, a useful one—that is, as a conceptual frame-work, providing us with a neat structure to operate from. But as we find out more about our theatre by way of research, the classification cries out to be modified and up-dated. The following two examples will serve to make the point. Contemporary Yoruba Travelling theatre, for instance, cannot be rightly classified under the literary tradition. If we must classify it at all under the broad divisions of either traditional or literary drama, Yoruba Travelling theatre ought to be classified as *modern traditional.* Not only are the plays not scripted (and therefore largely improvisational), but in tempo, in form, presentation, styles, indeed in their overall meaning, they are traditional. An appreciation of Duro Ladipo's theatre, as I attempt to show in my essay on him in this anthology is impossible without some familiarity with the conventions of traditional Yoruba theatre. And despite Hubert Ogunde's flirtations with European forms of the Variety theatre, he remains largely a traditional artist. "If I had attended a college or a University, I would have been cut away from my roots", he told an appreciative audience at the University of Ife in March of 1981. He continued, "the Nigerian theatre practitioner is not a product of any Drama School. He is a self-made man who found himself in the environment in which he was born—the ritual ceremony, the ritual priest and communal life".[13] These assertions about himself and his work are, no doubt, correct. But it is also correct to say that he is a modern artist. His contemporaneousness, the immediate relevance of most of his theatre work, the modernity of his vision make him a modern Nigerian artist.

Another area deserving of greater emphasis than has been given in J. P. Clark's essay is that of the inter-relatedness of the different types and forms of traditional theatre there are. For instance, as an example of what will presently be classified as a Popular form of traditional theatre, the Yoruba Alarinjo has a lot of tricks, acrobatics, pantomime, to say nothing of dance and song. And as I tried to show above, Alarinjo has sacred overtones, even though it is secular in character. So, in classifying Alarinjo, one would run into trouble if J. P. Clark's analysis is applied, since a dichotomy is drawn in his classification between religion and recreation, between the sacred and the profane. Even if we were to ignore the first category of classification, that is, between the religious and secular and place Alarinjo under Professor Clark's secular drama, the problem would remain unsolved. Is it to be considered an example of trick drama, dance drama, pastoral or civic drama, since it could be any one of these?

Given the foregoing problems, it would seem that a modified classification is required. Still taking our cue from J. P. Clark, we suggest two broad classifications—traditional and literary forms of drama. The traditional forms can be further split into three sub-sections, Dramatic ritual, the Popular tradition and Yoruba Travelling theatre. Dramatic ritual will include traditional festivals, whether they be held in celebration of cult or ancestral heroes, ritual ceremonies where drama is patently discernible, serious masquerade plays (as distinct from the light ones) etc. The term "popular" applied in describing the second category of traditional drama is used in its usual sense—that is, art intended to be popular, art that is commonly approved and widely liked by the "common" people in an ever-growing urban culture. The term is used in the finest tradition of a genuinely popular theatre where all that a living, popular performer needs is, not necessarily a text or an elaborate stage, but rather, a place, a time, an audience and himself. Unlike in the European tradition where the popular theatre such as vaudeville, burlesque, circus and musical comedy, is distinguished from what is considered legitimate, high artistic theatre, the popular in our context must be considered complex even as it involves an expression of physical pleasure and joy. In this category one must include all those plays in which amusement and entertainment are cited as the foremost functions. Among these are the Annang drama of the Ibibio, Yoruba Alarinjo theatre, Kwagh-hir and Bornu Puppet shows, the Hausa comical art of *Yankamanci*. Contemporary Yoruba Travelling theatre, the theatre of Ogunde, of the late Ogunmola, the late Duro Ladipo and the hundred or more such groups that now exist, is classified separately, essentially for reasons stated above.[14] And finally, the literary tradition would mean the literary plays that have been written since Ene Henshaw's *This is our Chance* (1956), while not excluding those, if any, that were written prior to 1956.

Quite apart from the changes made in places, this classification has the advantage of being less constrictive than J. P. Clark's, and so allows us to include other examples of Nigerian drama into the frame-work as continued research work throws more light on them. With a frame-work such as this one, it becomes easy to identify, as broadly as possible, even at the risk of oversimplification, the important characteristics of Nigerian drama.

Except for Hausa drama, it seems that the incipient focal point of most forms of traditional drama in Nigeria is the masquerade. Examples abound whether among the Kalabari, Yoruba, the Ibibio, the Opobo, the Efik, etc., of the inextricable link between the masquerade and the ritual play. Horton's extensive study of *Ikaki*, the Kalabari tortoise masquerade, is one example of the dominance of the masquerade in traditional drama. The occasion for the presentation of these performances varies from ethnic group to ethnic group, indeed from a particular festival performance to another. Generally, however, they are held during festivals, usually annual or seasonal festivals of cult groups, societies or even professional groups. As J. P. Clark quite rightly states, most of the rituals that are dramatized at these festivals may involve the representation of spirit, ancestral or mythic heroes, either in a symbolic, and therefore non-mimetic representation of the powers of these ancestral figures, or in a more dramatic impersonation. And always, these dramatic presentations are over-whelmingly interwoven with songs, drumming, extensive improvisation and dance. The role of dance as a fundamental concept of performance in Igbo festival theatre has been extensively explored by several Igbo scholars, among them Dr. James Amankulor and Dr. Meki Nzewi.[15] It is needless to add, of course, that the setting for these performances is generally an undefined area, usually the village square.

The nature of the preparation and execution of these festivals varies a great deal. Among the Igbos, Dr. Nzewi identifies four kinds of preparation, namely, religious, material, artistic and political, with each representing different stages of the activities that occur prior to the festival.[16] However, J. C. Messenger's study of Ibibio drama suggests that *Ekong* drama undergoes a period of meticulous, detailed preparation, far surpassing that of most examples that have been recorded or experienced. The extract deserves to be quoted in full because it also reveals the splendour and beauty of one of the most elaborate and complex examples of traditional dramas in Nigeria. After a carver is hired to produce all the needed materials for the six-year cycle, rehearsals begin:

> Rehearsals take place in the square for several hours during the afternoon on a specific day of each eight-day week for forty-six weeks of every year or six years, and performances are given publicly during the dry season of the seventh . . . . During the six-years of rehearsals a complete seven-hour routine was worked out and mastered to perfection by the Ikot-Obong players. The

routine included music played by an eleven-man percussion orchestra; dances performed by a chorus of eighteen men; songs
sung by the musicians, dancers, and marked soloist; plays enacted
by puppets or a group of fourteen men, some wearing masks;
dances on stilts by two costumed performers; and the mystifying
movements of a life-size carving of the principal female fertility
spirit, *ekanem*, enwrapped by the coils of a phyton.[17]

Ibibio drama deserves to be examined more closely because it
stands as one refutation of the claim that in non-literate, traditional
African societies, "drama is not a developed form". When the
advocates of this view suggest that traditional African drama hardly
exists, they mean that it does not exist in the form of European
drama, as if that is the only yard-stick for determining what drama
is. Said Ruth Finnegan: ". . . though these performances possess
certain of the elements we associate with drama, the emphasis is
very different from that of modern European drama". Continuing
in the same section of her book, she concludes, "Though there may
be no 'plays' *in quite the Western sense*, these indigenous artistic
forms nevertheless possess some of the elements *we* associate with
drama"[18] (my emphasis). The fact is that in its intensity, contained
not just in the preparation as we showed above, but also in its
amplitude and profundity, its brilliantly executed farcical skits, its
penchant for spontaneity, vigour and extemporization, Ibibio
drama surpasses the slippery, fluffy smoothness of much of what
passes for modern European drama. A closer examination of its
format amply bears that out.

According to Messenger, there are two forms of drama organization among the Ibibio. There is *Offiong*, which is a smaller,
secular association and entertains only social gatherings such as
burial, wedding and other feasts. The other is *Ekong*, which is a
sacred and more established association and performed only in
village squares before the entire populace. Unlike other forms of
traditional drama which tend to reflect only myths and stories,
Ekong reflects contemporary realities. This is especially so, since
"social control and providing amusement are the major and
manifest functions of *Ekong*".

The successful production of a performance depends largely on
the joint efforts of a team of professional actors who have to

memorize their lines, rehearse them; a large orchestra whose instruments consist of slit gongs, hollow wooden drums; a team of community members who construct an arena-type stage, complete with dressing rooms; and the carver whose duty it is to provide the props required for the performances.

The dominant features of *Ekong* are the skits and sketches which exploit "family and social tensions, rivalries and jealousies" and incisively satirize ethnic groups, social types, behaviour types and disapproved individuals. What is the format of these sketches and skits? "Among all the forms of aesthetic expression, only in drama is amusement cited as the foremost function by the Annang," Messenger has written.[19] But *Ekong* also seeks, through the plays and songs, to impose a pervasive social control, not only over persons, kinship and political groups, but also over foreign missions and government.

Broadly, the satire is of two kinds—specific and general. When it is specific, particular individuals and groups or institutions are castigated, the action being preceded by a calling-out of the specific name being satirized. A famous, greedy lawyer from Aba who appears in court to represent both the plaintiff and the defendant, obviously, after getting his fees from both of them; a dishonest trader who is cursed by the Hausa trader whom he owed money causing his two wives to bear twins (multiple births were dreaded among the Annang Ibibio); a corrupt native court judge who readily grants divorces to housewives after extracting promises from them that they will remarry him—all these are gleefully satirized on stage. Missionary christianity and the "spiritualist" churches also attract satirical barbs from *Ekong*.

In the more general skits and sketches, types of behaviour and conditions are derided. These behaviours include drunkenness, sexual jealousy, suicide, physical ugliness, poverty, mental illness, domineering wives, promiscuity, corruption, theft, stupidity, lack of skill, mistreatment of kin, etc. In one example of these, two singers tell and re-enact the story of a man who was said to have sold his grand-children and in-law into slavery to some traders. Since he "talked out of the side of his mouth to people," *Abasi* (the supreme God) punished him by causing him to "twitch at the mouth".

From the foregoing, it is obvious that *Ekong* also thrives immensely as spoken art presented in a dramatic form. This is one quality, among others, which it shares with other kinds of the popular tradition in Nigerian traditional theatre. In this respect it readily brings to mind *Yankamanci*, for instance, the comic Hausa craft of the spoken word, although *Yankamanci* is slightly different in its emphasis. While questions can be raised about the validity of *Yankamanci's* inclusion in a collection such as this, there is no doubt that as a form of minstrelsy it thrives on performance. In the end, the *Yankama* is a jongleur, a minstrel whose success as a performer depends not only on his skill to wed the word to the gesture and language to attitude, but also his skill at pantomime. But the real importance of *Yankamanci* for us lies in the way it has influenced contemporary Hausa drama, especially as the craft, in the state presented in this anthology, is fast in decline. Admittedly, its major elements, such as pantomime, the bodily attitudes needed to effect communication, pastiche of comical songs, parodies of songs, the nonsensical play on words, etc., can be incorporated into full-blown Hausa theatre. And as evidenced by the nature of present drama programmes on NTV (Kano) and NTV (Kaduna), much of contemporary Hausa drama thrives a great deal on the spoken art.

The other forms of popular traditional theatre deserving of mention are the Kwagh-hir Puppet theatre of the Tiv and the Bornu Puppet play—both of them being forms about which little is known. With Bornu Puppet plays, the problem is compounded by the fact that it is a form that may have virtually gone defunct. Kwagh-hir, on the other hand, is still very much practised and is the topic of study for a higher degree of the Ahmadu Bello University by Mr. Hagher. There is a strong likelihood that the Tiv tradition of puppetry came from the more Northern Hausa provinces, where they were originally imported, possibly by Arab traders. And although the facts of such origins are not conclusive, they are plausible.

An important feature of Arab theatre is the Shadow play which was first mentioned in travellers' narratives and muslim literature in the fourteenth century. These were popular puppet shows, distinguishable from marionette performances since the figures were manipulated behind illuminated curtains, such that the audience saw only the shadows moving on the curtain. Under the Turks, shadow plays became extremely popular throughout Turkey, Syria, Palestine, Egypt and much of Muslim North Africa. Considering Bornu's pre-eminence as "the indisputed mistress of the eastern section of the central Sudan",[20] during the early part of the nineteenth century and El-Kanemi's extensive foreign connections with Medina and Egypt, it is not surprising that puppetry was introduced in Bornu in the nineteenth century. Although the example which Ellison observed in 1935 is different from the Arab prototypes, it comes across as equally dramatic. Compared to Kwagh-hir, the Bornu Puppet play is distinctly more successful as drama. For whereas in Kwagh-hir we are presented with short vignettes, with the Bornu Puppet play we have scenes, lasting two or three minutes each, supported with background music.

Another interesting dimension of traditional drama, one which has been visited again and again by anthropologists is the relationship between spirit mediumship and the drama, between trance or possession and theatre. Unfortunately, much of what exists by way of information and material has been written, not from a theatrical viewpoint, but rather from an anthropological and sociological position. The two essays reproduced here—Andrew Horn's piece on Bori and Mr. Adelugba's on trance and the theatre—are leading attempts to situate the discussion in the Nigerian context, in the area of drama and the theatre.

As Andrew Metraux has argued in his "Dramatic Elements in Ritual Possession", "every case of possession has its theatrical side".[21] But this is certainly not to mean that theatre can be equated with ritual possession. Is a person in a state of trance no more than an actor? Horn cautiously approaches the question from the point of the intersection between ritual and drama, since ritual and drama possess identical "spectacular, theatrical qualities". As a medium, a man possessed must be viewed as the spirit incarnate of the very spirit which takes possession of his body. This makes the possessed more "profoundly involved in his 'character' than is the actor of drama" who must, of necessity be in control of the character he depicts on stage. The difference between them is in degrees, Horn seems to be saying, at least with reference to Bori. With the Kalabari, the situation is different. Possession, which is often difficult to identify by an outsider to the community, is one of the three ways of compelling the presence of gods to come into a community, the other ways being mime and masquerade. In effect, it is an integral part of traditional theatre. But still, the precise nature of the difference between "acting" and possession are difficult to establish. Until more is known about this area of our ritual and drama, our conclusion will remain speculative and tentative.

The Modern Tradition

By 1863, Britain had secured a foot-hold in Nigeria, through its annexation of Lagos. Prior to 1863, the twin face of British colonialism, the Church Missionary Society had, under a broad policy of the so called three 'C's'—Christianity, Commerce and Civilization—pursued a systematic policy of producing an elite class of Nigerians who would be leaders in church, commerce, and politics. As early as 1839, the first batch of immigrants, freed slaves and their children, who had acquired some form of Western education, had started to arrive and readily provide "a vigorous impetus to the realization of the objectives" of both the church and the British government. This set of immigrants, later to be joined by Brazilian emigrants, formed the very nucleus of a nascent Nigerian educated middle-class. It is interesting to note that this class of Nigerians imported the Western and European forms of the concert and the drama which were to constitute the basic framework of early modern Nigerian drama.[22]

By 1866, the population of Lagos had risen from 25,000 in 1861 to 38,000 and with it, came a corresponding rise in the need for recreational facilities in Lagos. In direct response to this need, the top cream of the Lagos elite—Bishop Ajai Crowther, J. A. Otunba-Payne, Robert Campbell, Charles Foresythe, J. P. L. Davis and a host of others—got together on October 24, 1866 and opened "The Academy", as it was called, "as a social and cultural centre for public enlightenment, dedicated to the promotion of the arts, science and culture".[23] Between 1866 and 1910, several groups, after the fashion of "The Academy", were founded, dedicated in one way or the other to the promotion of culture and the arts. Among the most successful were the Philharmonic Society which was founded by Otunba-Payne in 1873, the Lagos Grammar School Entertainment Society (1872), the Rising Entertainment Society, the Orphean Club, founded by J. Otunba-Payne, the People's Union (1904), the Lagos Glee Singers (1910), the United Native Progressive Society and the Brazilian Dramatic Company under the management of P. Z. da Silva. There was also the Annual Coker Concerts, organized by Robert A. Coker, the "Mozart of West Africa", which became extremely popular in entertainment circles in "Victorian" Lagos.

Practically all of these groups organized shows of their own. Quite predictably, the programme format and contents of these performances were based on those of the English music halls that were prominent in England in the late 1860's and the early 1870's—comic songs, love songs, duets, solos, glees and recitations, usually excerpts from plays, novels and comic sketches. Somehow, music tended to dominate in these performances.

However, there existed in Lagos at this time, other types of entertainment in which drama was fully presented, productions in which music was not the main emphasis. The Roman Catholic Church was the pioneer of this tradition. Faced with the complex challenge of having to conduct church business in Yoruba to a predominantly Yoruba-speaking community and a Portuguese-speaking Brazilian emigrant group, in an English-speaking colony, the French Order of Catholic Priests (Sociétés des Missions Africaines) which arrived in Lagos in 1867, was compelled to rely on the power of the theatre for a more effective communication. So that from 1881 when St. Gregory's School was founded by the French priests, to the end of the century, annual end-of-year performances were held. In 1882, Moliere's *He would Be a Lord* was staged, interspersed with farces, songs, recitations, etc. But crucial as these contributions were, they did not, in fact, could not lead to the beginning of a truly modern Nigerian drama. Ironically, the impetus to that came from within the Church.

By 1890, a major schism had occurred within the Protestant Church in Lagos, which led to the establishment of several secessionist churches in Lagos—fourteen, to be more precise, by

1917. The reasons for this situation must be understood within the context of the wave of a Yoruba cultural nationalist movement, itself the consequence of the disillusionment and alienation experienced by the educated elite of Lagos. The disillusionment was predictable and perhaps, even inevitable. Separated from these men by almost half a century, Frantz Fanon understood better. This period under consideration corresponds partially with the second phase which he identified in the evolutionary panorama of the colonized (native) African intellectual. Wrote Fanon:

> In the second phase, we find the native is disturbed; he decides to remember what he is . . . . But since the native is not a part of his people, since he only has exterior relations with his people, he is content to recall their life only. Past happenings of the bygone days of his childhood will be brought up out of the depths of his memory; old legends will be reinterpreted in the light of a borrowed aestheticism and of a conception of the world which was discovered under other skies.[24]

Not only was the call made for independent African churches where Yoruba music and language could be freely used, there were beginning to emerge attempts to blend Yoruba and European materials in entertainments. The lead for such "innovations"[25] came from Abeokuta and Ibadan, but especially from Abeokuta where, for instance, traditional masquerade songs were re-worked into church songs as a means of winning over converts from traditional religions. It is therefore hardly surprising that the first examples of truly Nigerian dramas came from these African Churches. Thus, in 1902, under the joint sponsorship of the Bethel African Church and St. Judes Church, Ebute-Metta, a play written by D. A. Oloyede, *King Elejigbo and Princess Abeje of Kotangora* was performed by the Egbe Ife at the Bethel African Church School-room. On April 22, 1904, the play received a public performance at the Glover Memorial Hall, thus earning for itself the distinction of being "the first appearance of a church drama group in a public hall".

For nearly two decades, *King Elejigbo* became the prototype of most Yoruba drama being written in Lagos and between 1904 and 1920, some twenty or more such plays were written.[26] Structurally, the plays were similar to the tradition which Hubert Ogunde was to inherit two decades after—the mild satires, the dialogues mingled with songs, the hymn tunes immersed in Biblical themes, the opening and closing glees, the insertions of sometimes unrelated sketches, etc. Under the aegis of the Lagos Glee Singers, headed by Dr. Obasa, the tradition waxed stronger in Lagos.

It ought to be noted, however, that in spite of all the bustle of those years, of all the hue and cry about the indigenization of the church, the well-meaning, if sometimes misguided surge towards a cultural nationalism, in spite of all that, the activities around the so-called "native" theatre,[27] were not popular affairs but rather the exclusive concern of only a circle of "Victorian" Lagosians. A majority of the "natives" were "illiterate and uncultivated" and quite naturally, cut off from the cultural life which the elite group promoted and acutely supported. In studying the population figures of Lagos between 1861 and 1866, Professor Echeruo concludes that only a tenth of the population could be regarded as "educated",[28] a generous figure which would normally include such working class persons as teachers and junior government officials. However, teachers were poorly trained at the time and so were hardly considered educated in the sense in which the word was used at the time. To be educated in nineteenth-century Lagos was synonymous with the acquisition of a "Victorian" taste, complete with all its vacuity and superciliousness. Numerically, the Lagosians who belonged to this group were infinitesimal—they were the wealthy merchants, those Lagosians who could afford to, and actually did send their children abroad, in some cases, after their own fashion, so they could get into the right professions, law, medicine and the arts, those Lagosians who, suffused in their elite pretensions, associated "themselves with the usual recreations of a 'sophisticated' Europe and so went to the races, to fancy dress balls . . . and to cricket".[29] It was this class of Lagosians who patronized the theatre and gave it support. It is needless to add, of course, that the theatre catered to their tastes. And yet, ironically, the cultural nationalist movement which provided an important impetus for the founding of this theatre, was sometimes initiated and massively supported by working-class Lagosians. For instance, the 1896 call by Lagos teachers for the wearing of native dresses was derided by 'educated' Lagosians. The Lagos editor of *Lagos Observer* saw it as a demand for "recurrence to primitive quasi-nudity".[30]

One of the many ways in which the mass population was excluded from these theatres was by charging exhorbitant gate fees for performances. For instance, the performances held at the St. Gregory's School were relatively very expensive, ranging from three shillings (30k) to five shillings (50k) for gate fee with the printed programmes going for three to six pence a piece. Considering the earnings of the average Nigerian worker in 1900, those gate fees were extremely expensive. For instance, under Henry McCallum, who became Governor of Lagos in April 1897, Public Works Department workers' weekly wage of one shilling and three pence (15k) was to be scaled down to nine pence (9k)![31] In 1900, the commencing salary for "native clerks" was £24 (₦48) per annum, which comes to about ten shillings (₦1) a week. Asking a clerk who earned £2 (₦4) a month in 1900 to pay five shillings (50k) for a performance is roughly equivalent to asking a man who earns ₦100 per month (before taxes) today to pay ₦7.50k for a performance. It is not surprising to read accounts of how some of these theatre houses were attacked and vandalized by those who felt excluded and cut off by the exhorbitant gate fees.[32]

So, in effect, the theatre of this period was anything but popular and it relied for its survival on the support of the tiny class for which it catered. Once that support was no longer forthcoming, the theatre was bound to collapse. And collapse it did. "When professional, commercial and later political interests diverted the attention of this elite, the spirit of these concerts began to fade away." And although the Lagos Glee Singers continued its activities well into the 1920's, the combined effects of the coming of World War I and that of the Cinema in 1914 finally served to dampen the sparkle of the preceding years. It took a Hubert Ogunde to revive that interest some two decades after. But the conditions leading to such a revival manifested themselves long before Ogunde came to the scene.

The ripples of the Great Depression of 1929 were felt in Nigeria, particularly in Lagos, which remained the economic out-post of British imperialism by the early 1930's. The unemployment which ensued from the effects of the depression meant a corresponding gain in strength for the numerous evangelical and spiritualist churches which characterized the period. These churches, through their unorthodox technique of instant results of healing, prophecy and spiritualism, provided solace for the working-class, a majority of whom were then unemployed. It is therefore not an accident that the future growth of a truly popular theatre of some sort, should be linked at this time in Lagos with the growth of the Aladura Movement.

After a period of initial hesitation to use the theatrical format in its propagation of its brand of the gospel, the Aladura Movement plunged into it completely. Driven by a belief in spiritualism as the very essence of religion, and as if aware of the close links between trance, drama and religion, the Movement resorted to music, dance and songs "as a means of impelling its members to express their religious experience".[33] Although the movement took a stand against the use of the Yoruba talking drum, its methods of basing church plays on stories taken from the Bible and setting them to music and dance was innovative enough to start a new phase in the development of Yoruba theatre. By the mid-thirties, a new kind of drama, Native Air Opera as it was called, had become popular, due largely to the efforts of the church movement; but more specifically, due largely to the efforts of A. K. Ajisafe who started "to relate church hymns to 'native airs' at the United African Methodist Church". He was followed in that tradition through the years by such renowned theatre artists as E. A. Dawodu, Ajibola Layeni, A. B. David, G. I. Onimole and A. A. Olufoye. This was the situation in the early forties when Hubert Ogunde arrived in Lagos as the organist and composer of sacred songs for a break-away church from the parent Aladura Movement, the Church of the Lord at Ebute-Metta.

Ogunde's arrival on the scene in 1944 was to determine the course of Yoruba theatre for over three decades. Freeing the so-called "Native Air Opera" from the strict confines of the church and monotonous church rhythms, Ogunde imbued the "opera" with a sprinkling of Yoruba music and dances. The fact that the Church of the Lord, which had been founded in 1931 in Ogere by Josiah Oshitelu was less fundamentalist in its approach than the parent body, was a contributory factor towards Ogunde's innovations. In 1946, encouraged by the warm reception to his first two plays, *The Garden of Eden and The Throne of God*, which was first done as a church play and *Worse Than Crime*, which told the story of the slave trade, Ogunde resigned from the Police Force and decided to go professional. With only £9 (₦18) in his total savings after eight years in the Force, he inaugurated the African Music Research Party, marking the advent of modern professional theatre in Nigeria.

As Ebun Clark has shown in her historical documentation of the development of Ogunde's theatre, Ogunde was from the beginning, actively involved in the struggle for self-rule, an involvement which is not only reflected in the subject and themes of his works, but led to his several brushes with the colonial authorities. Working from the premise that theatre must "reflect the reality of its society",[34] he boldly retold, sometimes at great risk to himself and his safety, the tragedy, the hopes, dreams, triumphs of his time and age. Not content to confine himself to Lagos, he hit the road and carried out extensive gruelling tours of the country. Evidently, the tours made their impacts. One of those who came to see him perform in Ado-Ekiti was a young school teacher. His name was E. K. Ogunmola. Ogunde remembers the details well:

> Ogunmola started in 1948. But before he started, the first thing he did was to come to Lagos. I saw him. I did not even know who he was. Then he told me that he had been working at Ado-Ekiti, at Ikare, at Akure and he thought we could do the same thing. . . . So he asked us to help him build costumes for his new play. So we built some costumes and he started from there. And from that time up to the time of his death, he had connections with Ogunde theatre. . . . And many a time, he would come and watch my play and offer suggestions and I would watch his own play and offer suggestions. In fact, I would say that we were together until his death.[35]

So started a long tradition of influences, from Kola Ogunmola, through Duro Ladipo to even the comic Yoruba artists such as Moses Olaiya. For instance, it is not generally known that the group that was later to become the Moses Olaiya Company (the Alawada) was in fact, a splinter group from the Ogunde theatre.[36] Nor is it always appreciated that Ogunde had first established most of the theatrical techniques which other artists of the tradition have relied upon.

What is remarkable about Yoruba Travelling theatre today is not merely or only the nature of Ogunde's pervasive influence on the tradition, but rather how fully established that tradition had become. It is believed that there are some one-hundred Yoruba Travelling theatre groups which make up the Association of Nigerian Theatre Practitioners—that is, not counting the groups stationed in the Republic of Benin where these groups perform to Yoruba-speaking Beninois. And as was seen at the 1981 mini-Ife Theatre festival where some of these groups participated, standards today are appreciably high.

Although much remains to be known about the techniques and working-methods of these companies,[37] there seems to be a current trend (again after the fashion of Hubert Ogunde) towards film-making. In recorded interviews carried out with scores of these groups, there seems to be a general interest in that direction. Already, Ogunde has filmed two of his works, *Aiye* and *Jaiyesimi*. Both Duro Ladipo and Oyin Adejobi featured in another film, *Ija Ominira*, an adaptation of *Omo Olokun Esin*, Bayo Faleti's novel, and produced by Ade Afolayan. *Kadara* has also been produced by Ade Afolayan. Although both of Ogunde's films have been uncritically popular with the mass audience of especially Yoruba speakers, they are surprising departures from his courageous and combative tradition of confronting realistically, without mystification, without recourse to the supernatural, the burning issues of contemporary society. In the world of both films, the diabolical forces of evil, symbolized by witches and witchcrafts, are after a momentary victory, magically destroyed by the forces of good, represented by a well-meaning medicine man. No longer does he ground the problems and implicit solutions of our time on the bed-rock of reality, as he is known to have done in some of his finest works—*Tiger's Empire, Strike and Hunger, Bread and Butter* etc., but rather on a supernatural, animistic, intractable world. Whether this trend in film-making will lead to the abandoning of theatre work by Ogunde and the other artists, and whether the standards of these films will be one that will sustain them and consequently the tradition itself, remain factors to be seen.

Before discussing the more contemporary forms of Nigerian drama—the drama of pre-independence and after—it would be useful to mention, if only in passing, the other kinds of drama that emanated from the 1940's, the drama of the Onitsha market literature. Although hardly mentioned in the studies of Nigerian Drama, and with condescending tolerance, if at all, yet as dramatic literature, Onitsha market plays provide us with useful insights into the meaning of the lives of an important segment of a part of the Nigerian society.

What has come to be known as Onitsha market literature was the product of several socio-economic and historical factors.[38] Among these factors were the growth of Onitsha in the 1940's as an urban economic centre and the upsurge in the acceptance of an egalitarian form of education at the end of World War II, one which may have filtered down through the 1930's following the influence of Dr. Azikiwe and the other American-trained Igbo graduates who subsequently set up popular mass media of information. Essentially, Onitsha market literature are pamphlets, novelettes, playlets and stories written by members of an emergent literate class of traders, artisans and working-class persons for a mass literate audience. Interestingly, the first pamphlet said to have appeared in Onitsha was Cyprian Ekwensi's *Ikolo, the Wrestler* (1947). The erroneous impression gleaned from studies of Onitsha Market literature is that a majority of the pamphlets are novelettes, short narratives and stories. The fact is that some of its most interesting pieces are plays. In Obiechina's bibliography of pamphlet literature, next to narrative genres, plays come next in number, closely followed by romances, essays and biographies.

Generally, the plays (going strictly by their titles now), deal with a wide range of subjects and themes, from the imprisonment of Adolf Hitler, through dramatized biographies of African leaders, love themes, to straightforwardly didactic pieces. Obiechina identifies three or four broad themes in Onitsha market literature—didactic love themes (Western style), marriage and family tussles and religious and moral themes. All these themes are adequately dealt with in the plays. The most prolific playwrights of this tradition are perhaps Thomas Orlando Iguh and O. A. Ogali. Iguh's titles include *John in the Romance of true love: A tragical drama of West Africa for Schools and Colleges, Dr. Nkrumah in the struggle for Freedom.* However, Ogali's *Veronica, My Daughter* and *Elizabeth, My Love* are definitely the two best known plays of this school.

Since it is not known if these plays were put on stage or even meant for the stage in the first place, it is not known exactly how audiences reacted or could have reacted to them. But one obvious delight intended to be derived from the plays is in the area of language. A strange blend of the Bible, Shakespearean syntax, vacuum-concealing American lingos and long-winded Victorian rhetoric, these plays allude freely to, and imitate unabashedly, an admixture of literary texts, sources and titles. So that in the hands of an Onitsha market playwright such as Uzoh, Shakespeare's *Troilus and Cressida* becomes *Tribus and Folida*. But always, there is an auditory effect reached for by these playwrights, sometimes even at the expense of meaning. Obiechina quotes a fine example from Ogali's *Veronica, My Daughter*, this being the speech of a character named Bomber Billy: "I assure you that this is nothing but a cocified agency antipasimodical producing nothing but voscadum, miszcandum and tiscomo. This medicine that I have in hand is called the Grand Electrical Punchutical Demoscandum which cures all diseases incident to humanity!"[39]

Some people have argued that there is little merit to these works as literature, lacking, as it were, the depth and polish of more sophisticated writing of better skilled and more accomplished Nigerian writers. Perhaps that is so. But this is not to claim that there is no value in referring to them in a study such as this. These plays, as I indicated above, tell us a great deal about the class of Nigerian whose stories it recreates, and for "anyone who studies society and the evolution of cultural patterns and behaviour among these new literates"[40] they remain a vital source material. But even more importantly for our purpose, these plays provide our theatre historians and critics some clues towards understanding the earliest forms of contemporary Nigerian literary drama. For example, in language and style, the dramas of Onitsha market literature are coarser prototypes of James Ene Henshaw's better constructed and more popular plays. The village school teacher, Bambulu, who says in Henshaw's *This is our Chance:* "If I may interrupt, Your Grace, if the old lady fell into a pit and broke her neck, death in that case would not be due to vitamins. It would be due to asphyxia and respiratory paralysis consequent upon the fracture-dislocation of one or more of her conical vertebrae"[41]—surely comes across as a surer and more-skilful version of Bomber Billy!

This comparison does not detract from the important contributions of Henshaw to our theatre. Henshaw's contributions lay, ultimately in the area of example—the example of simple plays, simple characterization, of uncomplicated plot and even predictable resolutions. While these attributes are not necessarily enduring artistic qualities, they help explain, in part, his immense popularity as end-of-year favourites in Nigerian schools. His attempt to give African treatments to subject-matter, sometimes taken from English bedroom comedies, helped "both to stimulate and fill the demand" for badly needed dramatic texts in schools and colleges. And the moment that demand for texts started to be filled by the more competent artists who emerged at the dawn of Nigeria's independence, critical attention turned away from Henshaw to more serious drama.

In discussing serious contemporary Nigerian drama, the year 1960 is taken as a starting point—the year in which Wole Soyinka founded "The 1960 Masks". But the facts are not as simple as that. The flurry of activities of the three years preceding 1960 ought to be understood and put in perspective because in the last analysis, the founding of the "Masks" depended immensely on the events of those preceding years. It also ought to be stated that "The 1960 Masks" was not the only important Nigerian amateur group to emerge on the scene. There was in the East of Nigeria, John Ekwere and his Ogui Players which he revived in 1960 and later called the "Eastern Nigerian Theatre Group". Quite apart from the Yoruba Travelling theatre, much of what existed as serious theatre was centred around the then University College, Ibadan. The impetus to this factor came from the introduction of drama and theatre courses at the University in 1957 as part of an Educational Theatre programme, organized jointly by the English Department and the Education Faculty. In the same year, a group of expatriates, mainly university teachers and civil servants resident in Ibadan, got together with their Nigerian friends and colleagues and formed the Arts Theatre Production group which sought to awaken interest in theatre and drama as entertainment and serious art. At about the same time as when the Arts Theatre Production group was being formed, the students of the English Department were also forming a Drama Society. A third amateur group, The Players of the Dawn, was formed in 1959, drawing its membership from the young University graduates of Ibadan University who were based in Ibadan.

Between these three groups, audiences in Ibadan and the environs, were thrilled to a wide range of plays, from Greek classics, through Shakespeare, Sheridan to old and long-forgotten sensations of London West End! Said Soyinka in his essay reproduced in this anthology: ". . . The Players of the Dawn (have) in spite of the intelligence of the leaders, consistently succumbed to the dictates of the British Council prehistoric strictures and are incapable of seeing theatre as an activity which did not petrify with Galsworthy at the start of the century!" The real impetus to serious theatre may have come from the University's Dramatic Society's production of Wole Soyinka's *The Swamp Dwellers* and a cut version of *The Lion and the Jewel* in 1958, directed by Kenneth Post and Geoffrey Axworthy, plays which were distinctly different from other kinds of Nigerian plays that theatre enthusiasts were used to at the time. The task therefore of initiating what was a new movement was left to Wole Soyinka.

Wole Soyinka's return to Nigeria in 1960 coincided, not unexpectedly, with a new wave of national consciousness, one which permeated aspects of Nigerian cultural life. Driven by that euphoria and by the desire to evolve an authentically Nigerian theatre to express a new national consciousness, Wole Soyinka proceeded to absorb the members of the erstwhile Players of the Dawn into a new group, "The 1960 Masks". Beyond completing work on a new play, *The Trials of Brother Jero*, he also produced in 1960 his independence-sponsored play, *A Dance of the Forests*.

Perhaps, what is remarkable is not so much the founding of the theatre itself, especially as there had been essentially others like it prior to 1960, but rather the intensity and dedication with which the concept was executed. For while the "Masks" was physically based in Ibadan where Wole Soyinka resided, a majority of its members were based in Lagos. Made up of such individuals as Yemi Lijadu, Ralph Opara, Segun Olusola, Ms. Funlayo Asekun, Olga Adeniyi-Jones, Ms. Tola Soares, Francesca Periera and joined later by Patrick Osie, Femi Euba, Elsie Olusola, Jimmy Johnson, Tunji Oyelana and Wale Ogunyemi, the group self-lessly dedicated itself to the development of a truly Nigerian theatre, in its conception and design. Femi Euba tells us in his own contribution that "The 1960 Masks" was "hailed as the nucleus of our National Theatre". Combining an energetic career which included variedly profuse writing, some acting, constant directing, some teaching plus extensive research tours across the country and the coast of West Africa, Wole Soyinka placed everything, skill, material and all, at the service of the group.[42] By 1964, the group (now called Orisun Theatre) had done some fifteen full length plays in all, among them *A Dance of the Forests*, *My Father's Burden* (a television play), the premiere perfor-mance of J. P. Clark's first play, *Song of a Goat*, an anonymous commedia dell'arte script, *Three Cuckolds*, Soyinka's *Camwood on the Leaves* and Sarif Easmon's *Dear Parent and Ogre*.

Further impetus was given to the new movement by two other events—the activities of the University of Ibadan Dramatic Society and the founding of the Mbari Centre in Ibadan. Both events served to popularize the nature of the growing national-cultural identity. As part of the Student's Union Independence year programme, the Dramatic Society planned a country-wide tour of which Moliere's *Les Fourberies de Scapin* was to be presented in its adapted form as *That Scoundrel Suberu*. "Due to the exigences of time and money",[43] according to Mr. Dapo Adelugba, the idea was shelved. The tour was successfully undertaken in 1961 after the campus experiments in which plays were taken round to different halls of residence and held on make-shift stages. Evidently encouraged by the successful country-wide tour of *Suberu* in 1961, the Dramatic Society undertook another country-wide tour in 1962 with Ernest Ekom's adaptation of Shakespeare's *The Taming of the Shrew*. During that year, a two-year diploma awarding School of Drama was initiated and continued the touring tradition, one which reached its climax in the group's presentation of the stage adaptation of Nkem Nwankwo's *Danda*.

Those years at the Ibadan University, particularly the seven years between 1958–1965, were highly productive years and marked by an excitement of creative activity. In a period of intense superciliousness, laced with the surface individualism of an emerging privileged class at Nigeria's premier and hitherto, only University, the more active drama and English undergraduates of those years must have cut a different image for themselves. Goaded on by a collective vision of some sort, they tried out new ideas and experimented with novel concepts. For instance, it is worthy of note that some of the plays the students presented were joint projects by the students themselves. *Suberu* was, for instance, a collective effort between Dapo Adelugba, Alfred Opubor, and Brownson Dede, while the adaptation of *The Taming of the Shrew* was written by Ernest Ekom, with some assistance from Mr. Geoffrey Axworthy. But even more laudable was the first genuine attempts to take theatre to the people, away from the narrow confines of a pretentious and stuffy University of Ibadan atmosphere. Their audience was a mass audience, their stage, in the words of Axworthy, "a Town Hall, a Law Court, an open air cinema, the table tops of a school dining-hall, or the studio of E.N.T.V. in Enugu"[44]—just about anywhere their performances could be adapted to the audience and the conditions of performance.

Recently, a controversy over who should take credit for particular projects carried out during these years, has surfaced among the major participants of the events. Disappointed that many publications of the events of those years have tended to attribute the period's most important achievements solely to Geoffrey Axworthy, who was first director of the School of Drama, Mr. Adelugba has, and with justification, it seems, sought to put the records straight.[45]

In periods of innovation in the theatre, one that is marked by a flurry of activities, it is not always possible to single out individual contributions. Nevertheless, key figures can be identified, their contributions highlighted for acknowledgement, against the background of the entire movement. To be sure, Mr. Axworthy encouraged and supported the students immensely, putting his technical and constructing skills at their disposal. But the records indicate that a bulk of the bold experiments of those years were initiated by these young men and women. Ernest Ekom's account of those years are a corroboration of Mr. Adelugba's views.[46]

But even more questionable is Mr. Axworthy's veiled suggestion that he introduced Wole Soyinka to the Nigerian public and the implicit presumption that but for his own intervention, Wole Soyinka would have remained unknown for a longer time to the Nigerian public. Again, here, one fact obscures a more substantial one. It is a fact that Mr. Axworthy was the first to do a Soyinka play on the Nigerian stage. But even at this time, Wole Soyinka was not totally an unknown quantity to the Nigerian theatre, having tried his hands at writing for radio before his departure for Leeds in 1954. While at Leeds, where he completed work on *The Lion and the Jewel*, he participated actively in theatre work both inside and outside the University. In 1958, he participated in the National Students' *Sunday Times* drama festival where he had entered a successful performance of *The Swamp Dwellers*, one which was widely reviewed and received.[47] And as he himself admitted in private discussions with me, his eventual return to Nigeria was already in the pipeline. Therefore, his inevitable introduction to the Nigerian stage was purely a matter of time, certainly not requiring the "foresight" of an Axworthy or a Ken Post, to introduce, in the words of Axworthy, "a Nigerian author (who) had not been seen or expected before".[48]

Perhaps, the one indisputable fact in the midst of all these, is the contribution of the Ibadan University towards the development of theatre and drama, first through its School of Drama, and subsequently as a fully-fledged department of its own. It remained for some time the only training ground for theatre practitioners in Nigeria. For instance, the School of Drama Acting Company which Wole Soyinka set up as Director of the School at the start of the 1967/68 academic session and could hardly get in motion before his detention, served as a laboratory aimed at producing actors in an ensemble fashion. To achieve this, students and actors were exposed to a wide variety of plays, drawn as it were, from the world's repertory. Equally important was the initial, though short-lived attempts made to bridge the gap between the "academic" and the professional theatre, between the elitist theatre and the mass, popular tradition. The collaboration between Ogunmola and the School of Drama, in the joint stage production of Tutuola's *The Palmwine Drinkard* was a highly imaginative experiment. And then, in the Summer of 1971, in what is considered the highlight of the Company's life, it spent six weeks at a workshop at the Eugene O'Neill Theatre in Connecticut, rehearsing and presenting Soyinka's *Madmen and Specialists*. Shortly afterwards, Wole Soyinka resigned as Director. The Trinidadian Technical Director, Mr. Dexter Lyndersay, took over as acting Director of the unit.

Mr. Lyndersay's task was to keep the boat afloat against great odds. Obviously, he had inherited an almost unmanageable set-up—a theatre Company and a degree-awarding department, without the Rockefeller funds which had come in handy in the previous years and was discontinued in July of 1967 without the full complement of staff needed to run the set-up. Then came the Civil War, which marked the beginning of government cut-back of funds to Universities. Under such trying circumstances, the Company floundered and had to be disbanded. It is possible that Ibadan has not quite attained its former heights ever since.

But in another respect, Ibadan's contributions lay not only in the fact that it provided a forum for the growth of theatre but also the fact that the University helped produce some of the most renowned writers of the earlier period, among them J. P. Clark, Nkem Nwankwo, the late Christopher Okigbo, and of course, Chinua Achebe. Of these writers, J. P. Clark was to distinguish himself in the theatre.

It used to be the case to affirm that J. P. Clark and Wole Soyinka are Nigeria's foremost and best-known playwrights. That may have been correct only up until about 1975 or thereabout. That view would be contested today. Certainly, Wole Soyinka remains Nigeria's most versatile and enduring dramatist, standing above the others, not only in his prolificity but sometimes, in the depth of his perception. Clark's stature seems to have dwindled somewhat. For instance, as against Soyinka's fourteen published plays, J. P. Clark's reputation as a major dramatist rests principally on his first four plays—*A Song of a Goat, The Masquerade, The Raft, Ozidi*. Perhaps, what ought to be clearly stated in any attempt to re-examine the young history of our literary drama is the fact that so much has happened to Nigerian theatre since Soyinka and Clark came on the scene, so much since the audience on that night of February 1959 was treated at the old University College, Ibadan to a performance of *Swamp Dwellers* and a cut version of *The Lion and the Jewel*, indeed, so much to compel a studied revaluation of our earliest contemporary literary dramatists, their works and their role in the development of our theatre and drama.

For his part, and in consonance with the literary fervour of the late fifties at Ibadan University, J. P. Clark read widely, wrote prolificly and founded and edited a students' poetry magazine *The Horn*, in which the works of many young writers were first published. In addition to his four plays mentioned above, he has just written a new play, *The Boat*, which was produced in April of 1981. In each of these plays, an array of restrained, simple archetypal characters are portrayed as almost helpless victims of forces over which they have little or no control. In an imagery-laden language that is deceptively simple in the manner of the best of traditional oral poetry, the traditional Ijaw setting of his plays is transformed into one of relentless, recurrent disasters and doom. This tragic world-view bespeaks a cynicism, one which seems to characterize much of the Nigerian writers of J. P. Clark's age-group, a cynicism which sometimes lacks the compassion and hope which ought to accompany our perception of reality, considering that reality, even in its darkest moments, is not totally bleak. Although a skilled artist, his plays sometimes come across as stilted on stage, obviously suffering, if inconsiderably, from his own lack of practical theatre experience.

By contrast, Wole Soyinka brings to bear on his works in the theatre an experience of practical technique which goes back to his student days in Leeds and his career at the Royal Court theatre in London. No short summary of Soyinka's works could do justice to his enormous contributions to our theatre.[49] Without any doubt, the range, the variety and vitality of his writing career in the theatre—the dramatic monologues (*Salutation to the Gut*, 1962), the television plays (*My Father's Burden*, 1961; *You in Your Small Corner*, 1964; *Night before the Hunted*, 1964), the radio plays (*The House of Banigegi*, 1959; *Camwood on Leaves*, 1964), the sketches and revue (*The Republican*, 1964; *Before the Blackout*, 1965; *Before the Blowout*, 1979); the comic satires (*Lion and the Jewel*, 1957; *The Invention*, 1959; *The Trials of Brother Jero*, 1960); the tragi-comedies (*Kongi's Harvest*, 1967; *The Road*, 1965; *A Dance of the Forests*, 1960; *The Strong Breed*, 1969; *Swamp Dwellers*, 1959; the more sombre works of the post-civil war years (*Madmen and Specialists*, 1970; *The Bacchae of Euripides*, 1973; *The Jero's Metamorphosis*, 1973; *Death and the King's Horseman*, 1975; *Opera Wonyosi*, 1977), and a body of critical and theoretical writing—all these are a testimony to his abilities as a highly skilled and versatile craftsman. And if Wole Soyinka is today increasingly under attack from radical younger Nigerian critics for not going far enough in his analysis of the Nigerian society, he himself must take a lot of the blame for that. For he had himself, by the very stimulus of his example as writer and social critic, indeed, by his courage, set such high standards by which he is now being judged. Among the several writers whom he had unwittingly encouraged, by the sheer power of his example, was Ola Rotimi.

At the outbreak of the Nigerian civil war in July of 1966, when Wole Soyinka was being detained by the Gowon administration, Ola Rotimi was completing a Master of Fine Arts degree at Yale. Although his first play, *To Stir the God of Iron* had been produced in Boston in 1963 and the late Jack Landau had directed *Our Husband Has Gone Mad Again* at Yale in 1966, his reputation did not firmly become established until *The Gods are Not to Blame* in 1968. This is so, partly because it is his most performed work, both at home and abroad, and partly because of the play's immense popularity with audiences. In 1969, *The Gods* won the *African Arts/Arts d'Afrique* annual prize for playwriting. Between that play and when Ola Rotimi took up his job at the University of Port Harcourt in 1977, he wrote some seven major plays, appearing to favour historical tragedies. His last performed work, *If. . .*, is markedly different from his historical tragedies; for here, Rotimi is concerned with the socio-economically fatal consequences of false electioneering promises in a society that lacks direction and purpose. This is a far cry from the more conventional interpretation of historical events to be found in his history plays (*Kurunmi* and *Ovonranwen Nogbaisi* for instance), an interpretation which ignores the creative struggles of the masses and concentrates historical events in the hands of single individuals, implying in the process that single individuals, alone, make history.

However, to my mind, his most important contribution to Nigerian theatre may well not be in the area of playwriting but in the area of real theatre practice. His directional skill is perhaps unmatched in the country—his ability to literally create "magic" on stage is one of his strongest points as a theatre practitioner. Although he has attributed some of his directional skill to influences from the late American director, Jack Landau, I think it is a little bit more than just that. A man of tenaciously stubborn artistic convictions, Ola Rotimi has an eye for details in the theatre and a sagacious ability to know what can, and will work theatrically. It is, perhaps, not an accident that of all our *major* playwrights, he alone has received formal training in the areas of playwriting and directing. That training is evident in his practice.

A look at the nature of that practice must begin with the Ori-Olokun theatre which he helped to found, "as an organ in the University's (then) Institute of African Studies concerned with the practical expression of music, dance and drama in the Nigerian cultural context".[50] What was unique about the Ori-Olokun was not the fact that it was for a long time in the country the only professional English speaking theatre company, although that fact is worth noting. Its uniqueness lay in the ideology underlying its objectives, as reflected in its membership, a membership drawn from all walks of life and all classes of society, a membership which affirmed the notion that the struggle for a meaningful cultural liberation is not the exclusive concern of any one select group in society, but rather that of all. In the hands of Ola Rotimi, the Ori-Olokun became a real experimental theatre,

providing the much needed meeting point betweeen the traditional artist and the trained University mind.

This attempt to seek to provide a meeting point between the
University trained artist and the traditional artist seems to have also
taken some root at both Nsukka and Ahmadu Bello Universities. At
post-civil-war Nsukka, for instance, Meki Nzewi, among others, has
carried out extensive research works in traditional theatre material
by working in collaboration with traditional artists in the field.[51] His
own dance-dramas are attempts to incorporate, in as less rigid a way
as possible, traditional materials into more "structured" situation for
urban audiences. Hence, his *The Lost Finger* is subtitled, "folk
mythological opera-drama" while his *The Third Coming* is subtitled
"a revue-dance-music". At Ahmadu Bello University in Zaria,
under the direction of Michael Etherton in the English Department,
students' drama groups have taken their works in Hausa to small
villages on the outskirts of Zaria. Also the experiments of Mark
Ralph-Bowman with drama students at Bayero University, which I
refer to later on, are of particular interest.

The post civil-war period has also witnessed the emergence of a
different crop of playwrights, inadequately referred to as second
generation playwrights. The finest of this crop of playwrights are
set apart from their first compatriots not necessarily by any
substantial age difference (where it does exist at all) but rather by
temperament and vision, hardened, as it were by the wounds and
trauma of the civil war. Among these writers are Fela Davis,
Comish Ekiye, Soji Simpson, Kole Omotoso, Bode Sowande,
Meki Nzewi, Laolu Ogunniyi, Bode Osanyin, Zulu Sofola,
Ahmed Yerimah, Femi Osofisan. Wale Ogunyemi, who is by far
the most prolific of these writers, is a half-child of both "generations" being himself a founding member of the old Orisun theatre
and currently one of Nigeria's most active playwrights. However,
his own works did not come to limelight until about the outbreak
of the civil war. The same is true of Femi Euba.

Unfortunately, some of these writers have not been accorded
the recognition they deserve, even in Nigeria. For one thing, they
have not "benefited" from the kind of foreign critical acclaim and
astoundment which became factors in the growth and exposure of
the first crop of writers. In some cases, these writers, out of an

ideological commitment, have shunned or at best, been indifferent to this "acclaim" by refusing to publish with foreign firms, believing firmly that the production of literature cannot be divorced from its content and over-all objective in a neo-colonialist economy. Others still, are more renowned in other areas of artistic endeavour. For instance, Kole Omotoso who has written two fine plays, *Shadows in the Horizon* and *The Curse* is a more accomplished novelist than he is a playwright.

This is not the place to do a major critique of these writers—that is work for another time and place. Suffice it to say, however, that some of these writers have distinguished themselves as highly competent craftsmen and deserve to be mentioned if only passingly. One such writer is Femi Osofisan, well on his way to becoming one of our finest playwrights. His eight major plays to date, among them *Chattering and the Song, Once Upon Four Robbers, Morontodun, Who's Afraid of Solarin?* are some of the finest works to come out of the contemporary Nigerian repertory. Eclectic as he is original, Osofisan has sought to reshape traditional Yoruba mythology and ritual in the light of contemporary realities, to squeeze out of old myths fresher meanings, in the belief that Man, in the last analysis, makes his own myth. Not content to merely expose the ills of the society, he has dared to provide us with glimpses of his vision of a new society. It is interesting to note that Osofisan's plays are popular fares at institutions across the country.

However, in spite of such popularity at institutions, it is debatable whether Femi Osofisan is eminently a popular playwright, indeed, whether any of Nigeria's literary playwrights can be said to be genuinely popular. The question can be put differently: Can the Nigerian playwright, based in a University setting, writing in standard English be effective and popular in a society where the mass audience (some seventy per cent of the entire population) is not literate in English? Will such a playwright ever strike a responsive chord in a mass audience, when such an audience comes from his immediate community? Will he be understood and his message comprehended? Do our literary playwrights reach out to mass audiences? The fact that the last five or more essays in this anthology touch on these crucial issues, is indicative of the controversial nature of the subject.

Perhaps, no playwright seems better suited to discuss the problem than Femi Euba, a playwright whose cryptic use of symbolism and language can be said to have been problematic for a thorough grasp of his plays. Unfortunately in Femi Euba's contribution to this anthology, his essay on the Nigerian playwright, he shies away from confronting concretely the whole question of the function and role of the playwright vis-à-vis his immediate constituency. Such an omission may not be accidental. There is an underlying presumption in his over-all position, namely, that "the prideful individualist position" (to use his own words) of the artist limits any attempts on our part as critics to make adequate judgements about the artist's vision. That view can be safely put to rest by stating unequivocally that even conservative schools of criticism do readily concede today that the artist being a product of a particular society, a particular historical epoch of a particular class, cannot and does not have his meaning alone—he speaks not only for his time and place, but also for his class. Euba ignores Ibsen's caution which he himself quotes in a footnote: no poet lives through anything in isolation.

None the less, he puts his thumb on one important problem. Put simply, his position can be summarized thus: in contrast to contemporary Yoruba Travelling theatre groups, for instance, why are works by our playwrights not popular with mass audiences? Why is it that although Ogunde can fill a large hall in, for instance, Lagos, our literary playwrights cannot do the same? In carrying the argument one step further, Mr. Euba zeros in on Wole Soyinka and Ola Rotimi. His questions here are also straightforward enough: whereas Wole Soyinka is a finer playwright, in Euba's view, than Ola Rotimi, why is it that Ola Rotimi is more able, even within a moment's notice, to fill a theatre hall in Nigeria than Wole Soyinka can claim to do? Is this not partly because most Nigerian audiences are intellectually lazy and therefore cannot make the extra effort needed to appreciate the sophisticated theatre of Wole Soyinka? Or is this the case of Ola Rotimi writing down to the audience, pandering to its taste?

First let us correct a few wrong assumptions. While it may be correct that Ola Rotimi will fill more halls in Nigeria, perhaps, more than Soyinka can, that is a view that can hardly apply to all Soyinka plays. As Mr. Euba aptly points out plays such as *The Trials of Brother Jero* and *The Lion and the Jewel* are immensely popular plays, to say nothing of *Before the Blackout* sketches which drew large audiences in Lagos and Ibadan when they first appeared. Neither is the problem simply that of an intellectually lazy Nigerian audience which refuses to do its extra work. Similarly, the problem cannot be reduced to a simple matter of not having enough competent Nigerian directors with the vision of realizing these works on stage. The problem seems deeper than these. Implicit in the responses and attitudes of most Nigerian audiences to the two playwrights, is a critical judgement of some sort, a critical judgement derived from the different stated objectives and practical approaches of both writers, vis-à-vis their relationships with their audiences.

Let me clarify. In his search for the most appropriate language to use in his work, Rotimi seems to have the Nigerian audience in mind. Rotimi's approach in a majority of his works has been that "of winnowing, selecting, and finding words, phrases and images that run close to vernacular parlance".[52] When asked pointedly for what kind of people he wrote, Ola Rotimi's response under-scores the point being made.

> English, as you know, is the official medium of communication in Nigeria. Inevitably, I write for audiences who are knowledgable in this language. However, in handling the English language in my plays, I strive to temper its phraseology to the ear of both the dominant semi-literate as well as the literate classes, ensuring that my dialogue reaches out to both groups with ease in assimilation and clarity and identification.[53]

When asked a similar question, Wole Soyinka replied:

> . . . quite frankly, I do not think of any audience when I write. I write in the firm belief that there must be at least a hall full of people who are sort of on the same wave-length as mine from every stratum of society and there must be at least a thousand people who are able to feel the same way as I do about something. So when I write, I write in the absolute confidence that it must have an audience.[54]

Even if we gave room for the creative writer's blarney and ignored the first part of Wole Soyinka's reply, since we know that he has mostly written with a Nigerian audience well in mind, his response raises questions. We must admit that Wole Soyinka's belief that at a production of, shall we say, *Madmen and Specialists* at the Mapo Hall, Ibadan or the assembly hall of Federal Government College, Okposi, there could be some one thousand people who operate on the same wave-length as he, is an exaggerated expectation. It is wishful thinking in a predominantly non-literate society where the majority of the people are not equipped to understand, let alone digest the highly sophisticated and cryptic English language of that play. It may well be an awareness of the predominantly non-literate nature of our society that has determined Ola Rotimi's more persistent experiments with language. For, while seeking to capture the nuances of Yoruba oral speech processes, he uses the English language in a manner "which renders his poetry prosaic".[55] There is a danger, though, that if not properly handled such an experiment could be flat. This may have caused Adelugba to describe the result of such an experiment as "blandness of language" in the supposed unsurer days of *The Gods are not to blame.*

The solution, seems to me, to be something of a middle ground between the high "sophistication" of language evident in some of Wole Soyinka's more "difficult" works and the delicate brand of English which Ola Rotimi has made popular. Ironically, Wole Soyinka tried out such experiments, even with far greater ease, in his earlier works such as *The Lion and the Jewel* and *The Trials of Brother Jero.* In *Brother Jero* he added the dimension of "pidgin" English thereby showing, quite early in his career, a brilliant awareness of the use of different levels of English in correspondence with the reality of what exists in the society itself. It is perhaps, not an accident that these two are his most popular plays before a majority of Nigerian audiences.[56] This adoption of a brand of English with a wider appeal seems a reasonable way out, especially as there is a growing expansion of persons who are literate in the various levels of English, "pidgin" standard and colloquial.

One of the strongest proofs that this is one way out is the

success of such experiments on contemporary television drama. The emerging national response since 1980 or thereabout, to such immensely popular television serial dramas as *Village Head-master*, *Cockcrow at Dawn*, *Adio Family* and the antics of Chief Zebodaya Okorigwe-Nwogo, (alias four-thirty!) in *Masquerade* is phenomenal. Not only does the response cut across class lines, it cuts across age and ethnic groups. The approach in most of these dramas is to use the various levels of English, with a preponder-ance of "pidgin" English and the substrates of English words drawn from different ethnic groups and coloured by the nuances of speech inflection of the different Nigerian ethnic languages.

Another way to look at the issue is to advocate that the playwrights write in our national languages, as a sure means of ensuring that their works are accessible to the greater number of our peoples. Once considered an unpragmatic and unrealistic position, that view is fast gaining ground today as more African writers revaluate their position and their effectiveness as artists. Ngugi Wa Thiong'o and Ousumane Sembane have been in the fore-front of the case for African literatures in African languages. Ngugi's decision to do a major production in Gikuyu was a conscious ideological one. Ola Rotimi completed (in 1980) work on a Yoruba version of *Kurunmi* due to be produced soon. It is also interesting to note that in a letter published in *Transition* (November, 1963), Wole Soyinka expressed a possibility at the time of performing his plays in Yoruba. Unfortunately, the possibilities have never been realized. Any doubts about the possibility that the use of national languages would ensure far wider popularity for literary plays is dispelled by the facts at our disposal. At a production of Akin Isola's *Efusetan Aniwura* in early 1981 at the Olubadan Stadium, an estimated crowd of 40,000 people watched a single performance of the play! A crucial appendix to this position, of course, is the fact that most African writers are victims of a historical circumstance and reality which makes this proposition almost impossible. Most African writers who operate in a European linguistic medium cannot write as fluently in an African language. So while we cannot in any seriousness demand of most of our contemporary playwrights the use of African languages, we can at least argue that the future of our literature ought to be in that direction. Steps towards the long term realization of that objective must begin now. This means that the teaching and learning of a national language must be made mandatory at our high schools and universities.

But will language by itself do it? When all is said and done, will it ensure the mass popularity of our literary playwrights? Are other factors not also crucial—the factor of physical theatre, their locations, their objectives, their management and operation? While these are all important, it seems that the nerve centre of the issue remains one which we raised earlier on: for whom do our literary playwrights write? About whom do they write? The real importance of Dr. Jeyifo's essay in this anthology is his identification of these problems, one which provides the answers to the questions Mr. Euba raised. After accurately stating that our finest literary plays have not (thank goodness for that) shied away from some of the acute concerns of contemporary Nigerian society, he concludes with characteristic incisiveness:

> But precisely because they (our literary plays) have not been consciously written for, and about the popular urban and rural masses, these crucial groups and classes play a passive, almost invisible role in these plays. And these plays have all, more or less, been heavily imbued with a mood and a spirit of despair, disillusionment and even sometimes with a savage, cynical misanthropic vision. *The literary drama will become popular theatre only if and when the popular audiences see themselves, their concerns and aspirations sharply and movingly related in this drama.*[57] (my emphasis)

The task therefore, seems to be on the broad logistics and methods of how to embark on this search for a really popular theatre. Tentative suggestions form the basis of the final section of this essay.

Towards a Theatre of greater Relevance

The search for, and the ultimate acquirement of a people's theatre must be our goal, a theatre which must become an instrument in the hands of the greater number of our people in their struggles for better working conditions, for more rights, for more land on which to grow food, indeed, for better lives. Such a theatre must build on the history of our peoples' songs, their drama, dances, drumming, masquerades, puppetry, etc., used in resistance against several forms of oppression in the past, political, traditional and economic. Such a theatre needs to provide a means of building a critical consciousness in the masses of our workers and peoples, or even mobilizing them for action, of engaging them in struggle and reflecting on the struggle. Because such a theatre would necessarily draw on the skills and creativity of the people, expressing their problems and concerns, it would reinforce the growth of identity in the people and instil far greater self-confidence in them.

The kind of theatre we speak of here is not a cathartic one where the masses of the people get a chance to get their bitterness and frustration off their chest. Neither is it the type of theatre where the people are presented with prescribed solutions to their problems. This is, in a manner reminiscent of the best of Bertolt Brecht, a theatre where the people are challenged to look critically at their situation and compelled to want to change it, a theatre which will debunk the myth that reality is unchangeable and the world cannot be transformed. Far from being the passive recipients of finished products, the "audience" is acutely engaged in the production of meaning. Reading from a paper presented at an International Theatre Conference held in Angola in January 1980, Ross Kidd, an adult educator and researcher who has been engaged in the search for a similar approach to theatre experience in Botswana said:

> In this approach the theatre performance is not the total experience; it must be linked with critical analysis, organization and struggle. The performance can provide a dialectical view of the world but this must be consolidated and sharpened through dialogue and action; it must be part of a continuing process in which past action (struggle) provides the dramatic material (a historical view of reality) for analysis and strategizing leading to future action (struggle).[58]

This approach to the theatre is being used extensively in many third world countries, especially in Latin America and Asia, in the struggles of small farmers and landless labourers.[59] By far the most publicized of these attempts are those by the Mexican educator, Augusto Boal, whose experiments with theatre as a weapon in class struggles, are published in his important book, *Theatre of the Oppressed*.[60] Believing acutely that education, particularly in the situation of the third world, is a cultural action, Boal works from the premise that the process of conquering oppression requires collective struggle and the development of revolutionary consciousness and awareness—the awareness that people, by themselves, create cultures.

Boal's task has been to show how, through various stages of training, education and collective work, theatre can be used to create a revolutionary consciousness. Specifically, he identifies four crucial stages in the process. The first two stages are those of physical exercises during which the participants, mainly peasants and farmers, are, through bodily contacts, made aware, first, of their bodies and subsequently of their capabilities to use their bodies for self-expression. During the third stage, the stage of theatre as language, the participants are introduced to a means of developing a critical understanding of reality and of how it can be changed and transformed. This stage involves three exercises which Boal further breaks into *simultaneous dramaturgy, Image theatre* and *Forum theatre*. In "simultaneous" dramaturgy the spectators or participants "write", so to speak, the scenario, telling a group of actors what to do in portraying solutions to a problem. Since the participants can intervene at any given time to change the action, to "rewrite" the scenario, they are in control of the situation. In the "Image" and "Forum" theatres the spectator/actor dichotomy is virtually obliterated. The spectators not only intervene, but do take over the action from the actors, inserting themselves in the roles of the actors. The fourth stage which he identified is that of "theatre as discourse", simple forms in which spectator/actor creates spectacles to discuss certain themes and rehearse certain action. In the end, participants and actors alike, are able to make their own theatre, use it as a means of developing their own ideas, trying out various options for overcoming oppression.

At first contact, Boal's experiments and theories seem farfetched, extreme and impracticable for our situation, especially as the experience of Latin America is different from ours. For instance, landless farmers and peasants are better organized than the best of our organized labour force and have a longer tradition of struggle from the clutches of a coalescence of a readily identifiable class of land-owners. However, the broad principles he identifies and frame-work outlined in his book are not only applicable, but known to have been applied, even if infrequently, in Kenya and even Nigeria.

When Ngugi Wa Thiong'o collaborated with peasants in his home in Limuru to put together a Gikuyu language play, *Ngaahika Ndeenda*, basically what he did was to *describe* and *discuss* details of the "scenario" with the peasants who then "restaged" the details for the rest of the community. The simple and direct approach of the play and its production drove many points home for the peasants. And here was a play, which, in the words of Ngugi, "correctly reflects the true social conditions in Kenya today, especially in its comparative depiction of the styles of the privileged thieving minority and the labouring majority".[61] Not unexpectedly, the play was banned by the Kenyan government shortly after it opened in Limuru and Ngugi himself was interned for reasons connected with the play.

Nearer home, Wole Soyinka's short-lived Guerilla Unit of the University of Ife theatre was a most welcome departure from the dominant tradition of our contemporary literary drama. The object of the Unit was not dissimilar in certain respects to those of Ngugi, for instance. The Unit was assembled during the political campaigns and well-rehearsed and well-equipped to present short satiric sketches. *Before the Blowout*, as the sketches were known, were performed before local audiences in the heart of Ife township. Although the sketches were loosely scripted, much of the "playing" was improvised by the actors, the duration and style of presentation was determined by the street audiences and the venue of presentation. The sequence of events for a particular performance was simple enough. Usually one of the performers would announce, at a street corner, for instance, in the manner of a town crier, the presence of the group and its intention to perform an event. As the unsuspecting crowd gathered, the short, pungent sketch which always dealt with various aspects of the corruption of the incoming politicians, would commence.

Unfortunately, the effectiveness of these sketches were attenuated by two crucial factors—the fact that they were written in English and performed before predominantly Yoruba speakers in the ever ancient Yoruba town of Ife. The second factor has to do with the fact that there were no attempts consciously made to involve the spectators and the actors alike in a critique of the sketches—no forum for critiquing some of the issues raised by the sketches. And to that extent, its format remained rigid. Nevertheless, Wole Soyinka has continued to demonstrate an awareness of the capabilities of a mass popular theatre as a powerful codification for conscientization purposes. During the Road Traffic Safety Campaign in 1980 organized by the Oyo State Road Safety Corps, which Wole Soyinka heads, theatre was used to *teach* traffic rules. An adaptation of a Yoruba language play, *Gbekude*, by Adegoke Durojaiye, was taken round urban centres in Oyo State with very successful results.

But, perhaps, the most publicized example of this kind of experimental theatre was the 1981 production of *The Project*, a play *devised* and performed by the Writer's Drama Club of the Bayero University, Kano. What was significant about this production was not so much the fact that it was a collective students' effort, with each student contributing bits and details to the overall play, but rather, the production style and the fundamental message of the play. Prior to the "writing" of the script, individual students went back to their villages to gather material on the incalculable effects, psychological and otherwise, of the developmental projects being financed, usually by International Agencies such as International Monetary Fund and the World Bank. The materials gathered over a long period of time was, with the assistance of Mr. Mark Ralp-Bowman, carefully put together as a play. One of the play's important messages, according to Isaac Yongo, who had also worked on it was the view that "the masses need to be politicized in order to ensure a healthy economic and moral development of the nation".[62]

Although highly instructive, and quite welcome in their refreshing approaches, each of these experiments mentioned above—the University of Ife theatre and the Bayero University Drama Group—have been limited in impact by two factors, that of being institutionalized and the fact that they have not been carried to the next logical step, that of concretely relating the problems the plays highlight to the current struggles of the greater number of our peoples, the urban and rural workers and peasants. As Ross Kidd put it, "It is not enough simply to express problems through theatre if this is not linked with critical analysis of and action on the underlying causes and structures; it is not enough to rehearse struggle if this does not lead to struggle."[63] The question then is: how can this be achieved today in Nigeria within the existing socio-political framework? How can the theatre, as a medium of social transformation be "woven into an on-going process of critical analysis, organization and struggle?"

There can hardly be a single answer to these questions. The clear option *now* seems the establishment of truly community theatres, removed from institutional settings such as universities and governmental bodies. The reason for this is obvious enough. Governmental organizations are by their very nature, apprehensive about challenging the *status quo* and no theatre movement under its umbrella can be meaningfully engaged in the struggle to bring about real change. Ngugi's decision to leave the University of Nairobi theatre setting and move to Limuru and base himself concretely where the peasant group he opted to work with was situated was a courageous, conscious, ideological decision. Therefore, a fundamental pre-requisite for the kind of movement we envisage is the establishment of small community theatres in small communities, theatres run by these communities and controlled by them and linked with organized labour. In fact, the most appropriate body that can finance the establishment of such community theatres is organized labour since it stands to gain the most from them.

However, the example of Nigeria is compounded by the fact that organized labour is not as organized as it seems, and the fact that the organized labour there is has no proper grass-roots connections and links. But even more sordid is the fact that organized labour in Nigeria does not as yet understand the close relationship between organized struggle and the cultural weaponry involved in such a struggle. What needs to be done urgently, is the fostering of links between our peasantry, farmers' cooperatives, our urban and rural workers, students' groups and organizations and organized labour. Beyond that, a process of education must be embarked upon. The role of courageous individual effort is important, individuals who can initiate such movements, at least at the stage of organizing because the establishment of the theatre we advocate calls for courage. It calls for the courage to break away from existing theatrical traditions and habits and face up to the risks of failure, of non-survival and annihilation, but above all, the courage of conviction needed to succeed. And beyond individual effort, in the last analysis, the task is a collective one requiring the concerted efforts of all trained theatre personnel in this monumental programme.

By all means, the existing cultural organizations located in institutions must be allowed to flourish, side-by-side with the efforts towards a popular cultural movement. But the cultural policies in our schools of drama, our university theatres, and Arts Councils must change radically. These institutions will need to be radically restructured in order for them to help create a truly relevant culture. To take one example, there is need to bridge the dangerously unhealthy gap between our universities and the countryside, between our intellectuals and practical labour, between rural and urban centres. The universities must initiate moves towards a meaningful and conscious merging of the best traditions of Western oriented textual dramaturgy and the vibrantly contemporary indigenous theatrical techniques. Beyond merely making their facilities accessible to small regional traditional groups, that is, on an equal basis of exchange and participation, our universities *must* involve themselves more actively in the creative struggle of our peasants and farmers by physically going to the countryside. Our drama undergraduates must be made to do a substantial part of their work in rural centres, learning from the traditional artist, while the traditional artist learns from them. And as I said earlier on, the teaching of national languages must be intensified in our universities.

The road to be walked is a tortuous, long one involving political and social work, the reconciling of opposites, of theory and practice, even the combining of disparate groups, peasants, farmers' cooperatives, teachers, educators, artists, politicians, students, etc., into one concerted push towards a society in which art serves the interest of all, where art and culture create the basis of the formulation of a common destiny and the collective cooperation in pursuing such a destiny, a society where art is meaningfully relevant and culture is not confined by the limitations of ethnicity or class. Only then can the search for a genuinely popular theatre be said to have begun, and perhaps, attained.

Notes

1. For one thing, it can be argued, and with justification, whether a truly Nigerian theatre does exist. Would it not be right to speak of Nigerian theatre and drama as a conglomeration of several ethnic dramas, each with distinct qualities of its own, even if it manages to share a few basic features with the others? So that while one can speak of 'Kalabari drama', 'Igbo ritual drama', 'Yoruba Travelling theatre', 'Kwagh-hir Puppet theatre of the Tiv', one can hardly speak of a single Nigerian theatre. The term itself becomes a convenient one for the purposes of studies such as we attempt here.
2. George Thomson, *Marxism and Poetry*, New York, International Publishers, 1946, p. 15.
3. J. A. Adedeji, "The Origin and Form of the Yoruba Masque Theatre", in *Cahiers D'Etudes Africaines*, Vol. XII, No. 46 (date not provided), p. 255.
4. Ibid., p. 255.
5. Ibid., p. 255.
6. Ruth Finnegan, *Oral Literature in Africa*, Nairobi, Oxford University Press, 1970.
7. See M. J. C. Echeruo's "The Dramatic Limits of Igbo Ritual", reproduced in Chapter 7 of this anthology.
8. Quoted by Meki Nzewi in "Traditional Theatre Practice", *Nigeria Magazine*, Nos. 128/129, 1979, p. 15.
9. See Meki Nzewi, "Some Social Perspectives of Igbo Traditional Theatre", in *The Black Perspective*, Vol. 6, No. 2, Fall 1978.
10. Ulli Beier, "A Year of Sacred Festivals in one Yoruba Town", *Nigeria Magazine*, (Special Number) 1959.
11. See J. A. Adedeji, "Folklore and Yoruba Drama: Obatala as a case study", in *African Folklore* edited by Richard Dorson, New York, Doubleday and Company, Inc., 1972, pp. 321–339.
12. In fact, Prof. Clark used the term "modern drama" when referring to the non-traditional drama. I prefer the term "literary" because it seems to me to be a most crucial difference between the two traditions, even though I am aware of the unfortunate qualitative differentiation implied in that choice, one which Dr. Jeyifo adequately deals with elsewhere in this anthology. The difference in terminology still agrees with J. P. Clark's classification since

there is evidence that he meant "literary" when he spoke of "modern"—"drama that usually is first seen in print before it is seen on the stage". I am eager not to be misunderstood here. I do not suggest that the traditional and the modern in Africa are antithetical—in fact, my classification of contemporary Yoruba Travelling Theatre as "Modern Traditional" bears that out. I am not unaware of Chinweizu's valid quarrel in a different context, with the erroneous insinuation made sometimes that the indigenous is always African while the modern is always European! *The West and the Rest of Us*, New York, Random House, 1975, pp. 296–297.

13. Hubert Ogunde at a public lecture at the University of Ife, March 19, 1981.
14. A nagging problem persists here! Yoruba Travelling theatre can quite rightly be considered popular in the sense already stated. That does not obviate the point being made, however, namely that Yoruba Travelling theatre is in a class by itself, the product of a specific historical situation as I attempt to show in this essay.
15. See James N. Amankulor, "Dance as an Element of artistic synthesis in traditional Igbo Festival Theatre", in *Okike: An African Journal of New Writing*, No. 17, Feb., 1980, pp. 84–95.
16. Meki Nzewi, *op. cit.*, p. 170.
17. John Messenger, "Ibibio Drama", *Africa*, No. 41, 1971, pp. 210–211.
18. Ruth Finnegan, *op. cit.*, pp. 515, 517.
19. *Op. cit.*, pp. 208–209.
20. See "Bornu under the Shehus", by G. C. Ifemesia in *One Thousand Years of West African History* ed. by Ajayi and Espie, Ibadan, Ibadan University Press and Nelson, 1965, pp. 289–298.
21. Alfred Metraux, "Dramatic Elements in Ritual Possession", *Diogenes*, No. 11, 1955, pp. 18–36.
22. See Lynn Leonard, *The Growth of Entertainment on non-African Origin in Lagos from 1800–1920*, unpublished M. A. Thesis, University of Ibadan, 1977. I am heavily indebted to this penetrating work for much of the details of this period of Nigerian theatre history. Other useful studies include: M. J. C. Echeruo's *Victoria Lagos*, London, Macmillan, 1977 and J. A. Adedeji, "The Church and the Emergence of the Nigerian Theatre, 1866–1945", in *Journal of the Historical Society of Nigeria*, Vol. VI, Nos. 1 and 4, December, 1971, and June 1973.
23. Quoted by J. A. Adedeji in "The Church and the Emergence of the Nigerian Theatre, 1866–1914", *op. cit.*, p. 28.
24. Frantz Fanon, *The Wretched of the Earth*, New York, Grove Press, 1963, p. 222.
25. J. A. Adedeji, *op. cit.*, p. 41.
26. Lynn Leonard, *op. cit.*, p. 165.
27. " 'Native' was in those years, a necessary word. It was used primarily to separate the indigenes from both the immigrants and the Europeans", Echeruo, *Victoria Lagos*, p. 29.
28. Echeruo, Ibid., p. 29.
29. Ibid., p. 30.

30. Ibid., p. 39.
31. See Segun Osoba, "The Development of Trade Unionism in Colonial and Post-Colonial Nigeria", in *Topics in Nigerian Economic and Social History*, Ife, University of Ife Press, 1980, p. 190.
32. Prof. Adedeji quotes an 1886 *Lagos Observer* account of how Catholics "were labelled 'dishonest supernumeraries' and youths who could not afford these exhorbitant gate-fees indulged themselves in the unfriendly exercises of throwing stones on the corrugated roof of the building"—"The Church and the Emergence of the Nigerian Theatre", p. 37.
33. Adedeji, "The Church and the Emergence of the Nigerian Theatre", p. 390.
34. Hubert Ogunde, Ife Lecture, *op. cit.*
35. Ibid.
36. Ibid.
37. Fortunately, Dr. Biodun Jeyifo of the University of Ife Department of Literature in English is presently carrying out extensive research on the companies with a view of publishing his findings in a book billed to appear in 1982.
38. See Emmanuel Obiechina's *An African Popular Literature: A study of Onitsha Market Pamphlets*, Cambridge, Cambridge University Press, 1973, *passim*.
39. Obiechina, *op. cit.*, p. 81.
40. Ibid., p. 120.
41. James Ene Henshaw, *This is our Chance*, London, Hodder and Stoughton, 1956, 1979, p. 16.
42. For instance, the first prize money offered by the British monthly *Encounter* for the entry of *A Dance of the Forests* went into the paltry coffers of the nascent company.
43. Dapo Adelugba, "Nigerian Theatre Survey", in *New Theatre Magazine*, Vol. XII, No. 2, footnote No. 5.
44. Geoffrey Axworthy, "The Performing Arts in Nigeria—A Footnote", *New Theatre Magazine*, Vol. XII, No. 2, p. 18.
45. Ibid, pp. 15–16. For G. Axworthy's position see the same source, pp. 17–18 and "The Arts Theatre and the School of Drama", *Ibadan*, No. 18, Feb. 1964.
46. Ernest Ekom, "The Development of Theatre in Nigeria (1960–1967)", *New African Literature and the Arts*, Vol. III, 1973, pp. 265–283.
47. There is an interesting footnote to this production. The well-known doyen of British newspaper drama critics, Mr. Harold Hobson, had written a review of the production. Soyinka objected, to Mr. Hobson's face, to the review as being patronizing and lacking an understanding of the world-view purveyed in the play, causing Mr. Hobson to admonish Mr. Soyinka for being "too sensitive a young man". Mr. Soyinka was 23 years old!
48. *Op. cit.*, p. 17.
49. Already, four major critical studies on Soyinka exist and provide valuable information on him and his works: Gerald Moore, *Wole Soyinka*, London,

Evans Brothers, 1971. Alain Richard, *Theatre et Nationalisme: Wole Soyinka et Le Poi, Jones*, Paris, Presence Africaine, 1972. Eldred Durosimi Jones, *The Writings of Wole Soyinka*, Ibadan, Heinemann, 1973; Oyin Ogunba, *The Movement of Transition*, Ibadan, Ibadan University Press, 1975.

50. From the programme notes of the 1969 University of Ife production of *Kurunmi*.

51. See Kalu Uka's, "New Directions in Theatrical Practice at Nsukka, 1970–1975", unpublished paper.

52. Ola Rotimi, in interview with Mrs. Margaret Folarin, New Theatre Magazine, *op. cit.*, p. 6.

53. Ola Rotimi in *Dem Say: Interviews with Eight Nigerian Writers*, ed. by Bernth Lindfors, Occasional Publication, Afro-American Studies and Research Centre, University of Texas, Austin, 1974, p. 60.

54. Wole Soyinka in *African Writers Talking* ed. by Dennis Duerden and Cosmo Pieterse, London, Heinemann, p. 177.

55. J. A. Adedeji, "The Nigerian Theatre and its audience", Paper presented at the Conference of Professors of Theatre Research, Venice, 4–6th September, 1975.

56. There is a cautionary footnote to this section of the essay. The presumed conclusions reached here, on which of the artists is the more popular than the other, or on which of the works of the individual artist is the more popular, is based on personal experiences and observations over a long period of time in this country. I do not know of any statistical studies that have been carried out on the subject to ascertain that such conclusions are accurate. But I think most people will accept them as close enough to a correct picture of the situation.

57. Biodun Jeyifo, see Chapter 23 of this anthology.

58. Ross Kidd, "People's Theatre, Conscientization and Struggle", unpublished paper.

59. See *Caribbean Contact*, "Sistren-Jamaican women in New kind of Theatre", May 1979.
    Yohan Devananda, "Rural Theatre and Conscientization in Sri Lanka", *Asia Action*, No. 7, March/April, 1977.
    Ross Kidd, "Popular Theatre and Formal Education in Africa: Liberation or Domestication", *Educational Broadcasting International*, Vol. 12, No. 1, 1979.
    Melechor Morante, "Experiments in Community Theatre in the Philippines", *Asia Action*, No. 7, March/April, 1977.
    Farley Richmon, "Theatre as Revolutionary Activity: The Escambray", in *Cuba: The Second Decade* ed. by John and Peter Griffiths, Writers and Readers Publishing Co-op, London, 1979.

60. Augusto Boal, *Theatre of the Oppressed*, London, Pluto Press, 1974. For all those who believe in the power of art as an important instrument in the process of change in any society, this work is highly recommended.

61. Ngugi Wa Thiongo, "Prison Diary: Ngugi Wa Thiongo", in *South: The*

Third World Magazine, No. 7, April/May 1981, p. 38 being extracts from *Detained: A Writers Prison Diary*, London, p. 38.

62. Isaac Yongo, "Resettlement Drama: A Review of *The Project*", in *West Africa*, No. 3323, April 6, 1981, pp. 745–746.

63. Ross Kidd, *op. cit.*, p. 8.

PART II
GENERAL

ASPECTS OF NIGERIAN DRAMA
J. P. Clark

If drama means the "elegant imitation" of some action significant to a people, if this means the physical representation or the
evocation of one poetic image or a complex of such images, if the
vital elements to such representation or evocation are speech,
music, ritual, song as well as dance and mime, and if as the
Japanese say of their Noh theatre, the aim is to "open the ear" of
the mind of a spectator in a corporate audience and "open his
eyes" to the beauty of form, then there is drama in plenty in
Nigeria, much of this as distinctive as any in China, Japan and
Europe. But what form? In what language? And are its functions
solely aesthetic and of entertainment values as in the West today
or have these functions, in addition, ceremonial and spiritual
relevance for both actors and spectators? To shed a measure of
light upon a subject so much in the news these days and yet so
much misunderstood by so many, there must be satisfactory
answers found for these queries, and I dare say, several besides.

Of the origins of Nigerian drama very little is known that is
reliable and precise, for the simple reason that no comprehensive
study has been made so far of the subject either by the old
government sociologists or by the new drama experts of today.
But one fact is certain. Contrary to what some seem to think,
Nigerian drama did not begin at the University of Ibadan. The
roots go beyond there, and one hopes, they are more enduring
than that. Very likely, they lie where they have been found
among other peoples of the earth, deep in the past of the race. Sir
James E. Frazer writes in *The Golden Bough*:

> . . . . according to a widespread belief, which is not without a
> foundation in fact, plants reproduce their kinds through the sexual
> union of male and female elements, and that on the principle of
> homoeopathic or imitative magic, this reproduction is supposed to
> be stimulated by the real or mock marriage of men and women

who masquerade for the time being as spirits of vegetation. Such magical dramas have played a great part in the popular festivals of Europe, and based as they are on a very wide conception of natural law, it is clear that they must have been handed down from a remote antiquity.[1]

We are told later this magical theory of the seasons became supplemented by a religious theory.

> For although men now attributed the annual cycle of change primarily to corresponding changes in their deities, they still thought that by performing certain magical rites they could aid the god, who was the principle of life, in his struggle with the opposing principle of death . . . *The ceremonies which they observed for this purpose were in substance a dramatic representation of the natural processes which they wished to facilitate* for it is a familiar tenet of magic that you can produce any desired effect by merely imitating it. And as they now explained the fluctuations of growth and decay, of reproduction and dissolution, by the marriage, the death, and the rebirth or revival of the gods, the irreligious or rather magical dramas turned in great measure on these themes.[2]

We have drawn extensively upon that well-worn handbook because we believe that as the roots of European drama go back to the Egyptian Osiris and the Greek Dionysius so are the origins of Nigerian drama likely to be found in the early religious and magical ceremonies and festivals of the Yoruba, the *egwugwu* and *mmo* masques of the Ibo, and the *owu* and *oru* water masquerades of the Ijaw; dramas typical of the national repertory still generally unacknowledged today.

Now Nigerian drama falls into two broad groups. One we may call traditional, the other modern drama. Of the first, still very much in the original state described by Frazer, we can again determine two main sub-groups. One of these is sacred because its subjects and aims are religious, while the other is secular drama shading from the magical through a number of sub-kinds to the straight play and entertainment piece. Within the sacred species there are again two types: one grouping together what have been variously termed ancestral or myth plays, and the other which are masquerades or plays by age groups and cults. The dramas of *Obatala* and *Oshagiyan* performed annually at

Oshogbo and Ejigbo provide indisputable examples of the first sacred kind. Against this set are the masquerades, for example, the *ekine* plays of Buguma.

Covering the Oshagiyan festival at Ejigbo, M. Pierre Verger, the French ethnologist, shunting between Brazil and here, reports that a "miniature war" opens the festival with a real bang. This is fought between the twin wards of Isale Osholo and Oke Mapo. "Composed of attacks, hasty withdrawals and offensive sallies," the battle "is interspersed with periods of comparative calm, during which the combatants" standing up their special fighting sticks "no longer attack their enemies but shout invectives and insults at each other worthy of the age of Homer." In earlier times, the fighting was simply symbolic, being staged between two priests. But the epic staging today calls up all able-bodied men of the clan so that they can taste of the injuries their ancestors administered on the Rainmaker who denied them rain. It is this version that M. Pierre Verger found still observed in Bahia today.

The annual ritual imprisonment of Obatala at Oshogbo is even more dramatic. The following is an account of the festival given by Chief Ulli Beier:

> "The second day of the festival has a feature not unlike a passion play. There is no spoken dialogue but singing accompanies the performance and the entire action is danced.
>
> "The story is of a fight between the Ajagemo and another priest, bearing the title of Olunwi. Ajagemo is taken prisoner by Olunwi and carried off from the palace. The Oba, however, intervenes for his release. He pays ransome to Olunwi, and Ajagemo is liberated and allowed to return to the palace. The return gradually attains the qualities of a triumphal procession.
>
> "The dancing of this simple (story) as performed at Ede takes only a few minutes. But it is intensely moving largely because of the qualities put into his part by the Ajagemo. There is no question of mere acting. The ability to suffer and not to retaliate is one of the virtues every Obatala worshipper must strive to possess."[3]

These virtues of Obatala are not unlike those of the crucified Christ. Obatala in fact is the creation God of the Yoruba. Though all powerful he is gentle and full of love for all creation. In the legend, against the advice of the Oracle Ifa, Obatala, on his way to Sango, the God of thunder, relieves Eshu, the God of mischief, here disguised as old woman, of a pot of oil. The pot breaks in the process with an effect like a sacred vessel break-ing—which is not unlike that of opening Pandora's box! Thus Obatala, his white dress all dripping with oil, arrives at the court of King Sango at Oyo, and since nobody recognizes the God, he is thrown into jail when he protests at the ill-treatment of a horse. As a result, drought and famine befall the earth. And it is not until King Sango consults the oracle and is told he must make reparation to an innocent man wrongly punished in his Kingdom that the general curse is lifted. This is the story re-enacted in the annual ritual at Oshogbo and other Yoruba towns, a story which has informed my own problematic poem 'The Imprisonment of Obatala'.

In each case given above, the story derives directly from an ancestor of founder myth well-known to the audience, and the development is not so much by logic and discussion as by a poetic evocation of some religious experience shared alike by performer and spectators. For them the act is therefore one of worship and sacrifice.

A similar drama is described with tremendous power by Mr. Chinua Achebe in *The Arrow of God*. This is The First Coming of Ulla, as celebrated in the market-place of "the six villages of Umuaro" to the clamorous beat of the *ikolo* and *ogene*. The precipitate entrance of the protagonist priest Ezeulu, all got up in his regalia and waving his terrible *Nne Ofo* ahead of his assist-ants, the pantomime he breaks into, the monologue and incanta-tion he says while the participating audience wave leaves of pumpkin in offerings of prayer, the dumping of these into a heap in burial of the sins of the land to the crescendo and crash of the kome, and the sudden stampede of the six settlements of Umuaro out of the square now inherited by spirits, this is highly stylized drama indeed. One can only hope that the great havoc and tornado that was Winterbota, I mean, Captain Winterbottom, Her Britannic Majesty's Political Agent accredited to one of the primitive tribes of the Lower Niger in their own interest and pacification, did not irrecoverably blow down this splendid institution of Ullu of the Six Settlements.

In all this the elements of pleasure and entertainment cannot be neatly pared from the devotion and ecstasy of religious worship. In the masquerade and age plays the aesthetic experience of the art undoubtedly is dominant. In fact the anthropologist, Mr. Robin Horton, more or less states they are purely so. He writes of the New Year Festival of Buguma:

> "The ekine plays are overtly religious in purpose, and those of the young men more or less unashamedly secular; both traditional and modern performances contain a very large element of sheer recreation. As art, all these masquerades are best judged as ballet rather than drama: though there is a plot of sorts running through many of them, it is at best very slight—rather a framework upon which to hang a dance sequence than something of value in itself. The leg of the dancer, not the story he enacts, is what Kalabari praise and criticize."[4]

Mr. Horton makes the same point in respect of the Amagba Festival at another Ijaw settlement, that of Kula, a point with which we are not wholly in agreement and hope to take up later.

It is in a similar vein the novelist Mr. Onuora Nzekwu, reports in *Nigeria Magazine* on the production of the *Mingi Oporopo*, that is, the water-pig, at Opobo:

> "The drama . . . reveals a high standard of play-acting . . . the various parts fit the daily life of the actors and tend to make the whole performance more real and natural. The play was enacted not in the river, but in the Amayanabo's compound. Of course, there was a canoe, paddles, a fishing net, representations of the shrines to the god of fortune. Fish and the monster were represented by masquerades whose carved headpieces told the role each played. The headpiece, a large fish, depicting the monster and which can open and shut its mouth at will is a credit to the creative ability of these people."[5]

On the secular plane the stage is equally crowded. First, there are the 'magic' or trick plays and secondly the pastoral or puppet plays of Calabar described with such mixed feelings by that pro-consul and anthropologist P. A. Talbot. Incidentally, his works are quite a jungle—as thick as any he wandered through in Southern Nigeria at the beginning of the century. The interesting thing is that they carry in their labyrinthine way pathways that often lead to unexpected clearings and discoveries. One such surprise is his record of a number of plays performed for him during his tours among the Efik and Ibibio people. There was *The Tight-rope Dancer* or *The Second-Born Excels*; there was also *The Pole Play*.

He thought some of these mere "conjuring tricks"; others he found to be gruesome plays, especially those in which either a baby was professedly pounded to death in a mortar and then brought to life again whole, or the decapitated head of a man was slapped back on his neck without apparent harm, or a man was impaled upon a spit without causing disgorgement of his bowels. Another was staged by ventriloquists. According to Talbot, this carried an incest interlude too "vulgar" for entry into official files.

> "I am happy to say that this is the only occasion on which we have encountered an instance of real vulgarity among primitive African peoples. Up till now, even when turning on subjects usually avoided by Europeans on account of difficulty of treatment, the perfect simplicity of manner and purpose with which such were mentioned or explained robbed them of possible offence. In this one case, most unfortunately inexcusable and irrelevant coarseness showed itself, naked and unashamed, and we could not but wonder as to the influence to which the innovation was due."[6]

What was this innovation that riled the old resident so? We gather it was open copulation between father and daughter-in-law. Obviously at that point of performance, life had overcome art!

But the day was not completely lost; in fact it had a splendid finale, one well worth the dangers of the expedition taken in a hammock.

> "After the garishness and coarseness of the performance above described, we were quite unprepared for the beauty of that which was to follow."[7]

This was the Akan play *Utughu* or *The Spider Play*. Preparations for it were always intense for 'as in every African, Tragedy walked close upon the heels of Comedy'. Obviously very moved, Talbot goes on to describe the Female Figure in the special costume she wore at the point she does a death duet with her partner in this "puppet" play.

> "She wore a mask, brightest gold in colour, which, from the distance, looked as though it might have come straight from some Egyptian tomb. Here were the same long diamond-shaped eyes as those which gaze from old papyri or the walls of many of forgotten sepulchre, newly opened to the light of day, or such as are depicted on painted sarcophagi or the papyri of *The Book of the Dead*."[8]

After the performance, Talbot's wish to have his wife photograph "the loveliness of the gold-painted mask worn by the bird-wife" was granted by the Ibibio "on the payment of the requested dash". But then comes the shock.

> "Our disillusionment may be imagined when the actual objects were laid in our hands. Carved from a solid block of wood, almost grotesque in outline, the whole glamour and beauty of the thing seemed to have disappeared by magic. . . . Thinking over the difference, scarce believable save to those who had actually witnessed it, a memory wave brought to mind visions of masks worn in the drama of old Greece. There, too, the conditions were not unlike. Given here, in the open—possibly also with a background of swaying palms—may not the glamour of air and sky have lent to these masks also, when seen from a distance, a beauty and aloofness which not only heightened the effect of the glorious text, but gave to the whole an atmosphere in which great men and women lived and acted greatly—far removed from the commonplaces of this work-a-day world".[9]

The point to remember in this gorgeous piece of rhetoric is that about the thin line existing between reality and illusion in the theatre. If as both Dr. Johnson and Coleridge enjoin us, we never quite lose all our consciousness while willingly suspending our sense of disbelief, there will be no cause to rush the stage at the point Hamlet is hacking Laertes to death. This is a custom and convention strictly observed in many of our societies, else what prevents the housewife or child from telling the man from the mask? It will be good too to recognize a point about such comparisons. The implication is not that one group of people borrowed this and that property from another but that there can, and, in fact, there do occur areas of coincidence and correspondence in the way of living among several peoples separated by vast distances and time, and who apparently are of distinct cultures, practices and persuasions. For example, the orchestra and the leader-chorus arrangement of characters occupies as much a principal part in Nigeria theatre as it did in Greek theatre. But this is not to say one is debtor to the other. It is a matter of correspondence and coincidence. Yeats observed this to be true, seeing in every Irish beauty a potential Helen full of havoc to the race. And the husband and wife team of Herskovits underline the fact with obvious excitement when in Dahomey they discovered in *The Lover and the Initiate*, a cult drama, the old Greek story of Alcestis.

> "(here) the conventional unities are observed. The place is the cult-house; the action occurs during one day; the theme is love and the courage to defy the Vodum and Death in its name, until both are moved to pity."

This leads us directly into our third class of secular drama—the civic kind. Mainly drawn from myths and rituals telling the history of the tribe, they serve a common civic purpose as do tales and fables, namely, that of educating and initiating the young into the secrets and moral code of society. It is interesting to note that both the period of eight years the Dahomean initiate was interned in the forest away from female contact and the purpose of turning him into a responsible citizen are themes that feature in the gradation drama of Isiji or *Ipu Ogo* performed by the Ibo people of Edda near Afikpo in Eastern Nigeria.

Another beautiful drama of the same class, associated with a figure of antiquity and now observed more or less as a vegetation festival is the annual *Igogo* at Owo in the West. The central figure is Orosen, wife of the founder of Owo. A changeling creature from the forest, the story of how her rival spouses eventually encompass her downfall by tricking their man into revealing the true identity of his favourite wife throws vivid light upon the conventional day to day conflicts and complexities obtaining in every house of polygamy.

Our fourth class of the secular kind consists of dance or song dramas such as the *Udje* of the Urhobo. The *Udje*,

> "is straight entertainment. That is, it is all art and little or no ritual and religion . . . performance is by age groups, wards and towns, each using the other as subject for its songs."

More often than not, the songs are straight satirical pieces, although a good number are parables passing oblique social comments and criticism. Supplemented with imitative action and movement, however much on a linear level, these song and dance dramas never fail to reach their audience, members of whom break out from time to time to mix in with the cast. Quite similar to these are the seasonal dance-dramas of the Ijaw, *Ekpetese*, being easily the best known of the lot. But that was thirty odd years ago, and besides, its stars and fans are all either faded or scattered.

Finally, the narrative or epic dramas which go on for days (seven is the magic number!) and which, because they demand so much energy and time, are more or less dying out today. A ready example is the Ijaw saga *Ozidi*. Out of this half drama, half narrative work I have just made a marathon play soon to be released by the Oxford University Press, while work is in progress now to publish the original story both in the Ijaw and English.[10] It is the story of a posthumous son brought up by a witch grandmother to avenge an equally famous father killed at war by his own compatriots to spite their idiot king, his brother. But the hero overreached himself in the course of his quest for vengeance, and in a turn of dramatic irony that knocks one over, he just narrowly misses his doom at the hands of Smallpox. In its roll-call of characters, range of action, and tone of poetry and colour, this is classic drama which we have shot on film and which we hope will show beyond the shores of Ijaw.

So much for the various kinds of traditional drama. Now how many are there of the type we have called modern? Two, if our count is correct. One is the folk theatre of Hubert Ogunde, Kola Ogunmola, Duro Ladipo and their several imitators, and the second is what some have called literary drama. Some would say the latter has its heart right at home here in Nigeria and its head deep in the wings of American and European theatre. The works of Wole Soyinka and my own plays, I am told, clearly bear this badge, but whether of merit or infamy it is a matter still in some obscurity. Of the former kind, however, Ulli Beier, writing lately for *Nigeria Magazine* under the assumed name of "critic", is pleased to echo British opinions that *Oba Koso* by Duro Ladipo is representative of "a new art form . . . neither opera, nor ballet nor poetic drama but all the three perfectly fused together".[11]

The emphasis in the above statement really ought to be on the fusion process, for the fact is that music, dance, and poetry have been the constants of true Nigerian drama from the earliest birth-marriage-and-death-cycle ceremonies and rituals to our own trials by error of today. The traditional theatre of sacred and secular dramas we have tried to outline here, from the ancestral to the epic plays, really is this "closely unified combination of the arts" lost to Europe and America a long time ago. The difference has been in the variation, that is, the degree of the mixture these vital elements to drama undergo from play to play, place to place, each according to the purpose motivating the act. Thus for most, the ascendant elements are those of music, dance, ritual and mime, that of speech being subdued to a minimum. This minimal use of dialogue probably is due to the fact that a good number of these plays belong to some particular group or cult in society and therefore require a certain atmosphere and amount of secrecy and awe. Silence can be an active agent in this. And because there is often little speech between characters outside of the invocations and incantations, it is easy to dismiss many traditional pieces either as simple pageants and processions or at best as forms close to opera and ballet.

The achievement then of the folk theatre of the Ogunmola and Ladipo kind is that it has found the happy means between these ancient constants and the much newer ones of overall speech and plot or the lack of it demanded by modern theatre. They have invented no new form. The English translation of Duro Ladipo's plays by Chief Ulli Beier in fact shows these to be no more than simple poetic dramas dependent on the accumulated image and utterance realized on a linear progression. These are no different from others of their species. But in the Yoruba, when not stripped of their concomitant music, dance, and ritual, the total effect is terrific and different, and for a white man who has seen nothing like that since Boadicea and the Valkyrie, the impact is like a clean knock-out.

Very likely, the so-called literary theatre of Nigeria is beginning to miss this complete identity of purpose and response enjoyed increasingly by the folk theatre in Yoruba. Its latest plays show a definite tendency towards this composite art of the folk theatre. *Kongi's Harvest* by Mr. Wole Soyinka, Mr. Frank Aig-Imoukhuede's *Ikeke*, and my own *Ozidi* provide concrete evidence for this view. Whether this is a deliberate adoption of a principle, and whether working in English as these playwrights do, they will succeed in wedding that medium to Nigerian drum, song and dance is another matter and one for their individual talents.

An aspect of Nigerian drama acclaimed by even those who do not as yet acknowledge the existence of this art so expressive of our culture is the wealth and variety of its masks, costumes, and make-up. Talbot at the turn of the century went lyrical over the fact. Today the apparatus, a super-admixture of the symbolic and the naturalistic, still inspires instant applause and awe in the Nigerian theatre, indigenous or imported. As against this is the minimum use of sets and props outside the ritual paraphernalia, a fact that is also well known for giving imagination full play.

But two aspects not so well noted by many are the use of the interpolated exclamation in Nigeria drama and the regular phenomenon of "possession". One is the spontaneous, independent outburst of cheering, directed to group or self, by members of the audience and players themselves. Together with music and dance as well as common story, which are obvious properties shared by all, this provides the spectator with what direct means of participation in the production which are so remarkable in Nigerian drama.

The other is the incidence of "possession". This is the attainment by actors in the heat of performance of actual freedom of spirit from this material world, a state of transformation which has been given the rather sniggering name of "possession" or "auto-intoxication" by those outside its sphere of influence and sympathy. This phenomenon features regularly in secular plays, especially the masquerade kind. It was a constant cause of hold-ups in any filming of the *Ozidi* saga at Orua! And such is the fear of the possible danger an actor may cause himself and others, when in this state of complete identification with his role, that leading irate masquerades in Ibo and Ijaw are usually provided with leashes held back or paid out accordingly by attendants. Nor could that state be a totally passive one, for at that stage when as the Ijaw put it, "things unseen enter the man," the actor may become a medium, a votary or some ancestor spirits or divine powers filling him with the gift of prophecy.

Quite tied up with this phenomenon is the observance of certain taboos in a number of plays within the Nigerian repertory. Thus priests and worshippers of Obatala must not eat certain meals, nor wear any dress other than white. Performance of sacred dramas like that of Oshagiyan at Ejigbo cannot just be fixed for any day of the week. It must fall within only those that are holy to the deity. In *Ozidi*, the story-teller/protagonist may not have anything to do with women in the course of the seven-day production! This seems to be a carry-over of habits from the character to the player, a practice perhaps also applicable to other parts and other plays subject to particular taboos.

Now what are all these in aid of? Why the precarious preparations so fascinating to old Talbot? Why the risk of observing taboos the breaking of which means punishment and possible death? In the conventional Western theatre, the life, though hazardous, is led for pure commerce and entertainment. Nigerian theatre, that is, its modern department, naturally now inclines that way. But traditional Nigerian theatre, so very much part of the contour of life in this country, what functions does it fulfil? Let us return to Mr Robin Horton with whom we said we had a little bone to pick.

> "The masquerade belies the easy and oft-heard generalization that in traditional West African culture there was no such thing as Art for Art's sake. For although its performance is intimately associated with religious activity and belief, here it is the religion that serves the art, rather than vice versa. It is possible that some studies of West African culture have not found art practised for its own sake, simply because they have not looked for it in the right

direction. This brings us to the second point. In describing the masquerade performance, I took pains to stress that its central element was the dance, and that the apparatus of costume and headpiece filled a subordinate place in the whole. I also stressed that the sculpted mask was first and foremost an instrument for securing the presence of a spirit, and not something produced as a work of art. This in fact is true of Kalabari sculpture generally. Now it would be dangerous to generalize on the basis of this one example. But taken together with reports on some other West African cultures such as that of the Ibo, it does make one suspect that, at least in certain areas of West Africa, the dance overshadows sculpture, painting, architecture and literature as the leading traditional arts."[12]

Mr. Horton's area of reference is rather wide. But it is true as he says that there is pure art in these parts. Limiting ourselves to a more compact area as we have tried to do, we can point straight at our popular Agbor dancers and several seasonal dances of the kind staged by the young everywhere in the country. Mr. Horton, however, is unfortunate in his choice of illustration. The Ijaw masquerade, that of Kalabari included, has always served a religious purpose quite apart from its entertainment value. In every Ijaw settlement there is a corpus of masquerade for every age-group of men. This ranges from the toddlers in an ascending order to the grizzle-headed elders, the degree of religiousness being in direct proportion to the position each occupies in the age hierarchy. The virgin palm fronds girding the headpiece of the chief masquerade, the fences of similar fronds this masquerade cuts through in his initial passage, and the actual sacrifice of gin and cockerel his priest makes to it on the field of play, these certainly are conscious acts of worship without which there can be neither performance for pleasure nor peace for the age-group. What is more, the chief masquerade of the eldest group to which all adult males eventually graduate provides in many places the centre for a prominent communal shrine. The Oguberi at Kiagbodo and the masquerade of Kikoru at Okrika are such gods sporting powerful priests and to whom members of the community are asked by oracles in times of trouble to send daily prayers and individual offerings. Mr. Horton is therefore somewhat playing it down when he gives the Ijaw masquerade as an example of art practised for art's sake in West Africa.

Indeed, it is doubtful whether any of the examples we have given of traditional Nigerian drama serves such dilettante ends. Firstly, as Mr. Horton himself admits, the very myths upon which many of these dramas are based, so beautiful in themselves, serve to record the origins and *raison d'être* of the institutions and peoples who own them. Secondly, dramas, like the Ijaw masquerade and Ullu ritual, represent spirits and gods which their worshippers seek to propitiate in the manner described by Frazer. They are therefore manifestations of a special religion. Thirdly, they serve a civic and social purpose by educating and initiating the young into the ways and duties of the community. In the process they help to knit together persons of similar background, giving them a common identity. Fourthly, as the historian Dr. E. J. Alagoa pointed out, masquerade dramas foster good relations between members of one village and another. A people famous for their performance will always have spectators pouring in from everywhere to see their show. In other words, the masquerade can in fact become a town's best advertisement. Fifthly, these dramas, whether sacred or otherwise, often provide the one occasion in the year that brings home all true native sons and daughters resident and scattered abroad. This is the occasion for thanksgiving, allowing celebrants the double opportunity to report home and show off whatever priceless possessions they have won from their labours abroad. Sixthly, some induce that state of mind when the spirit is temporally freed of its flesh shackles and the medium is invested with extra tongues that can foretell any imminent disaster and if possible prescribe prevention. A seventh use that Nigerian drama is put to is to be found in the Urhobo drama-dance, Udje which is a vehicle for social comment, satire and sheer spread of meaty gossip. And last but equally vital, like all good drama, the Nigerian one is robust entertainment. Can a critic, starved though like Oliver Twist, ask for more?

One aspect of this drama is still left to examine, that of language. It is a mixed blessing that no text exists of many of the several examples we have given of Nigerian theatre. Mixed blessing because it saves us on the one hand the trouble of proving any special point, while on the other, it underlines the said fact that there are such mines of material lying around to be dug up for our national enrichment. But it can be safely said that each traditional piece does pride to the language of its people at all levels of meanings such as T. S. Eliot outlined for poetry in the theatre. So we believe does the folk theatre, at present mainly in Yoruba.

The difficulty and controversy come when we move into the department of modern drama in Nigeria—drama that usually is first seen in print before it is seen on the stage. The dispute has to do with that irascible hobby-horse of scholars like my friend Mr. Obiajunwa Wali who foresees a dead end to African literature written in European languages. But I would not like now to be taken on such a John Gilpin ride! Can it be valid and authentic literature? asks Mr. A. Bodurin in the *African Statesman*. He goes on with the voice of dogma:

> "In literature content and expression determine each other so fundamentally that the validity and authenticity of a work suffers as soon as the native content is expressed in a foreign language. This dissociation of content from expression is partly responsible for the difficulty in appreciating Wole Soyinka's plays. I am strongly convinced that if *A Dance of the Forests*, the most intriguing of his plays, were written in Yoruba, much of the obscurity would disappear."[13]

Now let me quote another piece of castigation, this time of me.

> "The usual criticism of Mr. Clark's plays is that he has not quite found the kind of verse suitable for the presentation of dramatic action. This is, in my view, a just criticism. It is probably not consoling to add that Shakespeare did not begin to write good dramatic poetry till 1599, that is, till his tenth year in the theatre. No one ever begins by tossing off masterpieces. The delineation of character which is one of the springs of dramatic poetry is naturally a late accomplishment. One has to be much more than a gifted lyricist even to create ordinary dialogue that is resourceful, natural, and imaginative while dealing with the drab details which are bound to find their way into a play."[14]

That is Mr. Ben Obumselu reviewing my play *The Raft* (or was it Mr. Soyinka's production of it?) in *Ibadan*. After citing a passage which he never stops to analyse, he romps home

> "Mr. Clark has not, as a dramatist, been fortunate in the kind of poetry he has admired. The . . . actors found it difficult to decide whether they were uneducated Nigerian lumbermen who spoke English indifferently, or poetic personages to whom imaginative poetry came naturally. Occasionally, they strayed into pidgin English rhythms as lumbermen. I doubt whether Mr. Clark considered this matter sufficiently."[15]

Let me assure Mr. Obumselu here and now that I considered the matter most sufficiently. The characters in *The Raft* and in other plays of mine are neither "poetic personages" nor the kind of Cockney he has in mind. They are ordinary Ijaw persons working out their life's tenure at particular points on the stage. And they are speaking in their own voices and language to an audience, members of whom they expect to reach with a reasonable degree of sympathy and conviction. At this point, I would like to quote a letter I wrote from America in 1963 on this very subject to Mr. Gerald Moore:

> "Education and class consciousness which presuppose and actually create levels of speech and language in European societies have, thank God, not done that havoc to the non-literary tongues like Ijaw. Style, imagery, etc., these are what tell one user of a language from another—not grammar or class; for we haven't that. And you very well know that all I consider myself is a letter-writer for my character."

In other words, the task for the Ijaw, and I dare say, any Nigerian or African artist, writing in a European language like English, is one of finding the verbal equivalent for his characters created in their original and native context. The quest is not on the horizontal one of dialect and stress which are classifications of geography, society, and education. It is on the vertical plane of what the schoolmasters call style and register, that is, the proper manner, level and range of dialogue and discussion. And this is a matter of rhetoric, the artistic use and conscious exploitation of language for purposes of persuasion and pleasure. If in the process, there occurs no "dissociation of content and expression" as Mr. Bodunrin puts it, and I understand that term to mean, say, the discussion of food prices by market-women in the jargon of biologists, but on the contrary there is a faithful reproduction of the speech habits of one people into another language as Mr. Chinua Achebe does significantly in English with the Ibo dialogue proceeding by technique of the proverb, then I think the artist has achieved a reasonable measure of success.

In this connection, I would like to draw attention to the use of another language device, that of indirection which features prominently in my own play *Song of A Goat*. That doctor and patient in that play do not approach the business on hand with the directness of an arrow does not mean the playwright is unappreciative of the importance of speed and despatch. Rather, it is recognition by him of a living convention observed among the people of the community treated in the play, namely, that you do not rush in where angels fear to tread for the simple reason that the flying arrow either kills promptly of sends the bird in flight. Accordingly, delicate issues are handled delicately by these people. This approach is evident in their manner of negotiating marriage between one family and another and of announcing the news of death to the persons most affected. Each subject is tackled by indirection.

This is not to say the Nigerian playwright and novelist writing in English will not sometimes use the old gradation of speech as understood by all of us from our reading of European literature. Indeed some do use pidgin, like Mr. Wole Soyinka in his play *Brother Jero*, Mr. Cyprian Ekwensi in his novel *Jagua Nana*, and Mr. Chinua Achebe in his latest terrifyingly prophetic and exact story *A Man of the People*. But the character using pidgin must be in a position to do so in actual life, and there must be a special purpose served. That is, there must be propriety. Thus the houseboy will speak to his master in our new urban social set-up in the pidgin that his education and class dictate. Similarly the Warri market-woman selling to a cosmopolitan clientele will use the pidgin that really is the *lingua franca* of that section of the country. In Mr. Wole Soyinka's *Brother Jero*, however, the disciple Chume oscillates between "pidgin" and the so-called standard or Queen's English. The excuse might be that at one time the situation demands that he speaks straight in English that is Pidgin English as befits an office messenger, while at another it requires him to speak in his original Nigerian tongue here translated into appropriate standard English as we have said. Well, there it is; but will it do for the critics? One of them, I think Mr. Bodunrin, actually repeats the advice Mr. Harold Hobson of the London *Sunday Times* was kind enough to give modern African playwrights free of charge, which was that they should forget they have been to universities. Perhaps, the critics themselves should first take that advice! At the moment, many of them are encumbered with conventions and critical theories that pile up good grades in the old English schools, but then are thoroughly good for nothing thereafter. This is why, like the foreign "rigorous teachers who seized their youths", these Nigerians require the special aid of programme notes setting out all strange practices as in Chinese and Japanese theatre. But then it is the lot of the artist often to be misunderstood.

Notes

1. *The Golden Bough*, London, Macmillan.
2. Ibid.
3. Ulli Beier, "A Year of Sacred Festivals in one Yoruba town," A Special *Nigeria Magazine* production, 1959, pp. 13–14.
4. *Africa*, xxxiii, No. 2, April 1963.
5. *Nigeria Magazine*, No. 63, 1969.
6. *Life in Southern Nigeria*, London, Frank Cass, pp. 72–86.
7. Ibid.
8. Ibid.
9. Ibid.
10. The book has since been published. See *The Ozidi Saga*, collected and trans. by J. P. Clark, Ibadan University Press and Oxford University Press, Nigeria, 1977.
11. *Nigeria Magazine*, No. 87, Dec. 1965.
12. *Op. cit.*
13. *African Statesman*, i, No. 1, 1965.
14. *Ibadan*, No. 19, June 1964.
15. Ibid.

Reprinted Nigeria Magazine No. 89, June 1968

PART III
TRADITIONAL THEATRE
I: Dramatic Ritual

THE DRAMA IN AFRICAN RITUAL DISPLAY
Ola Rotimi

The term DRAMA has been used so frequently—at times, freely, perhaps—to describe happenings in African ritual ceremonies that it now seems necessary for some objective criteria by which to identify in that sometimes deluding melange of forms that is Africa's culture, what really is drama, and what is not.

The standard acceptation of the term Drama, within a cultural setting, at any rate, implies "an imitation of an action . . . or of a person or persons in action", the ultimate object of which is to edify or to entertain. Sometimes, to do both.

Some African ritual ceremonies reveal instances of "imitation" either of an experience in life, or of the behaviour-patterns of some Power. Others merely re-present certain Powers without the mimetic impulse to recreate the ways and details of those Powers. What could be, and has frequently been, mistaken for Drama in most African traditional displays, appears when this latter type of non-imitative ceremonial effervesces with movement, rhythm, and spectacle, beyond the ordinary. It is at such a point as this, that some objectivity in concept might help in the detection of what really is Drama.

Ritual displays that reveal in their style of presentation, in their purpose, and value, evidences of imitation, enlightenment and or entertainment, can be said to be Drama.

Thus, while the exciting series of "abebe" dance processions that highlight the seven-day long Edi Festival of Ile-Ife cannot be called Drama, the mock-duel scene preceding the festivities is Drama.

Usually performed on the eve of Edi, known as *frekete*, it involves two traditional chiefs: Obalayan and Obalufe. The former represents forces of Peace and Fair-weather; the latter an "embodiment" of Discord and Unrest. The Power of Evil, Obalufe, and the Power of Peace and Goodwill, Obalayan, engage in a duel at the end of which we see Obalufe subdued and taken captive. He offers a ransom, and he is later released. Obalayan then bears this ransom to the lord of the land, the Oni, who upon receiving it declares the Edi festival open.

In this mock-duel, one sees the essentials of Drama at work. The scene is an *imitation* of an action: the action of FIGHT. That this encounter is *entertaining* is beyond doubt. And as for *enlightenment*, the formal presentation of Obalufe's ransom to the Oni of Ife, is a symbolic endorsement of the people's loyalty to the lord of the land, a lesson in allegiance.

These criteria would rule out any classification of the Gelede masquerade display as Drama. Gelede masquerades who dance purposely to appease the Witches (*awon iya wa*) only portray the make-believe externals of drama. Excitingly rhythmic as their dance movements are: more so under the accent and grandeur of costume and mask, there, however, is hardly any suggestion of "mimesis" directed at a specific human experience or at some supernatural habit.

By contrast, aspects of the Egungun "apidan" display, such as the "mutation-scene" in which a masquerade "becomes" a serpent through the magic of adroit costuming, and then goes on to make aggressive strikes at spectators, can be called Drama.

The I-Njoku elephant ceremony of the Bakwerri peoples of the Cameroon Republic becomes Drama when, after the "Veambe" dance procession, masquerades clad in sack, palm-fronds, raffia fluffings, and wearing headpieces fitted with wooden projections for tusks between which hang long sugar-cane stems representing uprooted trees, dance about with the trampling gait of elephants, and sometimes make ferocious jabs with their "tusks" at spectators or into the ground.

The same label of Drama can be attached to the Ekpe ritual dance of the Efiks of Nigeria, in which the masquerade, costumed in black, reticulate overalls, imitates the predatory habits of the leopard.

On the other hand, the Eyo festival of Lagos which features masquerades representing Spirits of dead ancestors, cannot be rightly called Drama, since hardly any action is consciously imitated in the whole processional thrill of "eyo" turn-out.

Coming to rituals with less entertainment intent, one identifies Drama in such solemn events as the Puberty Ceremony of, for instance, the Sherbro natives of Sierra Leone. Here, the Cult-priest, masked as "Min" the Power of Life and Death, goes through the motions of symbolic killing of the adolescent candidate. Later on, "Min" "vomits" his "bath" until adulthood takes place.

Similar initiation rite, known as "ala suwo" by the Nembe, and as "iria" by the Okrika peoples of Nigeria, in which maidens dance to celebrate the formal transition into womanhood, cannot be termed Drama. Again, as with the Eyo, or the Gelede, specific imitation or recreation of an experience is missing here. ⸓ This all argues that not every action that highlights dancing or some involvement in an action measured to the tune of chants or to the rhythms of drum can pass for Drama. ⸗

If we are to further accept the immanence of PLOT, with its implied vitals of SUSPENSE and CONFLICT as another criterion, we find that the number of ritual displays that can be labelled Drama whittles down considerably. For whereas the I-Njoku, the Min, the Ekpe, and others of that type do relive observations on life, their creative patterns have been more or less rooted in the set formalism of religion. In this regard they stand on the same pedestal as did the Quem queritis Easter mime of the Medieval Church, in which priests impersonating the three Marys and the Angel, re-enacted the story of Christ's resurrection, and no more. There was no conflict of goals between characters.

Traditional displays that inhere instances of Suspense and or Conflict in their action are much fewer than those that merely re-enact observations. The annual Obatala festival in Ede offers the example of suspense-conflict Drama. Very similar in form to the *frekete* duel-scene of Ile-Ife's Edi, this drama is staged on the second day of the Obatala festival in the palace of the Timi of Ede. The characters are: the Ajagemo, as protagonist, the Olunwi, his opponent. They engage each other in a duel, the Olunwi wielding a whip and attacking, the Ajagemo mainly parrying off the strokes in self-defence. Eventually, the Ajagemo is defeated, taken prisoner, and hustled off into the interior of the palace. Next, the Timi himself intervenes with a ransom, and the Ajagemo is set free.

Without necessarily probing into the historical or mythological source of this act, one recognizes points of Conflict, mock conflict, true, but in essence, Conflict. While the feints and counter-moves of the combatants provide moments of Suspense.

From the preceding analysis and examples, it is only appropriate that the word Drama when used to refer to traditional displays should imply an immanence of Suspense and or Conflict within the body of the approved action. Where Suspense or Conflict is absent, then the meaning of the term must needs rest on the broader sense of mimesis in the performance.

Reprinted Nigeria Magazine No. 99, December 1968

THE GODS AS GUESTS
An Aspect of Kalabari Religious Life
Robin Horton

The Kalabari people live in some thirty villages in the tidal zone of the eastern Niger Delta. Linguistically they are part of the great block of Ijo-speaking peoples, but they form a distinct sub-group both in dialect and in culture.

So far as the evidence goes, the majority of these villages have always lived by fishing. One or two communities with a fortunate geographical position near the mouth of the New Calabar estuary abandoned this occupation about four hundred years ago for trade with Europe in slaves and oil—whence the great city-state of New Calabar or Owome. But although the switch in economy had some marked effect on the scale and political organization of the groups concerned, they still retain a culture which is basically the same as that of the villages whose inhabitants remained fishermen.

The Kalabari village settlement commonly appears as a mass of mangrove-pole or wattle houses jostling each other in wall-to-wall confusion on a cramped patch of raised mud—though migration inland beginning about seventy years ago brought some villages into tracts of more truly dry land and enabled them to spread out a little. Each village, however cramped, has nevertheless a large central square used for sessions of the village assembly and for religious festivals. Each is made up of a number of descent-groups, whose founding ancestors are generally seen as unrelated to each other, and are often thought to have converged on the present site from very diverse directions. Instead of looking to descent from a common ancestor as the basis of its identity, the Kalabari village looks to a culture common to all its members and distinctive set of laws. Government was traditionally carried on by an assembly of the entire adult male population of the village, which sat in three age-grades and had both legislative and judicial functions. The assembly was presided over by the *Amanyanabo* or village head, who also led the community in war—at least whilst he was young. The *Amanyanabo* was generally chosen from a single descent group, though changes of dynasty were not unknown.

Of the villages who went into trade with Europe, the first and foremost was Owome or New Calabar. The most marked consequence of this change of livelihood was a great increase of population through the buying of slaves for integration into the community as well as for resale, a development probably facilitated by the stress on learnable culture rather than descent as the criterion of membership of any Kalabari community. There was also a concentration of power in the hands of the great traders and their successors. Each of these built up a team of slaves to operate his trading canoes, and when he died his successor assumed authority over these slaves and their descendants. If the trader himself had no sons of adequate ability, an outstanding man of slave birth might succeed him. In the internal affairs of such a trading corporation of "house", its head had a high degree both of authority and of responsibility for collective welfare. As the house's representative to the state at large, its head also sat in the assembly under the presidency of the *Amanyanabo*. It is a significant pointer to the concentration of power that took place with the change in economy that this assembly consisted no longer of the total adult male population, but of the *Amanyanabo* and house heads only.

But although the City State of Owome was a very different kind of political organization from the fishing village, much else in the culture defied change. The general picture of the world and its working remained essentially the same, and so therefore did ideas about the world of the gods and their relations with men. Although the hectic competition for power and wealth which followed the economic revolution in Owome brought an element of ostentation into those religious practices which were carried out on a house-by-house basis, nothing in Owome religion would be unfamiliar to a fishing villager. Indeed, in fishing village and city state alike the festivals which are the subject of this monograph were once among the culminating events of the year, prepared for and looked forward to for months ahead, remembered and gossiped about for months afterwards. In this intensely pushful, virile culture where the skills of ruthless political struggle, war and head-hunting once engaged every normal man's attention, it may seem strange that so much enthusiasm could be spared for religious activities, and so much admiration spared for those who excelled in the dancing and other skills involved in them. I hope I can convey in the ensuing pages enough of the quality of these occasions to dispel this mystery.

An understanding of the Kalabari world-view, and of the gods' place in it, is essential if sense is to be made of the great festivals of Kalabari religion.

Kalabari divide their universe into two great orders of existence: that of *oju*—the bodily or material, and that of *teme*—the spiritual or immaterial. Things that have *oju* can be seen and touched by anyone suitably positioned to do so, and they are thought of as having definite locations in space. Things existing in *teme* only can be seen by ordinary people when they are very young, but after the first few years of life the accumulated pollution of the material world spoils their senses and they are no longer clairvoyant. To regain this lost faculty, one must submit to a special herbal treatment known as "clearing the eyes and ears". (A number of people do this in order to become diviners, since it enables them to carry on conversations with *teme* and to ascertain their will.) Though one can talk about *teme* coming to a certain place and staying there, in other contexts they are spoken of as if they were anywhere and everywhere at once. In this respect, they are "like the breeze".

Many *teme* exist without any bodily counterpart—for instance those of the dead and of the village hero-gods. Such *teme* are sometimes referred to as "the people we do not see". On the other hand, all things having *oju* also have a counterpart in *teme*; and if they lose this they die (if living) or disintegrate (if non-living). This is true for all objects of the everyday world, and even for certain of the gods, i.e. the Water people. In these cases, it is the *teme* that controls the behaviour of the *oju*, and in this Kalabari compare it with the helmsman of a boat.

Any *teme* can in principle be given prayer and offerings by way of worship or placation. This is one point of the Kalabari saying that if one cuts a stick and pours wine before it, the stick has become a god. In practice, only a limited selection of *teme* are powerful enough to warrant such attentions, though different people will draw different lines between those which are negligible and those which are not. Thus some men will make prayer and offerings to the *teme* of the various parts of their house: whereas the more tough-minded will consider these of too little power to be worth troubling about. It is often stressed, however, that the extent of human attentions can itself influence the power of the god: as Kalabari say, "It is men who make the gods great". Fervent worship will add to a god's capacity to help the worshippers; and just as surely the cutting-off of worship will render the god impotent or at the very least cause it to break off contact with its erstwhile worshippers. This fact has more than once been used to put an end to the influence of a god which has started to act maliciously towards its congregation. In one case during the last century, the Owome city-state practised regular cult of a Water Man known as *Owu Akpana* who materialized from time to time in the form of a great shark. After an unusually large number of people had been eaten by sharks in a small space of time, diviners laid the blame on *Owu Akpana* and the council of chiefs decided they must put a stop to his unwelcome attentions. To do this, they had a shark caught and its blood poured into the village well. Everyone was then ordered to drink of the water and this symbolic act of communal rejection was allegedly sufficient to destroy the god's power either for good or for ill.

Kalabari explain the effect of worship on the god by analogy with human beings, whose *teme* become strong and forceful or ineffectual and apathetic in proportion to the approbation they receive from their fellows.

In general, correctly worded invocation and correctly chosen offerings are believed to have an automatic effect in securing what benefits have been asked of the gods. Where prayer and offering fail, a diviner may be blamed for directing suppliants to a god who is not in fact concerned in the situation, or blame may be put upon the incorrect performance of the ritual. "Man proposes, God disposes" is not a proverb that would make much sense to a Kalabari priest.

Despite individual differences as to what merits worship and what does not, there are two distinct systems of gods whose influence on man and nature is so great that no one disputes the need to take heed to them at every turn.

The first of these systems comprises those gods whom we may call the Arbiters of Form and Process. In giving a broad explanation of the origin and course of the world, Kalabari attribute its creation of the female principle *Tamuno*, and the control of its subsequent course to the male principle *So*. Both of these are thought to be closely associated with the sky: *So*, indeed, seems to be the sky personified. In other contexts, *Tamuno* and *So* are treated as many. Thus everything in the material world has its particular *Tamuno* and *So*. This applies, for example, to each level of social group, where *Ama Tamuno* and *Ama Teme So* (i.e., *Ama* making *So*) respectively control the creation and life course of the *Ama* or village, *Polo Tamuno* and *Polo Temeso* the creation and life course of the *Polo* or compound. *Mbo Tamuno* and*MoSo* the creation and life cours of th individual. In the latter case, a person's *teme* is supposd to gobefore birth to his *Tamuno*, telling the latter what course of life it chooses. *Tamuno* keeps its words in her care: personified, they are the *So* of the individual whose *teme* came before her to speak hem. The *teme* itself she sends to combine with a bodywhich she had created in a mother's womb. This is why an individual's destiny or *So* is also referred to as *o fiee boye*—lit. "What he spoke before he came".

Kalabari often say that all the various *Tamuno* are yet one great *Tamuno*, and that all the various *So* are similarly one *So*. The paradox in this statement is resolved when we see that what is postulated here is a system in which both *Tamuno* and *So* act in a distinct (and distinctly-named) role towards each entity in the material world. And just as in everyday life we tend to treat the several roles played by a single person as if each were a distinct personality in its own right—think of one's friend who is also a policeman!—so too the several roles of *Tamuno* and *So* are treated in some contexts as if each were a distinct person.

What has been said above should make it clear that the state of everything in the material world can in principle be explained in terms of the system comprised by *Tamuno* and *So* acting in their various roles. In this respect, the system is virtually self-contained. The style of thought behind it is also quite distinct from that which sustains the other great system of gods. Thus *Tamuno* and *So* are defined in terms of functions of an austere and abstract kind—i.e., creation and the control of process. These functions apart, their lives and characters remain blank. No passions, no prejudices, no human quirks. In austerity, they come near to the sort of gods approved of by modern atomic physicists.

The second system of gods is made up of the Village Heroes, the Water People and the Ancestors. Each of these groups is concerned with its own particular range of human and natural situations; but in this each is complementary to the others, and together they too can provide an explanation of everything that goes on in the Kalabari world. Let us look at each group in a little more detail.

1. *ORU*—the Village Heroes. Although *oru* exist today in *teme* only, at the times of founding of the various Kalabari villages they lived among men in the material world; and a rich mythology tells of their lives and characters during their bodily existence. According to this mythology, most of the *oru* of any village came to live there after leaving some distinct and frequently unspecified community. Each of the more important *oru* excelled in some particular activity which he or she proceeded to teach their new neighbours. Thus in the city-state of Owome, *Owamekaso* brought and taught the skills of trade, *Ekine ba* the skills of dancing and drumming for the masquerade, *Okpolodo* and *Siriopubo* the skills of various types of war and hand-hunting, *Amakarasa* and *Kugbosa* various types of curative and cleansing rite. Sooner or later all the *oru* became tired of life in the village, often because the villagers refused to keep certain taboos which they had laid down as essential to the skills in which they specialized. After warning their people several times without effect, the *oru* vanished one by one, sometimes just disappearing and at others flying off as birds into the sky. Before going, however, each of them laid down instructions that prayer and offering should always be made to them, in return for which they would continue to look after the community from the plane of

teme. Although they often entrusted responsibility for their cult to the descendants of certain individuals whom they had befriended during their bodily existence, this cult was to be carried on for the benefit of the community as a whole.

2. *OWU*—the Water People. Whereas *oru* are closely concerned with the invention and maintenance of human skills, *owu* are concerned with the control of Nature, and especially with those of its fluctuations which human skills are seen as powerless to command. Thus they control the water level and the waves in the creeks, and the movements and depths of the fish shoals. Every *owu* is associated with a particular tract of creek, generally one with clearly-marked geographical boundaries, and people who fish in this area must pay special attention to it if they are to be successful.

Like the *oru*, the more important *owu* are described in a rich mythology. This recounts their life in the town of the Water People below the creeks, and the circumstances in which they first met their worshippers. Unlike the *oru*, however, these gods never lived with men in their villages. Their contacts with men were loose and transitory. Whereas the Village Heroes are concerned exclusively with the collective welfare of their particular human communities, the Water People are not strongly committed to the welfare of particular groups. They can in fact be approached by anyone of any provenance; and they will sell their favours to the highest bidder. This makes them particularly useful in satisfying individualistic aspirations, for which neither the Village Heroes, nor the Dead cater.

3. *DUEN*—The Dead. These are the *teme* of human beings which escaped from their bodies at death and continued existence on the immaterial plane. They are believed to retain the character and values they held when alive, and to participate in a society not unlike those of living Kalabari. Like Village Heroes and Water People, the Dead too are portrayed in a detailed mythology describing their life-time in the world of men. The Dead concern themselves with neither villages nor individuals, but with the collective welfare of the descent-groups to which they gave birth; all questions of the rise and fall of the various descent-groups in a community are generally explained by reference to the Dead.

It will be clear from these summaries that Village Heroes, Water People and the Dead are neatly complementary in respect of the social contexts to which their powers are relevant. Village Heroes and Water People are also complementary in their respective influence over human skills and environmental variation. Together, then, these three groups offer means of explanation and control of every situation in the material world. As a system of explanation, they are as self-contained as the system made up of the Arbiters of Form and Process. Indeed, they form a complete alternative to it. Even more remarkable, however, is the utterly contrasting style of thought which lies behind them. In place of the faceless austerity of *Tamuno* and *So* in their various roles, we find a system permeated by a full blooded sense of personality.

Why, we may well ask, this duality of explanatory systems? And why the contrast in the styles of thought underpinning them?

An answer to the first question comes readily enough to mind. In the Kalabari view of the world, certain techniques of invocation and offering correctly carried out are thought to bring automatic response from the gods. Clearly enough, the prospect of such automatic response is a mainstay of men's peace of mind in a difficult and threatening universe: and the inevitable failure of invocation and offering are a nasty threat which presses for some solution, however wishful. One way round this is to lay the blame for failure on mistakes in a very complicated sequence of ritual: room for hope can then be held out in the form of a corrected performance. Such reasoning is very characteristic of the Navaho Indian religion of the New World, whose rituals are by and large of such intricate complexity that possibilities of error are endless. In Kalabari and many other West African religions, the complexity of detail in the procedures of invocation and offering is not great enough to give much scope for this line of thought. Instead, by acknowledging that more than one system of gods is potentially concerned in any given situation, Kalabari are enabled to face and explain failure of worship by the knowledge that they may have been addressing themselves to the wrong person. Who is in fact the right person, in any case, can only be discovered by consulting a diviner. Now any diviner can always be mistaken or fraudulent in his diagnosis; so after a failure one can always hope that another expert will "see more clearly" and so put one in contact with the god really concerned.

Although this makes the duality of explanatory systems in Kalabari religious thought more understandable, it does not tell us why the two self-contained systems we have outlined above should differ so much in the style of thought that lies behind them. Here, perhaps, we should remember the truism that the gods of any community are caught up in the pressure of a great diversity of human desires and interests; for different interests may press the gods into incompatible moulds.

Both of the two systems of Kalabari gods are activated in people's thoughts by the desire for explanation of some situation as a prelude to its control. But in Kalabari communities as elsewhere, some people at least have an interest in explaining the world which is quite independent of their concern with controlling it. Anyone who has lived in an African village knows that it has as many wiseacres as an English village. Now what interests such people is neatness, simplicity and economy in explanation—everything that happens in the world should be deducible from a few clear cut postulates of great generality. The system of Arbiters of Form and Process—the faceless gods of Kalabari religion—is a perfect answer to their needs.

On the other hand, pressure of a very different kind comes from the desire to participate in a wider-than-human society. This is something weak in some cultures and strong in others, weak in some members of some cultures and strong in others. Witness a culture like that of Nupe where the gods are uniformly treated as pure instruments of environmental control, and never as persons in any fuller sense of the word. In Kalabari, where the reverse is true, there is a great pressure for the elaboration of gods as persons in their full panoply of passions and prejudices, as tangible characters.

The desire to develop the gods as full people must conflict with the desire for neatness and simplicity of explanation. However, by accepting the co-existence of two systems of gods moulded in utterly contrasting styles, Kalabari are enabled to give full vein to both types of interest.

This basic cleavage in the tenor of Kalabari religious thought makes intelligible the difference in approach to the gods of the two great systems. More especially it makes clear why the kind of ritual dramatizations which are the main theme of this essay are developed only for the second of these systems.

On the one hand, with *Tamuno* and *So*, the faceless gods, we find intercourse of a restricted and somewhat arid kind. An invocation is made, an offering given, and the matter is closed but for the awaiting of results. But with the Village Heroes, the Water People and the Dead, approach to them becomes a more elaborate affair, altogether richer in the sentiments it draws upon. As the time of the rituals draws near, a chorus of singers (generally women) chants the praises of the gods in songs which allude constantly to their characters and achievements. Then, after the invocations and offerings, there follows the most notable part of Kalabari religious practice. This involves the dramatization of the gods' presence by human actors who go through sequences of behaviour which in some way or other typify their characters and attributes—a procedure seen by Kalabari as bringing the gods as guests into the village. During such a dramatization, they react as if the gods were human guests of an exalted kind whom it was their business to greet and entertain: and on such occasions Kalabari often talk of people "playing with their gods".

It is not difficult to see why such ritual dramas are limited to one of the two systems of gods: of the Arbiters of Form and Process, *Tamuno* and *So*, are not defined by the sort of attributes that could be acted out in any of the ways which we shall shortly describe. On the other hand, the tangible personalities of Village Heroes, Water People, and the Dead cry out for dramatic presentation.

There are three different ways in which human actors are thought to "bring the gods into the village". First of all there is the simple mime, in which a man or woman runs through behaviour that exemplifies the character of a god or illustrates an episode in the god's life. This is perhaps the least widely used technique, and is usually subsidiary to the other two. Then there is the masquerade. In this, a man once more mimes the character and attributes of the god; only now he is covered in clothing and a mask, which also symbolize the god. Finally, there is possession, in which the god is alleged to "come into the man's head" and displace the *teme* in control of his body.

All three kinds of behaviour are closely related in Kalabari thought; for all alike serve to bring the gods into contact with their people. How this can be so is not at once evident to the outsider: for although it is clear in what sense inducing possession brings the god to the community, we need to know more about Kalabari premises before seeing how mime and masquerade can be thought to have the same effect.

The key idea here is summarized in the maxim "It is with their names that the gods stay and come". By "name" in this context is implied any word, object, or act which can be taken to symbolize the god—either its name in the literal sense, the sculpture, the masquerade and its carved head-dress, or the sequence of action by means of which a human being represents it. For all of these, the fact of their presence or occurrence in a given place is enough to secure the presence of the god they refer to. Whether one utters the name of a god three times, drums it three times, makes a new sculpture, purifies an old one, dons a masquerade or acts out behaviour attributes to the god, one is doing something which brings him automatically close because it is his symbol. This is why the mime and masquerade are just as effective means of bringing the gods into the community where they are performed as is the induction of possession. By "playing" with his imperson-ator, the villagers are playing with the god himself no less surely than when they confront a possessed medium.

Given their close similarity of meaning for Kalabari, it is not surprising to find that these three means of compelling the presence of the gods are apparent cultural equivalents. Thus ritual for the head of the Village Heroes may involve induced possession in one village and mime or masquerade in the next. Again, someone performing a mime or masquerade may sud-denly take leave of his senses and become possessed by the god he has just been impersonating. In this system of thought it is but a small distance from the close presence of a god brought about by mime or masquerade to actual possession by him.

A mimer representing an elderly merman suffering from elephantiasis.

The various models of dramatization of the gods must now be described in greater detail.

1. THE MIME—This, the simplest of the three modes of dramatizing the gods, is generally found as a subsidiary device in rituals where the principal god is brought to life by masquerade or possession. Nevertheless, there are various occasions when it is used alone to great effect.

Most striking is the ceremony of the coming of the "Dead without Houses", something which formerly took place in several Kalabari communities, either before or after rites for the founders of the various descent groups of the village. Prestige and contentment in the world of the dead depend on the size of one's descent group in the land of the living: the "Dead without Houses", forgotten and neglected in this world because they have no descendants, are therefore assumed to be the most despised and embittered denizens of the other world. Hence they too must be collectively entertained, lest in their bitterness they upset the feasts of their better-favoured companions. Impersonation of the Dead without Houses is laid on by members of the *Ekine* society, an association I shall mention at greater length in connection with the masquerade.

After the coming of the Dead has been announced by a village crier at sundown, women cook the evening meal and shut themselves and their children into their houses for the night. Then *Ekine* members assemble quietly in the dancing square. A senior member allots the rest to various parts of the village, where one by one they start to call and answer in the weird nasal voice of the dead. Tapping their throats and holding their noses, they give vent first of all to harsh, querulous staccato cries. Gradually they become more coherent, falling into the refrain "We who cry with tearful voices, we are hungry." After a while the actors emerge from their various corners and troop around from house to house demanding food and drink from the inmates. Women answer sleepily and crawl off their mats to get out a dish of soup or a bottle of gin put by for this contingency. As they come to the door with their offerings, *Ekine* members scuttle out of sight until they have gone back to bed again, then seize gleefully upon the things put out for them. They wish a loud nasal blessing upon the housewife for health, children and a powerfully amorous husband. Their tour of the village complete, they take its fruits to the house of one of their members and eat them with a good deal of joking about the reluctance of women to get out of bed for them, and some heated discussion about how to proceed against the odd women or child who defied their curfew.

In all this the victims of the mime are as much in on its secret as are the performers. No woman and few children of talking age are under any illusion that their callers are other than human— nor are they supposed to be. Yet when they are ordered to get off their mats and bring out food, they do so with an acquiescence which they never show on other occasions when they consider themselves genuinely imposed upon by the menfolk. Their atti- tudė makes sense only when one remembers the doctrine that "the gods stay and come with their names". For the mime here is one form of "name" for the Dead without Houses and its performance compels their presence. In the sense that the dead are "with" the human actors, giving food to the latter who are known to be merely greedy is giving food to the spirits, who may be helpful. This too is why the women must keep themselves from confronting the human actors; for in a sense they would also be confronting the gods, and the contact would be one of great danger where such potentially malicious personalities are in- volved.

2. THE MASQUERADE—Village Heroes, Water People and the Dead are all on occasion represented by means of the masquerade; but those most frequently treated in this way are the Water People. The reason for this is lost in unrecorded history, so we need not waste time in speculating about it. However, we shall take the Water Peoples' masquerades as representative of this technique generally.

In every Kalabari village, responsibility for these masquerades is vested in *Ekine*, an association containing most of the adult members of the community and named after the hero-goddess who is supposed to have been shown the secret of their dancing by the Water People themselves. Entry to this association is secured by finding oneself a member who has been impressed with one's dancing abilities, and who will sponsor one before his associates. A small payment and seven bottles of palm gin must then be given. One of these bottles will be taken to the priest of *Ekine Ba*, who invokes her on the new member's behalf. He asks her to protect her child and to give him strength to "play her game". Then he pours a glass of gin to her and smears kaolin on the candidate's forehead. This symbol of association with the gods signifies entry into the association. Finally, the other members escort the novice to his house, where he must entertain them.

In the small fishing villages, *Ekine* is generally concerned with the masquerades of thirty or fifty Water People, whilst in the city-state of Owome the number is probably a little higher. Today, the list of Water People masquerades varies only a little from village to village, though in most cases a single village is cited as the point of origin for a given play. The reason for this seems to be that prominent players in every village have always scoured other communities for new performances with which they could outshine their rivals: after a player has purchased the cult-rights of such a new *owu* from its previous masqueraders, his community can add it to the list of Water People tended by its own *Ekine*.

Each of the Water People tended by the *Ekine* has his own festivals at which he is entertained by the members. The whole cycle of festivals unfolds in a fixed order, which must be rigidly kept. It is generally opened after the periodic festivals in honour of the Village Heroes and Dead have been completed; and the character of the Water People as lords of the creek rather than of the village is dramatically illustrated by the nature of the opening rites. When the time is ripe, *Ekine* members take out a large canoe and go with it to a spot some way away in the open creeks known as the Beach of the Water People. Here they offer a goat to the Water people, begging them to come in from their various creeks as their entertainment is about to start. Getting into the boat again, they return to the village singing *Ekine* songs; the Water People are thought to return in *teme* with them. A day or two later, a dog is given to their patron goddess *Ekine Ba* by her priest. Then in the night the great *Ikiriko* drum which is her special instrument is lowered on to its side; and on the next day the first of the cycle of masquerades comes out to dance to its beat.

Every one of the Water People tended by the *Ekine* is masqueraded and entertained in turn (the lapse of time between one festival and the next may be anything from four days to some months). Then when the whole cycle is complete, a crier comes out one morning and calls upon all the Water People who have been entertained to gather in the dancing place, as their season has come to an end. Soon after this a player of every masquerade comes out into the central square; and now all the masquerades are danced together instead of one at a time as before. This ceremony is known as *Owu Aro Sun*—"filling the canoe of the Water People". Finally the whole body of maskers goes down to the special beach known as *Owusera*—"the resting-place of the Water People". Screened from the eyes of women they take off their masks. Then they dip themselves in the water—a symbolic gesture designed to speed the *owu* back to their homes in the creeks. *Owu Aro Sun* has been completed and the dancers go home. That evening the *Ikiriko* drum is put down into the village well and the season of the Water People is at an end until the next round of festivals for the Village Heroes and Dead has finished.

In most Kalabari communities the cycle opens with festivals for three or four of the Water People whose masquerades are the property of the community and are produced by the *Ekine* as a whole. These are followed by a succession of festivals for those whose masquerades are the property of a particular descent group; the latter's ancestor either was the first to encounter the god in question or else purchased rights to his play from a neighbouring community in the distant past. In such cases, though the whole village takes part in the festivals, members of the owning group actually make the offerings and don the masquerades. (Although the cults of these *owu* are organized either on a communal or on a descent group basis, such cults can be transferred from group to group in a way that is never seen in the case of the Dead and the Village Heroes. The most rigid social attachments implied in the definitions of these two categories of god rule out any sort of transfer from one group to another.) The final festival of the cycle is generally a communally-owned masquerade—often that of the most powerful *owu* known to the village. Before the Pax Britannica it seems that the whole cycle seldom took up a whole year, though now for various reasons it may be many years in completion.

The festival of any particular *owu* comes in with a great deal of activity for those who have to sew together the cloths and decorate the wooden head-dresses which cover the dancer as symbols of the god. On the evening before the masquerader comes out to dance, those responsible for the cult come together in the shrine where the head-dresses are painted ready for the performance. A cock, or sometimes a goat, is killed for the *owu* in front of its head-dress, with a prayer which asks that the pollution from those who have handled it should be taken away by the blood of the animal, that the *owu* should spare the dancer any accidents, and that peace, prosperity and issue should come to the owners of the cult. Often a long procession, mostly of women, files in and out of the shrine. Each brings a few pennies to drop before the head-dress with a request that the *owu* take sickness away from her children or protect an unborn child still in the womb. The men of the group concerned bring out their palm gin and as the spirit warms them they start to chant the praise songs of the *owu*. Even if the cult is the property of a single descent group, members of the *Ekine* will nevertheless come round to visit the shrine and swell the noise. Sometimes the whole congregation will sing through till morning, carried along on a mounting tide of euphoria, welcoming in the Water People.

A little after dawn, the *Ekine* drummer calls the maskers to the dancing field. Male helpers crowd into the shrine, sewing and strapping the dancers into the many cloths they must be burdened with. As each vanishes slowly into his cloths, he falls into a nervous silence at the gruelling prospect ahead, and a thoughtful helper gives him a glass of gin for his courage. Where the *owu* is known to be a powerful one, there is added to the prospect of physical exhaustion that of the close presence of the spirit, readily angered at any mistake made. Even if the dancer avoids all error, he may become possessed by the spirit as a consequence of his virtuosity, and this too is a little fearful. Dancing an important masquerade is work for a man of strong *teme* and dancing it successfully one of the most admired achievements in the community.

At last the cloths are sewn and the head-dress secured, and with praise shouts of *"Owu* has come out! *Owu* has come out!" his people take the dancer to the square. As the procession leaves the shrine, an old man of the dancer's family will pour a small libation to the ancestor who first introduced the cult, telling him, "This your child is going out to the field in your name; give him a quick ear, a smart leg, and let no ill thing harm him in the dance".

Before he takes to the field, the masker must first go to the tree where stands the shrine of *Ekine Ba*, patroness of the masquerade. Beside the tree waits her priest to whom he gives a small bottle of palm gin. With this the priest invokes the goddess: *"Ekine Ba, Ekine Ba, Ekine Ba!* This is what you have said, that at any time the dancing people are going to bring out *owu*, every one of them who is going to play the *owu* should come before you to give you drink in case he has been polluted by women or some other things. This is *Karibo*: please open his ears to understand the meaning of drums; open his eyes to see everything that may come before him; give him strength to dance the *owu*; let his legs and hands be nimble."

After the invocation the priest pours a libation of gin before the shrine. The masker cautiously opens his face and the priest tips a glass of gin down his dry throat. Then he bends down, dips his finger in the earth moistened by the libation and smears it on the forehead and chest of the masker. As he puts on the mud, he soothes the dancer, telling him that with this he is receiving strength and has nothing more to fear. Now, with all pollution gone from him, the masker steps out into the field as the drummer calls the god's name. Out in the middle, with the eyes of all the village on him, the dancer's heart grows big. As he starts into his step, joyful shouts of "The Water People have come" greet him from all sides. Though in cold blood he acknowledges the distinction between himself and the god of the mask, it is his every movement that compels the presence of the god with him in the dancing arena. It is not hard for elation to blur the boundary of his identity a little, and not far to go before

his everyday consciousness gives place altogether to something
quite alien to it.

The variety of performances carried out by maskers dancing
to represent the Water-People makes a summary of their characteristics very difficult. At one extreme we have graphic portray-
als of character. There is *Igbo*, a lascivious good-time "bluffer"
who can never resist using up all the family funds in buying the
favours of a woman when his father sends him up-river to buy
yams; in masquerade, he continuously falters in the serious
business of dancing and rushes off for a lecherous advance upon
some pretty girl in the audience. There is *Ngbula*, the ugly, deaf
and paranoic water-doctor, whose masquerade stares at people
as if to read their lips, then rushes savagely at them because he
thinks they must have been insulting him in his infirmity. There
is *Igoni*, the self-pitying old woman whose own troubles are
insufficient and who therefore takes up everyone else's sorrows
to slake her thirst for misery: in masquerade, she wanders
mournfully about alternately dirging her own misfortunes and
those of members of the audience.

Another common content of masquerade is not so much
character summary as straight episode from the life of the *owu*.
Thus in part of *Ngbula's* play as performed at Teinma there are
a series of sketches of dramatic events in his history. Among
these are the conflict between *Ngbula* and the fisherwomen of
Degema, who mistakenly set out their fishing fences in *Ngbula's*
private domain; then there is the mounting of King *Amakoro's*
boat by *Ngbula* as the King was crossing the New Calabar river.
In the *Agiri* play in the village of Bile, there is a conflict
between *Agiri* and *Sabo*, the brother of *Agiri's* girl-friend *Data*
who unsuccessfully tries to prevent her marriage because of
Agiri's ruthless nature. In such episodes, the tone is comic as
often as it is serious. Sometimes as with *Agiri* the *owu* being
entertained is the hero of the fun, sometimes as with *Igoni* the
butt of it. Although it is generally the lesser *owu* who are
portrayed in a ridiculous light, even the more powerful do not
escape a few shafts. But these are occasions of joy for both god
and audience, and the god seems to tolerate the laughter of his
hosts.

Yet another element, often the one that supplies the heights of climax in these visits of the Water People, is a game of risk played with the young men of the village. A common form of this is where the masker slashes at the audience with a matchet, whilst the young men compete in creeping as close to the menacing figure as possible. It is brought to its most exciting pitch in the *Agiri* play at Bile, where the masker alternately slashes with a matchet and hurls heavy staves in long, well-directed volleys—the supply being kept up to him by a retinue of attendants carrying bundles of these staves.

A typical Kalabari masquerade festival tends to alternate such high-tension bouts in which the Water People show themselves as powerful and ruthless with lighter-hearted sequences involving character sketch and comic episode. Often, as indeed in the *Agiri* play, the principal *owu* dominates the high-tension phases, whilst his followers and minions among the Water People come on for the interludes. This setting-off of successive climaxes of tension with a series of relaxed interludes is a favourite pattern in Kalabari ritual.

Perhaps the most striking development of the masquerade is one which makes use of the custom of which any god or its human representative must always salute other gods when their names are called in the drum. He must do this by pointing either to the appropriate shrine or in the direction of the god's abode. In a few masquerades this has been developed into a competition in the correct answering of drum calls—notably, as one might expect, in the city-state of *Owome*. In this type of performance, several descent-groups of houses bring out their maskers at once, and these are put through their paces one at a time. The central square of the community is generally surrounded by thirty or more shrines of the Village Heroes, whilst yet others lie out of sight; and when each dancer comes out, the drummer dodges about those shrines with his calls until he has run through the lot. Tension mounts as the dancer successfully calls shrine after shrine. When the last one is called there is a wild commotion and the dancer's own housepeople rush on to the field, hoist him on to their shoulders and rush him back to his house to strip the cloths from him before he suffers heat stroke. But whatever his prestige as the result of this performance, his disgrace had he failed would have been far greater. The reason for this is that the masquerade is not only the representation of the particular *owu*; it is also a symbol of the ancestor who introduced it; a symbol, indeed, of all the dancers' ancestors who performed it before him. This association with the ancestors is vividly illustrated by the memorial screens made for the chiefly dead in *Owome*. In these, the human figure is individuated and identified not by portraiture but by a miniature replica of the masquerade head-dress which the ancestor in question introduced or danced outstandingly. In a culture where such store is set by virtuosity in the masquerade, and where a man's prowess with a particular *owu* is one of his most important attributes, this secondary significance is hardly surprising. For the dancer it means that a serious mistake will amount to "spoiling the name of his ancestors".

Not only does this imply public shaming of the dancer's whole descent-group. Worse, it puts this group in danger of ancestral anger. Little wonder, then, that a mistake in these performances is so disgraceful. But the very extent of the risk creates just the sort of high-tension ordeal that appeals to Kalabari and undoubtedly adds to their fascination with these drum-answering competitions.

In much of the ritual drama in this culture, religion and recreation are inextricably blended. Men play with gods. In some of these developments of the *owu* masquerade, however, recreation seems to have broken loose from religion. The motives of dancers and audience in the drum-answering competitions are no longer focused on concern for the gods; even less so were the motives of nineteenth century *Owome* chiefs who combed the Eastern Delta for new plays to devastate their rivals. True, most of the performances involved are preceded by prayer and offerings to the gods represented. But in some cases these seem to have become little more than precautionary measures to ensure that no accidents mar the play. Although this applies only to some *Owu* masquerades and chiefly to the *Owome* community, there is little doubt that a secular dramatic form was beginning to emerge from the religious practice. How far this development would have gone had the culture received no violent jolts, we shall, alas, never know.

Although by sheer weight of numbers masquerades for the Water People tend to eclipse those for other gods, some of the latter are of great importance. Perhaps the most striking example here is one that unfortunately died out two or three decades ago. However, as I have cross-checking accounts from two or three old men who attended it in their youth, the outline of the performance seems worth giving.

The festival in question was held for *Opu So*, head of the Village Heroes in the large village of Ke. The nature of the proceedings is expressed in its name—the Creek Swimming festival. When it fell due, the whole community cooperated in preparing a large canoe. At its completion, a day was decided, and, on the evening before, an offering was made to *Opu So*, begging him to help them in what was to come. Next morning the canoe was dragged into the water, and mounted by a masker representing *Opu So*. At once a dozen young men dived into the water, caught hold of long ropes which had been tied to the canoe and started to tow it across the creek. As the canoe got under way, all the younger age-grades of the village who could swim jumped in after it. The canoe was first of all towed across the creek, then down along the opposite bank; all the while *Opu So* as represented by the masker on top poured libations of gin to the Water People of the area. At last, on reaching the mouth of a smaller creek, the canoe came to a halt. The towers simulated inability to pull it any further. Great excitement ran through the audience, for this was the spot commanded by the most powerful of the local Water People—a deaf man who had heard no news of the festival and so refused to let the canoe pass. For some time, *Opu So* continued to invoke him and pour libations; but in vain. Finally, several of the young men swam back to the village, secured new stocks of gin and returned with it to the canoe. Now at last the invocations had their effect on the *Owu*, and there was a wild shout of joy from the entire village as the canoe slowly got under way again and returned to the water-side. That evening the priest of *Opu So* made a further thanksgiving offering to the head of the Village Heroes, and the festival closed with three days' dancing.

This dramatic sequence, however bare the outline now available to us, is a particularly fascinating one; for it gives a vivid, almost diagrammatic statement of the complementary parts played by Village Heroes and Water People in man's struggle with his environment. Man, guided by the Heroes, strives to impose his skills upon the waters, whilst the controllers of the creeks continually oppose him until both he and his village gods recognize their dependence on them and pay respect accordingly. But this is not the whole story. It is clear from my informants that this, like the other dramatic representations of the gods, secured their presence in person. *Opu So* himself was in the canoe; and the safe passage and return of canoe and swimmers despite the opposition of the Water People was an example of his willingness to support the people in their life on the creeks during the coming year. If there were an accident to the canoe or, as indeed happened from time to time, a swimmer failed to return, the god had failed to exert his power over the forces opposed to him, and this was a sign of his anger. In such a case diviners would have to be consulted as to the human errors which were responsible for this, and steps would have to be taken to set them right before the villagers could count on further help from *Opu So*.

Here, then, we see yet another angle to the ritual drama—its use as a device to make the gods show their hands to men. This oracular element is even more important in possession, the last of the three modes of dramatization.

3. POSSESSION—Where mime and masquerade produced very close association between the dancer and the god represented, inducing possession means compelling a god to take over control of a man's body from his own *teme*. A new personality temporarily guides his behaviour; and when his own *teme* returns to control, it naturally enough knows nothing of what happened in its absence.

Possession is induced in rites for Village Heroes, Water People and more rarely for the Dead. For most of these rites, there is a medium who has been appointed by the cult group after divination to ascertain the god's choice, and who holds this office until death. The man (or woman) must present himself at the beginning of each festival for his god and submit to certain techniques of "calling the god to enter his head". Such techniques make use once more of the Kalabari doctrine and "the gods stay and come with their names". First of all, as the rite approaches the time appointed for the god's appearance, the medium is dressed in clothes which symbolize the world of spirits—the red woollen cap, the fishing eagle's feathers, the *Ekaki* cloth about the waist. He is taken and made to stand before the shrine of the god where often he is given to hold one of the latter's material symbols. Thus Water People's media are often made to hold paddles bearing reliefs of the python—the usual materialization of this group of gods. Finally, the drummer starts to call over and over again the drum-names of the god; and after a few minutes the god comes. For the outsider, Kalabari possession is often difficult to identify: the gods manifest themselves as more or less coherent actors, and often only a knowledge of the normal personality of the medium shows the way in which the possession is taking place. This difference in personality, however, is often very striking, especially where a normally placid medium changes into a dominating and aggressive god. Unlike the Yoruba, who stress, at least as an ideal, a harmony between the personality of the medium and that of the god, Kalabari stress the fact that a god may select anyone for his medium, even a person of the most improbable character. Indeed, it is those cases where a placid, temperate human being is transformed into an intransigent and aggressive god which Kalabari seem to find the most thrilling of the possession rituals, and which they stress most in reminiscing about such things.

The variety of themes coming up in possession sequences is similar to that encountered in the masquerade. As in the latter, behaviour summarizing the character and attributes of the god bulks large. Thus in the case of the Water People, their connexion with a particular stretch of creek is emphasised in rituals where the medium not only becomes possessed when the canoe carrying him enters his god's domain, but also tries to throw himself overboard into the water beneath which the god is thought to live. Again, the ability of all Water People to materialize as pythons is emphasised in possession dances where the god turns from acting like a man to writhing on the ground and even slithering about in the rafters of houses as the great snakes do. Often there is a demonstration of the relationship between several gods—as in the rituals for the Waterman *Duminea* of the village of Soku, where the god's wife also possesses a medium, and acts as would a human wife preparing her husband for day's headhunting. Thus she carries a platter down to the waterside where her husband is waiting to depart in his canoe, and in the act of giving it to him as a vehicle for the meat he will kill, she tries frantically but successfully to get into the boat with him. Attendants drag her off, since this is a man's work; and *Duminea* and his helpers paddle off into the creeks alone. Once in *Duminea's* domain, they kill a goat for the god; and the remains of its meat are taken home in the platter brought down to the canoe by his wife. As they return to the home waterside, she is there waiting for *Duminea* like any good wife. She rushes to the canoe to embrace him, and receives on her platter the goat's head—the traditional wife's share of the head-hunter's prey. With this she tears through the village excitedly showing it off, then finally goes back into *Duminea's* shrine.

An element of comedy is not uncommon, especially in the rites of individual Water People's cults started by self styled media. As the rites connected with these are not under public control, the opportunity for innovation during possession is much greater, and comic elaboration of these performances is probably one of the more effective forms of propaganda for the building up of a clientele. As festivals for the *Owu Ojoye Adamu*, the subject of one of the most important and successful private cults, the medium's body is invaded by a rapid succession of minor Water People—generally a different collection of them at each festival. These minor gods show all sorts of bawdy traits and infirmities such as uncontrolled lechery and elephantiasis of the scrotum; and their antics keep the audience in a storm of laughter between the greater tensions of the festival patron's appearances. They are the clowns which the patron brings with him as his foil.

As in the masquerade, the game of risk is an important feature of possession behaviour, especially where the gods concerned are patrons of headhunting or some other aggressive activity. Typical of such games is the spectacular *Iju Ti* which *Feni Be So*, the patron of headhunting, plays with the young men of Soku village. On the day after an offering has been made to the god, he is called to the head of his medium on a trio of special drums. The young men, dressed in their best clothes and each equipped with a matchet, line out around the cult house clashing their weapons once upon the other to "shake the god up". The medium stands impassively at the door of the culthouse, waiting for the drums to take effect. As the drumming and clashing goes on, the whole village streams expectantly into the square. Many take care to station themselves suitably close to half-open doorways or side-lanes in case the game becomes "too hot". After some minutes of waiting, tremors start to pass down the medium's body; the young men redouble their clashing and the drummer his beat. Suddenly an enormous shudder racks the man, and he rushes out into the square with *Feni Be So* on his head. Whirling an old and villainous sword about him, he nearly decapitates one of the young men, plunges his weapon deep into a house-post, then tears at the drummers and chases them off their pitch. The inflammatory beat silenced, he becomes calmer. Then begins *Feni Be So's* game. As the god approaches each of the young men participating, the latter must hold out the blade of his matchet towards him. If the youth has the nerve to stand his ground, the god may bring down his sword on the matchet with a bone-jarring vertical blow that sends a ring through the village and is answered by a roar of approval—a point of honour. On the other hand, the god may make a sudden horizontal swipe aimed at reaching the body, and the youth must be ready for instant flight if he sees this coming. A variety of nasty wounds awaits the slow and unalert; and several of the older dancers can show a scar from *Iju Ti*. This hectic sport goes on morning and evening for three days; then on the last evening there is a dance of all the players, whose sweethearts and other admirers vie in throwing them coins in token of their admiration. The art of *Iju* playing is to score as many points as possible with the maximum of impudent clowning at the god. The more impudent the player the more pleased *Feni Be So*; for this is a sign of prowess in the pursuits of violence which he patronizes. And although these pursuits are a thing of the past, an outstanding *Iju* dancer is still a notable in the village.

As we mentioned before, the oracular element in ritual drama is best developed in possession sequences. Every one of these gods must be in good humour for him to enter a man's head at all, so his very arrival is a sign that nothing major is wrong between himself and his worshippers. The god who refused to come to the medium's head when called would be a portent of major trouble requiring immediate divination and diagnosis. Each such sequence, then, is a way of forcing a god to show his hand; and his reception when he arrives owes to this an intensity of feeling seldom paralleled by the other two modes of dramatization.

Mention has already been made of the possibility of both mime and masquerade passing into possession behaviour. In the case of the masquerade, not only may this happen during an actual performance; the closeness of association established between a really accomplished masker and the *owu* he generally represents is sometimes such that he becomes possessed from time to time even away from his mask. Singing a snatch of the *owu's* songs or even dancing one or two of his steps may be enough to bring the god into his head.

In some masquerades, the performer is expected to await possession before dancing, the god being called to his head by a drummer as in a simple possession rite. This happens in those more violent types of masquerade involving duels of matchet and spear with the young men of the village. In such cases, the idea that the masker is also possessed would seem to enhance the effect created by the masquerade pure and simple; for the implication is usually that the god will be restrained by none of the scruples which might deter a more human impersonator from injuring his fellow villagers or even his close relatives during the course of the play.

These possessed maskers give rise to some curious instances of double-thinking. Thus despite the official dogma about them, they are often treated by individuals as though the masker was in his everyday senses. In one case, a prominent villager who wanted to show off gave a masker money just before a big festival at which the latter was to dance the principal *owu*. The idea was that this would secure him immunity from pursuit during the matchet play, so that he could pose as a figure of nerveless calm whilst all about him dashed hither and thither. The festival came, and the man was all-too-obviously exempt from chasing by the god. Afterwards the village elders, who were angered by this, showed just the same attitude to the masker as had the giver of the money. Instead of regarding the whole thing as the coincidence it must have been had the possession been genuine, they gave both briber and dancer a furious reprimand for spoiling the play.

This may sound like an exhibition of cynicism about the whole religious basis of such masquerades; but on Kalabari premises the enactment of the *owu's* representation nonetheless implied his presence. So the action of the elders is more accurately looked at as stemming from a concern from the dramatic impact and vigour of the play and not from a desire to keep up a religious pretence over something they knew to be secular.

In other cases, where the notion that a mimer or a masker is possessed does not play such an important part in maintaining the full impact of the proceedings, people are apt to be little concerned as to whether he is or is not dissociated. Some people may judge from the fervour of the play that he is. Others may disagree. Anyway, since for Kalabari mime, masquerade and possession are three ways of accomplishing the same thing, the matter is often of little consequence to anyone but the performer.

All three modes of the ritual drama—Mime, Masquerade and Possession—use much the same range of themes in presenting the gods to their audience. Individual gods are referred to by character summary, biographical incident or allusion to important attributes. Often several gods are referred to by a vivid presentation of the relationship they bear to each other and to the world of men—as where the respective roles of Village Heroes and Water People in the battle of human skill versus environmental forces are given illustration in the Creek Swimming festival at Ke. In all these themes there is a close correlation with doctrinal portrayal of the god's characters and place in the world.

Except where secularization has started in some of the masquerades, the most remarkable feature of these dramas is the intimate blend of religion and recreation to which they so often give rise. It is no coincidence that when they are used to bring the gods to the village as guests, there is generally an important part of the performance of which the word *ti* is used. For the concept *ti* has exactly the same range of application as the English concept of play. It is used in opposition to the idea of work, of games, and sometimes of frivolous treatment of things that should be taken seriously. Thus an angry person may say: *E na ti ma*— "Do not play with me!"

But it should not be thought because of this that Kalabari religion is a light-hearted one. Not a few of these dramas, as we have seen, conceal the taking of omens about matters of vital importance to the community's very existence. The grim moods of the religion are all too apparent in another type of rite known as *agba*, whose intention is to beg a god to take away some misfortune for which he has been diagnosed responsible. In making *agba*, people go to an appointed place with an offering which they tie up for the god to take away. They make a brief demand that with this he should "take his hand from them". Then they disperse without thought of cooking and sharing the meat. The *agba* are not entertainments of the gods: they are more like the grudging payment of blackmail.

By contrast, the *alali* (festivals) which are the theme of this essay are naturally called *ti* because they are occasions of joy for the congregations giving them. Often they are held in thanks for some benefit already received. At other times the joy is in a confident assurance that the gods will continue to see that things prosper as they have done to date. On such occasions, the appropriate way to receive the gods is a light-hearted one, in which the respect due to them is tempered with gaiety and even teasing—as when the young men taunt a matchet-twirling masker. Since the gods are greater in every way than men, the scale of entertainment due to them is correspondingly greater than anything due to one's fellow human beings; and so it is that many religious rites are at the same time the most elaborate and flamboyant recreation periods of the Kalabari year.

During *alali*, one sees the particular style of Kalabari living intensified almost to the point of caricature. Notable in all of them is the predilection for building up every situation into a series of climaxes of increasing tension set off with periods of relaxed calm. At festival times this pattern is magnified tenfold, people go about like sensitive guns ready to be triggered by the slightest vibration; and the living of four months seems compressed into the four days of the ritual week.

One salient feature of Kalabari ritual drama is the relatively poor development of straight acting as compared with masquerade and induced possession. The reason for this may be that such acting lacks characteristics which serve to maintain the distinction between the actor's everyday person and his dramatic role.

In the European theatre, it is possible to maintain this distinction using straight acting alone (a) because the actor is in general not personally known to most of the audience, and (b) because it is possible to use the apparatus of stage and stage-set to emphasize the discontinuity between the performer at work and off-duty. In Kalabari religious dramas the performer is always personally known to his audience; and the value set upon audience participation precludes the use of any device like the stage. Some additional contrivance must therefore be used to preserve the distinction between the actor's role in the drama and his role outside it. One very simple way is to carry out the acting at night—as is done for the Dead Without Houses, and for the night parades of some of the masking Water People. It is much easier for an actor to emphasize the break with his everyday self when his audience merely hears him without seeing him as well; and this perhaps is why most instances of pure acting in Kalabari drama are in fact nocturnal. Presentation of the gods in daytime requires something extra—either the total extinction of one's everyday appearance and style of behaviour imposed by the masquerade; or the striking discontinuity in behaviour which marks the personality dissociation of a genuine possession episode.

It is not for nothing that the mask is often associated in the European mind with so-called "primitive peoples". For if they have nothing else in common, people labelled "primitive" are always dwellers in small-scale societies. Now this smallness of scale creates a grave problem of social organization: it means that one man must often be required to take up several very different roles toward the same set of people, and that these people in turn are required to accept the differences and behave accordingly.

Religious drama is by no means the only context in which this problem arises. It is just as urgent where an ordinary villager has intermittently to act as executive of the village body politic, and where people who have known him as a friend suddenly have to accept him as a public disciplinary agent. In such a situation the masquerade is as valuable an aid as it is in the religious drama; and it is not surprising to find a great many small-scale societies in all parts of the world, where the maskers who represent gods in ritual drama also act as executives of the communal authority. Examples near at hand are the maskers of the *Odo*, *Omada*, and *Mmo* cults in Iboland, those of the *Ekpe* cult at Old Calabar, and those of the *Poro* cult in Mendeland. In West Africa, indeed, Kalabari and other Ijo maskers are somewhat exceptional in their lack of political function.

In the large-scale societies of Europe such extreme devices as these are unnecessary. The theatrical actor is scarcely ever a personal friend of his audience members; and the executives of the state have very limited outside acquaintance with members of the public whom they control, discipline and direct. By and large, a change of clothing suffices to do here what masquerade and induced possession are called upon to do in a small-scale African community.

The picture of the world that makes sense of Kalabari ritual dramas is still a very live one. As a system of explanation and control of the universe it is constantly drawn upon even by many of those who have had contact at secondary school with a very different world-view. Nevertheless, in all Kalabari communities today one sees a steady stripping-down of traditional religious practice to its bare essentials. The various techniques of making the gods manifest in person at the time of their rituals are among the first items to be dispensed with; and the peculiar intensity of feeling which they bring to religious occasions may soon be a forgotten experience.

This decline is a consequence as much of the Pax Britannica as of the spread of Christianity. Formerly, relations between one village and another were often so hostile that people venture no further than necessary from their home creeks for fishing trips. Now, with violence outlawed, people are free to follow the logic of their production methods: when the fish shoals move unpredictably from one estuary to the next, so now do the fishermen—even if it means moving into quarters where they breathe down the necks of traditional enemies bent on the same quest. The relentless pursuit of constantly and capriciously migrating fish now keeps many people as much as thirty miles of creeks and estuaries from their home village for much of the year. The festivals that previously demanded nothing more than four days' holiday from fishing excursions based on the home community, now require tedious journeys back and forth from the fishing camps plus equally tedious packings and unpackings of possessions; so a growing reluctance to attend festivals is inevitable. Its result is that the personnel required for proper performance of a ritual is seldom available nowadays. People content themselves with contributing money which priests or their substitutes in the home town can use to make offerings to the gods whilst they themselves remain out at the camps.

The truncation of religious practice resulting from all this has left a big gap in Kalabari culture. As to what will fill it, or as to whether it will be filled at all, at the moment there are few clues.

Reprinted Nigeria Magazine, Special Issue

EKPE FESTIVAL AS RELIGIOUS RITUAL AND DANCE DRAMA

J. N. Amankulor

Introduction

Among the Igbo of Nigeria, there is a wealth of cultural heritage manifested in ceremonies connected with marriages, births, farming and myriad of other social institutions. These cultural activities contain the germs of rich poetry and prose, excellent music and lively drama which have not been raised far above their traditional level, although present-day scholars—sociologists, anthropologists and literary researchers—are showing sufficient interest. The *Ekpe*[1] festival, an action-packed festival full of song and dance, is one of such cultural events, a deeper investigation of which would reveal its great significance as religious ritual and potentialities as dance-drama.

The *Ekpe* festival is very popular among the Ngwa of Igboland. It is also widely celebrated in neighbouring areas such as the old Umuahia and Owerri Provinces. As a festival, *Ekpe* is celebrated every year because it is an important cultural event in the life of the people being the culmination of their Year Rites. Its roots are deep in traditional religion and ritual. It is only a tragic event such as the death of a village hero, or a permission from the gods that can stop the staging of *Ekpe*.

Ekpe (tone-marked - -, low-low) should not be confused with Ekpe (tone-marked - -, high-low). The latter is a secret society which is exclusive to men, and which is also called *Okonko* in many parts of Igboland. This Society is equally popular among the Efik and Annang of Nigeria. But *Ekpe*, the former, enjoys communal patronage and participation with women and children forming part of its choric force.

The Ekpe Ritual Cycle

In order to fully appreciate or understand the importance of

113

Ekpe as a religious ritual, it might be necessary to trace what should rightly be called the "Ekpe Cycle" (fig. 1). *Ekpe* is the seventh and the last of activities and ceremonies within the religious-ritual year.[2] I will go through these activities briefly.

The first of these ceremonies is called *Ikpa Unwu* (famine ceremony). It is done in April after crops have been planted and nothing is left in the barns. This ceremony is dedicated to the gods to protect the people from famine till the new yams are ready.

The second ceremony which takes place about June is called *Ira Ugu* (eating fluted-pumpkin vegetable sauce). It is a ceremony of hope, because soon it will be time for the harvest of new yams. On an appointed date, each family cooks large quantities of fluted-pumpkin vegetable sauce which is doled out in large measures to everybody.

The third ceremony, *Iwa Ji* (yam-slicing ceremony) is done about July by the chief-priest of each compound who dedicates the new yam to Njoku, the yam-god. Only after this ceremony are the people free to eat the new yams. With *Iwa Ji*, the people are free from famine and hunger. From now on merriments can begin. That is why *Igba Ogbom* (Ogbom Dancing), the first of the year's popular out-door activity, comes at this stage.

Igba Ogbom continues from July to September or October. It is first done at the *Ogbom* Shrine before the dancers tour the different village squares. During the *Ogbom* dance, the people are virtually thrown into uncontrolled ecstasy with rhythmic body jerks and twisting of waists and breasts. Highly-trained chorus leaders lead during *Ogbom*. It is a time for competition in excellence during which the best dancer-artiste for the year is honoured.

Apart from the religion-ritual level, *Ogbom* possesses all the basic elements of drama. It has good music, song and dancing. The costuming is gorgeous and the action mimetic. The performance is strictly communal. But *Ogbom* has not passed through the transition necessary for it to become drama because dialogue and word sequence remain merely repetitive and unelevated beyond the sphere of traditional ritual.

The ceremonies of *Itu Aka* (Thanks-giving Prayer) and *Ize Mmuo* (Dedication Ceremony) are of very serious ritualistic significance.

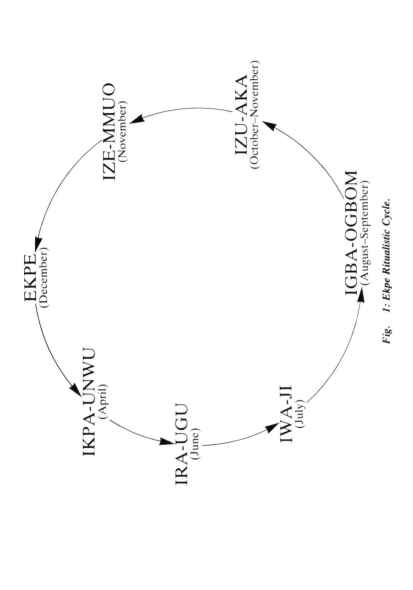

Fig. 1: Ekpe Ritualistic Cycle.

During *Itu Aka* each family priest thanks his ancestral gods for protecting his family during the year. He begs favours for the coming year and reprimands the gods for the misfortunes of the passing year. The sacrificial victims are usually he-goats and cocks. The chief priest of each compound co-ordinates and unites all other sacrifices by lesser priests.

Ize Mmuo, the sixth ceremony, has overtones of tragedy. It is a ceremony in which the chief priest for the village goddess, *Alumerechi*, is chosen. One is not merely chosen by other priests, but *Alumerechi* herself selects whom she pleases through the oracles. Her choice is unpredictable and never refused once done. It must be accepted. Because this service involves pain and suffering, it is tragic in the true sense of the word. But the "hero-servant" and everybody else must be reconciled with this painful mission. This reconciliation we could regard as temporary suffering which is bound to be resolved into eternal harmony. The spirit of the sacrifice is one of obedience unto a higher authority because the candidates of *Alumerechi* ceases to have anything physical in common with every one else in the community, but there is "inexhaustible joy" in the end when the suffering must have been meekly borne. In confrontation with *Ize Mmuo* the community (audience) is caught by that strange contradiction of pleasure through pain which is the basic element in tragic pleasure.

The servant-hero of *Alumerechi* although now specially dedicated, represents the entire village. In a sense it is communal service through the physical pain of one man for the spiritual regeneration of the community. Food for this priest is collected by the entire village. *Eze Alumerechi* appears only at night to deliver messages from *Alumerechi*. Such messages are shouted from the compound gates of whoever they are meant for. Although *Ize Mmuo* is celebrated each year, it is not necessary to choose a new *Eze Alumerechi* every year. The serving one continues till his death which is marked by thunderstorms and heavy down-pour of rain, the signs which mark triumph for *Eze Alumerechi* and the people.

In the terms of significance as dance-drama the movements for *Ize Mmuo* are as follows:

(a) The consultation of the oracle of *Alumerechi* by the village priests among whom is the would-be *Eze Alumerechi*. *Alumerechi* speaks through the thick and dark wood that is her shrine, answering questions put to her and giving directives:

Eze Dibia: Alumerechi, anyi abiala!
                Onye nwe ala Umuode,
                Futa gwa anyi ihe bu eche ghi.
                Ura churu anyi l'anyasu,
                Anya di anyi l'ama
                Biko, gwa anyi uche ghi.
Alumerechi: Ekelee m unu umu m
                Unu emee-la!
                Ije unu abughu ije ojoo
                Ama m ihe di unu l'obi, —
                Onye yara Alumerechi di-ibi.

The speeches are made to *ogele* (gong) accompaniment and when *Alumerechi* speaks nobody raises his head because she is "invisible".

Translation:

Eze Dibia: Alumerechi we have come!
                The owner of Umuode-land,
                Come out and divine for us
                Sleep forsook us last night
                We are very expectant,
                Please tell us your mind.
Alumerechi's Greetings my children!
Voice: I owe you thanks
                Your visit is not a bad one.
                I know the contents of your mind, —
                A servant for Alumerechi.

The consultation ends when *Alumerechi* walks out of her shrine and calls the name of the elect who answers and follows her into the shrine.

(b) The second movement comes when the new servant-hero takes farewell of the village never to be seen again. The spiritual conflict comes at this stage—to go or not to go. The elders encourage and he affirms, "what *Alumerechi* has ordered cannot be changed".

(c) At the entrance of the shrine, the chief leaders with the elect move right, move left, move forwards and then backwards, then forwards again. They bid the new servant-hero good bye! All the time there is music and movement but not the uncontrolled dancing and merriment as in *Ogbom*.

When there is no new *Eze Alumerechi* to choose, the events of the preceding choice are re-enacted and dramatized with plausible impersonation.

The Ekpe Dance-Drama

The successful conclusion of *Ize Mmuo* means that *Ekpe* festival, the final of the year's activities can go ahead. In essence, *Ekpe* combines the tragic and the comic aspects of the proceeding ceremonies. There is ribaldry and great exuberance as in *Ogbom* but there is also anxiety and spiritual purgation as in *Ize Mmuo*. *Ekpe* takes place on Eke day. It is preceded by the *Ekpe* eve, a free-for-all-night of dancing and rehearsals for drummers, dancers, chorus leaders and their choric groups.

(a) *The Choric Groups:* On *Ekpe* day, many choric groups perform, ranging from groups of elderly men or women to children's groups. But the most important of all these groups is the group comprising men drawn from different quarters of the village who accompany the masquerade dancer and chief actor. Before noon on *Ekpe* day, this group rouses the village and begins the series of a circular movement designed to take them to the village square and out of it. It is led by a choric leader who in the Greek sense is the *epheboi*. The *epheboi* sings in praise of the village ancestors, especially those of them who had been chief actors, soliciting their blessings for the current chief actor and the village.

Other choric groups of young men, women and children perform in the village square. They tour the village with the main drummers and not with the chief actor. They move into the village square minutes before the *epheboi* and his group lead in the chief actor. The participation by these minor choric groups goes to add up to the communal significance of *Ekpe*.

(b) *Staging:* The only staging device of *Ekpe* is the "Arena Staging" in its most traditional form. There is no raised platform for the chief actor or the drummers. Everybody is on the same level including the spectators who have to peep over a forest of heads to see what is going on in the innermost circle enclosing the chief actor and masquerade dancer. Nearby tree branches help to form the auditorium.

On the stage, there are four or more concentric circle formations comprising an innermost circle of the *epheboi* and main choric group. This circle encloses the drummers, the sacrificial spot and the main actors. (See fig. 2.) Immediately following this group is the circle of men, then the women's circle and the circle of young boys and girls. There is another circle of village stalwarts who act as policemen for the day by watching the behaviour of spectators. The spectators form the outermost circle.

It is significant that the old village shrine forms a background for the stage with the drummers backing it and the chief actor facing it. It reminds one of the traditional Attic theatre thousands of years ago. It is a symbol that the people are engaged in the act of religious celebration even though interest in the dancing might make this significance appear rather remote.

(c) *Dance Movements:* The dance movements of *Ekpe* are the vehicles of plot advancement. In *Ekpe* there are three main dance movements (i) the Entry Dance, movement which leads the chief actor to his ancestral shrine where, as it were, he obtains blessings for a successful day's performance. This however takes place outside the arena.

(i) In the Entry Dance, the *epheboi* who in essence is a second actor because of his direct communication with the chief actor, sings the entry songs some distance from the main village square where the stage of the day's drama is located:

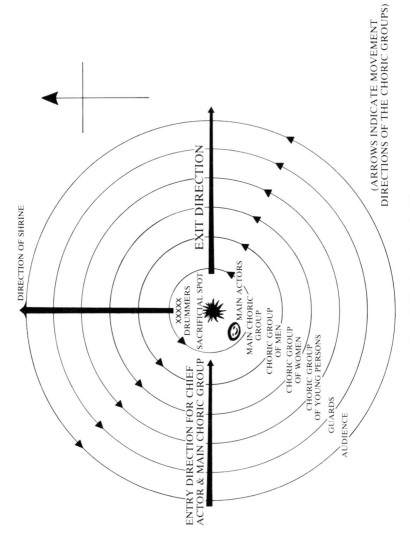

DIRECTION OF SHRINE

ENTRY DIRECTION FOR CHIEF
ACTOR & MAIN CHORIC GROUP

EXIT DIRECTION

XXXXX
DRUMMERS

SACRIFICIAL SPOT

MAIN ACTORS

MAIN CHORIC
GROUP

CHORIC GROUP
OF MEN

CHORIC GROUP
OF WOMEN

CHORIC GROUP
OF YOUNG PERSONS

GUARDS

AUDIENCE

(ARROWS INDICATE MOVEMENT
DIRECTIONS OF THE CHORIC GROUPS)

Fig. 2: The Arena Stage for Ekpe.

Alumerechi ndi Umuode . . .
Akwuwa nwa Wipi . . .
Chigbu nwa Enyia . . .
Ndi gbara ekpe la mbu . . .
Anyi afuwala ama . . .
Duru—nu anyi ga-wa
Alili eleghi Umuode

The choric refrain for each line is

Ehe-e n-ye
Ehe-e n-ye

Translation:

Alumerechi of Umuode people
Akwuwa the son of Wipi
Chigbu the son of Enyia
Chief actors of Ekpe in the past
We are moving to the square
Lead us on to arrive
Shame shall never touch Umuode

Refrain:

Ehe-e n-ye
Ehe-e n-ye

Getting closer to the village square, the chief guide of *Ekpe* runs forward towards the dancing groups recounting as he moves the farm fame of the village. He runs back to the chief actor:

Uzo di nma
Ujo atula ghi
Gaa mee ihe nna ghi mere
Alumerechi no ghi l'ukwu

Translation:

The way is clear
Don't be afraid
Go forward and perform like your father
Alumerechi is your guide.

The chief actor usually hesitates but he is urged onwards till it appears he has passed through the crisis of conscience. He runs forward with full speed into the centre of the square and dances to the aja music. The choric participants shout joyfully and dance more gracefully.

(ii) The Second Dance Movement is the climax of *Ekpe*. It marks the critical stage of the performance and it is here that the chief actor's role as a communal representative becomes clear. As the music changes from "aja" into a more vigorous type, a sharpened knife is handed over to him. The chief guide admonishes him, "The village looks on you." The chief actor shakes his head as he looks at the knife and although dancing continues it is not with the same gusto as before. This is the time of spiritual and emotional crisis because nobody knows what will be the fate of the village. If the sacrifice is successful, then it is great promise for better things in the coming year. If not, there will be woe!

When the actor takes the knife, he moves round and round the sacrificial goat tied to a peg on the sacrificial spot trying to make a decision. As in all traditional dance-drama and ritual the goings-on in his mind are those of the whole village. That he is re-enacting an ancient sacrifice by which the people recall an adventure by their forebears during which a human being was sacrificed to appease the gods, is known by all. If he succeeds in despatching the goat with one stroke ofhis knif, ther is hope that the village tradition is in progress. Otherwise, something is wrong somewhere which may ieed the consultation of the oracles. It is of dramatic significance that the sacrifice must be performed and cannot be shirked but there is the conflict as regards how the stroke is to be administered and the result.

After the chief actor has taken so many tours round the goat, he appears to make up his mind. He waits for the opportunity for the goat to stretch its neck, a propitious moment. All of a sudden he takes a stance, bends and rises—the sacrifice is done! The head of the goat is thrown up to show the audience amid volleys of gun-shots and wild ecstasy. The sacrifice has been successful and the village can expect increases in crops, livestock and children during the coming year.

(iii) Finally the chief actor does the *Okoro-Oji* after which he exits north from the square. The *Okoro-Oji*, a dance movement supposed to have been borrowed from Ohafia and Aro-Chukwu, spells out the drama just performed. It recalls the ancient past when the village sacrificed a friend for the first time when a conflict arose as regards loyalty to *Alumerechi* or to the friend. The chorus leader intones it:

> I mere enyi-e
> I mere enyi-e

and the group replies:

> I mere enyi
> L'enyi mere enyi ya,
> I mere enyi,

Meaning: You did a friend
             A friend did a friend

"did", here standing for a bad turn meted to that unfortunate victim-friend when the villager was confronted with a choice of loyalty. Singing and dancing here assume an ominously suppressed atmosphere.

As the *epheboi* leads the chief actor out of the arena, he introduces more satirical or comic lyrics:

> Anyi mara ndem ugha o-
> Ndem amuta ugha ga - enwe e-
> Onye ukwu le - erughu ala e-
> Ihe ndi ya l'ukwu e-

while the chorus replies:

> Owe nye nye
> E - hee, E - hee
> Owe nye nye.

Translation:
We taught women to tell lies—
Women learnt lies and became experts—
One who cannot bend down,
There's a fault in his waist!

Members of the chorus dance according to indications of their leader. For example, everybody bends as low as possible in "Onye ukwu l'erughu ala" to avoid being accused of waist pain, a sign of impotency.

On the other hand, other choric groups continue to enjoy themselves singing praises for the village:

Ode-Ogu bu enyi
Ehe - e
Ode-ogu bu enyi

meaning that *Umuode*, the great fighters, are great. At this stage women groups satirize men, women who behaved immorally during the year or those found guilty of stealing.

In terms of emotional involvement of both audience and the communal participants of *Ekpe*, there is traceable an emotional triangle with the sacrificial movement at the peak. The first level marks the merriment and song preceding the sacrifice which forms the climatic level, and the final level, one of resolution which comes after the sacrifice has been successfully or otherwise performed. (See fig. 3.) If the sacrifice is unsuccessful, the ceremony continues with unwilling participants who go home eventually with sad hearts.

(d) *Costuming, Make-up and Props:* As in most traditional African ceremonies, the costumes used for *Ekpe* are very colourful indeed. The chief actor wears a white net-like mask covering from head to ankles. He carries a wooden figure of *Ngwu* on his head. *Ngwu* is one of the deities in the service of *Alumerechi*. He is the symbol of traditional

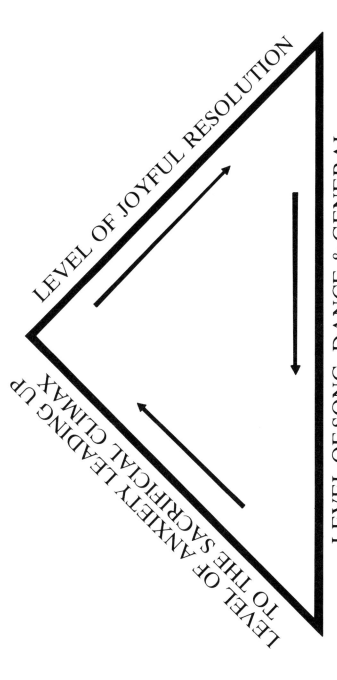

Fig. 3: *Emotional Triangle in Ekpe.*

strength, power or magic. The *ufo*-bearer carries a magical concoction believed to destroy the power of charms. He guards against any foul deeds or intentions by any member of the audience. His costume consists of tattered rags and he smears his body with charcoal. A real devil incarnate! Some comic asides are provided by the bow-man and his wife or mother. The bow-man carries a bow and some arrows and frightens the audience as he pretends to shoot into it. He looks funny with his white and black face and charcoal-smeared body. His female counterpart wears the same make-up in addition to a pair of tattered trousers and a shirt but the bow-man ties a jute bag only around his waist and wears no clothes except for his charms. The pair dance in a truly comic fashion.

The element of disguise or impersonation is very strong in *Ekpe*. Young boys usually disguise themselves as young girls by wearing ladies' dresses. The trick is so exquisitely done that a spectator cannot find out the truth. Other participants—men, women and children—dress in the traditional fashion by tying large pieces of colourful cloth in addition to singlets or shirts for the men and blouses for the women. Young ladies simply cover their breasts with broad cloth exhibiting the intricate design of the tattoo on their skin. They wear large beads around their waist and their hair-do is strictly cultural. Make-up and costumes worn in *Ekpe* prove that these branches of art are no problems for the African traditional artist.

The Ekpe Cycle and the Greek Dionysia

Although comparisons may be misleading, yet there are striking similarities which can be identified between the *Ekpe* cycle, and the Attic ceremonies in honour of Dionysius which gave rise to the birth of classical Greek tragedy and comedy. Within the *Ekpe* cycle there are ceremonies, such as *Ogbom* Dance, which are comparable to Rural Dionysia, or the Lesser Dionysia, or the Dionysia or the Fields, which were held in many country districts of Attica when the harvests had been completed in December each year, as festival of dedication and thanksgiving to the fertility god for the first fruits of the year.[3] *Ogbom* also resembles the Lenea festival of fifth-century Greece because the ceremony is a platform for competition in choric verse. The laurel won in *Ogbom* may be as high as woman given to the choric victor as wife. These festivals do not have any tragic overtones. It is the comic or the satirical that dominate. To be declared the best composer-singer of the year is a great honour coveted by everyone.

Ekpe itself is like the Greek City Dionysia during which visitors from all parts of the world visited Athens. Like the City Dionysia, *Ekpe* enjoys communal participation. Both occasions are dedicated to fertility gods. But whereas Ekpe appears an odd mixture of serious and comic elements, the City Dionysia is performed on one place only, that of religious-ritual dedication. In movement *Ekpe*, follows closely the three ritualistic movements of the Greek Chorus. The entry movement of *Ekpe* could be regarded as the Greek prologos, the sacrificial movement, its stasimon, and the exit movement, the Greek exodos, the three stages in the primary act of religious ritual.

From the drama-theatre development point of view, *Ekpe* contains the same germs which housed the plays of Aeschylus, Sophocles and Euripides. What remains to raise it to the Aeschylean level of drama is a reconstruction of its dialogue to provide for greater communication between the chorus and the chief actor. The Greek idea of the chorus is present in *Ekpe* and it does the same function of communal representation. In terms of formation, the early Greek dithyramb was also sung in the arena formation, which enclosed the officiating chief priest in the middle.

It has to be stressed however that *Ekpe*, like all "primitive" African drama, has not followed any clear and known process of development and the absence of records in the past makes any categorical statement on the issue misleading. We cannot however expect an carbon-copy similarity between it and its Attic or any other counterpart, at least because of cultural differences. As T. S. Eliot put it in a broadcast in the year after the first production of *Murder In The Cathedral*, ". . . There is a good deal about Greek theatre that we do not know and never shall know. But we know that some of its conventions cannot be ours . . ". And, although I have tried to point out possible similarities, we still cannot regard *Ekpe* having as developed in the same way as the Greek dithyramb, but one thing is certain and that is that both have their roots in religion and ritual.

The seeming odd mixture of elements of tragedy and comedy in *Ekpe*, while not borne out in Greek drama, is however vindicated in Shakespeare's tragedies where comedy mixes freely with tragedy. Perhaps such mixtures must have developed in *Ekpe* as a result of the people's wish to bring the year's events to a climatic peak, and to have the best in the seemingly different worlds of suffering and enjoyment. There is also the strong implication that the people over the years have played down considerably the elements of tragedy and sacrifice in *Ekpe* because of the introduction of the Christian religion.

Conclusion

Ekpe as dance-drama stands in dire need of structural reconstruction to lift it above the level of traditional art. Happily enough, it possesses the germs of good drama and the third quarter of the twentieth century is fast producing some sense of awareness in Africans who are constantly asking themselves the same question which Oedipus asked himself thousands of years ago "who am I?" The answer to this question for the African is a return to the roots of culture and back to the realm of tradition, ritual and religion. In this sphere, there are great potentials in African music, drama, art and religion. Like all great developments, in drama especially, the sphere of tradition, religion and ritual, housing "ceremonies designed to solve practical problems by putting the worshipper in rapport with the forces that controlled him",[4] are store-houses for the quest. *Ekpe* provides a possibility for this exercise in reconstruction. Through its media of song and dance, great drama could be forged.

Notes

1. Among the various communities which perform the *Ekpe* festival, the people of Umuode-Nsulu, in Ngwa, have retained the traditional and original attributes of *Ekpe*. I will therefore use this particular *Ekpe* tradition for my illustrations in this paper.

2. The figure 7 is a magic figure of ancient fame. That *Ekpe* marks the climax of the year's activities is significant.
3. See Anthony Caputi, Master Works of World Drama: *Classical Greece* (D. C. Heath and Co., Cornell, 1968), p. x.
4. Master Works of Drama: *Classical Greece*, p. ix.

Ijele Masquerade, Anambra State.

MASQUERADE
Onuora Nzekwu

Entering a small Eastern Nigerian village one morning, I was surprised by the pandemonium which had replaced the usual calm that precedes dawn. Men, women and children rushed towards their houses and disappeared through doors which they slammed behind them. One of the men who passed by me stopped long enough to ask what I was doing just standing and staring. Did "a deaf and dumb" need to be told when a battle was on?

In the general confusion his metaphor was lost on me and I stood listening for the clash of weapons which would warn me of the direction of the battle. Instead my ears picked up the faint sound of a bull roarer. Its noise increased every minute. I hurried to the nearest house smiling, for just then I had the answer: masqueraders, ancestral spirits on a visit to mankind, were entering the village. This group of masqueraders only appeared at night and was to be seen by man under the pain of death. They were obviously returning from a funeral to which they had been invited by a nearby village. That was ten years ago.

Today masquerading has lost most of the religious ideas which brought it into being and sustained it. Yet, at first sight it still appears to have all the essence, vitality and prestige which characterized it not so long ago. In the rural areas, one sees only a reflection of its more glorious past, but even that is dwindling in importance as the people become more and more used to Western ideas. In urban areas, the change, though greater, is veiled. There non-initiates feign the awe, born of traditional usage. They watch him giving his display at close quarters. They pay him the due respect which traditional etiquette prescribes and run away when he approaches them. Yet they do this not because they are afraid of him, but because they dislike being "disgraced". They cannot take revenge if they are assaulted, for that would bring a charge of wilful exposure of the secrets of the cult against them, and such severe punishment as, in more recent times, has replaced the customary sentence to death. Even an initiate keeps well out of the way of a masquerader belonging to a cult from another community, partly out of respect but more from the fear of falling a victim to the magical powers which are worked into his mask or costume and which he falls back on in times of stress.

Unfortunately nowadays masquerading is often scorned and misrepresented by the younger generation who decry it as a mere fraud, a clever device of the man desiring to terrify and dominate his womenfolk. The truth is that the manifestation of ancestral spirits is a vital facet of ancestor worship. Traditionally, like everything else of any importance, masquerading and its secrets are the prerogatives of the men—and only initiates at that. Women have been excluded from sharing in the secrets for they are weak and fickle and are therefore not fit to take part in them. They are also mysterious and sometimes unclean. They cannot therefore approach these ancestral manifestations, whose character is diametrically opposed to their own. Any meeting between them would have adverse effects on both parties. Much harm would come to the women and masquerades would lose something of their virtue. Apart from this fear, there is the desire to avert the wrath of these spirits whose condescension to visit mankind in the form of masqueraders is a great honour which must not be abused. They are mindful of the fact that ancestral spirits are superior to mere mortals and constitute an unusual phenomenon when they assume physical forms.

In a few places however, very elderly women of means may become initiates—but they are not allowed into the masquerade house when preparations for a display are going on. Generally women watch a masquerader dance from a distance, admiring the beauty of his costume and performance. They know that masqueraders are men dressed up in strange costumes; yet they are forbidden to tell of this or discuss it. Their knowledge is however challenged by the masqueraders' voice and occasionally by some extraordinary performance of a masquerader. The secret of the masquerader's voice was the most jealously guarded of all the secrets of the cult for, among most tribes, it is the voice that is really the masquerade. Yet it is a simple device, a hollow cylindrical reed some two or three inches long and about three tenths of an inch in diameter, over one end of which a spider's cocoon is drawn taut and secured in position with a thread. This device will disguise a man's voice, giving it a harsh, grating quality, something like the sound of a gramophone record played with a worn out needle.

Despite the change which has overtaken masquerading and left it a monument to a vital principle of traditional religion among these peoples, it is developing along other channels. It has now become an entertainment and a source of amusement in their lives. To understand this new development, one has to look back to the glorious days of masquerading among the tribes of the Region. For the purpose of this article, they are the semi-Bantu tribes, the Niger Delta and coastal tribes and the Ibo tribe who inhabit the central and northern parts. The semi-Bantu peoples live in the eastern parts of the territory and comprise the Cross-River tribes, the Efik, the Kwa, the Ibibio and their sub-tribes. Amongst them the greatest factor in masquerading is its development into a most effective agency of government. *Ekpe*, their principal cult, was a mysterious overlord who became more significant than any king or government. At its height, it assumed legislative and judicial control of the community. Its messengers were masqueraders who, to most of the people, became synonymous with the overlord himself. These went about proclaiming laws and enforcing them on behalf of their master. The fear of *Ekpe* was exploited for their private ends by officials of the traditional secular government, who were invariably members of the cult.

The Niger Delta and coastal tribes are made up of the Ijaw sub-tribes and the Kalabari. Among them, masqueraders represent gods, water spirits, village heroes and the dead. In many cases they symbolize the ancestors who introduced them. The bulk of their masquerades however represent manifestations of water spirits. They believe that in some of their masquerade displays, the masqueraders, whose identity may be known, are possessed by the spirits they are representing.

There is a second interesting aspect to masquerading in the Niger Delta area: There is a myth behind each masquerade performance, a short and very simple story which is usually dramatized. Occasionally one comes across a long and elaborate story, but this is never performed even where it concerns a water spirit actually portrayed in mask form. For since it serves as a frame upon which other art-forms such as music, dancing and dress are hung, the details of the myth would spoil the masquerade just as too elaborate a plot would spoil an opera or ballet.

These non-religious, "purely aesthetic" values which keep the art going nowadays were extremely important even before traditional religion went into decline. Before the great changes of outlook brought about during the colonial period, people like the Kalabari recognized that masquerading, as ballet and drama, had an intrinsic value quite apart from its worth as a means of coercing the gods. So much so that by the nineteenth century some traditional performances had already reached the stage where rites addressed to the gods connected with them had become mere precautions against accident or bad weather marring the play.

Among the Ibo, masquerading is of foreign origin, having been introduced along with some cults from among the Igala to the north, the semi-Bantu to the east and the Niger Delta tribes to the south. But they have adapted them to their own conditions. The adaptation varies from place to place depending on the source of the cult in each Ibo community and its degree of development. But all of them have cut down the power of the masquerades to suit their own administrative system.

In borrowing the art from other peoples, they have left out the myths which surrounded individual masquerades in their original setting. What is more they never gave them any themselves. The result is that while the basic principle—that masquerades are physical representations of ancestral spirits—has survived to control their display and their relationship with men, masquerade displays have become more of a social appendage to the religious festivals and observances to which they were attached. This explains why the Ibo were the first in the country to make masquerade displays and traditional dances the high-lights of such Christian feasts as Christmas and Easter.

Among all these three peoples, but particularly among the Ibo, masquerades are intended, by their performances, to convey certain attributes and qualities of ancestral spirits—power, strength, speed and knowledge. Such masqueraders as those wearing two-faced masks, those that carry swarms of bees or smoke-belching fires in their masks, and those that perform other almost impossible feats tell their own tales.

The traditional carver who has found a strong source of patronage in masquerading, has contributed towards the accentuation of these qualities. The masks he produces are such that they are essentially communicative and symbolic of them, for his intention is not to represent but to communicate. His efforts have resulted in distor-tions, strange compositions and unexpected symmetry as he intro-duces and accentuates some feature of an animal or thing endowed with these qualities. For example, large pointed teeth represent the jaws of a leopard and therefore strength, a long pointed nose represents a European, signifying knowledge and wisdom.

The masquerade displays in Eastern Nigeria take place mainly in the dry season, that holiday period following the rain and farm-work season, when food is plentiful—when men and women assess the result of their labour under the hot exhausting tropical sun over the past months, when all can afford to relax and divert their energies and resources towards the celebration of thanks-giving festival and the advancement of their social status within the society by traditional initiation and other rites.

It is at such times that Eastern Nigeria exhibits its ample store of masqueraders with their varied activities. They sing, dance, become possessed, keep order, gossip and tell the future. Some-times their performances are as remarkable as their appearance, but the degree of importance attached to both factors vary with each locality. Unfortunately quite a good number of masks which enhance their looks have been taken out of the country and more are being stolen away. It is indeed heartening to know that the Government is now doing something towards the preservation of these art-forms.

Reprinted Nigeria Magazine 1960.

THE DRAMATIC LIMITS OF IGBO RITUAL
M. J. C. Echeruo

Introduction

This paper is a very tentative statement of a view which I have held for some time but which I have hesitated to advance because more extensive field research than I have been able to undertake seemed required for its full validation. I present it now because this seems to be as good an opportunity as one could ever want for securing the reaction of those who have been engaged in Igbo and related studies for a much longer time than myself.* I should hope, in any event, that my argument will be found not only valid for the study of Igbo traditional literature but also helpful to our creative writers who may wish to exploit our traditions for contemporary uses.

My approach has been inevitably determined by my interest in myth-criticism, that is in the archetypal meaning derivable from the structure of ideas and action in a given work of art. Accordingly, I have tended to look at the Igbo festival in gross, as an event whose structure has meaning in itself. Drama lends itself very naturally to this critical approach because its outlines of action are usually clear and the sequence of its events invariably of a deliberate kind.[1] For this reason, also, I have not concerned myself at this stage with the language of the festivals, nor with Igbo dramaturgy—that is with the Igbo *style* of presenting action. These are important aspects of the subject which, for me, follow only after the more general and theoretical argument has been established.

African Drama

It is generally agreed these days that drama is an important element in traditional African culture. In Nigeria, the Yorubas,

*This paper was read to the Seminar on Igbo Language and Literature organized by the Institute of African Studies, University of Nigeria, Nsukka, November 24–27, 1971.

Ijaws, and sometimes the Efiks, are usually singled out as illustrating this contention.[2] In these studies, attention is drawn to the elements of song, dance, and costuming which in various combinations have resulted in such dramatic forms as heroic drama, burlesque, satire and ribald comedy. "The Ijaws, perhaps more than any other people in Nigeria", one writer has argued, "have developed over the centuries a form of dramatic art which is religious in purpose but which has become weighted heavily on the side of skilful performance and artistic values."[3] Similar studies have not been carried out in detail among the Igbo, but from the evidence already in print, indications are that the same conclusions are likely to be reached with regard to the place of drama in Igbo culture.[4] It will also be found that the Igbo do not lack adequate mythologies, that they have a keen sense of stylized representational action, and that they certainly do not lack a feeling ceremony.

While asserting this, we should not lose sight of the argument recently advanced by Ruth Finnegan that "it would be truer to say" that "there are certain dramatic and quasi-dramatic phenomena to be found" in African traditional festivals. This is important, she holds, in view of what she regards as the absence of "linguistic content, plot, represented interaction of several characters, specialized scenery", etc. in these indigenous drama.[5] Her argument is borne out, in part, by statements made by some of those who champion the idea of a fully-developed indigenous drama. Writing of the *Ekine* dramas, for example, Robin Horton says that "the masquerade is not intended as the enactment of verbal narrative. Its dominant symbols are those of rhythmic gesture, dictated by the drum; and in so far as its verbal commentaries have a use, it is one of directing attention to the broad area in which the meaning of the dance gestures lies . . . it is left to the language of dance to fill in the detail which makes the masquerade rich and satisfying to its audience."[6] If this is true, then, there is reason to re-examine our use of the word "drama" to describe these events, since for example, the "recitation" and "performance" of epic poetry in chorus can also have most of the characteristics of the indigenous festival and still not be drama.

Drama and Society

Drama, in its very many manifestations, including its ritual manifestations, is very specifically communal in character. More than any of the other arts, it requires a group audience at all stages of enactment; quite often, in fact, it demands the participation of the audience in the action of song. For this reason, some theorists have argued, quite convincingly, that drama flourishes most in a society that has developed a strong consciousness of itself *as a community*.[7] We should, however, add that drama flourishes best in a community which has satisfactorily transformed ritual into celebration and converted the mythic structure of action from the religious and priestly to the secular plane.

On the level of theory, this is the explanation often advanced for the development of Greek drama. It is maintained that the plays depended on the identification of Greek civilization with its common religious and cultural roots and the transformation of that identity from its strictly Dionysian or Apollonian origins to the equivalent secular experience which, nevertheless, still retained something of the original religious implications.[8]

Where this happens, drama becomes the ideal festival, communal feast which features re-enactment and rededication for every individual in the community. In Greek and similar societies, drama, as festival, reinforces common values, shared bonds and common taboos. It re-established links with the past and compels the living to participate in hilarity and comradeship of a communal happening.

Drama, Ritual and Myth

If, therefore, the festival is a celebration, drama is a re-enactment of life. Drama is to the society what ritual is to religion: a public affirmation of an idea; a translation into action of a *mythos* or plot just as ritual is the translation of a faith into external action.[9] A divination scene, for example, is not in itself drama, though it may be dramatic. It is ritualistic or liturgical. That is to say, it is a representation in action of a faith or a dream, like communion or baptism. The pattern of action does not tell a story; it reasserts the essence of the faith in *symbolic* terms. Drama, on the other hand, allows for the reinterpretation of life through a pattern of ordered events, through that fragment of history we usually call plot.[10] Hence it is that myth gives substance to narrative just as faith gives substance to ritual. It is myth—i.e., plot—that gives mass and duration to ritual (and thence to faith), and leads it ultimately to drama.

Anthropologists have not been very helpful in sorting out these interrelationships. The so-called Cambridge School which argues that "myth arises out of rite rather than the reverse", that myth is "the spoken correlative of the acted rite" has misled many investigators by encouraging them to assume that rituals, especially among the so-called primitive peoples, have yet to evolve a conceptual embodiment in myth. Accordingly, they see ritual action simply as unorganized and perhaps spontaneous reaction of primitive peoples to the mystery of life. Other investigators, however, have tended to deny the relevance of any distinction between ritual and myth and identify them fully with the idea of the festival. They thereby, quite unjustifiably, give the impression that there is no special and important limits to the interpenetration of drama into the festival. A New Yam Festival, for example, is a great ritual and festive event. Behind the ritual activities of the festival is almost certainly a *mythos* of a returning and beneficent god who is both welcomed and propitiated. But the festival itself, together with its associated ritual acts, is not drama which only emerges from the selective elaboration, re-enactment and reinterpretation of significant aspects of the festival myth.

We need, therefore, to distinguish between drama and festival, not on the basis of their external "dramatic" characteristics (including dance, song and costume) but their elaboration of action, whether or not this action is supported with dialogue (as distinct from speech). The masquerade, for example, which has strong roots in Igboland[11] is drama only to the extent that its mime element carries with it a narrative or plot content. But, basically, the force of action of the masquerade is ritual or symbolic. Behind the masquerade is a dream of faith.[12]

Greek and Ancient Sumerian Analogies

Analogies with Greek tradition are common in discussions of the nature and origins of drama. Some of these analogies can be misleading. Arthur Koestler argues that dramatic art has its origins in ceremonial rites—dances, songs, and mime—which enacted important past or desired future events: rain, a successful hunt, an abundant harvest. The gods, demons, ancestors and animals participating in the event were impersonated with the aid of masks, costumes, tatooings and make-up. The shaman who danced the part of the rain-god *was* the rain-god, and yet remained the shaman at the same time.[13]

Speaking of the origins of Nigerian drama, J. P. Clark says "they lie where they have been found among other peoples of the earth, deep in the past of the race. We believe that as the roots of European drama go back to the Egyptian Osiris and the Greek Dionysius, so are the origins of the Nigerian drama likely to be found in the early religious and magical ceremonies and festivals of the peoples of the country."[14] It is true enough that there are close analogies between, say, the Nigerian New Year (February) Festivals and early Greek Dionysian festivals which usually preceded the planting season and lasted 5–6 days. (J. P. Clark says "seven is the magic number!") But there the comparison ends, because early Greek dramas were, in fact, *one* item in the programme of the festivals. In their dramas, the Greeks provided for a special presentation or enactment of a *mythos* within the framework of the larger (and generally ritualistic) festive event. In other words, the early Greek play was a dramatization of a myth undertaken as part of a festival. The play was never synonymous with the festival itself. As Cornelius Loew has put it, the dramatists resurrected the rich tradition of myth that all the people held in common and through a free manipulation of familiar themes they contributed more than any other group to the Greek Awakening.[15]

The difference being emphasized here becomes even clearer in the case of the ancient Sumerian New Year Festival which lasted some twelve days between March and April and again between September and October each year. This festival never led to drama, as was the case in Greece, in spite of the presence of ritual, dance and song. In the Sumerian Festival, the first four days are devoted to the purification of the entire community in readiness for the general atonement or cleansing which takes place on the fifth day of the Festival. The next five days are taken up with the arrival of the gods, the liberation and subsequent coronation of their Supreme God, Marduk, his triumphal entry to the city and the consummation of his return in a sacred ritual sexual orgy. The last two days of the festival are devoted to the blessing of the community by the gods who return on the twelfth day to the other world.[16]

There is, thus, no lack of event, even of dramatic event, in the Sumerian Festival. But unlike the Greek Festival, the enactment, for example, of the arrival of Marduk is embodied in the Festival itself as a ritual incident. That is to say, the drama is absorbed in ritual action and the *mythos* is subsumed in ritual. Hence, though the Festival has a great deal of dialogue, action, music, dance and decor, it does not crystallize in drama.[17]

The Igbo Festival

The Igbo Festival, it seems to me, is at present structured in Sumerian rather than Greek lines. If this is so, then the emergence of Igbo drama based on our indigenous traditions will depend on how effectively it can be moved beyond the rich but ritual character of the festivals themselves.

(a) The "Mbom Ama" Festival

I take my first illustration from the Mbom Ama Festival in my own town, Umunumo. The festival is held between the first and second weeks of October each year and lasts about eight days. There is the usual feasting, dancing, and drinking; the invocations, propitiations and sacrifice. But the heart of the festival is the clearing of all footpaths leading from every homestead to the shrine of *Ebu*, the ancestral god of the town. In general, the festival has the following features:

(i) All paths in the town are weeded and swept clean in anticipation of the sixth moon and the departure of *Ebu* from the town;

(ii) The chief-priest of *Ebu* announces the sixth moon and fixes a day for the celebration.

(iii) Led by the chief-priest and his assistants, the town makes communal offerings at the *Ebu* shrine; families specially favoured by Him also make their offerings.

(iv) On the appointed *Afo* market day, which is also the eighth day of the festival, the town gathers at the market square for dances, wrestling competitions and various masquerades. There is general merriment and out-of-town guests are particularly well-catered for.
(v) The merriment becomes ecstatic and unruly as evening approaches. The day ends with a bitter verbal contest of insults. This takes place by the river separating the two sections of the town and is said to represent one way of accusing and chastising each section of the town for its crimes of the previous year.
(vi) *Ebu* leaves town with his consort, *Lolo*, during the thunderstorm which is expected to follow the end of the festival.

The overall structure of the *Mbom Ama* Festival is thus essentially ritual in character. Behind this ritual action is a suppressed (or at least, an unexpressed) *mythos*. When one unscrambles the rites, one finds that the Festival, in fact, celebrates the departure from the town of the ancestral god with his mate, *Lolo*. *Ebu* is the bringer of good fortune, not only of wealth but also of offspring. The special gifts presented to him are tokens of appreciation from those whose children born in the preceding year were divined to be reincarnations of one of *Ebu*'s two principal subordinates *Oparannu* and *Oparaocha*. It becomes evident, then, that the preliminary clearing of the paths is an anticipatory rite to make the path ready should the god and his queen choose to dwell with any of the suppliants in their several homes.

Implied or suppressed in the *Mbom Ama* Festival is the entire mythology of the town: the ancestry of *Ebu*, of his consort, *Lolo*; the circumstances of their domestication in the town; the crises of the past; the circumstances surrounding their annual departure from the town; the reason for propitiatory and thanksgiving sacrifices. Each detail is a plot or the germ of drama; each is liable to a thousand varying interpretations and reinterpretations, depending on the choice of fact and detail. Without this elaboration of the hidden myth, there can be no drama; only ritual and spectacle.

(b) The Odo Festival

A more elaborate festival is the *Odo* Festival in Aku, a small farming and trading community some fourteen miles from Nsukka. The festival is held between February and July every two years. In a sense, this festival is not unique to the Aku community but it is to be found all over Udi and Nsukka Divisions where it is sometimes called the *Omabe* Festival and is then held every four years. Nevertheless, there is no ritual link between the Aku *Odo* and other *Odo* in the Nsukka area, perhaps because for each community, the *Odo* (in spite of the common name) is a local phenomenon.

This is all the more important because the *Odo* is not a god, but the spirit of the departed returning for a six-month stay of communion with the living. Hence, there is no reverence and no worship of the *Odo*, but instead a kind of respectful familiarity. There is good explanation, perhaps, for this. The Aku people, though a very republican community, accept a common ancestral god, *Diewa*, who is quite clearly distinguished from that supreme Igbo deity *Chukwu* whom the Aku people (like most other Nsukka people) call *Ezechitoke*. But even so, *Diewa* is only a supervisory god in Aku. Most of the active gods are located in the thirteen village units of the town, and the only one for whom there is an Aku-wide festival is *Ojiyi*, the local or paternal god of Use, one of the six villages in the Eka-Ibute complex. Even the professional gods of Aku (war-god, *Nshi*; god of justice, *Egwu*; god of agriculture, *Fejoku*; goddess of the hearth, *Usere*, and of water, *Ujere*) belong, in the first instance, to one of the village units. The *Odo* festival is thus not even a festival of worship or even of propitiation of a god even though the ceremonies take place just after the planting season. It is, nevertheless, of sufficient importance for the community to bestow on the non-god, *Odo*, the second most respected festival in the town.

(c) The Ojiyi Fertility Festival

The next thing to notice is that the *Odo* festival is not a fertility rite. By a fertility rite I mean a ceremony designed primarily to ask the gods for children and good harvests. A fertility festival is usually associated with some actual or symbolic consummation of a union between male and female, earth and sky, benefactor-god and consecrated suppliant. Such ceremonies are accordingly Bacchanalian in character and feature orgies of one kind or another. There is a period of apparent sexual licence in the ritual pattern of these ceremonies deliberately meant to anticipate the hoped-for abundance of Nature and the gods.[18] Such a festival is the *Ojiyi* festival in Aku, held during the "eighth month" of the Aku year.[19] The *Ojiyi* festival begins with a long procession of children, women, young men (with guns), priests, sword-bearers who receive the *Ojiyi* and move with him along the dried-up valleys to the accompaniment of heroic *Ikpa* music through every village unit of Aku. But the crucial act of the festival is the offering and dedication to the god of several young women. Through these women *Ojiyi* bears children the next year in confirmation of His continued interest in the community. These children are fully respected as *Ojiyi's* offspring, and though they are not regarded as sacred, they are admitted to all assemblies as freeborn.[20] This sexual consummation (or marriage) ritualizes the meaning of the festival and is followed by general merriment.

The Odo as an Apollonian Festival

In the *Odo* festival, then, the emphasis is not on consummation but on communion. This communion is, in the first place, between two levels of existence: between this and the "other" world; between the living and their departed kinsmen. There is thus a spiritual quality to the festival which is why it may be described, even if a little inaccurately, as an Apollonian event in order to distinguish it from a Dionysiac festival which usually commemorates the death of a hero, a god or a kinsmen (Prometheus, Orpheus, Christ). The *Odo* festival celebrates the return of a lost or wandering hero, god or kinsman (Easter Sunday). The mood is that of rejoicing though, inevitably, this is associated with holy fear. It is important to appreciate this because it explains why every village unit of the Aku community has its own *Odo*, one of its own sons returning from the spirit world.

Broadly speaking, there are five distinct structural divisions in the festival: (i) Preparation, (ii) Welcome and Return, (iii) Communion, (iv) Dedication, and (v) Departure and Blessing.

(i)   *Preparation:*
      This actually begins early in January with the preliminary celebrations known in Aku as the *Egorigo* festival. The *Egorigo* is a light-hearted festival which ushers in the first *Odo*, called the *Ovuruzo*, a scout spirit whose arrival on the last but one *Afo* day in the "eleventh month" marks the beginning of festivities.

(ii) *Welcome and Return:*
      Following the successful return of the *Ovuruzo*, the other twelve *Odo* begin to return. They are welcomed on successive *Afo* days with drumming, feasting and dancing. At this stage, though the people speak of the *Odo* in the singular, there are in fact as many *Odo* as there are village units and each village organizes its own additional reception festivities at the local level.

(iii) *Communion:*
      The *Odo* now withdraw to the sacred groves said to be under the protection of a kind of conservative but vigilant and well-meaning god, called *Uhamu*. From here the *Odo* maintain contact with the living. First some chosen young people take specially prepared food from the women and rarest palmwine from the men to the *Odo* in their several forest or hillside shrines. Secondly, in return, the *Odo* visit each household very early each morning in a gesture of reciprocation and communion. The *Odo* do threaten violence but this is generally understood to be playfully meant and to be their way of re-establishing communion without too much familiarity. During these visits, the womenfolk again prepare very delicious meals for the *Odo* and their escorts.

(iv) *Dedication:*
      The dedication precedes the return of the *Odo* to the spirit world. The ceremony takes place this time before a massed gathering of all the village units of Aku. One *Odo* now represents all the others. The main shrine at Umudiku is specially decorated and the entire community, including women and children this time, are allowed to take part or witness. The official *Odo* drummers and

trumpeters are on hand and there is most impressive
singing of *Odo* praise chants by the womenfolk. The
climactic event is the *Odo's* first race: a part playful, part
deadly-serious contest between the spirit and a representative group of able-bodied males (between the ages of 14
and 30) from all the thirteen village units. It is a gesture of
solidarity, the *Odo's* last act of identification with the
community.

(v) *Departure and Blessing:*
The departure of the *Odo* begins on another *Afo* market
day. Its significance is to be seen quite clearly in the ritual
character of the events. First comes the *Odo's* meeting with
the oldest woman of the town. This meeting takes place
about midnight under a bridge across a very deep gully at a
village called Legelege (Lelege). This old woman presents
the *Odo*, now fully naked and stripped of his heavy
six-foot-high headpiece, with a symbolic gift of fish (the
Odo's favourite) and a piece of white cloth. After this, the
Odo makes his round of visits to all thirteen units in Aku.
At each stop, the host village provides a young man to
replace the previous "spirit". The new *Odo* then stages a
competition with youthful runners from the next village.
This is a highly stylized event designed to generate a lot of
bad blood but also structured to end in a free-for-all race of
both *Odo* and people to the next village. At the end of
these visits, the *Odo* retires again to the grove, waiting for
the final all-night drumming and vigil which will precede
his being escorted out of the town by a choice group of
youths on his way back to the other world. It is at this point
that the *Odo* gives his final blessing which usually material-
izes in a propitious July thunderstorm.

Conclusion

This structure is the vehicle for the meaning of the festival. It
will be noticed that the narrative line is that of the festivity, not of
the events provoking or sustaining it. Behind the ritual meeting
of the *Odo* with the oldest woman of Lelege, for example, there
is a story. But that story is not dramatized, and one can only

derive the meaning of that action through older men or kind interpreters. The dramatic content is, in other words, buried in the ritual purity of the festival. What is needed then, it seems to me, is to force that ritual to yield its story; to cut through the overlay of ceremony to the primary events of the *mythos*. Ritual is, and has always been, a dead end, it cannot grow. It only shrinks steadily into inevitably inaccessible (though powerful) symbolism. The Igbo should do what the Greeks did: expand ritual into life and give that life a secular base. That way, we may be able to interpret and reinterpret that serious view of life which is now only so dimly manifested in our festivals.

Notes

1. Friedrich Nietzsche, *Philosophy in the Tragic Age of the Greeks*, tr. Marianne Cowan, Chicago, 1962, passim.
2. J. P. Clark, "Some Aspects of Nigerian Drama", *Nigerian Magazine*, No. 89, 1966; Robin Horton, "The Kalabari Ekine Society", *Africa*, 2, 1962; Ulli Beier, "Yoruba Folk Operas", *African Music*, 1, 1954; "The Oba's Festival at Ondo", *Nigeria Magazine*, No. 50, 1956; "The Egungun Cult", *Nigeria Magazine*, No. 51, 1956; "The Oshun Festival", *Nigeria Magazine*, No. 53, 1957; S. A. Babalola, *The Content and Form of Yoruba Ijala*, Oxford, 1966; O. Ogunba, *Ritual Drama of the Ijebu people: a study of indigenous festivals*, Ph.D. Thesis, Ibadan, 1967.
3. Margaret Laurence, *Long Drums and Cannons*, London, 1968, p. 79. See also pp. 12, 18, 78–80.
4. G. I. Jones, "Masked Plays of South-Eastern Nigeria", *Geographical Magazine*, 18, 1945; J. S. Boston, "Some Northern Ibo Masquerades", *Journal of the Royal African Institute*, 90, 1960; J. P. Clark, *op. cit.*; Ruth Finnegan, *Oral Literature in Africa*, Oxford, 1970.
5. Finnegan, pp. 500, 501.
6. Horton, p. 98.
7. Northrop Frye, *Anatomy of Criticism*, Princeton, 1957, p. 249.
8. Cf. Arthur Koestler, *The Act of Creation: A study of the Conscious and Unconscious in Science and Art*, New York, 1967, p. 309: ". . . though modern theatre hardly betrays its religious ancestry, the magic illusion still serves essentially the same emotional needs: it enables the spectator to transcend the narrow confines of his personal identity, and to participate in other forms of existence."
9. Frye, p. 107.
10. Cf. J. Melville and Frances S. Herskovits, *Dahomean Narrative: A Cross-Cultural Analysis* Evanston, Illinois, 1958, p. 106: "A rite is—it must never be forgotten—an action redone (commemorative) or predone (anticipatory and magical)."

11. Finnegan, p. 510, G. I. Jones, p. 191; J. S. Boston, passim.
12. In my view, the masquerader is a performer; he requires only a plot-based role to become a character-in-drama.
13. Koestler, pp. 308–309.
14. Clark, op. cit.
15. Cornelius Loew, *Myth, Sacred History and Philosophy: The Pre-Christian Religious Heritage of the West*, New York, 1967, pp. 239–240.
16. Ibid., pp. 33–34.
17. The re-enactment of the coming of the god, *Ulu*, in Achebe's *Arrow of God* would be drama, in any sense of the word.
18. As one Ebenezer Ozo, an Aku student formerly at Ahmadu Bello University, says of that matter, there is a proclivity to become drunk. Women and children are no longer hindered from drinking wine. This freedom, together with many other shelved restrictions, augurs well for a happier celebration."
19. Another fertility festival is the *Alu* (or *Ani*) festival which is held in the "third month", within the period of the *Odo* ceremonies.
20. In recent years, this practice has been held responsible for the unusually high incidence of prostitution among some of Ojiyi's wives who can thrive, as one source put it, "without molestation or discrimination" because they are sacred to the god and are "unable to secure alternative husbands".

Reprinted Research in African Literatures, Vol. 4, No. 1.

MYTH, RITUAL AND DRAMA IN IGBOLAND
Ossie Enekwe

There is a serious effort among Igbo scholars to define the
relationship between Igbo myth, ritual and drama. M. J. C.
Echeruo who expresses the view that myth is the main substance
of drama, argues that Igbo drama cannot evolve until this myth is
freed from the ritual in which it is buried.[1] Echeruo's article has
generated much controversy, especially at the University of
Nigeria in Nsukka where the article was first presented at a
seminar on Igbo language and Literature in November, 1971. A
battle line seems to have been drawn:

> So far, two schools of thought seem to crystallize around the
> question deriving from attitudes which one could reasonably call
> evolutionary and relativistic. The evolutionist theory is well repre-
> sented in an article by Professor M. J. C. Echeruo called "The
> Dramatic Limits of Igbo Rituals". Professor Echeruo uses the
> *Odo* festival to illustrate his thesis. His central proposition is that
> the *Odo* festival, like the Greek Dionysian and Apollonian
> festivals contains dramatic elements capable of future develop-
> ment into full-bodied drama. Ritual and myth, in his view, would
> first of all be shorn of their coagulating sacredness and rendered
> sufficiently mobile for use in a secular drama built on the destiny
> of differentiated, individual characters.
> The relativistic view flatly contradicts the evolutionary one and
> insists that the ritual festivals in Africa represent full and authenti-
> cated drama that should be recognized as such; that they are
> communal dramas which differ from secular, individuated modern
> drama with its precise separation of its stage from the auditorium,
> of actors from the audience and stage time from the duration of
> the experience enacted on the stage.[2]

While Obiechina thinks that the evolutionists are right in
comparing the *Odo* and *Omabe* festivals in Nsukka to the Greek
Dionysiac and Apollonian festivals, he rejects their position that
modern Igbo drama must follow "identical linear development of

149

the classical Greek drama from the Dionysian and Apollonian festival".[3] Obiechina insists that African drama cannot develop like the classical Greek drama, because Africa has a history and a culture that are different from those of the Greek. As one goes deeper into Obiechina's paper, one cannot help concluding that he is in the relativist camp, for he argues that the *Omabe* and *Odo* communal performances though different from modern, individualistic and literacy-mediated dramas, are drama all the same. He thinks that "the evolutionists have been misled by their too great reliance on writing and the facilities it provides and too little confidence in an oral tradition".[4] Obiechina points out that the Greek situation is not paradigmatic of every dramatic development, and argues that there is no incontrovertible reason why the Greek example must be repeated everywhere else.[5] He then wonders:

> Is there any particular reason, except that of meeting the specifically practical pressures of the present age, why an enactment should last only two or three hours instead of six months? Is the sense of organic unity which we assume in the modern theatre and its conventions not possible on an extended scale among a people whose sensibilities are trained to absorb more diffused ritual and symbolic significance of action? Is a broad communal canvas not more suitable for painting more inclusive social and emotional action than the mere mouse-tongue platform called the modern stage?[6]

The preceding query from Obiechina has been motivated by Echeruo's view that myth is an indispensable element that develops into drama through selective elaboration, reenactment and reinterpretation.[7] Against this view, Meki Nzewi has noted that there is no reason why ritual should be forced to yield its story, except to serve audiences that are strangers to the latent nuances and symbolisms of Igbo rituals.[8]

Elsewhere, I argued against Echeruo's opinion that myth is the soul of drama, pointing out that drama does not have to evolve from myth, and that if it contains elements of myth, the myth is not used for itself, but, rather, for social restructuring. In other words, "myth is important in terms of an ideological position, that is, the ideology of the moment".[9] In this paper, I intend to advance my argument by considering the relationship between myth, ritual and drama with particular reference to Igboland.

Since Echeruo bases his view on the classical Greek tradition, it is necessary for us to turn to that tradition, and to others, for comparison. Greek mythologies were not presented in their pristine form by Homer who was mainly occupied in entertaining an essentially patriarchial and military audience. About much of the nocturnal, and funeral side of Greek religion and mythology, Homer says very little. About Dionysus, the Greek god of wine and vegetation whose worship is said—perhaps, erroneously—to have brought about tragic drama, Homer makes only an allusion to an incident of his childhood.[10] In Greece and elsewhere, myth remains a malleable material in the hands of artists. In the making of literature, myth in its broadest sense, provides material and, perhaps, structure, but it plays a very subordinate role in the theatre where impersonation and interactive activity are of the essence. As for the origin of Greek tragedy, there is no convincing proof that it evolved from myth extracted from ritual.[11]

Myth as Infrastructure (Myth = Plot?)

Echeruo attaches much importance to myth or story partly because it gives form and meaning to experience. Myth, he argues, gives clear outlines to dramatic action whose sequence of events is "invariably of a deliberate kind".[12] From his talk of "a pattern of ordered events", it is obvious that he is concerned with the Aristotelian unified plot-structure, with logical cause-and-effect progression in time. However, the implied syllogism has nothing to do with dramatic experience. There is ample evidence in theatre history to show that linear plot is not essential to good drama, and that function determines the form of drama in every culture.

Lack of space restricts me to mentioning names of very few movements and traditions in the theatre. There was, for instance, the Doric mime which together with its later counterpart—the Italian *Commedia dell'arte*—was characterized by improvisation. In mime, whether European, Asian or African, literature always takes a subordinate place.[13] What is the significance of dance in the theatre? Dance, which is organic to the life of the Balinese, is also the foundation of the Balinese theatre in which stories are suggested tenuously. The Balinese *Legong* drama is so far removed from narrative that it is almost pure dance. Generally, Balinese theatre does not present ideas in a clear, predigested form, nor is the audience expected to derive an intellectual pleasure from a working out of the subtle meanings of the drama.[14] In the Indian Sanskrit drama, oldest of the major theatre forms in Asia, the main purpose is the portrayal of emotional states of *bhava*, not the narration of human action as in Greek drama. Similarly, the Japanese Noh drama "is not a story-teller's art; it does not often present the unfolding of a human action. Rather, through recollections of the past, it evokes a mood, an emotion, a religious state".[15] The knowledgeable spectator perceives the performance, "not as emotionally bound human actions but as elegantly formed patterns of sound and colour that impinge on his emotions peripherally if at all".[16] The Elizabethan theatre of Shakespeare was not what it was because of the clear outlines of its stories. Because the Elizabethan playwright concentrated a great deal more on the effects of action on his characters than on the causes of the action, he substituted a rhythmic framework for dramatic causation.[17] He selected scenes which would contrast with, or echo, others or which would illustrate various facets of a single experience.[18] This accounted for the looseness of Elizabethan plays. The scenes of an Elizabethan drama often appear to be hanging from a thread of narrative, instead of being lineally connected to other scenes.

We have pointed out that function determines the nature of drama in every culture. In 5th century B.C. Greece, for instance, poetry was central to drama because for the Greeks it was the most desirable and perfect art form. In Asia and Africa, on the other hand, dance, mime and music are of the essence in the theatre. While the mainstream European theatre is syllogistic in form, the Asian and African theatres are ritualistic. In Greek tragedy where moral rhetoric is emphasized, the moral order must be reflected by the order of events—"the right of the story".[19]

Nigeria has numerous examples of drama that are structured on dance. Robin Horton writes that the real core of the Kalabari *Ekine* masquerade drama is dance and that "by and large other elements are only considered important in so far as they contribute to it".[20] The sketchiness and brevity of Kalabari *Ekine* plays are explained by Horton:

> . . . . the masquerade is not intended as the enactment of verbal narrative. Its dominant symbols are those of rhythmic gesture, dictated by the drum; and in so far as its verbal commentaries have a use, it is one of directing attention to the broad area in which the meaning of the dance gesture lies. Words here provide no more than a bare, crude outline of meaning, and it is left to the language of the dance to fill in the detail which makes the masquerade rich and satisfying to its audience.[21]

For those who have been nurtured in the tastes of European theatre, the *Ekine* performance is not drama, because it lacks linear structure and has little linguistic content. Thus, Ruth Finnegan says that "drama in Africa is not typically a wide-spread or a developed form, and that what Africans have are 'certain dramatic and quasi-dramatic phenomena',," for example, the celebrated masquerades of Southern Nigeria.[22] Finnegan is in search for African performances that are analogous to what she is familiar with in Europe, Echeruo appears to be doing the same thing when he calls on the Igbo to force their ritual to yield its story,[23] and seeks for a European meaning in the *Odo* festival.

The *Odo* festival is essentially a communion between the Igbo and their ancestors who "shed their munificence among the living, and then depart to reappear during the next cycle of ritual celebration".[24] It is the living who really need the communion, for the *Odo* ensure good harvest and wealth, increase in birth rate, and decrease in death rate. But, because of his interest in Myth-criticism, which seeks for "universal" or "archetypal" patterns behind particular events or phenomena, Echeruo describes the *Odo* in Apollonian terms: "The *Odo* festival celebrates the return of a lost or wandering hero, god or kinsman."[25] Echeruo (and Kalu Uka who shares his view, more or less) agree with Finnegan that absence of "linguistic contents, plot, represented interaction of several characters, specalized scenery, etc." in African traditional performances is a limitation.[26]

What these scholars fail to realize is that Africans are not interested in portraying an Aristotelian action that is whole and complete, with a beginning, a middle and an end, or in working out the subtle meaning of a play. While the Asian and African traditional theatres are not averse to intellectual activity, they are not interested in syllogistic action. Moreover, they are more presentational than their European counterpart. By presentational, I mean that there is considerable interest in activities that are designed to astonish and delight the audience—dancing, acrobatics, etc. Also, traditional African and Asian dramas are stylized. This means that the actors are not interested in exact or elaborate imitation of reality. Stylization means simply "approaching reality through a different perspective, choosing what is more significant, meaningful, pleasing, or dramatically effective".[27] Moreover, because of its importance in Africa, ritual is an integral part of the African theatre. Consequently, African traditional dramas are participative and celebrative.[28] It is also total, because it combines many art forms, music, poetry, dance, acting, miming, mask, painting, singing, dialogue, etc., hence, speech is not dominant as in the mainstream European theatre. This combination of various art forms is also an attribute of the Asian theatre. So also are ritualization and stylization. African theatre is closer to Asian theatre than to the European theatre. Critics of traditional African theatre should, therefore, not ignore the Orient as is the case right now.

It is surprising that most of our writers and critics are still enchanted by the European theatre that is considered by many Westerners themselves as effete, dull and mechanical. Some of these Europeans have even gone on to imitate the forms of Asian and African traditional dramas so as to bring their theatre back to life. Leonard C. Pronko, a European who is very familiar with both European and Asian theatres, has even gone as far as to question the validity of the former:

> The traveler who has feasted on the theatres of Japan, China, and Bali cannot repress the feeling, when he returns to the West, that the actors are exceedingly loquacious and singularly incapable of doing anything other than talking. Our hypertrophied rational faculties have led us in the past three hundred years, and particularly since the industrial revolution and the late nineteenth-century age of science, to a theatre that is most often as small as

life itself, a theatre that requires careful listening and intelligent understanding. We sit in plush seats, fatigued after two or three hours of dialogue interspersed with a bit of movement, then disperse to discuss the "issues" of the play, if it was a drama of any "significance". Our serious theatre is so sociology-psychology-philosophy centred that it begins to acquire (as Ionesco claims Brecht might wish) all the charm of a night-school course. Instead of a feast for all the senses and for the mind as well, we are given the intellectual scraps from the top of the table of theatrical history.[29]

When Echeruo talks of interpreting and reinterpreting "that serious view of life which is now only so dimly manifested in our festivals",[30] he is operating within the European theatrical tradition that is psychological, peripheral, ametaphysical and intellectual, against the traditional African one that, like the Asian theatre, is religious, integral, metaphysical and sensuous. The object of theatre is not the discovery and reinterpretation of meaning. Theatre is first and foremost an experience.

Ritual-Theatre Relationship

There is also a suggestion by Echeruo that ritual and theatre are mutually exclusive. How far is this true? Doubtless, ritual and theatre are, by strict definition, different as water and air. But, judged from their relationship, they are not antipodal. They are reciprocal in function and similar in structure. Richard Schechner argues convincingly that context, not fundamental structure, distinguishes ritual, entertainment and ordinary life from one another.[31] Hence, ritual can easily be transformed into theatre and vice versa—in a number of ways. A ritual becomes entertainment once it is outside its original context or when the belief that sustains it has lost its potency. There are many instances of the transformation of ritual into theatre, instances which disprove Echeruo's claim that ritual "is, and has always been a dead end", that it cannot grow.[32]

One example is the *Nwaotam* or *Nwatam* play that is performed during the new year at Opobo and Bonny. For most participants in *Nwaotam* at Opobo, the performance has no story or dogma. For them, *Nwaotam* is a pure aesthetic experience now, though it was a ritual in Ndoki from where the Opobo people took it. If *Nwaotam* has a story, what is its source of appeal? It's main appeal is abstract—its pageantry, its powerful music, its movements and groupings of more than three hundred participants and its change from apparent chaos to order. The movement, grouping and coordination of the several age groups—including males and women—are fascinating to the eyes. The age groups, differently costumed and each singing its own song with its peculiar music, move about the performance area. But, when *Nwaotam* masquerade enters with its own orchestra, all the other groups stop playing their instruments, as *Nwaotam* drums take over. At this point all the groups, except that immediately assisting *Nwaotam* become part of the audience. The culmination or climax of the performance occurs when *Nwaotam* suddenly appears on the roof of a house, and after long duel-like manoeuvres and gestures, jumps into the outstretched arms of the men in the age group sponsoring him.

Many of the participants in *Nwaotam* performance at Opobo work in distant parts of Nigeria. Most of those I interviewed in 1978 could not tell me the meaning of *Nwaotam*. People participate in it because it provides physical, emotional and psychological release. Many others enjoy it because it offers them opportunity to socialize, and meet or see people they have not seen for a long time. Some participants are merely perpetuating the tradition of their people. From the preceding, it is clear that *Nwaotam's* theatrical impact does not derive from its story or myth.

There is, however, a story behind *Nwaotam*, but it is not an elaborate one. *Nwaotam* is on the roof in order to bring blessings to the people. There, he is confronted by evil forces. The activities of *Nwaotam* on the roof symbolize and actualize for Opobo a struggle against the forces of Evil. When *Nwaotam* leaps into the outstretched arms of his followers, the mission is deemed to have been accomplished. Once this happens, the play is over.[33] Apart from demonstrating the phenomenon of ritual transforming to theatre, I have used this description of *Nwaotam* to further show that theatre is an experience, and does not have to be explained.

What makes *Nwaotam* a drama (without its mythical content)? I think one can reasonably say that it has the essential elements of theatre: an actor, and an audience conscious of itself as such. The individual in the mask is an actor, an impersonator recreating an experience or creating something new. Although knowing the story increases our appreciation and enjoyment of *Nwaotam*, the story is not indispensable, for theatre is more than stories and words. It is essentially a sensuous medium:

> . . . . long after typographic man is supposed to have been thinking by linear reasoning, that of words spaced syntactically upon a printed page the theatre persists in communicating by a simultaneity of sensory impressions. Now as then, it demands that its audience perceive its configuration, its Gestalt, of impressions.[34]

Let us return again to the call for the recovery of myth buried in Igbo ritual, a myth like one I have just come across in Akpugo, Uzo-Uwani Local Government area, Nsukka. Sometime ago in the distant past, in the ninth month of the year, a certain widow called Urunye, with her baby boy on her back, was going to collect firewood in the forest, when suddenly, she was confronted by a strange creature covered with young palm leaves. The creature ordered her to call his name, but Urunye could not do so. She was terrified. Thrice the creature demanded that she call his name, but she still failed. Urunye started to run home, but was obstructed by the creature who then asked her baby boy Ugwunyeke to call his name. Without delay, the boy called out "U-ii". Immediately, the creature disappeared. In fear, Urunye ran home and told her people of the strange apparition. After a month, the creature appeared again to the small boy, gave him *oji, opi, mbuba*,[35] and asked him to call him again. The boy called him "*Akawo*". Again, the creature asked the boy "What is my name?" Thereupon, Ugwuyeke called him *Odo*.

Odo began to appear to Ugwuyeke and the entire village from time to time for seven months. Two years after, the creature appeared in the early morning of *Afor* day, and began chasing people about. Ugwuyeke was asked to appease him. The little boy took a lump of *odo* ("glorizza" powder), alligator pepper and fresh palm wine in a calabash which had never touched the ground from the day such wine was put in it, and offered them to the *Odo*. From that day, the *Odo* ceased chasing people. Eventually, the *Odo* disclosed that he came from Nri, Igbo-Ukwu, the "real" and mythical home of the Igbo.

How important is this story or myth to the development of drama? Certainly, it offers a story which can be elaborated, reinterpreted and reenacted. But any other story or piece of experience can go through the same process. History, ritual or any form of activity can be used as material and structure for drama. Moveover, drama is more than story-telling. Drama is imagined act involving impersonation and the presence of a conscious audience. From the point of view of the European drama which is concerned with the portrayal of action and revelation of character, there must be dramatic choices and motivation.[36] From the point of view of African theatre which has ritual concerns, drama recreates or affirms models of familial and communal life. So, African drama is both mythic and ritualistic.

Of what significance is the *Odo* festival? It is both a re-enactment of a primordial event and an actuality. During the festival, "the protagonists of the myth are made present", and we become their contemporary.[37] When the *Odo* arrives, chronological time is displaced by primordial time.

What should we call the *Odo* festival, ritual or drama? I think one could say that it is a ritual drama. It is efficacious, bringing children, good harvest and wealth to the living who are united in a ritual communion. However, it also provides a great deal of entertainment.

The *Odo* festival contains many dramatic moments which will increasingly lose their efficacy as belief in *Odo* ritual declines. When this happens, the performances will become drama with or without some ritual associations. The *Odo* ritual can therefore become theatre without the aid of elaborate mythology.

But, we must distinguish between a ritual such as the *Odo* festival and the dramas it contains. As a festival, the *Odo* is essentially a ritual of communion between the living and their ancestors. But, as part of this reunion, and in keeping with the *Odo's* objective of teaching the people and ensuring social solidarity, drama is introduced as a model for meaningful and ethical life. An example of this drama is the *Odo* masquerade performance portraying a family in Abu-Ugwu festival at Okpatu in Udi Local Government Area. Through mime and songs, the *Odo* masquerade performers show the Okpatu people models of social behaviour.[38]

The play provides a good model for family life. It features Ezembo, the father of the family; *Ogolimaluihe* (or Ogoli for short) the mother; Akawo, two teenage sons, and Ada Odo, the daughter. They are all appropriately costumed to reflect their social roles. The father (Ezembo), beautifully costumed in colourful clothes and stripes of cloth with ribbons and ornaments hung around his head, appears like an elder and leader. He looks calm and noble, with his walking stick and a big fan. Ogoli's mask is delicately cut to reflect the beauty of womanhood. On her chest are two projections that represent breasts. Her costume is made up of very expensive materials. She wears expensive beads, and bangles, and carries a fan decorated with tiny mirrors. In the modern time, she may wear a wig. As her name suggests, *Ogolimaluihe*—literally meaning a sensible woman, she is a model housewife.

Akawo's costume is rough and unkempt, because he represents a troublesome youth. He carries a knife, canes, and other things with which he scares or attacks people. The Ada's costume, on the other hand, reflects the delicate and ethereal Igbo ideal of feminine beauty. This masquerade is the type generally referred to as *Agboho Mmuo* (Maiden Spirit).

The performance takes place, not in the *Eke Ugwu*, the ritual ground where the *Odo* reside, but in the central square called *Obom Oshaka*. Sheds for the audience are built around the arena. For the *Odo* family, there are about two huts at one end of the square. This serves both as a home and a dressing room. The *Odo* performance is accompanied with dance, music and songs. While Ogoli sings, the audience responds. Through song, she instructs the people and praises her husband.

Because of scarcity of space, let us go straight to the performance. A flutist blows his flute in praise of Ezembo, who, together with the rest of his family, is in the hut at the rear of the playing area. Ezembo steps out from the hut and moves round the arena slowly and majestically, surveying the ground to ensure that the environment is safe for his family. He returns to the hut, and comes out with his shy and beautiful wife whom he fans. As they take their seats, Akawo the rough son, dashes out of the hut and charges at the spectators who run back in fear. Ezembo chases his son, catches him, and drags him to a seat. There is an interlude of music during which Ezembo persuades his wife, Ogoli, to dance. She dances with slow steps, shaking her body and waving her hands sideways. Next, Ezembo asks her to sing for his guests (the spectators), but she declines, feigning headache. But, after a while, she gets up, kneels before her husband, who wipes her face with a cloth. She then stands up and sings in praise of him. As the audience sings the chorus, she starts dancing, and Ezembo, impressed and thrilled, pastes coins on her face, according to custom. The *Odo* escorts and the audience follow his example. Afterwards, Ezembo and Ogoli embrace each other, and the music stops. This scene shows how a father should control his family and how couples should live and love one another.

Another episode dramatizes the need for self-control in young people. Seeing a beautiful maid, a masquerade, Akawo begins to chase her about. Ezembo asks some of his aides to catch Akawo and drag the rough youth to him. This done, Ezembo pushes Akawo away—an expression of disfavour. Grumbling and pointing at his father, Akawo runs off to the family hut at the rear. Ashamed of what her son has done, Ogoli covers her face. Then, she goes to Ezembo (with his hand on his chin), kneels before him, and enquires what she should do to mollify him. But, he ignores her. Thereupon, she hurries to the hut and brings Akawo—who now is repentant—along to his father before whom they kneel as a sign of respect and Akawo's repentance. Ezembo signals that he has forgiven the son. Thereupon, Ogoli jumps and dances for joy.

Soon after, another female masquerade appears, passing along slowly, deliberately seductive. Although she is more beautiful than the one that Akawo chased, she is ignored by him. The audience cheers because the rough youth has at last improved.

The whole drama shows how the head of a family should lead and direct his wife and children. Ogoli illustrates the right behaviours of women, superlative loyalty to their husbands, and concern for the moral upbringing of their children. As a demonstration of the ideal unity that should exist in families, the *Odo*

Gargajiya"—traditional performances. Thus the word, *wasanni*, in Hausa is a general reference to all forms of performances. This provides us with a rough idea of our traditional concept of enactment. In its specific and definite form the idea of dramatic concept is contained in the Hausa descriptive term *"Wasan Kwaikwayo"*, literally meaning "imitation play". Our parallel traditional equivalent of the idea of drama and theatre is thus satisfied in both the general term *Wasannin Gargajiya* (traditional performances) and the specific term *Wasan Kwaikwayo* (dramatic plays). The modes of performance which can be drawn from the traditional concept as stated above may be grouped after the pattern given by E. T. Kirby. Thus:

Simple enactment.
Ritual enactment.
Story-telling performances.
Enactments of the spirit cult.
Masquerade performances.
Ceremonial performances.
Comedies.[3]

Says Kirby: "To be sure, a concept of theatre might well include dance and almost anything dramatic done before an audience."[4]

Although our concept of drama and theatre has been taken care of by the above categories, we are still left with the issue of classification of the dramatic forms in as much as they relate to the Hausa traditional society. In their social manifestations, traditional forms of Hausa drama as related to the above concept can be classified into the following forms:

Royal Court Forms.
Occupational Forms.
Domestic Forms.
Social Forms.
Religious Forms.
Ceremonial Forms.

There are numerous categories of dramatic forms under the above broad classifications and only one or two examples of the forms will be given in our later dramatic analysis of them.

Meanwhile, let us examine the factors involved in the above classification of the forms of dramatic performances. Crucial among the factors is the social factor. In this, the forms reflect the social setting and organization of the Hausa traditional community. However, the changing pattern of social factor imposes some measures of historical consideration. Since no society is static, social factor may involve changes through periodic historical experiences. In the case of the Hausa society, the social factors may cut across the pre-Islamic historical period through the colonial up to the present post-Independence period.

Another important factor hinges on purposes or objectives of performance. This is central to the classification of the forms. For example *Turu* dance is meant to entertain only the royal household.[5] It is usually performed on the occasion of royal installation or turbanning of a new *Sarki* (Chief). A more elaborate form of traditional drama meant to entertain the royal household or courtiers is *Wasan Gauta*.[6] So also are the burlesque shows of the court jester known as *Wawan Sarki*, the King's Fool. The main objective of this performance is to entertain the *Sarki*. It is not customary for him to perform for the "commoners" except for the courtiers who are connected with the courts or the royal household. These then are some of the variables that influence our classification of such performances under the royal court forms.

In the above case, the purpose and objectives are related to the social status, position or placement of the audience. Closely related to this factor is the environmental condition imposed by way of natural disposition. So the royal court forms are performed at court with, and for royal/patronage audience. In the same way, the Domestic Forms are the performances enacted in domestic environments, as for example, the homes of Hausa traditional setting. *Kidan Ruwa* is an example of this dramatic form. The audience is usually composed of women in purdah, the young, girls, maids, other women visitors, relations and children. The performing area is usually in an open space within the compound. It is important to note in this connection that other purposes and objectives of the performance of the domestic forms of Hausa drama include its uses in entertaining the

womenfolk in marriage or naming ceremonies, as pastime material for the sometimes boring situation of life in the purdah.

The Occupational Forms differ in modes, purposes, and setting. There are numerous examples of the Occupational Forms
and as the name implies, there are as many as there are
established and recognized occupations to be found in Hausa
traditional society. The drama of the hunters is performed as
Wasan Maharba, a form of entertainment unique to the hunters
occupational group only. So also is the *Rawar Pawa* which is
exclusive to the traditional butchers. The same is true of *Wasan
Makera*—blacksmiths occupational group play in which *dundufa*
music is rendered to accomplish the dramatic display.[7] Since
these forms of Hausa dramatic performances are unique to
occupational groups, the purpose or objective of their performances is also derived from the traditional calendar of events of
each particular group involved. Consequently, the performance
of the dramatic enactment by the *maharba* guild would take place
on occasions of ceremonial events which are of special recognition to the guild-group. For example the *maharba* occupational
group—hunters group—may decide to hold a special celebration
to mark the victory of a brave hunter over a deadly and powerful
animal such as a lion. When members of an occupational group
perform the installation ceremony of a new *Sarki* or chief for the
group, say the *mahauta's* group—butchers group, prominence is
usually given the dramatic performance unique to the group. The
communal social system of the Hausa traditional society also
provides an encouraging forum for the display of dramatic skills
unique to a particular group when a member of the group is
engaged in one of the traditional rites of passages such as the
naming ceremony, marriage ceremony, and even burial ceremony.

What dictates the place or places of performance is also
variable. For example, the performance on the occasion of an
installation ceremony of a new chief or *Sarki* may take place in
front of the house of the new leader of the group if the
arrangement is internal to the group. The performance during a
yearly feast or ritual festival of an occupational group, say, the
maharba group, may be held in a village square. When the group is

involved in a community oriented yearly festival, such as *Sallah* celebration, it is engaged in dramatic performances which shift from one place to another, along with other occupational groups engaged in the occupational displays. The nature of the theatrical function of some occupational groups is such that their area of performance depends on the movement of the group. The traditional boxers—*yan dambe*—go from one village to another in search of challenge performance. Say Madauci et al.:

> . . . . like wrestlers, boxers too are fed by the people of the towns they visit. As the boxers and spectators troop to the boxing area amidst drumming, the people in neighbouring villages and hamlets pour into the town to aid their neighbours against the visiting foe.[8]

A similar pattern of mobile performance is observable among the performing group of the *makera* occupational group. For example, *masu dundufa*—*dundufa* musical group—go from one place to another, sometimes on special invitation of a member of the patronage occupational group—the *makera*—who is holding a special party, say naming ceremony, for members of the group. Also *masu zari*—the special performing group of the *makera* (blacksmiths) occupational group—produce their performances in homes of their patron group within a town or move from one town to another to perform for the *makera* group.

The ceremonial forms are those dramatic enactments which take place on special occasions involving the entire members of the society. The term ceremonial is applied to them because they occur less frequently and are community oriented. Religious and the political events are usually the two main reasons for their performances. One of the pre-Islamic ceremonial forms is *Farautar Ruwa*.[9] This is a pre-Islamic form of dramatic ritual. Another pre-Islamic ceremonial form is *Wasan Su*, which is popular among the inhabitants of the riverine areas of Sokoto State. The *su* (fishing festival) is the climax of the pre-Islamic fertility rituals performed among the Kebbawa people and has been modified into a modern socio-political event (the *Argungu* Festival) organized by the government of Sokoto State and recognized all over Nigeria and abroad.[10]

Tashe is a very popular ceremonial form of entertainment to mark the period of the Islamic Ramadan. The Muslim Sallah celebrations are also marked with some forms of dramatic enactments, some theatrical expressions of dramatic moves and ideas, some representative reproduction of the past historical experience through the uses of dramatic elements such as costumes, music and props that are meant for only such occasions.

It is not easy to identify the social forms with a particular group of dramatic or musical entertainment than the developed multiple functions of any group beyond its primary aims and objectives. Thus the use of a particular form of entertainment may shift ground from its erstwhile exclusiveness for a particular social group to a wider scope or purpose. This can be illustrated with the extended use of *goge* music and dance for social purposes other than *bori* ritual. A similar development can be noticed with the multiplicity of the social forms of entertainment produced with the *kalangu* music though it tends to be associated with the *mahauta* occupational group. Several theatrical musical entertainment groups have been developed into social forms through the use of the *kalangu* (hour glass-shaped drum) music in Hausaland. Mamman Shata, the renowned poet of music and dance entertaining group, developed the melodic rhythm of his dramatic songs purely from the *kalangu* music.

It seems from the foregoing that in Hausa society, social forms of drama are performed principally for the entertainment of a public audience made up of different social groups.

In Hausa traditional society, before the advent of the colonial administration, there were traditional social forms of drama performed by the youths. These are known as *Yawon Magi* among the Kano people, and *Kalankuwa* in Sokoto State.[11] They are usually performed to mark the end of the rainy season. As the word *Yawo* implies, the first form involves movements of the youths from one village to another. The second form is performed at one place only and does not involve any *Yawo* movements. According to Ibrahim Yaro Yahaya, the main difference between the Sokoto and Kano forms lies in the composition of participants and places of performance as noted above. *Yawon Magi* involves both male and female youths, while *Kalankuwa* is performed by male youths only. In addition certain characters such as *Sarkin Butsu* which are featured in *Yawon Magi* are not included in *Kalankuwa*.[12] Although social forms of drama such as *Yawon Magi* and *Kalankuwa* are no longer performed, they have assumed different names and roles. This is because socio-economic organizations have assumed dynamic changes from the past. For example, agriculture is no more at the centre of the economic system. So that social activities such as *Yawon Magi* which were once produced to mark the end of the rainy season are becoming obsolete. Instead, new social groups have developed. Some are based on age-groups, some on trade associations and some on village groups for community development. On occasions such as naming and marriage ceremonies, the association members gather to do *Ajo*—contribute donation—and rejoice with the celebrant. Musical groups are usually invited to entertain the audience on such occasions. This is an opportunity for praise singing and for drumming the special *taake* of the individual members of the group. It seems the idea of producing dramatic plays such as observed with the Maitama Sule dramatic group of Kano actually developed from the traditional notion of entertainment among such groups of social associations. A similar example can be drawn from the current programme of dramatic performances in the NTV of Kaduna known as *Gidan Kashe Ahu*.

Performances on the programme include dramatic and musical episodes. The studio audience is usually of several social groups, clubs or associations invited for each programme. There are permanent stereotyped characters such as Alhaji—the landlord and chief celebrant and Hajiya Kasheta, his wife. A very popular character in the programme is *Tsumbuleke*. His role could be likened to that of *Sarkin Butsu* in the traditional performance of *Yawon Magi*. He behaves like a court jester and has a potential ability to make the audience laugh.

Having clarified some issues regarding the dramatic classification along basic social functions, aims and objectives of the performances, one can now concentrate on the descriptive analysis. Let us examine the nature and modes of production of the various forms. Consider the *Wasan Gauta*—the royal court form of the oral tradition. The royal court form of *Wasan Gauta* in the

Hausa society can be likened to the masques in the late medieval European court or the Elizabethan theatre from the performance patronage point of view. It is, however, a dramatic performance restricted to women actresses of the traditional palace households only. They receive active support and encouragement of the *Sarki*, the courtiers and officials of the royal administration. The performance takes place on an open space in the palace. In fact, it is believed among the traditional informants in Kano that the open space in the compound of Gidan Makama—a building presently occupied by the Department of Antiquities and used as a National Museum—was an ancient traditional theatre.[13] If that is true, it can be safely assumed that the performances were held in the homes of lesser chiefs also, apart from the *Sarki's* palace. Be that as it may, it is likely that that "open theatre" was used for a more spectacular drama which saw Kano through her period of political crisis before the emergence of the colonial administration. By way of digression, it may perhaps be necessary to state that the post of Makama is that of a traditional custodian of the oath of faith of allegiance to the *Sarki*. So in time of crisis, when Kano is attacked or waged war against her enemy, it is the duty of the Makama to administer the oath of allegiance to all Kano war chiefs. That was a highly dramatic event. Amidst the high tempo and rhythmic sound of *Kurya* music, each war chief was expected to step out boldly, and in a spectacular manner, say his "kirari" as the musician chanted his praises. As the warrior said his oath, Makama reminded him of the grievous implications of failure to adhere to the oath. That was the traditional way of emboldening the minds of the warriors while at the same time ennobling the cause of the war.[14]

Such was the politically dramatic tradition of pre-colonial Kano. *Wasan Guata* is, however, an elaborate and highly organized form of entertainment by the female members of the royal household. According to other sources, *Wasan Guata* takes place only once in a year. So it can in fact, be said to be a periodic form of traditional performance. It seems the periodical nature of its performance was due to the elaborate pre-performance preparation involved. Perhaps it also has something to do with the social status of the participants. It is likely that the status of the female participants who are mostly royal household servants would normally require some diplomatic negotiations before performance permission is granted and the date of performance fixed. However, *Wasan Gauta* is an official performance of the traditional social system.

Of great interest to this analysis are the dramatic elements in the performance. Since there is no written evidence of the nature of the performance, our sources are mainly from the oral tradition. Suffice it to say, however, that *Wasan Gauta* is a full-fledged drama in many respects. First the fact that *Wasan Gauta* is linked with the very concept of imitation in Hausa tradition makes it an object of dramatization. Basically, the concept of dramatic enactment was contained in the term *Wasan Kwaikwayo*, a specific reference to the nature of performance in *Wasan Gauta*.

The aim of the performance is to dramatize issues, usually based on those that concern the royal authority—the *Sarki* and his lieutenants such as Waziri, Galadima, the courtiers, etc. Since one of the basic objectives of the performance is to draw the attention of the ruling authorities to some important administrative issues in the society, the performance is usually built round an artificially contrived plot or improvised story outlined to be enacted by the cast. This is important to the inter-related dramatic nature of the traditional forms of performances. Whereas in traditional oral poetry, the dramatic communication is done by the lead and chorus singers mainly through songs and the use of musical rhythm to enhance its dramatic content, in *Wasan Gauta*, acting, dialogue, imitative gestures and satire are applied. It seems dramatic devices as observed in the delivery technique of the traditional story-teller have been explored with the additional advantages of multiple characterization as against the story-telling enactments by one person. Thus, in *Wasan Gauta* the characters in the dramatic enactments are well represented. In fact, the embedded idea of characterization in dramatic imitations as conceptualized by the Hausa term *Kwaikwayo*, is crucial to the elaborate preparations before the performance.

The suggestion that the dramatic plot or story is derived from the administrative or political issues in the traditional society is strong especially if one considers that the costumes used in the productions were collected mainly from the royal patrons. In fact, one of my informants said that the satiric imitation of the important personalities of the royal court is aimed at drawing their attention to issues that concern public opinion about them.[15] This opinion is confirmed by the subsequent development of *Wasan Gauta* into *Wasan Gwamna* during the colonial regime. According to Ibrahim Yaro Yahaya, the traditional form was adapted to suit the colonial situation.[16] A major aspect of the adaptation is the increase in the characterization which include the colonial ruling personnel such as District Officers, Education Officers, and members of the medical personnel. The expansion of *Wasan Gauta* outside the strict confines of the traditional ruling system transformed it into a more public event. It received the same form of encouragement from the colonial authority because it was perhaps recognized as a potential weapon for public enlightenment. One might also conjecture that since social problems were generally highlighted in the performance, the colonial administrators may have, through these performances, learnt more about the weakness of their administrative systems from the *Wasa* just as the traditional ruling authorities were able to do.

Let us consider one example of the occupational forms—*Wasan Maharba*. As the name implies, *Wasan Maharba* means hunters' play. The factors responsible for the periodic control of the performance has already been mentioned. Today, however, it is possible to get an occupational group to perform on a day or occasion not special to them because of the commercialized influence of the government policy of cultural regeneration. *Wasan Maharba* may be manifested either in the performance of a *garaya* musician in a special ceremony of the *maharba* (hunters) group or in the performance which involves the group in dramatic enactments. In either case, *garaya* music is an important feature although one cannot rule out other forms of music especially in non-speaking Hausa areas.

The *Maharba* performance dominated by the *garaya* music may be produced at the gathering of the hunters with *garaya* musicians plucking some musical tones from the cords of the instrument. The music is highly rhythmical especially when the rhythm is combined with the one produced by the rhythmic timing of the sound through the hitting of the (*garaya*) calabash base of the *garaya* instrument with some rings fixed on the thumb or/and fingers. Sometimes, a solo rhythm is produced; sometimes the sounds from the cords blend into rhythms of chorus sounds pulsating after the solo cord tune. Sometimes the *garaya* music performs the lead and the musician sings the chorus suggested. At other times, the solo rhythm of the cord's lead sound blends with that of the *garaya* player's voice, producing a vibration of emotional emphasis. The music is tuneful and the vibrations in the rhythmic sound is re-vibrated by the clinging, tinkling, silvery little sounds that emanate from the several rings fixed on the flat metal edges at the end of the long wooden bar holding the cords with the calabash case of leather cover. As the rhythm of the music rises so does the voice of the musician, chanting the heroic deeds of great hunters in their encounters with several types of animals.

The Hausa musical performances are usually produced in repertoire which in traditional concept is termed *taakee*, in which each song or musical composition is meant for a particular person, animal, thing or event. *Taakee* in most cases are not the same though they might be similar in rhythm, thought, concept, music or song. So when the *garaya* musician plucks a sweet *taakee* melody praising the heroic deed of a hunter, he sometimes applies onomatopoeia to enhance the rhythmic effect in the hunting encounter. Sometimes the music slows to the rhythm of the pantomimic movement and hunting strategy. Sometimes musical pace rises into sudden and quick rhythms presenting an aesthetic imagination of the rhythms, sounds and movements between the hunter and animal in the hunting expedition. Some of the hunters in the musical performance dance to the rhythm of sound and songs repertoire. Others simply sit listening in a cool emotional recollection of events being recounted in the repertoire. But occasionally in a sudden rise of emotion, a hunter, whose repertoire had touched his soft sensitive recollection of events, would jump up and chant his *kirari*—in a self-praise demonstration of prowess. It is a short enactment of prowess, a demonstration of heroic ability which is met with the spectators ovation. He shakes as if in a possessive trepidation, shouting along his *kirari* to the rhythm of *garaya* music. The other form of dramatic enactment of the hunters' occupational group is the mimetic form. In this form of enactment, music is also played but the emphasis of the dramatic entertainment is in the re-enactment of events during hunting expeditions. The enactment takes the form of movements. Strategies involved in hunting expeditions are displayed. Because of the limitation of space, a descriptive analysis of such performance is not possible here. Suffice it to say that the dramatic performance mentioned above is a rare example of an act of the theatre. It is not one of the common performances of hunters occupational groups in state and national festivals.

The domestic form of Hausa drama to be discussed next is *Kidan Ruwa*. This is a form of dance-drama. It is produced to the accompaniment of music produced by placing some calabashes in a bowl of water. The calabashes are beaten with small sharpened billets of wood to produce the musical sound. Different sounds are produced by *Kidan Ruwa* instruments due to the difference in the natural shapes of calabashes and water base containers. Like in all Hausa music, there are various *taakee* or repertoire in the performance of *Kidan Ruwa*. The rhythm of the music is, however, constant and regular with little or no varieties or diversifications as could be observed in the versatility of say, the *garaya* musical performance.

The dramatic impact of the performance derives from its song repertoire from where various themes are developed. There are songs for the jealous and envious rival wives—*kishiyoyi* (pl.), *kishiya* (sing.). There are those for the lazy and unfaithful ones. An important feature of such composition is the creative freedom. Thus a talented lead musician can increase her repertoire by composing songs based on events she has experienced or even improvised on the spot.

Kidan Ruwa is performed as part of a large domestic ceremony with simple sketches. As the lead singer chants her repertoire, the chorus supplement with a repetitive emphasis, usually, on one general theme of the song. The rhythm rises and falls in regular rhythmic pace as the various sounds blend to produce the melody. The re-enactment is done through a dance parody of the characters mentioned in the song. In the performance *Mai Soso Ke Wanka*[17] (only one with sponge takes bath) two actresses dance to the market in response to music, initiated by a lead singer and amplified by a chorus of performers. At the market, one of the two actresses goes to a sponge seller to purchase a sponge. The other does not buy any sponge. When they get home, they decide to wash. The one who purchased a sponge removes her sponge and initiates the action. Both of them imitate the act of bath-taking through various movements. However, the actress who did not purchase her own sponge stands aloof and watches in embarrassment. She later makes some effort to borrow a sponge from the other members of the performing group. They refuse to lend her one. She then decides to go to the market to purchase her own sponge. But it is too late, the market has closed. When she gets back home she meets the others already dressed up and ready for social engagement. They mock, jeer and laugh at her as a dirty pig who does not care about washing her body. It is, in event, a satiric sketch against dirty housewives.

Finally, the last two forms that will be discussed together are *Yawon Magi*—under the sub-heading of "social forms"—and *Wasan Bori* which could be both religious or ceremonial. These two are ancient forms in the Hausa traditional social setting or system. *Yawon Magi*, as has been mentioned earlier, is the public or commoners version of *Wasan Gauta*, the royal court form already discussed. *Yawon Magi* is also known as *Kalankuwa* in some parts of Hausaland such as Sokoto. Even in Kano State where it is generally known as *Yawon Magi*, there are places, such as Gumel, where it is referred to as *Wasan Samari*—youth play. The performance is usually periodical. It takes place generally after the harvest period on the farm. There are several versions of the dramatic nature of the entertainment. This is apparently natural from the different terms of reference to it in parts of Hausa-speaking areas. Currently, inconclusive research, however, unveils some important dramatic elements in the performance of *Yawon Magi*. It seems that in its ancient social setting when the performance was declared, some persons were selected as characters. The characterization is developed from the traditional system of organization. So the "characters" are put in charge of the whole affairs. From the Hausa traditional dramatic concept, the affairs of the "state" is temporarily in the hands of the selected persons. They then play the roles of *Sarki, Waziri, Galadima* and other important traditional personalities in the traditional ruling system. *Sarkin Samari*, the leading character, therefore plays the role of *Sarki* as it is perceived in the traditional social administration. He holds his court and presides over cases brought to him from the dramatic festival of *Yawon Magi*. The Waziri and other important councillors are supposed to sit in the *Sarki's* council and receive greetings from the citizens who will come to pay obeisance to the *Sarki*. Every character is provided with the appropriate costumes and is expected to be accorded the same type of honour and respect in true traditional social setup.[18]

Yawon Magi involves both the male and female youths of the society. Several forms of events are organized during the long-term period of the performance which runs for days. Several other characters are also appointed, such as Sarkin Butsu—a kind of foolery figure who takes care of children's orderliness during performances. The performances are marked with a series of traditional events, such as competitive dances, wrestling, and even boxing. The performances are done in the presence of the special guests who are themselves "characters" in the production.

The term *Wasan bori* means bori performance or play. It is derived from the *bori* ritual. This is a form of religious performance by the *bori* adherents known as *masu bori*. *Bori* ritual involves spirit-possession by *masu bori*—the *bori* adherents. Possession by spirits during a *bori* performance is an important factor in *bori* religious ritual. Since the ritual is performed for healing purposes it seems the spirit-possession is an integral part of the *bori* performance. This is not strictly so. *Bori* performance is actually done for other social purposes. This is why it is possible for us to refer to other forms of *bori* performance as *Wasan bori*—bori play or performance.

According to Fremont E. Besmer:

"the bori spirit-possession cult persists in Hausa urban centres because enough people believe in its usefulness in ritual healing, and still more view it as a lively entertainment for weddings, namings and other important events."[19]

The use of *bori* for entertainment purposes is the main interest of this section of the article. It is this use of *bori* performance that is here referred to as *Wasan bori*. Here *bori* is examined as a traditional form of drama.

It is perhaps important to stress that *bori* performance, irrespective of the objective, is highly dramatic. Such a dramatic nature of *bori* is derived from the use of elements of drama in its performance. So *bori* performance can be examined under two broad objectives, namely, as a ritual performance and as a performance for entertainment.

There are however some crucial observations on the nature of the *bori* performance when it is meant for each of the particular objectives mentioned above. One of such observations is the strictly controlled nature of the dramatic elements when it is performed for ritual purposes. Consequently, the basic elements of drama in *bori* ritual performance are not subjected to artistic creation. *Bori* music in a ritual performance is controlled. It is subjected to the accepted forms and structures which are relevant to each spirit of possession. That means that the music and song rendition for a particular spirit of possession, say, *Sarkin Makada* will be different from that of another spirit say *Sarkin Rafi*. That is why Fremont E. Besmer comments that:

"while variability might be expected in songs . . . where subject, rhythm, and structural relationships rather than set sequences are the relevant identifying factors . . . . it is judged unusual for praise-epithets, which in other contexts (e.g. the royal court) are identical from rendition to rendition."[20]

So the *bori* ritual performance places some forms of artistic restriction or control on the elements of drama employed in the process. As Turner puts it, "the symbols of ritual are, so to speak, 'storage units'".[21] It seems in ritual performance of *bori* the use of the elements of drama in the "storage units" is of exclusive importance to the artistic creativity of the participants.

The nature of the creative control when a *bori* performance is meant for ritual purpose could be viewed from the similar implication of this statement on Uban Dawaki by Fremont E. Besmer. Says Besmer

> "during a *bori* performance, the songs for Uban Dawaki are normally played immediately after those for Sarkin Makada. Uban Dawaki, who is said to be Sarkin Aljan's Madaki (an important title in a royal court), spends most of his time at the main gate to the spirits' city of Jangare, guarding the entrance. His other names include Kuturu (The Leper), Kyadi, Malam Musa, Goje, Madaki, and Kaura, the last three being reference to his royal title."[22]

It seems therefore from the above statement that although variability in the storage units could be employed for artistic versatility, it nevertheless cannot be carried away from the realm of traditional corpus. There is another element of control or artistic freedom in *bori* ritual performance. That is the power of symbolism of the elements of drama in ritual performance. Thus the ritual purpose of a *bori* performance achieves its meaningful objective only by the strict adherence to the use of dramatic elements in their symbolic connotations.

These are the basic situations in the analysis of the traditional forms of Hausa drama. One sees some direct links in the nature and forms of drama and those experienced in certain forms of the traditional system of Hausa social organizations. The links make us recognize the similarities especially in the basic elements of drama. However, a major consideration is the place of the dramatic forms in the traditional social entertainment. Since the concept of enactment is basic to drama, one sees in the traditional forms some elements and links with drama. For they are acts of the theatre, basically for entertainment and performed in theatrical enactments. Their entertainment values have been explored in recent Nigerian cultural festivals. So their performances outside the social setup has removed their local traditional objectives. This is what raised them as conventional acts of theatre and so recognized as traditional forms of drama.

Notes

1. Richard Southern, *The Seven Ages of the Theatre*, Faber & Faber, London, p. 25.

2. E. T. Kirby, "Indigenous African Theatre", *The Drama Review:* Indigenous Theatre Issue, Vol. 18, No. 4 to 64, 1974.
3. Ibid.
4. Ibid.
5. Festival of Traditional Dances of North-Central State, Programme, 1974.
6. Suwaid Muhammad & Ibrahim Y. Yahaya, *Darussa a kan adabin Hausa*, Institute of Education, A.B.U., Zaria, p. 43.
7. Mini-Festival Workshop, Centre for Nigerian Cultural Studies, A.B.U., Zaria, 1977.
8. Ibrahim Madauci et al., *Hausa Customs*, N.N.P.C., Zaria, 1968, p. 74.
9. An informant.
10. *Zaruma*—A Cultural Magazine of Sokoto State, 1979.
11. Muhammadu Bici, Adult Education Office, Kano State.
12. S. Muhammad & I. Y. Yahaya, *op. cit.*
13. Informant, Mohammed Sarki, Council for Arts and Culture, Kano.
14. Informant, Muhammadu Bici, Adult Education Office, Kano.
15. Ibid.
16. S. Muhammad & I. Y. Yahaya, *op. cit.*
17. Performance at Dutsin Ma, Kaduna State, 1977.
18. Informant, Muhammadu Bici, Kano.
19. Fremont E. Besmer, Harsunan Najeriya, III, C.S.N.L., Abdullahi Bayero College/A.B.U., Kano, 1973, p. 31.
20. Ibid., p. 17.
21. Ibid., p. 16.
22. Ibid., p. 20.

RITUAL, DRAMA AND THE THEATRICAL: THE CASE OF *BORI* SPIRIT MEDIUMSHIP

Andrew Horn

I. Introductory: "Theatre" and "Drama"

Much contemporary discussion of the nature and origins of drama and the other performing arts in Africa has been characterized by an unnecessary imprecision of nomenclature, an unfortunate tendency to identify any performance, regardless of formal or functional qualities, as drama. This curious refusal to acknowledge generic distinctions bears scant benefit. There is little point in calling a leopard an animal when we can call it a leopard, thereby differentiating it from pythons, planaria and men. Indeed, to refuse to distinguish between the leopard and the tabby-cat, however structurally similar they may be, allows us, in the end, fully to understand and be able effectively to deal with neither. The division of phenomena into genres (including sub-genres and "mixed" genres, like dance-drama, or mules, or uglyfruit) allows us better to understand the mechanisms, geneses and functions of the phenomena and their dialectical relationships with one another. The analysis of what a given genre *is* may often usefully begin with what it is not, perhaps with what preceded it, engendered it, but was not it.

The fundamental problem of nomenclature in the examination of African performance modes lies in the necessary distinction between "drama" and "theatre", between the "dramatic" and the "theatrical". Theatre, in its broadest sense, subsumes elements of most structured performances before an audience, including drama, dance, musical recital, group ritual, secular ceremony, even classroom lecturing. It is, essentially, *spectacle*.

In his brief but useful survey, "Indigenous African Theatre", E. T. Kirby classifies African traditional performances into seven general categories: "(1) simple enactments, (2) ritual and ritual-

181

ized enactment, (3) story-telling performances, (4) spirit-cult enactments, (5) masquerades and masquerade enactments, (6) ceremonial performances, (7) comedies".[1] Of these, all are essentially theatrical, some have elements of the dramatic, and some, at times, contain rudimentary forms of drama. Unfortunately, Kirby's categories are by no means as discrete as they seem. He finds himself unaccountably including amongst "civic-religious ceremonies", the strikingly dramatic, dialogued interactions of the spirit mediums in Yoruba *orisha* and Nago *vodun* cults.[2] Similarly, the *bori* performances of northern Nigeria would rightly fall into at least three of Kirby's classes: the ritual, the spirit-cult, and the ceremonial. All of which serves to demonstrate the serious analytical difficulties presented to the scholar by the myriad forms of traditional African performance.

Of the several theatrical and peri-theatrical modes mentioned above, amongst the earliest to appear in human society was ritual. It is here that we shall begin our discussion of the dramatic, for it is at the very interface of religion and art that drama and ritual intersect. To identify what occurs in that intersection—and what is excluded by it—will be the concern of this enquiry.

II. "Bori": A Spirit Medium Ritual with Dramatic Elements

1. Drama and Religion

It has often been argued—indeed, since Aristotle, who identified the beginnings of classical tragedy in the sacred *dithyramb* of the Dionysian sect[3]—that drama has its roots in religion. I would maintain that its roots, in fact, lie even deeper and, like those of all art, are to be found in the very origins of religion, in sympathetic magic, in the earliest attempts of man to comprehend, order and control his environment. When, for example, Richard Axion suggests that the development of church drama in early medieval Europe owed a great deal to "three profane traditions"—mimicry, the mock combat, and the dancing-game—and from this infers that "any easy assumptions about the 'evolution' of all Medieval and Renaissance drama from one ecclesiastical 'seed'" become "quite untenable", his argument remains incomplete.[4] For, while it is unlikely that medieval drama developed only out of liturgical patterns and that secular performance forms, largely unrecorded perhaps because discouraged and officially banned since the *Concilium Trullanum* (A.D. 692), did not significantly contribute to the process, the ultimate antecedent of both the sacred and secular traditions is ritual magic. Even these worldly entertainments must have grown out of vegetative and animist rituals which pre-date the Christian Church by millennia.[5] In the spirit medium cult of *bori*, as practised in the Hausa speaking communities of northern Nigeria, one can observe something of this process. *Bori* in performance *is* ritual magic and *uses* art. It relies on theatrical spectacle, but is not drama.

2. *Nature Religions and Their Rituals*

Before looking at how the arts and belief-system of *bori* are structured, it would be useful briefly to examine the general characteristics of nature religions, the manipulative qualities of which continue to be important both overtly in the major world religions and covertly in secular art. The forces which govern man's world are beyond his control. They are sometimes palpable—rain, earthquake, animals, disease—and sometimes impalpable—fate, luck, and the apparent breakdowns and discontinuities of causality. To most men, both why and how these things happen are impenetrable mysteries and their world may seem a menacing anarchy. The desire to order this confusion, as a means of influencing, if not totally controlling, the capricious forces, lies in the priorities of human communities second only to survival itself: to dominate nature and destiny, to be sovereign over their lives in their world.

Immediately man becomes aware of this desire, he is confronted with the forces' insubstantiality. While their effects may be material and observable, their mechanisms and ultimate qualities are not. Man, as a material being in a material world, fears what he perceives as immaterial, for it cannot be contained or dominated. His defensive impulse is to concretize, to make the invisible visible, the infinite finite, and the superhuman human. It is this last, the tendency to anthropomorphize, which generates the idea of gods. If it rains, it is reasoned, there must be someone who makes it rain, someone who, although perhaps invisible and mysterious, or visible and elusive, has a mind, feelings, motivations, and is, in some critical ways, like man himself. And if such a being controls the rain, there must be another who controls the rivers. So evolves an elaborate bureaucracy of gods, each with his own powers, personality, limitations, and social status. This divine heirarchy usually reflects the fundamental social and economic relations of the human community which generates it, as can clearly be seen in the *bori* pantheon.[6] There is also, it would seem, a progression in the emergence of these gods, from those which govern the more immediately observable phenomena (animate creatures, meteorological change, death, disease, and the like) to those who determine the more abstract forces, such as good or ill fortune in marriage or trade.

The individualizing and, to some extent, anthropomorphizing of these controlling agencies allow man to feel that he can communicate with them as he would with his fellow human beings, although in a more exalted and stylized manner. He begins to believe that he can plead with them, question them, argue with or even bribe them. But then, where does one direct these appeals? To the raindrops and lions and smallpox rashes of the palpable world? This is awkward, especially when one wants to anticipate the phenomenon: to bring on rain which has been long absent, or to prevent the disease before it strikes. So the god—the natural force—is objectified, physicalized in a sacred tree, a carved fetish, or even in a real human being who, by executing prescribed actions in a special, magical, ritualized way, may become the representative of the force or—as in *bori* and other spirit medium and possession cults—may for a time become the force itself. If the representative of the force or spirit, he has become a priest, a person with unique knowledge and powers who leads and supervises the worship of and ritual communication with the unseen agencies. But if the force itself, he has become a medium. Once possessed by the spirit he is effectively no longer himself and cannot be addressed by his accustomed name. His body and mind have been occupied by the force and he speaks with its voice, not his own. In such a state, he as the spirit can be directly approached for favours, information, or advice on human affairs. The *bori* spirit medium is such a figure.[7]

3. The "Bori" Belief System

Bori is a spiritualist cult originally of the Maguzawa, Hausa-phone animists whose religion seems to pre-date the introduction of Islam into the Hausa territories and to have survived Muslim, Christian, and British Colonial attempts to suppress it.[8] Its survival, within an overwhelmingly Islamic society, may be due in part to its syncretic character, the expansion of its pantheon to include Muslim spirits,[9] its absorption of the Muslim concept of the *jinn*,[10] and its acknowledgement of Allah's overall sovereignty of the spirit community.[11] It has even gained a modicum of acceptance in some Islamic quarters. But we are not here concerned with assessing either its ethical qualities, its legitimacy, or its relationship to any of the world religions, rather with *bori*, mediumship as a performance mode. And in order fully to understand this performance mode, we must first briefly survey the beliefs that lie behind it and the motivations for executing it.

The members of the cult, the "*yan bori*" ("children of *bori*") or *masu bori* ("owners of *bori*", sing. *mai bori*) are today mostly women,[12] a fact which significantly colours some of the social inversions—rather like those of the medieval European Feast of Fools and Lord of Misrule—evident in *bori* performances.[13] They are members of a fellowship requiring for admission the undergoing of an initiation ritual (girka),[14] which is, at least initially, meant to be curative[15] rather than primarily intromissive. Some of the initiates are Muslims, many are not, but they share a belief that the events in human life are directly controlled by unseen spirits, known variously as *iskoki* ("winds", sing. *iska*) or *aljannu* ("jinns"), who are very precisely individualized, each with specific powers, a defined domain in earthly affairs, and a unique personality. Some, largely the Muslim spirits, are restrained, benevolent, healing, while most of the "pagan" spirits are violent, malevolent, disease-causing.[16] Ba-Maguje, for example, is a Hausa *arnaa* ("pagan", "animist") who causes drunkenness and is physically realized as a reeling inebriate.[17] Malam Alhaji, on the other hand, the *sarki* ("king") of the Muslim *iskoki*, dispenses medicinal cures and is physicallized as a bent, learned old man, counting his prayer beads and reading from the

Qu'ran.[18] The female spirit *Yar Kunama* ("daughter of the scorpion") is typical of the pathogenic spirits, causing pimples and boils and moving her arms like a scorpion.[19]

In all, there are about a hundred such *iskoki*,[20] whose powers lie largely in the realm of disease. The cult is thus primarily concerned with the healing and prevention of illness, but also more generally with good and bad luck. The spirits reside in the invisible city of Jangare,[21] believed to exist somewhere in the real, physical world of Hausaland,[22] and from there may be enticed by the *bori* initiates. In Jangare the spirits are grouped into several discernable domestic communities or compounds, each with its own social hierarchy, congruent with that of the initiates' own society. Fremont Besmer counts twelve of these compounds;[23] while Ibrahim Madauci, Yahaya Isa and Bellow Daura, rather less systematically, mention eleven;[24] and Michael Onwuejeogwu tabulates six major groups of spirits: urban Muslims (*"yan riga"*), ritual "Pagans" (*babbaku*, including Farmers and Hunters), Warriors (*yan garki*), Youths (*samari*), Children or Smallpox (*yan zansanna*), and Bush Spirits of wildlife (*yan dowa*).[25] Each of these *iskoki* is so specifically individualized and both its metaphysical and social roles are so clearly perceived by the *masu bori* that Besmer is able, in his "Avoidance and Joking Relationships Between Hausa Supernatural Spirits", to attempt a parsing of the social interactions within Jangaro as if he were monitoring a real, human community.

A given *iskoki* of this elaborate pantheon, it is believed, can be called from Jangare by the playing of his personal theme-melody (*waj'ar bori*) and the reciting of his praise-epithet (*kirari*),[26] in an appropriate setting. He appears by inhabiting the body of the *bori* medium and can then, through her, be given gifts,[27] asked questions, or entreated to foretell the future. All of this occurs in the culminating event of the cult's activity, the ritual performance, to which we shall turn after noting some comments on spirit possession, spirit mediumship, and their central roles in *bori*.

4. *Spirit Mediumship and Spirit Possession*

As the executive aspects of *bori*, with which we are most concerned, are largely associated with spirit mediumship and possession, it would be appropriate here to mention something of these forms of religious manifestation. A great deal of extremely close research has been done by psychologists and theologians as well as by sociologists and anthropologists into the dynamics of religious ecstasy.[28] From these enquiries, it seems probable that in their stark displays of radical dissociation, such ecstasies as possession and mediumship are in some way related to the internal discordances which emerge pathologically in the psychoneurotic "multiple personality".[29] But for our present purposes, determining the relationship between drama and these ecstatic states, it will suffice to distinguish broadly between possession and mediumship and between the "real" and the simulated trance.

In his foreword to John Beattie's and John Middleton's *Spirit Mediumship and Society in Africa*, Raymond Firth explains:

> . . . I have found it convenient to separate the phenomena of spirit-mediumship in particular from those of spirit possession in general. In both, a person's actions are believed to be dictated by an extra-human entity which has entered his body or otherwise affected him. Both kinds of phenomena may often be regarded as instances of multiple personality, that is the individual concerned assumes another identity, refers to his normal self as "he" and sincerely differentiates this new identity sharply from his everyday self. But in spirit possession his behaviour does not necessarily convey any particular message to other people. It is primarily regarded as his bodily expression of spirit manifestation. In spirit mediumship the emphasis is on *communication*. The extra-human entity is not merely expressing himself but is regarded as having something to say to an audience. This implies that the verbal and non-verbal behaviour of a person who, possessed by a spirit, acts as a medium, must be more highly *controlled* than that of a person simply possessed. In some societies possession is a form of collective extravaganza, routinized and tolerated, though not as everyday behaviour. By common convention in many other societies a person regarded as possessed tends to be classed as a sick patient for whom treatment is necessary. But a possessed person who acts as a medium tends to be regarded as a hale person who is carrying out a special role. The behaviour of both tends to be largely stereotyped, to conform to a kind of code.[30]

Of all these determinants, it is, above all, the role of communication—especially communication through stylized behaviour—that is of significance in the study of drama. This points the central importance in our present discussion of the mediumship rather than the possession element in *bori* and further suggests the pivotal questions, which we shall confront in Part III: *what* is communicated and between *whom*?

But even within mediumship, a distinction must be made between those seances in which the medium actually achieves a state of trance and those in which trance is simulated. In terms of the medium-performer, it is not a problem, Firth argues, "of spiritual *versus* human phenomena, but of unconscious *versus* conscious production of symptoms",[31] between, in other words, compulsive and intentional mimesis. In the case of genuine trance, the psychiatric interests may be greater than the theatrical. But in consciously simulated ecstasies, the medium becomes a theatre artist, an actor who creates a character in a formal performance. It should, however, be noted that a trance simulation is not always perceived as such by the audience and that, even if it is, this may have little effect on the audience's sense of the value of the ritual or of the cult. Firth comments that "trance simulation undoubtedly occurs among peoples who have confidence in spirit performances and is known by them to occur. Though it may invalidate for them the efficacy of an individual performance, such 'faking' is not held to destroy the truth of the spirit cult as a whole".[32] Indeed, as Beattie and Middleton suggest, there are spirit cults in which "it is more or less frankly admitted that possession does not or need not really occur, but may be simulated".[33] In *bori* both genuine and assumed trance occur, as will be discussed in the next Section.

5. *The "Bori" Performance*

It is not within the scope of this enquiry to explore in any depth the social and material conditions which prompt a person in contemporary Hausa society to seek cure, community and catharsis in *bori* participation, rather than in other activities. These conditions evoke complex social, economic, and religious questions, including that of women's role in the society,[34] which are not immediately related to the study of theatre forms. We shall simply note that the *masu bori* are formed into fairly discrete groups, mostly of women, both married and divorced, using as their meeting-place—although not necessarily as their ritual site—the house of the cult leader (*magajiya*), which may also be a brothel.[35]

Besmer has observed four distinct types of *bori* performance, two of which are presented primarily for public amusement and two of which are intended to achieve communication with the *iskoki*. The former, which he identifies as *wasa* ("playing"),[36] is of two types: the *kidan bori* ("drumming for spirits"), "which includes a demonstration of trance by cult-adepts", and *kidan wasa* ("drumming for play"), "which does not include trance".[37] In the latter group, which he calls *"bori"*,[38] fall the two healing rituals: that of curative sacrifice in which no trance state is induced, and that of the medium trance, which is resorted to when sacrifice to the spirits is seen to have failed.[39]

Onwuejeogwu suggests an alternative division into the domestic *borin gida* ("home *bori*"), a small trance ritual attended only by women within the walls of a dwelling compound and today largely rural; and the public *borin jama'u* ("group *bori*"), attended by men as well as women, which may be either a *wasa* (entertainment) or a *bori* (trance) performance.[40] Whatever the most accurate scheme, we can readily see that it is those presentations involving trance mediumship, whether genuine or simulated, and performed before some sort of audience (i.e. not involving all those present as participants) which are of the most direct interest in our present discussion: the *kidan bori* and both forms of *borin jama'u*.

Bori performances occur most often at times of family or community crisis or transition: serious illnesses or epidemics, marriages, Muslim *eid* festivals, the opening of new markets, moments of national instability. They are usually held, when public, in an open area where all the local *masu bori* and whoever else may wish to attend, gather. At one end of this "theatre" space sit the male musicians, not themselves initiates but professional specialists in the unique music of *bori* and the theme-melodies of the *iskoki*. David Ames and Anthony King catalogue seven types of *bori* musicians,[41] but Besmer claims that the most popular musical ensembles in Kano include one *garaya* (two-stringed plucked lute) and two or three *gora* (calabash rattles), or perhaps a *goge* (singled-stringed bowed lute) and several *k'warya* (inverted half-calabashes beaten with wooden sticks).[42]

When the musicians begin to play the song of a particular spirit and its praise-epithet is declaimed, the *mai bori* who is regularly visited by that spirit moves into the performance area. She is likely to be dressed in clothing appropriate to the *iska*, perhaps of a particular colour, perhaps an elaborate costume.[43] She will carry an important hieratic fetish, the *tsere*,[44] which functions as more than a stage property, as it is the "vehicle"[45] through which the spirit possesses the medium. The *tsere* objects are, according to P. G. Harmis, "miniature replicas of implements and clothing necessary to the particular spirit": sandals for the Hunters, axes for the Bush Spirits, a "white gown and cap" for Malam Alhaji.[46]

The *bori* initiate then begins to dance, to move erratically, to jump in the air and land squarely on the buttocks with legs splayed apart, or to jerk wildly about. The spirit is now presumed to have occupied her body and, in the imagery of *bori*, she is said to be "ridden", "mounted" (*hawa*) by the *iska*; she becomes the "mare" (*godiya*) of the spirit.[47] If she has fallen into a state of possession, there will be no fully realized characterization of the occupying spirit and the performance will simply be a display of ecstatic hysteria with a musical accompaniment. But if she is a medium, the *mai bori* will assume the demeanour of the spirit and her movements, voice, words, knowledge and power will be those of the *iska* "riding" her. If Malam Alhaji, she will cough and stoop, reading from an imagined Qu'ran, like an aged religious scholar; if the fever-bearing Dan Caladima ("the Prince"), she will walk with noble dignity, sit on a mat and mime the proceedings of a royal court;[48] if, on the other hand, the rural Hunter Ja-Ba-Fari ('Neither-Red-nor-White"), the half-African, half-Arab spirit of madness, she will eat dirt and, either arousingly or grotesquely, mime copulation.[49]

The medium has now *become* the spirit which has mounted her and is treated as the spirit, not as herself, her own familiar personality suspended for the duration of the trance. It is at this point that the audience enter into the performance and make direct appeals to the spirit. Offered gifts which are placed on the mats before it, the *iska* may converse with the spectators, foretell individual fates, offer guidance in personal conduct, issue orders, or "speak in tongues". This, then, is the practical, functional heart of most public *bori* performances: a direct communication between spectator and spirit, between men and natural force.

It should be noted here that even when trance is simulated the spectators, whether or not aware of the quality of the trance state, may still treat with the medium as the *iska*. And while, as most commentators acknowledge, simulation is extremely common in the *bori* entertainments,[50] this does not necessarily invalidate for the audience, nor even for the medium, the supernormal claims of the *masu bori* and the efficacy of their rituals. In his study of spirit possession and mediumship amongst the Bunyoro of western Uganda, Beattie argues that:

> Even when there is limited or no dissociation, it would be an over-simplification simply to assert without qualification that mediumship is a fraud. A Nyoro ex-medium informant perhaps provided the clue. She knew, she said, that *kubandwa* was deception. "But", she went on, "I thought that all the same it would be good for the patient if I did what I was required to do". . . . What she saw herself as performing was, it might be said, a religious ritual or drama, and such a rite may be thought to be pleasing to the spirits and an effective means of influencing them, even when it is recognized (except, perhaps, by the very simple-minded) to be a dramatic performance, and not taken to be literally "true". This at any rate appears to be the way in which the matter is regarded in twentieth century Bunyoro.[51]

While this use of "drama"—rather than "theatre"—may be ill-considered (a problem to be discussed further in Part III), Beattie's Bunyoro testimony may help to clarify the performer-audience relationship in *bori*.

As the trance performance reaches its denouement, the *iska* signals that it is ready to "dismount" (*sauka*)[52] by a sneezing or coughing fit which seizes the medium, after which she is now again herself, is addressed with her own name and resumes her usual social persona. Her performance may be followed by that of another medium or by a sequence of music. The gifts offered to the *iska* were traditionally distributed to the professional musicians of the ensemble as payment and were not seen as a source of income by the *masu bori*.[53] The medium's personal rewards presumably lay in the social control she acquired, the emotional catharsis of role-playing (not unlike that of psycho-therapeutic "psycho-drama"), and the physical stimulation of ecstatic frenzy. But today, with the commercialization of the public *bori* and its not uncommon use in the promotion of prostitutes, the cash nexus has replaced the earlier mode of relations. Gifts are now often viewed as payment to the medium rather than as an offering exclusively to the spirit.

III. Ritual and Drama: Intersections and Divergences

In this cursory description of the *bori* cult and its performance modes, one can clearly discern elements which are theatrical, shared at times by spirit mediumship, drama, story-telling, dance, and the secular ceremony. Indeed, it is quite common amongst anthropological researchers into mediumship to note the theatricality of many presentations. Beattie and Middleton write that frequently there is a

> dramatic quality of cult behaviour. Usually it involves dressing in unfamiliar, often striking and colourful, attire, the use of a special spirit language or vocabulary, and the assumption, often with notable histrionic skill, of a pattern of behaviour accepted as appropriate to the spirit supposed to be present. It appears that it is the act, the drama, that is believed to be therapeutically effective; whether there is actual possession or not is not neces-sarily the major consideration. It is significant that so many . . . scholars have stressed the dramatic quality of mediumship.[54]

Pierre Verger goes even further in describing the rituals of the Nago-Yoruba ancestor cult:

> These festivals give the impression of a theatrical performance or even an operetta. Their cast, costume, orchestral accompaniment, solo, and chorus differ little in spirit from the Mystery and Passion Plays enacted in medieval Europe in the forecourts of the cathe-drals. The salient difference is that in the present case the actors, if we may so call them, are in a state of trance.[55]

Similarly, Michel Leiria speaks of "La possession rituelle et ses aspects theatraux" in Ethiopia;[56] Alfred Metraux, of "la comedie rituelle dans la possession",[57] and Leo Frobenius, of *bori* as "a skilful conjuring performance".[58]

But one immediately notices in these comments an imprecision of nomenclature, a tendency to use interchangeably the words "theatre" and "drama", ignoring the fact that drama (except for the anomalous literary form, "closet" drama) is a sub-group of theatre with specific qualities, both formal and functional, which distinguish it from other sub-groups. This might be better illustrated with the Venn diagram (see fig. 1).

Where the theatricality of drama intersects the theatricality of the spirit medium ritual, the following in various forms, may appear in both:

a "theatre",
an audience,
"actors",
a communication,
character
dialogue (speech),
movement,
gesture,
dance,
song,
music,
costume and masks,
properties, and
scenic settings.

Many of these fall into what Aristotle called "melody" (*moles*) and "spectacle" (*opsis*), and quite rightly identified as amongst the less valuable qualities of theatre art, elements of medium and manner rather than of content.[59] But their coincidence demonstrates that the formal husks of drama and ritual may be quite similar, despite important divergences of substance and function.

Of these shared elements, movement, gesture, dance, song, music, costumes and masks, and scenic settings need no extended discussion and have been mentioned in passing above. It should also be clear that both drama and rituals like the public *bori* use some form of "theatre" area, in the original Greek sense of

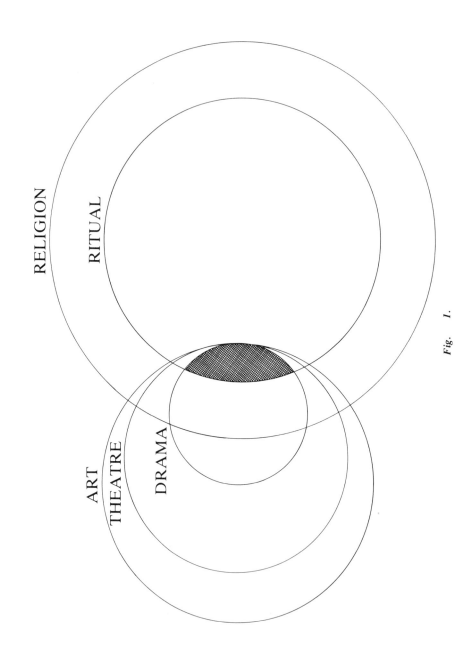

RELIGION

RITUAL

ART

THEATRE

DRAMA

Fig. 1.

theatron as a "seeing place". In both, an audience watch the performance but participate in it only to a limited degree. When the distinction between audience and participant entirely dissolves, the form has been transmuted and should no longer be called theatre, as there is no "seeing".[60]

This audience is presented with "characters", imagined people who can only appear and be active during a performance and are observable only as imitated by other people, by actors or mediums. The audience therefore simultaneously perceive two incompletely congruent beings, the bodily shell of the actor and the personality of the character.[61] These characters may speak and their "dialogue" may be amongst each other, or with the audience, or with characters unseen, and may even be in language incomprehensible to the audience. Of this last one may instance the medium's "speaking in tongues", Peter Brook's and Ted Hughes's "orghast" experiments,[62] and the distortedly vocalized antique Japanese of the Noh play. The characterization may also be augmented by stage properties, either naturalistic or symbolic, which help visually to identify the character. But in the case of the medium's properties, like the *tsere* of the *mai bori*, the object may have an extra-theatrical magical function, as, for example, the medium's receptor or the spirit's "vehicle".

There is, too, a communication achieved in both forms, whether between performer and audience, performer and spirit, or audience and spirit. But it is in the nature of this communication that we begin to see the most important divergences of drama and religious ritual. In ritual man attempts to communicate directly with the *supernatural*, with the world of forces beyond his control. Any communication he may make to the priest or the medium is not *to* that person but *through* him to the spirit, and it is through the medium that the supplicant is addressed by the spirit (hence the word "medium"). The diagram opposite illustrates these relationships.

In drama man communicates with *other men*. Human actors act upon and talk to other human actors, or to a human audience, which may even talk back to them. But the voices are always human, as are the perceiving ears and eyes. Whatever is being communicated is designed to be received not in the immaterial

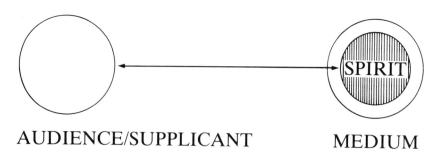

AUDIENCE/SUPPLICANT   MEDIUM

Fig.   2.

other-world but in the material human mind alone. Drama is, then, men acting out human situations for other men.[63]

Not only do the nexes of communication in the two forms differ, but so too do their operative functions. The ultimate end of ritual is to have an effect on the spirits, to make the god act. Even in *bori*, when human action may be guided as part of the *mai bori's* covert social manipulation,[64] it is so only upon the directive of a spirit and supported by that spirit's explicit threats The primary purpose, then, of ritual is magical effect.

But it is an effect only on man that drama works towards: to stimulate thought, feeling, perhaps even action in the human world alone. Even religious drama—plays on religious themes —is not magical but fundamentally human.

Ritual and drama also manifest differences in the role in each of the actors, in how the spectators see the actor and how he sees himself. In ritual the actor is seen either as a representative (a priest) or as another being entirely (a spirit). As a priest, he is rarely assumed to be someone or something other than human, but rather to be the repository of certain arcane knowledge and the skilled or even inspired master of magical processes. As a medium, he is presumed to become another entity, to cease entirely being himself. Whatever the degree of his dissociation, whatever the depth or duration of his trance, he is perceived by the audience, if not always by himself, as the spirit incarnate. He is therefore more profoundly involved in his "character" than is the actor of drama. Indeed, the stage actor must always be in complete control of his character, at a distance from it. He must never be possessed by it, never let it "ride" him as the *iska* rides its *godiya*. Part of the drama audience's pleasure derives from an awareness of this, of performance as conscious mimesis and of the performer as actor as well as character. The audience knows—and wants to know—that the actor is, after all, "only acting".

There is yet another area in which ritual and drama only rarely intersect, that of plot, of sustained, developed story enacted. Most ritual is not essentially story-showing, although it may sometimes involve bits of story, usually not fully enacted but rather recounted or recalled (in narration, recitation, oration, or song) and perhaps partly visualized in mime, dance, or tableaux.[65] Drama, conversely, is essentially a story form and, even at its most episodic, is plotted, is a narrative acted out.[66]

It is, therefore, in its spectacular, theatrical qualities that ritual most resembles drama, and in its capacity to entertain and give aesthetic pleasure, for these are present in even the most sombre of rituals. And, like most drama, most ritual is experienced communally encouraging a sense of community amongst members of the audience in addition to its more central purposes. But while it may in some ways be theatre, ritual is not drama. For, while *bori* and similar spirit medium displays demonstrate the kinds of human activities and compulsions which eventually generated dramatic art—and here one may cite the often noted relationship of Greek tragedy to the earlier Dionysian possession cult[67]—it has developed in a divergent direction, towards magical communication between man and the natural forces rather than worldly communication amongst men. It would greatly facilitate the understanding of both ritual and drama—religion and art—if generic distinctions between them are kept distinct.

Notes

1. E. T. Kirby, "Indigenous African Theatre", The *Drama Review* ("Indigenous Theatre Issue"), XVIII, 4, December 1974, 22.

2. Kirby, pp. 32–33. See Pierre Verger, "Trance and Convention in Nago-Yoruba Spirit Mediumship", in *Spirit Mediumship and Society in Africa*, ed. John Beattie and John Middleton, London, 1969, pp. 56–64.
3. Poetics, 1449a.
4. Richard Axton, *European Drama of the Early Middle Ages*, London, 1974, p. 12.
5. An interesting, if highly contentious, discussion of the "theatrogenic character" of cults and religions may be found in Benjamin Hunningher, *The Origin of the Theatre*, New York, 1961 (1955).
6. See Michael Onwuejeogwu, "The Cult of the Bori Spirits among the Hausa", in Beattie and Middleton, pp. 280, 288 et passim.
7. Fremont E. Besmer, "*Boorii:* Structure and Process in Performance", *Folio Orientalia*, XVI, 1975, pp. 101–130. A. V. King includes "other rural *arnaa*" ("pagans"), "A Boorii Liturgy from Katsina", *African Language Studies*, VII, 1966, p. 104. A. J. N. Tremearne claims it is also common amongst the Nupe and Egbirra, *Hausa Superstitions and Customs*, London, 1913, p. 149. P. O. Harris says it is closely related to the Yoruba *ofoshi*, "Notes on Yauri (Sokoto Province), Nigeria", *Journal of the Royal Anthropological Institute*, IX, 1930, p. 333.
8. See A. J. N. Tremearne, *The Ban of the Bori*, London, 1914, and Alhaji Hassan and Shuaibu Na'Ibi, *A Chronicle of Abuja*, trans. and ed. F. Heath, Lagos, 1962 (1952), pp. 64–66.
9. Onwuejeogwu, pp. 287, 293–295.
10. Onwuejeogwu, p. 288. Besmer 1975, points out the wide use of the Arabic word *aljan* in Kano, p. 102. See also Joseph Greenberg, *The Influence of Islam on a Sudanese Religion*, New York, 1946, passim.
11. Besmer, 1975, reports that *bori* is justified by its contemporary practitioners as "totally within the framework of Islam", p. 102. Onwuejeogwu argues that "the old pre-Islamic concepts of the world are now neatly interwoven with Muslim concepts, so much so that it is difficult to distinguish their respective strands very clearly", p. 281.
12. Onwuejeogwu says that male participants, except for the musicians, "are regarded as homosexual or impotent", p. 291. Beattie and Middleton point out that this female domination of a spirit cult is common in several cultures (they instance the Alur, Lugbara, and Bunyoro of Uganda, the Somali, the Segeju of Tanzania, and the Zulu of southern Africa), where it may lead to "an association . . . between male homosexuality, with transvestism, and spirit possession", "Introduction", in Beattie and Middleton, p. xxv.
13. Onwuejeogwu argues that in *bori*, women who occupy a subservient role in Hausa society and are legally minors (p. 281), experience in fantasy the trappings of officialdom and are thus able "temporarily (to) subdu(e) and humiliat(e) the world of men", p. 290. David W. Ames and Anthony V. King, in their *Glossary of Hausa Music and Its Social Context*, Evaston, 1971, note that the *bori* spirits are "headed by the spirit called *Sarkin Maka'da* ('The Chief of the Drummers'), in contra-distinction to the status hierarchy of real life", p. 117, in which musicians occupy the lowest

positions. The social contradictions behind these inversions resemble those which found expression in the medieval European role-playing festivals.

14. Ames and King, p. 117.
15. Hassan and Shuaibu Na'Ibi, p. 64, Besmer, 1975, p. 102.
16. King, p. 106. Harris divides the spirits into "active" (evil) and "passive" (good), p. 329.
17. Onwuejeogwu, p. 296.
18. Onwuejeogwu, p. 293.
19. Onwuejeogwu, p. 302.
20. Besmer counts ninety-nine active spirits and considers this "to be an important Muslim number rather than a *boorii* one, since there are ninety-nine beads on the Muslim rosary, symbolic of the names of Allah known to man". But he acknowledges that informants list nearly 275. "Avoidance and Joking Relationships Between Hausa Supernatural Spirits", *Studies in Nigerian Culture*, I, 1 (1973), 48n. Ibrahim Madauci, Yahaya Isa, and Bello Daura, in *Hausa Customs*, Zaria, 1968, claim that there are about 100 "devils", p. 79, and mention the gathering of "ninety-nine different roots" before the ritual can begin, p. 78. Onwuejeogwu lists, in his seven Tables, eighty-two spirits, pp. 293–303.
21. "Jangare" is so spelled by Besmer, 1973, p. 28 et passim, and 1975, p. 103, while Onwuejeogwu prefers "Jan gari", p. 287. This latter spelling suggests *aljan* ("jinn") and *gari* ("town") or "the town of the jinns".
22. Onwuejeogwu, p. 287.
23. "Theoretically, there are twelve compounds in Jangare, but many of these consist of two or three sub-sections", Besmer, 1973, p. 28.
24. Madauci et al., p. 83.
25. Onwuejeogwu, pp. 293–303.
26. Ames and King, pp. 62–63. See also Madauci et al., pp. 78, 82, 83: Besmer, 1975, pp. 103–104; King, p. 106.
27. Onwuejeogwu, p. 287; Harris, pp. 332–333.
28. See, for example, William James's early *The Varieties of Religious Experience*, Boston, 1902, the excellent bibliographies in Beattie and Middleton.
29. The neologisms (secret languages, "speaking in tongues", etc.) and the hearing of "voices" characteristic of hebephrenic schizophrenia, are often evident in spirit possession and mediumship. For discussions of these personality disorders, although not of their connections with religious ecstasy, see B. Maher, *Principles of Psychopathology: An Experimental Approach*, New York, 1966; H. C. Quay, ed., *Research in Psychopathology*, Princeton, 1963; C. Landis, *Varieties of Psychopathological Experience*, ed., F. A. Mettler, New York, 1964.
30. Firth, "Foreword", Beattie and Middleton, pp. x–xi.
31. Firth, p. xii.
32. Ibid.
33. Beattie and Middleton, xxvi. See also Beattie, "Spirit Mediumship in Bunyoro"; and Aidan Southall, Spirit Possession and Mediumship Among the Alur"; in Beattie and Middleton.

34. See Onwuejeogwu, pp. 281–285, 290–292.
35. See Alhaji Hassan and Shuaibu Na'Ibi, p. 64; Ames and King, p. 82, Onwuejeogwu, pp. 291–293; John N. Paden, *Religion and Political Culture in Kano*, Berkeley and Los Angeles, 1973, p. 47.
36. Besmer, 1975, pp. 103, 196.
37. Besmer, 1973, p. 27. I have here adjusted Besmer's Hausa spelling in order to standardize the orthography within this essay.
38. Besmer, 1975, p. 106.
39. Besmer, 1973, p. 27.
40. Onwuejeogwu, p. 286.
41. Ames and King, pp. 7, 8–9, 16, 41, 63, 70, 83–84, 109, 117.
42. Besmer, 1975, p. 104.
43. See Madauci et al., pp. 81–82.
44. Onwuejeogwu, p. 285. Comparable "symbolic objects" have been mentioned by Verger as common in the Nago-Yoruba spirit cult, p. 59.
45. Harris, p. 331.
46. Harris, pp. 331–332.
47. See Ames and King, p. 117; King, p. 106; Besmer, 1975, p. 103, Onwuejeogwu, p. 285. Similar mounting and horse metaphors have been noted by Robin Horton in the Kalabari *oru seki* ("spirit dancing") festivals, "Types of Spirit Possession in Kalabari Region", in Beattie and Middleton, p. 23; and by Verger in the Yoruba *orisha* cult, in which the medium may be called "*elegun orisha*" ("the one climbed on by the orisha") or *eshin orisha* ("horse of the *orisha*"), p. 50. The clearly erotic implications of this horse image in *bori* is of a piece with the cult's association with prostitution, with the intensity of its ecstasies, and with the various sexual role-inversions which are typical of the cult's practice.
48. See Onwuejeogwu, pp. 286, 293.
49. See Onwuejeogwu, pp. 287, 298.
50. Alhaji Hassan and Shuaibu Na'Ibi, p. 66; King, pp. 105, 107; Harris, pp. 332–333.
51. Beattie, p. 167.
52. Besmer, 1975, p. 103.
53. Harris, p. 332.
54. Beattie and Middleton, p. xxvi.
55. Verger, p. 64.
56. *La possession et ses aspects theatraux chez les Ethiopiens de Gondar*, Paris, 1958.
57. *Diogene*, 11, 1955.
58. Frobenius, *The Voice of Africa*, trans. Rudolf Blind, London, 1968, (1913), p. 563.
59. Poetics, 1450b.
60. See Axton on "theatre" and "game", p. 47.
61. This duality is central to the concerns of both Constantine Stanislavski and Bertolt Brecht. See Stanislavski, *An Actor Prepares*, trans. Elizabeth Reynolds Hapgood, London, 1937; and Brecht, "A Dialogue about Act-

ing" and "A Short Organum for the Theatre", in *Brecht on Theatre*, trans. and ed. John Willet, New York, 1964, pp. 26–29, 179–205.

62. See John Heilpern, *Conference of the Birds*, London, 1977, and A. C. H. Smith, *Orghast at Persepolis*, London, 1975.

63. "Human situations" here includes those enacted in the anthropomorphized animal—or god-play.

64. See Onwuejeogwu, p. 290.

65. Verger's description of the Nago-Yoruba cult enactments offer a striking exception to this. His transcript suggests a fully realized dramatic performance, with sustained dialogue exchanges and the situational development of interactions (plot), pp. 56–64. Indeed, the dialogue is so coherent that one wonders that it could really be performed by mediums in deep trance. His account seems good evidence for arguing a "mixed" genre of fully realized ritual-drama, although additional examples would be useful.

66. The student of theatre may find in the *kota koma nyaga* comedies of the Mande-speaking people of Mali an example of secular folk drama to contrast with the magical, spiritualist performances of *bori*. See Ruth Finnegan, *Oral Literature in Africa*, Oxford, 1970, pp. 505–509.

67. See Hunningher, pp. 29 ff.; Jane Harrison, *Ancient Art in Ritual*, London, 1948 (1913), pp. 135 ff.; Beattie and Middleton, p. xxvi; Beattie, p. 167.

A Selected Bibliography

1. *BORI*

Ames, David W. "A Sociological View of Hausa Musical Activity", in Harren L. D'Azevedo, ed., *The Traditional Artist in African Societies*, Bloomington, Indiana, 1972, pp. 128–161.

Ames, David and Anthony King. *Glossary of Hausa Music and Its Social Context*, Evaston, Ill., 1971.

Besmer, Fremont E. "Avoidance and Joking Relationships Between Hausa Supernatural Spirits", *Studies in Nigerian Culture*, I, 1, 1973, pp. 26–51.

——. "Praise-Epithets and Song Texts for Some Important Bori Spirits in Kano", *Harsunan Nijeriya*, 3, 1973.

——. "*Boorii:* Structure and Process in Performance", *Folia Orientalia*, XVI (1975, pp. 101–130).

Frobenius, Leo. *The Voice of Africa*, trans. Rudolf Blind, 2 vols., London, 1913.

Greenberg, Joseph. *The Influence of Islam on a Sudanese Religion*, Monographs of the American Ethnological Society, no. x, New York, 1946.

Harris, P. G. "Notes on Yauri (Sokoto Province), Nigeria", *Journal of the Royal Anthropological Institute*, LX, 1930, pp. 283–334.

Hassan, Alhaji and Shuaibu Na'Ibi. *A Chronicle of Abuja*, trans. and ed. F. Heath, Lagos, 1962 (1952).

King, A. V. "A Boorii Liturgy from Katsina: Introduction and Kiraaii Texts", *African Language Studies*, VII, 1966, pp. 105–125.

Kirby, E. T. "Indigenous African Theatre", *The Drama Review* ("Indigenous Theatre Issue"), XVIII 4, Dec., 1974, pp. 22–35.

Madauci, Ibrahim, Yahaya Isa, Bellow Daura. *Hausa Customs*, Zaria, Nigeria, 1968.

Onwuejeogwu, Michael. "The cult of *Bori* Spirits Among the Hausa", in Mary Douglas and Phyllis M. Kaberry, eds., *Man in Africa*, London, 1969, pp. 279–305.

Paden, John N. *Religion and Political Culture in Kano*, Berkeley and Los Angeles, 1973.

Palmer, H. R. "'Bori' Among the Hausa", *Man*, XIV, 52, July 1914, 116.

Price, J. H., "A Bori Lance in Accra", *West African Review*, Jan. 1957.

Reuke, Ludger. *Die Maguzawa in Mordnigeria*, Freiburger Studien za Politik und Gesellshaft uberseeischer Lander, Ban 4. Freiburg, 1969.

Smith, May. *Baba of Karo*, London, 1954.

Tremearne, A. J. N. *The Ban of the Bori*, London, 1914.

——. *Hausa Superstitions and Customs*, London, 1913.

——. *The Tailed Hunters of Nigeria*, London, 1912.

2. *SPIRIT POSSESSION*

Beattie, John. "Initiation into the Cwezi Spirit Possession Cult in Bunyoro", *African Studies*, XVI, 3, 1957.

——. "Ritual and Social Change", *Man*, new series I, 1, pp. 60–74.

——. "Spirit Mediumship in Bunyoro", in Beattie and Middleton, pp. 159–170.

—— and John Middleton, eds. *Spirit Mediumship and Society in Africa*, London, 1969.

Firth, Raymond. "Foreword", Beattie and Middleton, pp. ix–xiv.

——. "Ritual and Drama in Malay Spirit Mediumship", *Comparative Studies in Society and History*, IX, 1967, p. 190–207.

Gray, Robert F. "The Shetani Cult Among the Segeju of Tanzania", in Beattie and Middleton, pp. 171–187.

Harrison, Jane. *Ancient Art in Ritual*, London, 1948 (1913).

——. *Prolegomena to the Study of Greek Religion*, Cambridge, 1903.

Horton, Robin. "A Definition of Religion, and its Uses", *Journal of the Royal Anthropological Institute*, XC, 1960, pp. 201–226.

——. "Types of Spirit Possession in Kalabari Religion", in Beattie and Middleton, pp. 14–49.

Leiris, Michel. *La possession et ses aspects theatraux chez les Ethiopiens de Gondar*, Paris, 1958.

Metraux, Alfred. "La comedie rituelle dans la possession", *Diogene*, 11, 1955.

Southall, Aiden. "Spirit Possession and Mediumship Among the Alur", in Beattie and Middleton, pp. 232–272.

Thomson, George. *Aeschylus and Athens*, London, 1914.

Verger, Pierre. "Trance and Convention in Nago-Yoruba Spirit Mediumship", in Beattie and Middleton, pp. 50–66.

Zaretsky, Irving. *Bibliography on Spirit Possession and Spirit Mediumship*. Evanston, Ill., 1967.

TRANCE AND THEATRE:
THE NIGERIAN EXPERIENCE
Dapo Adelugba

The study of Trance and Theatre in the African context can be richly rewarding. The study of Trance itself as manifest in African religious, ritual and social practice is relatively new in the Western world. Beattie's book, *Spirit Mediumship and Society in Africa*, itself a pioneer work, only appeared in 1969.[1] In the introduction to the book, John Beattie and John Middleton submit thus:

> There is an immense literature on spirit mediumship, spirit possession, shamanism and related phenomena. Almost all of it relates to societies outside Africa, particularly to Asia and North America. The most comprehensive account is probably that by Eliade (1951). However, it contains relatively little African material, and it is not written from an anthropological or sociological viewpoint but rather from that of the historian or religion concerned with symbolic interpretation and the diffusion of items of culture . . . This volume of essays is an attempt to begin to fill this gap in the ethnography of Africa.[2]

If, as Beattie and Middleton rightly say, studies from anthropological and sociological viewpoints on this subject are few, those written from a theatrical point of view are even fewer. Pierre Verger's essay in Beattie's collection, "Trance and Convention in Nago-Yoruba Spirit Mediumship"[3] pays some attention to theatrical aspects of West African festivals and ritual practice. And Robin Horton's article, to some degree, does this too. African scholars of drama and theatre are exploring the field, but no full-scale studies have yet emerged on Trance and Theatre. The Dallas-based British scholar, Antony Graham-White, acknowledges the potential of such studies in his recently published *The Drama of Black Africa*,[4] but he wisely limits himself to speculations and careful restatement of other people's views. The present study too is exploratory and will be looked into in greater detail in the near future.

In this paper, I will look at the phenomenon of trance in three Nigerian societies: Hausa, Kalabari-Ijaw[5] and Yoruba, and relate this analogically to some of the Nigerian plays I am familiar with. I will end with some postulates about the interrelatedness of Trance and Theatre.

I will now discuss the phenomenon of trance in a well-established Hausa cult—the *Bori* cult—which I have had the opportunity of witnessing in Ibadan and aspects of which I have also seen at our Fourth National Festival of the Arts in Kaduna in December 1974.

I have largely relied on an essay, *The Cult of the Bori Spirits among the Hausa*[6] written by a Nigerian ethnographer, Michael Onwuejeogwu, and other publications on the subject of historical, social and cultural data. I am fully responsible for any errors of aesthetic judgement that may exist in this analysis. I have chosen to discuss the *BORI* in detail as this is one traditional practice in which possession and trance take a central place, and one in which movement and dance are paramount.

In his essay on the *BORI*, Michael Onwuejeogwu observes:

> In order to illustrate its dramatic and expressive character, I shall briefly describe a typical Bori dance. The woman puts on the colour appropriate to the spirit and in some cases carries the miniature symbolic object, bow or spear, etc., in her hand. She is now the spirit and acts as the spirit. If, for example, she is possessed by the spirit called Mallam Alhaji, she walks around bent and coughing weakly like an old learned mallam and reads an imaginary Koran. If she is possessed by Dan Galadima, the prince, she acts like a nobleman wearing kingly robes. She sits on a mat hearing cases, and people around make obeisance. If she is possessed by *Mai-gangaddi*, "The nodding one", who causes sleeping sickness, she dances and suddenly dozes off in the middle of some act and wakes up and sleeps again and wakes, etc. If possessed by *Ja-ba-Fari*, "neither red nor white", a spirit that causes people to go mad, she eats filth and simulates copulation. . . . In some cases she leaps into the air and lands on her buttocks with feet astride—thrice. She falls exhausted and is covered with a cloth. During this state she may foretell the future. Spectators

wishing to obtain a favour from or appease the spirit that has mounted her, place their gifts and alms on the mat. Then she sneezes, the spirit quits her, and she becomes normal. During this period she is never referred to as herself but as the spirit.

Bori dances are held in time of national or communal crisis such as epidemics, the abandonment of an old town or the establishment of a new one, crop failure, lack of rain, when opening new and closing old markets, and on market days. (M. Smith 1954: 218–22; M. G. Smith 1962.)

A woman starts from the event of possession by first screaming loudly. Immediately other Bori women living around hear the shrill cry, they proceed to the scene and in a matter of moments the inner compound is converted into a small Bori stage.

The women sing and beat calabashes turned upside down, while the originator and some other become possessed, each Bori dancing and acting according to the character of the spirit possessing her. *Borin gida* is correlated with the occurrence of crises in the marital life-cycle of the female occupants of the compound—marriage, death, illness, birth, ceremonials, quarrels and divorce.[7]

As may perhaps be inferred from the above, there are two varieties of Bori ritual, the public and the private. The Bori stage in public for the public is known as *Borin jama'u*: it is more elaborate than the *Borin gida* staged by individuals, in compounds, for personal purposes.

The musicians in the Bori cult are males and they consist of fiddlers, guitarists, and calabash-rattlers. Each spirit has its own music, praise-song and other special songs. The musicians occupy one part of the "performing" arena with mats spread in front of them. From behind the musicians, the *MASU BORI* emerge, in turn, to dance.

A few terms must now be explained. The *Masu Bori* are the Spirit Owners; the *Yan Bori* are Spirit Children. *Dwakin Bori* (literally, "Horses of Spirits") is the name used for those possessed by the Bori. To be possessed is to be mounted by a spirit, if male, and as a mare (*godiya*) if female. The spirit mounts the head of the possessed through a miniature object called *tsere* (a bow, for instance) which most *Masu Bori* carry. The spirit rides the person and the possessed is synonymous with the spirit for the duration of the possession. And so the Hausa will say, without any difference in meaning, either that the spirit mounts the person or that the person mounts the spirit. It should perhaps be pointed out that no pejorative connotations are attached to the terms "horse" and "mount", as the horse is a noble animal in Hausa society and indeed a symbol of aristocracy.[8]

The Bori cult, as currently practised, is more a female affair than a male one. To account fully for this fact would take more space than present exigencies of space would allow. However, it should be pointed out that current Bori practice is very different from the original manifestations of olden times in which men and women, it is believed, participated on a basis of near-equality. With Islamization, especially in the last century, there has been a rapid change in the status of women in the society. According to the school of Islamic law followed in the North of Nigeria, Hausa women, being legal minors, must not hold political office: their proper place is in the home. Their pre-Islamic political, legal and economic freedom virtually lost, dependent economically and legally on husband or kin, secluded inside the compound, women came to use the Bori as a weapon for subverting male dominance. As Onwuejeogwu writes:

> In Bori Hausa women experience in fantasy the trappings of officialdom. They experience the world of men, the world of political power, and the world of supposed splendour that society has denied them.[9]

Bori is also an occasion for self-display and a mechanism for expressing or suppressing rivalry between co-wives and strains and stresses in the marital relationship. Bori is, in addition, an opportunity for courtship. These aspects of the cult are generally believed to predate Islamic worship. However, as Onwuejeogwu points out, although in pre-Islamic days divorce was easily obtained by women, this is no longer the case:

> Indeed, the situation now is that, in order to escape from an irksome marriage, a wife has to run away from her husband's compound, taking refuge with a *Magajiya* (Bori cult leader). While waiting to gain a legal hearing for her case against her

husband, the refugee wife takes advantage of the public displays which Bori dancing affords. And if divorce is thus almost synonymous with Bori, these circumstances have stimulated a new pattern of courtly prostitution based on Bori. The *Magajiya* thus assumed a double role—at once local leader of the *Masu Bori*, and keeper of a brothel.[10]

Let us now look briefly at the ecological aspect of the Bori. Hausaland, like much of Africa, experiences epidemics and diseases such as cerebrospinal meningitis, relapsing fever, undulant fever, louse-borne typhus, sleeping sickness, leprosy, mental illness, heat exhaustion, eye disorders and various skin diseases. The symptoms of these diseases have many common features such as sudden onset, rapid rise in temperature, headache, rigour, weakness, giddiness, nausea, vomiting, convulsions and delirium. It is a matter of interest that these diseases are commonly attributed to Bori spirits, and the Bori dancers simulate their symptoms. It may also be noted that Hausa economic activities—agriculture, crafts and commerce—feature in Bori. Discussing Bori in relation to social change, Onwuejeogwu points out that some European spirits have been added to the Bori cosmology.[11] He also points out the use of Bori music and dance for self-display and sexual advertisement in the rapidly increasing brothels in urban areas. Writes Onwuejeogwu,

> From 1950, with the rise in nationalism the development of political parties in Hausaland, and the re-definition of the concept of freedom and individualism, Bori again took a new trend. The *Magajiya* and her followers became the core organization of the women's wing of political parties and rallies. These women now use Bori dance and music not only to win more clients but also to win over members for the political parties they support. These women, under the leadership of the *Magajiya*, are mostly practising prostitutes, new divorcees, those waiting to be granted a divorce, runaway girls, and the new girls from the rural areas seeking fortune and excitement in the urban areas.[12]

And now, if we look at Segi's women in Wole Soyinka's *Kongi's Harvest*, we shall find that they fit into these categories. Segi may be seen as a kind of *Magajiya* leading her political fortress of a night club as a counter-force to Kongi's tyrannical regime. The nightly vigil at Segi's club may be seen as prototypes of the *Borin Jama'u* in one sense and the *Borin gida* in another. The women's "performance" at the Harvest Square has the intensity, conviction and force of a *Borin gida* in its pristine, pre-Islamic fullness and glory. The climax of their "performance" comes at the end of the *Second Part*:

> The rhythm of pounding emerges triumphant, the dance grows frenzied. . . . Segi returns, disappears into the area of pestles. A copper salver is raised suddenly high; it passes from hand to hand above the women's heads; they dance with it on their heads; it is thrown from one to the other until at last it reaches Kongi's table and Segi throws open the lid. . . .[13]

Indeed the entire play, exluding the "Hangover", may be seen as a sustained Bori rite with all the entranced characters acting in consonance with the spirit they are possessed by. For, in a sense, Kongi, Danlola, Daodu, the Organizing Secretary, Sarunmi and the rest are entranced creatures, and Soyinka's comment in "Hangover" can be used to validate this interpretation. If Segi and Daodu are, by the Secretary's testimony, "mad",[14] "Roadside lunatics",[15] Danlola also thinks, Myself I drank from the stream of madness for a while.[16] Kongi is undoubtedly the most prototypically "Bori" of all the male characters in the play:

> Kongi, getting progressively inspired harangues his audience. He exhorts, declaims, reviles, cajoles, damns, curses, vilifies, excommunicates, execrates until he is a demonic mass of sweat and foam at the lips.[17]

No less than Segi's women are Daodu's farmers (*metallic lunatics*)[18] a cult group, and Kongi's Carpenters' Brigade are desperadoes who would dare the devil himself when mounted by the spirit of Kongi-ism. Their anthem is a good lead:

> Our hands are like sandpaper
> Our fingernails are chipped
> Our lungs are filled with sawdust
> But our anthem still we sing
> We sweat in honest labour
> From sunrise unto dawn
> For the dignity of labour

And the progress of our land.
For Kongi is our father
And Kongi is our man
Kongi is our mother
And Kongi is our Saviour
Redeemer, prince of power
For Isma and for Kongi
We're proud to live or die.[19]

Before we get too embroiled in Wole Soyinka's *Kongi's Harvest* and the Hausa Bori practice, let us move on to another part of Nigeria and consider spirit possession and trance among the Kalabari and Ijaw peoples. In a term paper/demonstration presented at the Arts Theatre in June 1975, Mr. Bob Manuel, then a second year student in our Department of Theatre Arts at the University of Ibadan, discussed the *Orukoro* possession dance, a ritual of the Ijaw people of Nigeria. Mr. Bob Manuel also presented for his design project a model of *Orukoro*.[20]

Orukoro is a "performance" of rites of worship of the deities of the sea—the mermaids. It is a popular religious movement which attributes the creative and controlling force of man's life to the mermaids or *Mammywota* as they are sometimes called. This phenomenon, however, is not exclusively Ijaw, as many other African communities, especially those inhabiting riverine areas, have some form of worship or other associated with the mystery beneath the water's surface.

Osun, for instance, is a deity of the Yoruba people related to the River Osun. What is important to note, however, is that it is primarily functional as a medium of expression of the people's beliefs. "Orukoro" therefore transcends the mere entertainment or secular function. The dance is essentially a performance of worship in supplication to the deity or in appeasement for a foreseen evil.

The Ijaw people in general have most of their deities associated with existence beneath the sea. *Mammywota* are referred to as *Oru* by the Kalabari people. There are several *Orus*, and each forms a deity making up the Kalabari pantheon. Robin Horton has done a great deal of work on the Kalabari, but the narrow scope of this paper does not permit more than brief, passing references to his monumental studies.[21]

Orukoro includes the worship of deities like *Okpolodo* (symbolized by the python) and *Adun* (also symbolized by the python).

Mermaids have been known among the Ijaws to betroth themselves to human beings of their choice. The deities here have sexes. Therefore, if it is a male deity, he betroths himself to a woman while the female deity betroths herself to a man. This is said to be due to the amorousness of these supernatural beings. Those to whom they are betrothed then become their chief priests, gifted with the inner eye for seeing into both the future and existence beyond the plane of the physical. At definite seasons of the choice of the god, the priest or priestess (*ORUKOROBO*) is possessed by the god. The possessed is consequently transformed into the essence of the god himself or the goddess herself, and during the trance, characterized by ritual sacrifices, incantations, music, song and dance, the possessed is capable of the prophet's sight, communicating with man as a first-person representative of the deity.

With the inspiration of the possessed, the worshippers who are versed in knowledge and are on constant vigil assemble and sing the praise-songs and chants of the god, while the possession deepens gradually into ecstasy. The possessed is thus transformed into the essence of the god. Thus a priestess who in ordinary life is known to be very effeminate, old and weak, can be transformed into a fierce, agile, bold and awe-inspiring character capable of commanding the whole worship.

This explains the initial down-to-earth personal dance of the priest or priestess who is soon to be possessed. During this stage the personality of the performer is still distinctly individual. Communication with fellow humans is possible and still obtains. But when the trance is achieved the possessed becomes oblivious of all existence, even of himself or herself. The musical instruments, consisting chiefly of graded tonal instruments of waterpots, play the special tunes of the worship of the particular deity, while worshippers chant or sing and clap to a point of hysterical involvement.

The priest or priestess made up with white paintings of ritualistic clay chalk on the face and body, is often dressed in two colours principally—WHITE and RED—most often a white band around the bust and another knee-length white loincloth worn on the waist and tapped with another thigh-length red cloth. Usually a coral bead hat is worn or some Indian bells are worn on the wrists and ankles. Coral beads are also worn on the neck and balanced in one palm is a saucer containing a fresh egg, some alligator pepper and, or, kolanuts and coins which significantly are part of the sacrificial offerings. In the other hand is an elephant tusk symbolic of authority.[22]

During this ecstatic possession, the priest or priestess prophesies with the voice of the god or goddess. Sometimes there are punishments meted out to the body of the priest or priestess during the process. On this occasion, the deity may choose to teach its lesson through strangulation. The possessed is thus contorted or strangled by unseen hands and there is no salvation except in the appeasement of the deity. This is the case when the possessed is the offender.

In the light of this analysis of *Orukoro*—a play like John Pepper Clark's tragedy, *Song of a Goat* (written in 1960 and first published in 1962),[23] starts to reveal multiple levels of meaning and significance, some of which have informed the present writer's three productions of it (in Los Angeles in 1963,[24] in Painesville, Ohio in 1964[25] and in Ibadan—at the Ibadan Grammar School[26]—in 1966).

Orukorere (the name is not accidental) is in a state of trance during large portions of the action. Tonye and Ebiere's incestuous love-act can be more readily accepted if we realize that they are in a state of trance during that section of the play. Tonye (the offender) suffers strangulation as in the traditional ritual. Zifa, who is also entranced at certain times during the play, walks into the sea.

My choreographic realization of the Ebiere-Tonye love-scene has, in my productions, emphasized their entranced states, and J. P. Clark's poetry in this section of the play has facilitated this kind of interpretation:

TONYE: Why, Ebiere, you are mad, so gone far
                Leaves-gathering, and you are hot all
                Over, oh so shuddering, shuddering
                So, you want to pull me down which is

A thing forbidden, now take that then, and
that—Oh my father!
EBIERE: So I am crazed, completely gone leaves-plucking
And you? Aren't you shuddering too, Oh,
So shuddering in you heat of manhood you
Have thrown me? Now, hold me, do hold on and
Fight, for it is a thing not forbidden
(*Cocks crow beyond.*)[27]

The short "cleansing" scene in the Fourth Movement[28] has the
veracity and ardour of the traditional "Orukoro" ritual but the
entire play can be (and indeed, one would suggest, should be)
performed like sequences in a traditional ritual.

"In Kalabari communities today", says Robin Horton in his
essay "Types of Spirit Possession in Kalabari Religion", "one can
see several kinds of possession behaviour in addition to the
traditional ones . . . —notably the various kinds associated with
the powerful and ever-proliferating separatist churches".[29]

The latter comment leads us naturally to consider Wole
Soyinka's use of possession and trance in his *The Trials of Brother
Jero*. The Penitent's fainting comes at the end of ecstatic dancing:
she is mounted by the spirit of God, or so it is believed. Her
performance lends variety to the congregational worship at the
beach with Chume as temporary officiator due to Jero's exit in
pursuance of one of the "Daughters in Discord".[30]

(*Jero is already out of hearing. Chume is obviously bewildered by
the new responsibility. He fiddles around with the rod and eventually uses it to conduct the singing, which has gone on all this time,
flagging down when the two contestants came in view, and reviving
again after they had passed.*
     *Chume has hardly begun to conduct his band when a woman
detaches herself from the crowd in the expected penitent's par-
oxysm.*)

PENITENT: Echa, echa, echa, echa, echa . . . . eei,
eei, eei, eei.
CHUME: (*taken aback*) Ugh? What's the matter?
PENITENT: Efie, efie, efie, efie, efie, enh, enh, enh,
enh . . . .
CHUME: (*dashing off*) Brother Jeroboam, Brother
Jeroboam . . .

(*Chume shouts in all directions, returning confusedly each time in an attempt to minister to the penitent. As Jeroboam is not forthcoming, he begins, very uncertainly, to sprinkle some of the water on the penitent, crossing her on the forehead. This has to be achieved very rapidly in the brief moment when the penitent's head is lifted from beating on the ground.*)

CHUME: (*stammering*) Father . . . forgive her.
CONGREGATION: (*strongly*) Amen.

(*The unexpectedness of the response nearly throws Chume, but then it also serves to bolster him up, receiving such support.*)

CHUME: Father, forgive her.
CONGREGATION: Amen.

(*The penitent continues to moan.*)

CHUME: Father, forgive her.
CONGREGATION: Amen.
CHUME: Father, forgive her.
CONGREGATION: Amen.
CHUME: (*Warming up to the task*) Make you forgive 'am father.

                  . . . .
                  Save us from trouble at home. Tell our wives not to get us trouble. (*The penitent has become placid. She is stretched out flat on the ground.*)[31]

Obviously there is a lot of work in this scene apart from the Penitent's possession, fits and fainting, but these are used as counterpoint by the adept playwright. When Brother Jero returns, bruised and battered from his encounter with the Tough Mamma, it is significantly the Penitent who has totally recovered from her trance, and who has since resumed her participation in the service, who recognizes him from a distance:

PENITENT: (*Who has become much alive from the latter part of the prayers, pointing . . .*) Brother Jeroboam![32]

Considering Brother Jero's lascivious looks at women it might be argued that the possession and trances of members of his congregation could be seen as their way of drawing the prophet's attention to them. (Some analogy with the functional use of Bori in Hausa practice suggests itself here.) But that is not our main concern now. What we wish to emphasize is Soyinka's use of trance in the theatrical medium which is a pointer to what can be done on a more ambitious scale by future dramatists on the African continent.

Looking at other Soyinka plays,[33] one finds equally exciting use in them of possession and trance. In *The Road*, for example, Samson, enacting Sergeant Burma, becomes possessed by Burma's "spirit" and enters momentarily into a trance out of which he has to shake himself, tearing off Sergeant Burma's clothes which he had put on to make his "acting" more realistic:

> (*Samson's face begins to show horror and he gasps as he realizes what he had been doing.*)

> SAMSON: (*tearing off the clothes*) God forgive me! Oh God, forgive me. Just see, I have been fooling around pretending to be a dead man. Oh God I was only playing I hope you realize. I was only playing.[34]

The Professor in *The Road* falls regularly into a state of trance; his mortal struggle with Say Tokyo Kid at the end of the play may be seen as a fight between two entranced people, and the Professor's final speech acquires greater force when seen as the statements of a "possessed" person. The enigmatic Murano is probably in a trance all through the action of the play, for, as the Professor, he has one leg in each world.

Even an early Soyinka play like *The Swamp Dwellers* lends itself to interpretations along the lines of possession and trance. Igwezu's litany during his question-answer confrontation may be seen as the inspired utterance of one possessed by his ancestor-spirit, for he begins significantly:

> Can you see my mask, priest? Is it of this village?
> (Yes.)
> Was the word grown in this village?
> (Yes.)
> Does it sing with the rest? Cry with the rest?
> Does it till the swamps with the rest of the tribe?[35]

When the litany is over, and the Kadiye, having proved himself an utterly corrupt and unworthy leader of the village, has run out of Makuri's house, Igwezu says with the conviction and inspired assurance of a divine:

> I know that the flood can come again. That the swamp will continue to laugh at our endeavours. I know that we can feed the serpent of the Swamp and kiss the Kadiye's feet—but the vapours will still rise and corrupt the tassels of the corn.[36]
> In a tired voice he says to his confidante, the Beggar:
> I wonder what drove me on
> ....
> Do you think that my only strength was that of despair?
> Or was there something of a desire to prove myself?[37]

We would like to suggest that perhaps there was something more—the strength of his ancestor-spirit—which made Igwezu, for the brief period of his confrontation with Kadiye, the Voice of the Village.

We shall now move on to make a few brief comments about possession and spirit mediumship among the Yoruba traditional ritual practices, but the phenomenon of trance as related to theatre is yet a subject for future systematic study. Pierre Verger in his essay, "Trance and Convention in Nago-Yoruba Spirit Mediumship", has indicated the all-pervasiveness of possession in traditional religious practice in Eastern Nigeria as well as in Dahomey. The theatricality of behaviour under a state of possession is stressed in his essay:

> *Ogun* (Yoruba) or *Gun* (Fon), god of blacksmiths, warriors, hunters, and all who was iron, is characterized by coarse and energetic manners; *Shango* (Yoruba), or *Hevioso* (Fon), god of thunder, by manly and jolly dances; *Orishala* (Yoruba), or *Lisa* (Fon), the creator god, by calm and serene behaviour; *Shapana* (Yoruba) or *Sapata* (Fon), god of Smallpox and the contagious diseases, by restless agitation; *Eshu Elegba* (Yoruba) or *Legba* (Fon), messenger of the other gods, by cynical and abusive attitudes. These examples show just a part of the total range of behaviour which the "horse of the gods" may adopt.[38]

Verger says of Yoruba-Negro festivals, *apropos* of our theme:

These festivals give the impression of a theatrical performance or even an operetta. Their cast, costume, orchestral accompaniment, solo and chorus differ little in spirit from the Mystery and Passion plays enacted in medieval Europe in the forecourts of the cathedrals. The salient difference is that in the present case the actors, if we may so call them, are in a state of trance.[39]

And it is the entranced quality of the performers in Duro Ladipo's *Oba Koso*[40] (especially in the version which recently toured the United States of America and Brazil) that recommends the production to audience both local and foreign.[41] Which perhaps would suggest that, in our particular kind of drama, directors and actor-trainers should seek inspiration for their work, among other sources, in the traditional phenomenon of trance and possession. For after all, the actor, to operate most effectively, should appear to be "possessed" (though not mastered) by his role.

That traditional festivals and rituals have influenced the form, content and structure of the artistic products of our national playwrights such as Wole Soyinka, Duro Ladipo, Hubert Ogunde, John Pepper Clark, Ola Rotimi, Wale Ogunyemi and 'Zulu Sofola is an undisputed fact. What is now being recommended is a more scientific study by drama and theatre scholars and a more coherent and meaningful use of our traditional inheritance by theatre directors and actor-trainers.

There is an element of "theatre" in trance as manifested in traditional African ritual and festival practice. How much is real and how much "acted" in the trances of the possessed is often difficult to determine. If trance has borrowed from theatre, as it quite clearly has done, we are suggesting that theatre can and should borrow from the veracity and soulfulness of trance.

Notes

1. John Beattie and John Middleton, (ed.) *Spirit Mediumship and Society in Africa*, London, Routledge and Kegan Paul, 1969.
2. Ibid., p. xvii.
3. Ibid., pp. 50–68.
4. Anthony Graham White, *The Drama of Black Africa*, New York, Samuel French, Inc., 1974, pp. 20–23 especially.
5. The Kalabari and Ijaw are two different ethnic groups some of whose traditional ritual practices are similar.

6. In Mary Douglas and Phyllis M. Kabberry, (ed.) *Man in Africa*, London, Tavistock Publications, 1969, pp. 279–306.
7. Ibid., pp. 286–287.
8. The terms "horse" and "mount" are not unlike what exists in the case of Voodoo. In a seminal essay which appeared in Diogenes in 1955, entitled "Dramatic Elements in Ritual Possession", by Alfred Metraux, he wrote as follows: "The relation between the god and the man of whom he has taken possession is comparable to that of a horseman to his mount. Thus it is said that the god 'mounts' or saddles his (cheval). Possession being closely associated with the dance, the image of a 'spriit which dances in the head of its horse' is used. The invader is a supernatural being who takes possession of the body; hence the current expression: 'the *loa* (the spirit) seizes his horse" (Editor).
9. Ibid., p. 290.
10. Ibid., p. 291.
11. Ibid., p. 292.
12. Ibid., p. 292.
13. Wole Soyinka, *Kongi's Harvest*, London, O.U.P., 1967, pp. 83–84.
14. Ibid., p. 89.
15. Ibid.
16. Ibid.
17. Ibid., p. 83.
18. Ibid., p. 71.
19. Ibid., p. 65.
20. The cooperation of Mr. Bob Manuel, and the Tutors of Dance (Miss Fidelma Okwesa) and Design (Mrs. Danielle Lyndersay) at the Department of Theatre Arts, University of Ibadan, is gratefully acknowledged.
21. Robin Horton's work includes, among others, 1962 "The Kalabari world view: an outline and interpretation", *Africa*, 32, (3), 197–220; 1963, "The Kalabari *Ekine* Society: a borderline of religion and art", *Africa*, 33, (2), 94–144; "Kalabari diviners and oracles", *Odu* I (I); 1965 "Duminea: a Festival for the Water-Spirits", *Nigeria Magazine*, no. 86; 1969 "Types of Spirit Possession in Kalabari Religion", Mary Douglas and Phyllis M. Kabberry, (ed.) *Man in Africa*, op. cit., pp. 14–49.
22. See model built by Mr. Bob Manuel for his final Design Project in a course in the Department of Theatre Arts, University of Ibadan.
23. The edition used for reference in this paper is in J. P. Clark, *Three plays*, London, Oxford University Press, 1964.
24. A production done with Black students (African, Afro-American and Caribbean) of the University of California, Los Angeles, and mounted at the Presbyterian Church in Westwood, Los Angeles.
25. A production done with theatre students (female) and members of the Painesville Community (male) at the Department of Theatre, Painesville College, Painesville, Ohio.
26. The present writer was a tutor of English and Drama at the Ibadan Grammar School, Ibadan, from January 1965 to August 1967.

27. Op. cit., pp. 27–28.
28. Ibid., pp. 33–42.
29. *Man in Africa*, op. cit., p. 14.
30. *Wole Soyinka, Three Short Plays*, London, Oxford University Press, 1969.
31. Ibid., pp. 62–63.
32. Ibid., p. 64.
33. The final set of speeches of Aafaa and Old Man in Wole Soyinka's *Madmen and Specialists*, London, Methuen, 1971, pp. 71–77, may be seen as speeches by entranced characters.
34. Wole Soyinka, *The Road*, London, Oxford University Press, Ibadan, 1965, p. 83.
35. Wole Soyinka, *Three Short Plays*, op. cit., p. 37.
36. Ibid., p. 39.
37. Ibid., p. 40.
38. *Man in Africa*, op. cit., p. 51.
39. Ibid., p. 64.
40. Published in Yoruba and English by the Institute of African Studies, University of Ibadan, in 1972. A disc of this version has also been made.
41. It is felt that some of the qualities of the 1972 version have been dispensed with in the current version, but that is a matter beyond the scope of this paper.

PART III
TRADITIONAL THEATRE
II: The Popular Tradition

"ALARINJO": THE TRADITIONAL YORUBA TRAVELLING THEATRE

J. A. Adedeji

Background

The first accounts of the Alarinjo, the traditional Yoruba travelling theatre, are contained in the journals of Hugh Clapperton and Richard Lander.[1] To mark their seven weeks' stay in Old Oyo (Katunga), the capital of the Oyo (Yoruba) empire, the Alaafin (king) of Oyo, invited his guests to see a performance provided by one of the travelling theatre troupes which at that time was waiting on the king's pleasure. The time was Wednesday, February 22, 1826.[2]

The Alarinjo theatre first emerged from the dramatic roots of the *egungun* (masquerade) as ancestor worship[3] and during the reign of Alaafin Ogbolu, who acceded to the throne at Oyo Ighoho about 1590,[4] as a court entertainment.

Alaafin Ogbolu, otherwise called Abipa,[5] was the fourth and last king in exile. He made a firm resolve to remove the seat of government back to Katunga, the ancient capital. But he did not find things easy. Most of his people, especially those who had been born in exile, could not be easily persuaded to accept the fact that returning to Oyo was a worthwhile proposition and venture. Ighoho had been well settled and had given a firm security to those who had spent a good part of their early lives wandering around the marshes of Borgu and Nupe on the lower banks of the Niger. The Oyo-Mesi, the king's council, was strongly opposed to the move. When they knew that the king could not be persuaded to change his mind, they resolved on using the element of disguise as a stratagem to foil the attempted move.

The Alapinni, one of the Oyo-Mesi and the representative of the Egungun Society on the king's council, was the brain behind the dramatic strategy. They knew that, as was customary, the king

221

would send emissaries to inspect the abandoned sites, propitiate the gods, and make sacrifices before the final move-in took place. As they were resolved on thwarting the king's will, they thought the move could be stopped by frightening the emissaries off the old sites by a company of ghost-mummers. They got masked actors (or ghost-mummers) ready and secretly despatched them to Old Oyo to precede the king's emissaries.

There were six stock-characters, each representing a councillor; the hunchback (Basorun), the albino (Alapinni), the leper (Asipa), the prognathus (Samu), the dwarf (Laguna) and the cripple (Akiniku).[6] Their presence at the sites, indeed, frightened the first batch of emissaries on the hill, Ajaka. "Abipa was at first distressed, but the Ologbo, the royal cymbalist and aroken (arokin), who had some inkling of the truth, advised him to send a group of trustworthy men from Ighoho to investigate the matter. Six famous hunters set out and they soon rounded up the bogus phantoms."[7] The king's Ologbo (Ologbin) would certainly be privy to the secret design of the councillors, he himself being a member of the Egungun Society. But his decision to reveal the secret of the cult in this regard might have gone to strengthen the clash of interests and personalities that had existed between the two clans which had been uneasily wedded together to form the society. Thus, the strategy of the reluctant councillors was destroyed and the king earned the nickname "Oba Moro" (The king who caught ghosts).[8]

On the king's orders the ghost-mummers were brought to court and placed in the charge of his Ologbo (Ologbin). They lived "in a special building within the Afin"[9] to entertain the king. At the weekly meeting of the king and his councillors for the Jakuta sacrifices, they retired into the banqueting hall for the usual refreshments that followed the religious ceremonies. Here, the king, in a mood to surprise the councillors, arranged for a show in which the ghost-mummers waited upon their creators! The councillors were dumbfounded by this but they took the show good-humouredly and departed. Those they thought to have been playing the "ghosts" at Old Oyo were in fact in the king's palace as a band of entertainers! The king thereafter called for a public performance of the ghost-mummers to enact the story of the "Ghost Catcher" under the management of Ologbin, his Ologbo. The councillors having been greatly incensed planned to ruin the show by evoking rain. But Ologbin stopped the heavy downpour, and his mummers carried through their improvisations with dances and chants. Upon this feat, he was hailed "Ologbo Ojo" (the king's Ologbo who has control of the rain!). From then on Ologbin became popularly called "Ologbojo".

The concillors could never forgive Ologbin for defying the *egungun* cult. Apart from revealing their secret plan of using the cult to stop the king from carrying out his plan to return to Old Oyo, he had blatantly converted to his own use, as a court entertainer, the six ghosts they had created. Nobody could so treat the cult with disdain and get away with it. They finally succeeded in their attempt and Ologbin Ologbojo died from their poison.[10] The king, saddened by the unfortunate end of Ologbojo, and "in order to show his love and esteem for the deceased, ordered for him a semi-state funeral, and had his body wrapped in an ass's skin to be taken to Oyo for interment".[11] When the final move back to Old Oyo was completed, Ologbojo's body was buried in a court dedicated to his memory and called Ode Ogboluke—Eni ti Ogbolu fi Ode-Ile ke (one whom Ogbolu honoured with a court).

The story of the "Ghost Catcher" was re-enacted at Oyo three times annually: firstly, during the Orisa Oko (farm god) festival; secondly, during the festival of Orisa Mole; and thirdly, at the Oduduwa festival. It was also enacted during the installation of a new Alaafin when it takes place privately in the royal reception hall (Aganju) at night.[12]

Old Oyo was reoccupied in the twentieth year of the king's reign, about 1610.[13] By the middle of the seventeenth century, the "Oje" or "egungun apidan", the names by which the ghost-mummers came to be called, had become well established at court. The group also took part in the annual *egungun* festival when commanded by the Alagbaa, the cultic head of the Egungun Society.

Thus, Ologbin Ologbojo founded the Alarinjo theatre. A worshipper of Obatala[14] and of the Oba clan, it is claimed that it was on account of his hybrid[15] son, Olugbere Agan, that he established the theatre as a permanent part of court entertainments. To launch him, Ologbin Ologbojo got Olojowon, the master carver, to carve a wooden face mask and Alaran Ori, the costumer, to build a set of costumes. With these Olugbere Agan careered as a costumed actor and a strolling player. Ologbojo himself served him as the masque-dramaturge or animator who handled the improvisations while the Akunyungba, the palace rhapsodists, provided the choral chants.

The Alarinjo theatre began as a lineage profession but with the demise of Ologbin Ologbojo, his mantle as head of court entertainments fell on Esa Ogbin, a maternal relation and to whom professionalism in masque-dramaturgy has been traced.[16] He was nicknamed Ologbojo and honoured to live in "Ode Ogboluke", the court set aside for the palace entertainment officer by Alaafin Ogbolu. Esa Ogbin has, in consequence, become the progenitor of all those who have taken to the profession of masque-dramaturgy. During the performance, every masque-dramaturge salutes him and submits his pledge. In consequence of Esa Ogbin's inspiration when evoked, masque-dramaturges have come to be known as *ap'esa* (called on Esa Ogbin).[17]

Esa Ogbin's troupe and repertoire surpassed those of Ologbin Ologbojo; while the latter had only entertained the court, flattered and amused the governing class, Esa Ogbin took the theatre to the masses, the grassroots. Through him the theatre became popular and attracted people from other lineages who wanted masque-dramaturgy as a career.

The masques flourished within a guild system which helped to ensure that the secrets of the art did not pass beyond the lineages which followed it. There never really emerged an all-embracing guild or actors' union until much later, and individualism markedly distinguished one lineage guild from another. Even though each group watched the others jealously and quickly picked up new ideas from them,[18] it was clear that certain lineages were identified with certain artistic specializations. For instance, the Lebe troupe was renowned for peotry (*iwi*) and dance; Eiyeba was popular for acrobatics and dance; Agbegijo was famous for sketches; and Aiyelabola for "tableaux vivants".

The masque-dramaturge was mainly an animator who had to rely on the carver for his artistic inspiration. The carved masks had to be bought as the carvers belonged to a different lineage craft guild. In most cases, the *bata* orchestra accompaniment was provided by a different lineage; historically, only the costumer had always been a member of the troupe's lineage. Of course, there were occasions when the masque-dramaturge built his own costumes. The *bata* leader, as a matter of form, collected fifty percent of all proceeds at the end of each performance since the success or failure of the performance depended largely on his part in the total pattern. He had to be involved not only with the shape of each act but also with the communication line that ran through the performance. He, in fact, formed the linking channel of communication between the actor and the spectator. He also had to show his skill in relating and reflecting the histrionic capabilities of the dramaturge. He therefore had to take part in training and was present in all rehearsals.

Professionalism had encouraged many an artist, whether he be a carver or a masque-dramaturge, to exhibit his own individualism through self-expression and experimentation. The element of competition, which became a functional part of the annual *egungun* festivals where every masque-dramaturge was expected to contribute directly or indirectly, had improved the general style and form of each group. On the other hand, by working within the general convention of the *egungun*, the extent to which an individual artist could carry his freedom had been limited. One significant breakthrough nevertheless, was the emergence of the profane element with its increased interest in the sketch or "revue".

The masque-dramaturge who, by demonstrating his genius, was able to move the taste of his spectator, had in a way, transcended the tradition of the *egungun*. His modification of the original concept was made possible by his venturing out from the court as well as from the fired pattern of the religious festival in order to appeal to and meet the taste of a wide undifferentiated public. In the past he had lived by flattering the elite; that is, the court and the nobility, for their amusement; now he could include them in his satirical sketches if he so desired.

The Theatre in History

The history of the Alarinjo theatre cannot be separated from the rise and fall of the Oyo-Yoruba empire. Its development and growth were closely associated with Yoruba political and social history. The expansion of the empire brought about a re-organization of the government and the extension of court activities to the provinces. This also meant an increase in the number of troupes in order to cope with a wider area of operation. Each metropolitan governor could keep a troupe and it was the custom to include a troupe in their entourage during their annual visit to pay homage to the Alaafin of Oyo.[19]

During the first half of the nineteenth century, the empire faced the rapacity of the slave trade, then the outrage of the Fulani invasion and collapsed under the spread of internecine wars. With this break-up came the disruption of court life and the movement of the masses southwards for new settlements. The place of the theatre in court and outside was thus affected but this led to a further development. Several new troupes sprang up beyond the Ologbojo lineage and these were free to entertain any individual or group of people who invited them. Names of troupes like Aiyeba, Lebe, Aiyelabola and later Agbegijo, Ajangila, and Ajofeebo emerged. They participated in the annual *egungun* festivals as was their custom and, on non-festival days, were able to satisfy the people's desire for entertainment and diversion; whether the occasion was a birth or a death, the troupes were specially invited to perform. In addition they organized their own itineraries and visited places. Thus began the period of intensive professionalism.

The gulf between the theatre and the cult that inspired it was further widened by the rise of professionalism in the theatre. Professionalism not only resulted in proliferation of troupes but encouraged competition which, in turn, improved the theatrical art.

From about the middle of the nineteenth century onwards, Ibadan had risen as a power quite independent of the Oyo hegemony. For the theatre, the rise marked a new phase of expansion. The troupes became an extension of the power of the *Ajele* (the Ibadan resident lords) in the various and vast areas in which they were located.[20] They waited on the *Ajele* and at their pleasure performed to the masses. This was the period when the troupes acquired their popular attribute, the "alarinjo" (the travelling dance-theatre troupe).

The corroding influence of such external forces as Islam and Christianity affected the existence of the theatre in the Yoruba society more than the disruption of political life. During the first half of the nineteenth century, the Moslems banned theatrical activities in the Fulani occupied areas of Yoruba to the north, thereby forcing the troupes to operate in the south. Also during the second half of the nineteenth and early part of the twentieth centuries, Christian missionary activities which moved up-country from the south had grave consequences on the traditional, social, political and religious institutions of the Yoruba. The missionaries found ritual ceremony intolerable, made no efforts to understand traditional forms of religion and set out to reform the mental outlook of their converts.[21] A Yoruba convert to the Christian faith was expected to renounce his membership in all secret societies and his participation in all forms of traditional rituals including dancing.[22]

This period marked the decline of the theatre. The missionaries became hostile to the Egungun Society which was used as an organized weapon against them.[23] Both the theatre group and the cultic group (two separate entities associated with the Egungun Society) were thus condemned by the missionaries as works of the devil without distinction. Apart from constant interruptions of their public shows by the die-hard Christian converts, the troupes also started facing privation. They were losing the allegiance of the womenfolk who used to constitute the chorus of every public performance. Both the Christian converts and the growing "elite" class in the Yoruba society maintained an attitude of indifference to the traditional theatre and looked down on this kind of amusement. Instead, they developed new forms of entertainment and these spread out with increasing Christian European civilization and education.[24] These, in consequence, dealt a disintegrating blow on the traditional theatre and the generality of its practitioners.

The Dynamics of Professionalism

One had expected the professionalism and individualism of the masque-dramaturges to have affected their style and their form to the ultimate emergence of "the actor without the mask". This

never happened. The masque-dramaturges still go by their original descriptive name, *egungun apidan*, and their classificatory
name, *oje*,[25] and do not even take kindly to being called the
Alarinjo—a name which originated as an abuse and which more
or less picks them out and labels them as "rogues, vagabonds
and sturdy beggars". For the purpose of appealing to their mass
audiences and influencing their psyche, it became expedient for
the masque-dramaturges to be identified as *Egungun*; as they
"cannot very well ignore the shaping and restraining influence of
the cult".[26]

The troupes were exposed to all kinds of dire situations and,
sometimes, awful experiences when they travelled from place to
place. They needed the cultus as a bulwark to shield them and as
a watchful eye to superintend their performance. They never
performed without the permission of the Alagbaa of the town or
village they entered. In fact, they lodged in his house and he
arranged for their feeding and, in most cases, helped with their
publicity. He was paid a certain percentage of all the proceeds;
but, sometimes, only a token or a gesture of appreciation was
made to him. To avert some of the dangers and temptations to
which the troupes were exposed during performance, the Alagbaa would provide them with masked bodyguards as *atokun* to
attend on them.[27] There are reports of charms having been used on
the performers by some unknown person in the audience especially during the performance of the *Masque of the Bao-
constructor*, the actor was unable to remove his costume at the
end of the act.[28] To maintain their prestige, therefore, the actors
also armed themselves with counter-charms. The *atokun* or
bodyguards could also wield the whip against any one suspected
of being too inquisitive. It is important that a performance is
opened with "a salute to earth".

> Earth existed before the gods (orisa).
> Earth is the mother to whom the dead return
> Earth and the ancestors are the sources of moral law.[29]

It was incumbent on the masque-dramaturge to be a member of
the Ogboni Society.[30] Since the Society is concerned with the
mystical aspects of Yoruba life, and the theatre troupes need the

guidance of the "earth spirit" when they travel out, membership of the Ogboni Society gives them certain privileges and advantages. The Yoruba adage, *Awo ni gb'awo ni gbọnwọ* (A cult member is the one to raise the arm (support) of another cult member) provides the necessary incentive for professional people to belong to certain cults or secret associations, especially the Ogboni Society. It is imperative that a cult member must not be let down. By seeking to support him, the secret of the cult is hereby protected.

Sometimes the masque-dramaturges were charged for vagrancy and robbery and were refused permission to perform on account of these allegations. Sometimes they were received with open arms and were well loaded with gifts including new wives! They were also notorious for being fond of women, even though, in most cases, the women were the ones who flocked to them out of sheer admiration for their performance. The following narration from "Odu Oturupọngbo"[31] accounts for the popularity or notoriety of the actor:

Oni bẹẹ ni ẹnyin o gbọ'fa
   ti nwọn peri yi bi?
O ni Oturupọngba, Oturu-pọn-kete
A difa fun ọmọ-atakiti-gbe-gbẹwa
Ti o t'akiti t'o re e do'yawo
   Ọlọfin l'otu-Ifẹ Ile.
Igba t'o t'akiti, ibi t'o ti gbe'ra
   jin gbun-gbun-gbun bi ọjọ;
N'bi ti o ta a si na
   jin gbun-gbun-gbun bi kanga
Ọlọfin wa d'aun pe oun ko mọ
   idi rẹ ti gbogbo awọn obirin
   oun ṣe l'oyun
Ni babalawo ni ko lo re e toju ẹgbẹwa owo
Nwọn ni ko ko jọ
Ko wa kesi awọn atakiti ti mbẹ
   l'Otu-Ifẹ Ile.
'Eni o ba le t'akiti ninu kaa
   ti o ba le tu s'ẹhin gbagede,
Oun ni yi o gb'ẹgbẹwa yi,
Gbogbo wa ẹ jẹ ka ma da'wo jọ.

Ni olokiti ba de lati t'akiti gbe'gbewa.
B'o ti gbera ninu ile, lo ba bọ sinu kaa.
Nwọn l'ẹni ti nfẹ 'birin Ọba re o
Ni wọn ba mu u
Oba ni ki nwọn lọ re e pa
Àwọn ilu d'oju ọna,
Nwọn l'awọn ko ni se iru eyi,
Atakiti ti d'Agẹmọ!

He said, "don't you understand what the Oracle is saying?"
He said the impersonator Oturu has carried his calabash, he has carried his receptacle.
Thus decreed the Oracle on the Acrobat, who receives two-thousand cowries for his show
Who went to display and later cohabited with the wife of the Olofin at the first Otu-Ife.
When he tumbled, he took off from a height farther than the sun;
When he landed, he ended up on a spot deeper than the well!
Olofin then remarked he didn't know why all his wives had become expectant mothers.
Then the Oracle priest asked him to find two thousand cowries and put them together
And then invite the Acrobat who lived at Otu-Ife.
"Whoever is able to tumble from the inner-chamber and land on the outer-wall
Shall receive this two thousand cowries."
Let us all collect our two thousand cowries and put them together
Then the Acrobat arrived to display and collect his fee
He took off from the house and landed in the inner-chamber.
Then they knew he was the man who had made love to the Ọbas' wife.
They grabbed him; the Oba ordered him to be killed.
When the chiefs set out, then they decided that action was beyond them.
The acrobat had transformed into the Agemo![32]

The troupes travelled mostly during the dry season and spent the rainy season as sedentary medicine-men after the manner of Olugbere, the first professional actor (ghost-mummer) and with whom they were all spiritually connected. They trafficked in charms and medicines and many people were easily gulled by them. It was difficult, of course, to resist their posturings, especially as most of the people they imposed upon in this way believed that their "transformations" were made possible by means of magic and charm. There were reports[33] of occasions when the troupes had been refused permission to perform in a place and had left, promising vengeance on the people; and later when the place had become infested with smallpox, the people had believed that the "Alarinjo" who were refused permission to perform, had sent the "god of smallpox" to finish them!

There were also cases of troupes who were banned from performing in certain areas on account of their unrestrained flair for social criticisms. Sometimes when their sketches were in bad taste, they were stopped in the middle of the act, chased out, and ordered never to return again. A classic example[34] was that of the troupe of Abidogun of Agborako's house, Oyo, in the 1920s. King Ladigbolu I, the Alaafin of Oyo, banned the troupe from further performance of the *Masque of Kudeju* because it was a satire on the institution of the *are'*. The play was a historical sketch on Kudefu, the famous *are* of Alaafin Adelu. Johnson, narrating the story of the act said:

> Kudefu, the king's favourite Ilari and head of all his slaves on the morning of the death (King Adelu) before it was officially announced, went to know of his master's condition, and learning he was dead he was going home sad at heart to die for his own accord.
>
> Alega the keeper of the gate on seeing him coming from the inner apartments, being inquisitive, approached him to learn of their master's condition. Kudefu at once unsheathed his sword saying, "You go before, I am coming at your heels to be attendants on our masters in the other world", and in one stroke he cut off his head and then coolly went home to die.[35]

In spite of the popularity of the masque with the audience, Abidogun was rounded up by the King's valets who protested that the masque-dramaturge had flagrantly exhibited a lack of respect for the Alaafin. Abidogun was summoned before the King who declared him guilty of disrespect. He paid the *itaje* (ransom fee) and was ordered to drop the sketch from his repertoire.

Whether he was hailed or denounced and chased out, the "Alarinjo" was undeterred in his desire to appeal to and amuse the masses. Sometimes in his enthusiasm, he violated the propriety of the cultures and had to face the penalty of the Egungun Society for having gone beyond the bounds of what they regarded as a "sacred art". A classic example was the incident at Ikirun after the Kiriji War in 1886. Balogun Ajayi Osungbekun had invited the troupe of Aiyelabola, then managed by Ọlọjẹde, to entertain him before the palace of the Akirun. Tijuku Ajangila, the leader of the Agbegijo troupe, who was a follower of Ọjẹlade Aiyelabola but had become famous since the death of the latter, was displeased that the invitation was not given to him. He demonstrated his resentment by ruining the performance. First, he invoked rain to stop the show; the Balogun, who was aware of what was happening, sent to Tijuku and warned him not to spoil his pleasure. Then during the *apada* dance, Ọlọjẹde overplayed himself and accidentally exposed his body to the full view of the audience. The officers of the Egungun Society dispersed the crowd and the show ended abruptly. At Tijuku's pleasure, the Society insisted that Ọlọjẹde should pay the penalty of death in the sacred grove. Ọlọjẹde reconciled himself to his fate.

The next day, the officers of the cult gathered at the sacred grove waiting for the culprit. Ọlọjẹde, prior to appearing before them, set out on a masque-parade round the town chanting his farewell "salute". When he reached the Aafin where the Balogun of Ibadan was staying, he was surprised to see the Chief and all the important Ibadan war leaders waiting with gifts and praises for his reception. In a moving and soul-subduing chant he narrated the story of his own end and that of the great Aiyelabola. The Balogun stopped him and said he recalled his (Ọlọjẹde's) father and his great contribution to the Jalumi War and remarked:

Ọjẹlade, a d'eegun d'enia
A d'enia d'eegun!
B'ọjẹ ba boode,
Ki paaka o ma a tele

Aiyelabọla d'ọjẹ Olubadan
lat'oni lọ!

Ojelade, one who becomes a masquerade and human being
Or a human being and a masquerade as he pleases!
When the Oje (masque-dramaturge) steps out,
Let all minor masquerades follow him,
Aiyelabọla has become the Olubadan's masque-dramaturge from
today onwards!

Ọlọjede never reached the sacred grove. News went out that he
and his Aiyelabọla troupe were, rather, on their way to live at
Ibadan, accompanying the Balogun and his team.[36]
The degree of independence of the theatre from the cultus
varied from area to area. It was clear from all accounts, however,
that the Ọyọ-Ibadan theatre groups, since becoming travelling
troupes and attaining a high degree of professionalism, had
ceased to have any strong obligations to the cultus though they
did not sever connections completely. The cult members and the
masque-dramaturges are still bound together by ancestor-
worship and meet during the funeral ceremony of any member of
the Egungun Society. The members of the various theatrical
companies can also, as individuals, carry the serious or the
eegunla masks without question. But the theatre guild is a
separate organization from the Egungun Society.
The masque-dramaturge built his repertory and filled it with
playlets especially with *efẹ* (satire)—items which diverted his
patrons and spectators alike. It is to them that he directed his
greatest appeal. He knew that "everything that breaks over the
social taboo is funny". His spectators reflected with amazement
when they saw the restrictions of the Egungun Society trampled
upon in the arena of play and laughed when their revered gods
were revealed in sketches as caricatures. His jugglery, acrobatics
and his skill in dance, chant and mime excited wonder and
admiration in his spectators. These were features for which the
"Alarinjo" was remembered long after he had tramped away and
until the next time when he showed his face once again.

Theatre Organization

Publicity

During the period of intensive professionalism, the theatre was organized by three types of promoter; the first was the Alagbaa of the Egungun Society who invited the troupes to perform. The two occasions when this happened were the festival of the Egungun Society and during the festivities following the death of a member of the Society. The second was a promotion by the court; when the players were required to entertain the court or the populace, the invitation came from the Ọba, the Baalẹ or the Chief. The third was when the troupe leader himself planned his own itinerary and toured the various towns and villages without having been previously invited. The publicity arrangement varied in respect of each term of promotion. There were no formal notices; instead, the troupes announced their shows through contacts and processions. Whatever the type of promotion, the role of the Alagbaa was important whether as a patron or an agent.

Performances sponsored by the Alagbaa were usually ritualistic in nature and were similarly organized. If the troupe lived in the same village or town, the Alagbaa sent the *Ope* (Caller), one of his officers, to invite the head of the troupe and put the proposal before him. If the troupe lived out of town, the same officer was sent with an *aroko*, a token, indicating that a proposal had been made calling for a performance. When everything had been decided upon as to date and time of performance, the publicity for the show was placed in the hands of the officers of the Society.

It was usual that the procession took place on the day of performance. It started from the *Igbo Igbalẹ* (sacred grove) led by the *Ope* to the *Ode* (open space) fronting the Alagbaa's compound where the performance took place. Costumed in their *agọ* (overall garment), the troupe processed, accompanied by the *Bata* orchestra, dancing and chanting. The chants were usually in praise of Esa Ogbin, the progenitor of the theatre, as well as in praise of the *egungun* in general. Before the procession wound up, the troupe paid a homage-visit to Ṣango's shrine.

The court promotions were usually meant for the pleasure of the Ọba and Baalẹ; whether the occasion was a commemoration, an anniversary, or just entertaining an august visitor, the troupes came with a view to entertaining a public. The Oba, of course, as a gesture, invited the Alagbaa to make the necessary contacts or consultations with the troupe manager. If they lived out of town, accommodation was arranged for them, usually at the palace. Sometimes they had to go with the Alagbaa who put them up for the duration of their visit. Since the occasion of such a visit was civic and non-ritualistic the troupe had very little to do with the local *egungun* cult. Only *bata* was used in publicizing their arrival. Of the two processions made, one took place as soon as they entered the town on the evening before the day of performance, although they usually looked tired and worn out having treked long distances. On the actual day of the performance shortly before they were due to set up, the actors, costumed in the *ago* and carrying their *ẹku* (dressing-up bags), were accompanied by the *bata* around the town. They chanted, danced and tumbled as they processed.

Lastly, when the troupes planned their own itinerary, they invariably sent an *aroko*, a token, to the Alagbaa of each of the places they planned to visit. If the visit was not welcomed, the Alagbaa sent word for them not to come; otherwise, when the troupes promoted themselves, they used the Alagbaa as their professional agent and placed in his hands all arrangements for publicity, accommodation and feeding. He in turn received a certain percentage of all the total proceeds after the engagement. As this performance was usually designed for the public, it was helpful to know in advance some lineage-heads and some important people who might be present at the public performances so as to have appropriate totem and praise chants ready. This the Alagbaa helped in providing. He also provided bodyguards in case something untoward happened to the troupe during performance.

On such itinerant visits, three processions were arranged. The first took place immediately the players entered the town; when the *bata* struck its music, everybody knew the troupes had arrived. While chanting the *oriki* of the place, they made straight for the Alagbaa's house where they lodged. In the evening the Alagbaa led the second procession to the Oba's or Baale's palace for formal introduction of the leader of the troupe and for a preview entertainment. They wore the *ago* but did not carry the dressing-up bag. After this formal introduction and the welcome ceremony, the Alagbaa led them around the town to visit some important local chiefs and nobles. They received gifts (usually money but sometimes clothing) from this outing. The third procession took place on the actual day of performance when the players were led by their own leader to the place of performance, the main market square, and then waited in a booth already set up for use as their "dressing room".

Presentation

Depending on who was promoting the show, the choice of programme varied tremendously. In each case the form of the performance was that of a "variety show" and the troupe manager relied on a large "repertoire" to pick and choose from. Usually, the religious performances sponsored by the Alagbaa took into account the sanctity of the *egungun* and, therefore, concentration was more on spectacle rather than on sketches. The secular performances, however, were the most popular and the troupe leader invariably took liberties with the cultus without fear of any sanctions.

The duration of any performance took into consideration the amount of money that had been paid by the promoter or sometimes, the extra amount of money the players expected to get at the end of the engagement. When they were invited to perform at births, marriages, deaths or some such social ceremonies, they usually charged a fixed amount for the engagement. However, they expected the patron to give them something more, and this encouraged them to spend extra time with him, and to give of their best. Some of these private performances were limited however, because not everybody was privileged to see them, especially if they were held for private showing in the courtyards of the patrons.

Staging

Performances were enacted in any of the following places, depending on who had commanded the performance: court performance (the palace quadrangle or inner courtyard, or the piazza in front of the palace); Alagbaa's performance (the *ode* in front of the gabled frontage of his compound); lineage-heads, chiefs and other important persons (in the courtyard or the *ode* in front of the gabled frontage of the compound). No raised platform was necessary for any of these performances. An open space was all that was needed. A "circle" was always formed by the spectators as they assembled round the open space (arena) to watch the show.

The "stands" were important features—the "royal" stand (in the case of a royal command), "promoter's stand", and the "orchestra stand". On each of these "stands" seats were provided. The orchestra stand was placed very close to the "booth" (dressing-room) of the actors, sometimes not too far away from the promoter's stand. The actor's "booth" was normally an improvised rig-up that could give shelter and privacy. In certain cases setting up a booth was not necessary; for example, at a royal performance, the palace had a *kobi* (portico) which was used for this purpose; sometimes a cult-house or hut nearby was used, and many times, especially during itinerant visits, the troupes improvised their own dressing-rooms by changing in their *ago*.

There were two types of "movement" in the action of the plays. One "movement" was circular; that is, the action moves round the "circle" or the arena from the booth in a clockwise or anti-clockwise direction. The other "movement" was straight; the actors came out of the booth and went directly to the middle of the "circle" and moved back again, describing a radius. The "circular movement" was used in the plays that involved audience participation (usually the sketches) whereas the "straight movement" was usually for the serious plays or spectacles, to enable the spectators to appreciate them from an aesthetic distance. In certain cases, for this movement, the actor or actors involved in the play, were shielded in the centre of the "circle" (which then became a temporary dressing-room) by other actors holding up a number of their costumes for concealment.

No scenery was necessary except that, occasionally, the genius of a masque-dramaturge manifested itself in the use of symbolic scenery.[37] But generally, the objective in staging was not the simulation of a locality but the creation of an atmosphere.

(a) The Chorus, called "Akunyungba", was an essential part of the performance. During the early part of the development of the theatre when the masque-dramaturge was yet an officer at court the chorus was composed mainly of the women of the palace. Later, when the theatre moved out of court circles and the troupe had to travel about entertaining the general public, the masque-dramaturge had to rely on his younger actors to play the chorus; sometimes his wives and spectators joined in, especially when the action involved a particular song that was familiar to them.

The chief function of the chorus was to provide the "song element" which was, invariably, part of the plot. It therefore helped to form links for full understanding of the episodes. In another role, the chorus, especially the chorus leader who was supposed to be a rhapsodist, acted as the interlocutor by participating in the dialogue and action of the play with both the actor and the spectator. The chorus leader was one of the wives or a daughter of the troupe leader. She went round the "circle" during the performance of each act and chanted the praises of the players and gave credits to the performance, among other things. The importance of the chorus to any performance was never in doubt since without it the drama was fragmented, episodic, and incomplete.

(b) The Orchestra was made up of the *bata* set. The set contains four drums: the *iya ilu*, the *emele abo*, the *emele akọ* and the *kundi*. The *iya ilu* is the talking-drum, but it is a stammerer and is difficult to follow without previous familiarity. It has two membranes and both are played together. A leather strap is used to strike the left membrane while the palm of the right hand beats the right membrane. The *emele abo*, the supporting drum, repeats what the *iya ilu* says. The other two drums are accompaniments.

It is said that *Bata* was a mythological ancestor deified and worshipped as an orisa after his death; and he was a relation of both Sango and Egungun; and that the three as ancestors are ritually inseparable. It is not known when *bata* became the orchestra of the Alarinjo Theatre to the exclusion of all other types of Yoruba drums. It is known, however, that the *bata* is the drum played for the ritual worship of "Orisa Sango" and that other forms of drums are played during *egungun* worship, especially the lineage masquerades.

The drama of the masques was essentially a poetic image; the actors indulged in very little dialogue or story-telling. The chief function of the orchestra was to provide the vital links. It streamlined the operatic form of the masques and furnished its life-line.

The *bata* leader had a number of duties during a performance. He served as the "call-boy" for the actors and communicated with the audience by announcing what scene or act they were going to see next. He also warned the actors when they were exceeding their limits with the usual:

Ma s'afara!
Bo ba buru tan
Iwọ nikan ni yio ku.

Don't get slack!
If the worst comes,
You'll be left to your own devices.

The *bata* leader pin-pointed the highlights in the action of the play (occasionally adding a few embellishments of his own; he always followed the action of the play around the "circle", and he was versed in Yoruba verbal art which he rendered by means of his drum. It was conventional that every "dramatis personae" had an *oriki* or attributive chant as part of the dramatic form. Besides, every act ended in a dance. As both the *oriki* and the dances were distinctive features of the masques, so they were also the essence of the orchestra.

(c) *The programme* for every performance was that of a "variety show" but, invariably, followed a particular order: the *Ijuba*, the Dance, the Drama Spectacle and Revue and the Finale.

The *Ijuba* was the formal or ceremonial opening very much like an "opening glee". It contained the "pledge" and the "salute"; both chanted together sometimes in a particular order of succession, sometimes in any order. The original pledge called *Ipesa*, was addressed to Esa Ogbin, the foremost masque-dramaturge and the founder of the first professional guild. The "salute", as a form of acknowledgement, varied from troupe to troupe. It was, however, important that the troupe leader paid certain respects or homage; first, he acknowledged the lineage from which he drew his inspiration or the leader from whom he received his training; he then addressed the unseen forces; and lastly, praised himself. Sometimes when a performance was called by special command or invitation, the important personage in whose honour the performance was being staged had his praise-chant included in the "salute".

The content of the pledge as well as the focus of the "salute" varied from troupe to troupe. At a performance in Otta and Imala both in the south-western area of Yorubaland, the *Ijuba* took the following form:

> The Bata-orchestra opened the show with an "evocation" and drew the attention of the actors to the fact that the audience was waiting for the show to begin. The Bata-leader then walked up to the booth or dressing-room, stopped at the threshold and beat the "oriki" of the masque-dramaturge. At this a masked actor came out of the booth, wearing the "ago". He knelt by the side of the Bata-leader facing in the direction of the booth and chanting, called on the leader to come forth. He called once, twice and at the third calling, the leader answered and emerged into the "circle" in his "ago" amidst the chanting of the other masked actors and the beating of drum.
>
> When he had seated himself in front of the orchestra, the music stopped. Then he began his homage. First he pledged his loyalty to Esa Ogbin, praising him and acknowledging him as his lineage-head. The orchestra broke in occasionally with complimentary ejaculations. Then came the "salute". He saluted the "earth", the owner of the land on which he was going to perform. He saluted the unseen eyes that were watching his performance—"Iyami Osoronga".[38] He introduced himself and finally praised his promoter.

This ritualistic opening was brought to a close with a dance tune by the orchestra. And with that the young actors trooped into the "circle" for the second item on the programme—the Dance.

The Dance was in two parts—ritual and social dance. The actors changed into the *labala*, the undergarment, which looked like a kilt

over a pair of pants. (This was the costume which the *Oje* wore when he strolled about as a gleeman or troubador.)

The ritual dance was an *orisa* dance. The *bata* played in honour of the notable deities of the locality in which the performance was taking place. The actors danced and at the same time chanted the *oriki* of each deity. After the ritual dance came the social dance. This was based on the current "beat" in fashion and was full of sex appeal. Social songs were also sung with the *bata* leading in every case. The dance finally dissolved into acrobatic display. Acrobatics, of course, may form an aspect of the specialization of a particular troupe. Not all the troupes are known for this feat.) While the acrobats performed, the *bata* described their skill as in the following chant:

> Alantakun! Alantakun!
> B'o ba f'inu ta,
> A f'ẹhin ta,
> Alantakun!

> Spider! Spider!
> When he spins with his inside,
> He spins with his back
> Spider!

(The *bata's* allusion to the spider is, of course, a compliment of the skill of the acrobat and a description of his "back and fore" spinning and tumbling in the air.) The Dance ended with the orchestra playing the "interlude" to enable the actors to get ready for the next part of the programme.

The Drama had two distinct genres—the "Spectacle" and the "Revue" and the presentation was in that order. The Spectacle was a form of theatrical presentation that was remarkable in dimension. It was performed chiefly by the troupe leader as a sole mime. Sometimes other minor characters joined but the masques concerned mainly mythological or totemistic characters. The mythological dramas were enactments based on myths of deities like Sango, Obatala and others, or some local heroes like Aroni. Sometimes, however, the masque of a mythological character could become a satirical sketch.

The totemistic dramas were animal "motifs". Totemism as a system seemed to have been practised in the Yoruba society in

the olden days when "animals had an effect on the imagination and thoughts of the people".[39] (But at present there does not seem to be any conscious link with the system.[40]) There is, however, no doubt that certain animals like the elephant, the lion, the leopard and others like the snake, the monkey, the crocodile or alligator and also some birds were at one time taken as family symbols.[41] Besides, the role of animals in Yoruba folklore is an indication of their significance for theatrical presentation. The folklore is full of tales about the closeness of Yoruba life to animal life. This has probably led to the belief that living persons could metamorphose themselves temporarily into birds and animals.[42] This belief was extended to the spectacular masques and made them very popular.

In each case, the characters were never really fully developed. Presentation was sometimes haphazard. Whether in pantomime or, as in some cases, as tableaux, the chorus and the orchestra supplied the missing links in the plot of the masques.

Added to the category of Spectacle was the "Pure Show" which was also performed by the leader mainly to demonstrate his manipulative skill. Examples of this were found in the *Apada* (changeling) and the *Ijo Ori Odo* (mortal-dance).

The "Revue" was a medley. As a comic sketch, music, dancing and singing were its main features. There were three categories of the Revue—abstract, sociological and historical. The abstract sketches were either solo or group mimes. Some represented odd physical features in the society while others were caricatures of human frailties. Examples included *Didirin* (Moron), *Elekedidi* (Mumps), and *Onimu Oru* (Nosey), among others.

The sociological sketches analysed the Yoruba society and highlighted its vices, pests and morals. "Stranger" elements in society were isolated and treated satirically—for example, in the Tapa (Nupe)—while "village" characters or "non-stranger" elements were sketched and treated humorously as a *Pansaga* (Adulteress).

The historical sketches, though at one time sociological, had psychological implications because they seemed to have been introduced to influence social cohesiveness as, for example, the

Atinga (a cult for exorcism) and the *Idahomi* (Dahomeyan General) masques.

All the revue-masques depended for their effect on "audience participation". The sketches were mainly improvised and capable of infinite changes. Their songs were topical and in most cases familiar. The dialogue included jokes and ribaldry. Lack of premeditation and any carefully worked out "scenario" affected the shape of the masques as, sometimes, the enthusiasm of both the actor and spectator resulted in unrestrained indulgence in farce.

The Finale, known as "Idan Apa-re'le", was usually the *Iyawo Masque* (the Bride). It was the most beautiful and the most expensive to dress and was always acted by the leader of the troupe to display his flexibility and versatility. The masque was improvised like the sketches and could vary from one performance to another. However, there were certain distinctive features in it which described the way the bridal procession was organized in Yoruba society in the past.

By the end of the performance, while the bride still continued her "song and dance" round the "circle", the other actors repaired into the "tiring-room", collected their properties and costumes into the *eku* (dressing-up box), and followed the *Iyawo Masque* out of the arena in a recessional dance round the streets of the community.

The Repertoire

The theatre operated on a form of repertory system; that is, a company could have several productions from a stockpile of plays ready at the same time. Every company had a stock of masques which were performed over and over and over again. It was not easy to divide the masques into the two basic classical dramatic genres, namely, tragedy and comedy. This was because, although most of the mythological masques were serious in nature, the artist was free to base his masque on a satirical motive and change the original popular conception of the deity. By comparison, however, the totemistic masques were tragic while the abstract and sociological masques were comic.

The masque-dramaturge used the masques of his "repertoire" to demonstrate two main aspects of his own skill, the use of the serious masques to assert his supernatural attainments, and the use of the comic masques to satirize. But his desire to dance and sing was by no means inhibited since he utilized both effectively to complement his total performance. Realistic acting and costuming were natural concurrences. All these combined to give the masque in performance their variety and vitality.

Conclusion

The theatre convention of the Alarinjo theatre can be validly appreciated against its own historical background, professional practice and system of operation as a travelling theatre. Its innate dynamism sustained it as a going concern during its span. In spite of the forces which had committed it to antiquity, its members are being raked up and its undying influence is now visible in the organizational and operational practice of the practitioners of the contemporary travelling theatre led by Hubert Ogunde.

Hubert Ogunde, who became the first Nigerian artist of the contemporary theatre to turn professional and assume the leadership of a flourishing theatre troupe, recalled that his experience and source of inspiration belonged to the Alarinjo theatre. "I was playing drums with the masqueraders in my home town when I was young, and these Egungun people gave me the urge inside me to start a company of actors."[43] What has been most significant in the Ogunde theatre since he became professional was the extent of his identification with the conventional theatre practice of the Alarinjo theatre.

Ogunde lunged into the hazards of professionalism with his African Music Research Party (the name by which Ogunde theatre was first called) in 1945. In the following year he took to the road.[44] As a travelling theatre, he adopted the repertory system and enshrined the tenets of the Alarinjo theatre especially with regard to certain aspects of its presentational procedures and theatre organization.

The significance of the *Ijuba* (salute), the entrance song of the traditional theatre, was in evidence in Ogunde's "Opening Glee"[45] at the early part of his career. Having adopted the spirit of the entrance song, Ogunde introduced some modifications which are a reflection of his Christian outlook and contemporary viewpoint.[46]

The nature and purpose of the Ogunde Theatre strikingly relate to that of the Alarinjo. In conformity with the practice of the traditional theatre as a lineage profession, Ogunde has worked his wives and children into his company in order to perpetuate it as a going family concern. To all intents and purposes, the popularity and success of the Ogunde Theatre is traceable to the extent of its leader's glorification of the dynamics of the Alarinjo theatre.

Notes

1. Hugh Clapperton, *Journal of a Second Expedition into the Interior of Africa*, London, 1829, pp. 53–56; Richard Lander, *Records of Clapperton's Last Expedition to Africa*, London, 1830, Vol. 1, pp. 115–121.
2. Clapperton, *op. cit.*, p. 53.
3. The Egungun Society was formed as a conjoint association of two choruses: Igbori (Tapa) and Oba (Yoruba) with the responsibility of the ritual worship of the ancestor and of organizing the ceremony of the materialization of the ancestor as a costumed figure.
4. R. S. Smith, "The Alafin in Exile: A Study of the Igboho period in Oyo History", *Journal of African History*, Vol. 6, No. 1, 1965, p. 74.
5. Abipa is a contraction of *eni-a-bi-si-ipa* (one born on the wayside). Abipa was born to one of the wives of Alafin Egunoju as the royal party was approaching Igboho from Saki. See Robert S. Smith, *Kingdoms of the Yoruba*, Methuen, London, 1968, p. 36.
6. These stock-characters are caricatures of humanity believed to have been created by Orisa-nla (Obatala), the Yoruba arch-divinity, under the influence of wine. They are called *eni Orisa* (those of the Deity).
7. Smith, *op. cit.*, p. 70.
8. Samuel Johnson, *The History of the Yoruba*, C. M. S. (Nigeria) Bookshops, Lagos, 1960, pp. 165–166.
9. Smith, *op. cit.*
10. Johnson, *op. cit.*, p. 166.
11. Ibid.
12. Smith, *op. cit.*, p. 73.
13. Ibid., p. 70.
14. The worship of Obatala has important consequences for the development of Yoruba ritual drama and finally, the emergence of the theatre. The impetus to create (and the fact that the first *dramatis personae* of the theatre as narrated above were all *eni Orisa* (those of the Deity)) has been identified with worshippers of Obatala.
15. Olugbere Agan was born half-ape, half-human. His mother was a Tapa woman, the daughter of Oloponda, of the Igbori clan. By masquerading he was able to disguise his features.
16. It is claimed the Esa Ogbin assumed the office of Ologbin Ologbojo through

a contrivance. See "Oriki Iran Ologbun" in Adeboye Babalola, *Awǫn Oriki Orile̩*, Collins, London, 1967, pp. 91–103.

17. It must be noted that the poetry of the Alarinjo theatre is called *e̩sa*, a hotchpotch of selected themes on various aspects of Yoruba life, from the lineages down to the smallest matter in the Yoruba world.
18. Beier, "The Agbegijo Masqueraders", *Nigerian Magazine*, No. 82, September 1964, p. 191.
19. Clapperton, *op. cit.*, p. 53.
20. What came to be called the Ibadan empire extended from Igana in Egbado (South-west Yoruba) through Ife to the Ijesha, Ekiti and Akoko districts (North-east Yoruba). See Bolanle Awe, *The Rise of Ibadan as a Yoruba Empire in the Nineteenth Century*, D. Phil. Thesis, Oxford, 1964, pp. 120 and 144–160.
21. E. A. Ayandele, *The Missionary Impact on Modern Nigeria: 1842–1914*, Longmans, London, 1966, pp. 329–331.
22. R. H. Stone, *Yoruba Concept of the Natural World*, Ph.D. Thesis, London, 1967, p. 58.
23. Ayandele, *op. cit.*, pp. 162–164.
24. Lynn Leonard, *The Growth of Entertainment of Non-African Origin in Lagos: 1866–1920*, M.A. Thesis, Ibadan, 1967.
25. *Oje* is a name associated with the guild of Egungun masqueraders. It applies to the individual member or the group. In the context in which it is used here, *oje* denotes a member of the guild who is a costumed itinerant dancer.
26. Denis Williams, "The Nigerian Image", *Odu*, Vol. 1, No. 2 (a review), p. 87.
27. "There are cases when outsiders or competitors of a different Egungun branch in civilian robes, test the miraculous power of the Egungun (theatre-troupes)." See Delano, *The Soul of Nigeria*, Laurie, 1937, p. 163.
28. Rev. Olumide Lucas, *The Religion of the Yorubas*, C.M.S. (Bookshop) Lagos, 1948, p. 139, refers to another account and said the actor was believed to have been affected by a tester who directed charms against him.
29. Morton-Williams, "The Yoruba Ogboni Cult in Oyo", *Africa*, Vol. III, No. 4, October 1960, p. 364.
30. Followers of Obatala claimed ownership of the earth on which the Yoruba race was established. Members of the Ogboni Society venerate the earth believed to be the creation of Obatala and maintain a mystical contact with it.
31. I am grateful to Mr. Wale Ogunyemi of the Institute of African Studies, University of Ibadan, for helping me to record this *Odu* at Oshogbo.
32. The Agemo is a cult among the Ijebu and manifests itself in a masquerade. In the theatre the Agemo is a satirical sketch. It is customary during the order of a theatrical performance for acrobatics to be followed by the Masque of the Agemo (Agemo Eleni). The incident explained in this *Odu* may have provided the original source of the order of performance.
33. According to my professional informants, they had themselves experienced such disgrace from one or two village heads.

34. This information was contained in the accounts of the Alarinjo theatre given to me by Alagba Ojebisi, one of my professional informants who is himself a masque-dramaturge and leader of the Ajofeebo troupe at Oyo.
35. Johnson, *op. cit.*, p. 397.
36. I am grateful to Alagba Ojeleke Aiyelabola for giving this account of his father and grandfather.
37. Beier describing the scene at a performance says, "The Leopard suddenly bursts out from underneath a pile of grass", suggesting a scenic background. See Beier, "The Agbegijo Masqueraders", *Nigeria Magazine*, 1964, p. 195.
38. The Yoruba mother superior, head of witchcraft.
39. G. J. A. Ojo, *Yoruba Culture*, O.U.P., 1966, p. 218.
40. Beier, "Before Oduduwa", *Odu*, No. 3, p. 10.
41. Parrinder, *Religion in an African City*, O.U.P., 1953, p. 173.
42. Ojo, *op. cit.*, p. 220.
43. Hubert Ogunde in a personal communication.
44. In an announcement inserted in the *West African Pilot*, 1 August, 1946, Ogunde listed the towns in his itinerary, his first excursion into the Western Provinces of Nigeria as a professional.
45. Ogunde once used a set of masquerades to perform his "Opening Glee".
46. See J. A. Adedeji, "Trends in the Content and Form of the Opening Glee in Yoruba Drama", *Research in African Literatures*, Vol. 4, No. 1, pp. 32–47.

Reprinted Theatre in Africa, ed. by Ogunba and Irele.

THE KWAGH-HIR THEATRE
Edith Enem

One of the important "discoveries" made during the festival of traditional dances held in all the states of the country between December 1973 and December 1974 was the kwagh-hir puppet and masquerade theatre of the Tiv communities settled in Gboko, Makurdi and Katsina-Ala.

Traditionally, the Tivs are farmers, but in modern times the young men have preferred careers in the army where the vigour and discipline of military life are presumed to be ingrained characteristics of every male Tiv. Their versatility and resourcefulness are also abundantly expressed in their dramatic arts—their music, dance, story-telling performances which, through time, have accumulated resources drawn from shared experiences and historical contacts with other cultures.

Kwagh-hir is a composite art which can take almost a whole night to perform in an open air, circular ground.

The audience assembles as early as 7 p.m. for a lively entertainment which they have seen many times before, but without any diminution of interest and readiness to participate.

An evening's performance witnessed at Gboko was held in an open school field with a fixed play area in the centre around which the audience arranged itself, some sitting and others standing. Had it been an unclouded night, the almost full moonlight would have served as perfect lighting. But as it turned out, it was darksome and overcast, such that hurricane lamps became necessary in order to obtain additional light. The narrator had to carry a lamp around as he moved over the play area to introduce each story. He told each story, always a fragmentary episode, without conscious display and his jokes which were well spaced helped to liven up the mood of participation. Sometimes, he had to intervene if the performance of a story was dragging or depreciating in impact, especially towards the end. He would step

249

up to the scene and engage them in some trivialities or exuberant business which occasioned instant laughter and huge applause as reward.

The technical means of illustrating the story, the mechanism of the puppet performance and the masquerades demand all the ingenuity and craftsmanship of the production crew as failure to strike a valuable effect at the right time creates false suspense even though some consider it great fun if a hitch occurs, particularly if another group has so disgraced itself. Embellishments in the form of coloration of carved puppet, accessories and masquerades help to reinforce the visual impact of the theatre.

The performance usually proceeds in this order. First the narrator will come out and tell the story and almost immediately the chorus of musicians and dancers seated with the audience but in group start their performance. When interest is sufficiently aroused, the cast moves up from the back of the group and starts acting as soon as they are in view, covering in their various moves, all sides of the circular staging area. At the climax or terminal point of the drama, the chorus starts singing again as flourish for the departure of the cast from the circle. After this, there is hushed excitement for the next story and to help the narrator's presence on stage the chorus begins in the background a song and dance to establish new atmosphere.

The paraphernalia of kwagh-hir are diverse in types and moral connotations. The puppets especially, are in different styles. Some are naturalistic, others grotesque and ridiculous, but all reflecting the moral prejudices and sanctions of the community. Historical awareness is shown in some puppets which represent events such as when the first motor bike was ridden in Gboko or the first policewoman emerged or when modern dress styles of European design gained local acceptance.

The Tivs recall a time in the early political days when kwagh-hir was prohibited as the satiric impulse of this theatre was exploited by opposing political factions to aggravate social strife. This again attests to the elastic structure of kwagh-hir which is capable of accommodating new experiences in addition to the traditional repertoire. This resilience and the people's passion for dance and drama which seems to thrive best on subjects that can be as commonplace as their drinking calabashes or the way a woman ties her scarf, make for the continuing vitality of this folk art form.

The quality of actuality is often achieved by the literal representation of essential details of a situation presented. For example, in the vignette of the execution of an armed robber by a firing squad, an actual shot is fired and at the same time the criminal's head jerks suddenly and drops to one side. An ironic edge in that situation is pointed by the presence of his helpless relations (presumably his parents) at his execution. In the master-drummer scene, the puppet is actually playing two drums with intense vigour and the music is unmistakably Tiv drumming. The mad man who is always beating his wife without respite is armed with a club which descends at intervals on the woman's head.

The animation of puppets is initiated and sustained in time so that a rhythmic pattern of repetition, suspense and spectacular action is achieved over the interplay of diverse situations in the total performance.

The unity of Kwagh-hir theatre is revealed in its artistic intention to abstract from reality those situations, attitudes and social behaviours which are to be found, not only in Tiv communities, but also in universal human situation.

Reprinted Nigeria Magazine No. 120, 1976.

A BORNU PUPPET SHOW
R. E. Ellison

The puppet show has long been established in Bornu as a form of popular entertainment. The puppets themselves, called *dogodogo* in Kanuri, take the form of rag dolls and slip on to the hand like a glove, fingers being inserted into the hands of the doll. When preparing for a performance, the manipulator, *dogodogoma*, plants in the ground a stout stick forked at the top. In front of this he places his bag of hyena skin containing the puppets (see fig. 1). He then sits down behind the stick and covers both the stick and the bag with his gown. His head and the forked stick provide supports for the tent thus formed, while he manipulates the puppets through the opening of the gown for the head (see figs 2 and 3). Some drummers stand behind the performer and beat their drums and sing songs while the puppets are being changed inside the tent.

The *dogodogoma* does the speaking, but it is almost impossible to distinguish the words since they are all uttered in a shrill whistle, far shriller than that of the English Punch and Judy performer. The whistle in this case consists of two pieces of ostrich egg shell, about three-quarters of an inch square, bound together with thread. This is half swallowed by the *dogodogoma*, and he declares that to perfect this whistling voice is by far the most difficult part of his craft and requires years of practice. The words of the puppets, being almost indistinguishable, are repeated by one of the assistants standing by.

The performance consists of about eight short scenes, each lasting for three or four minutes. Each scene is complete in itself and has no connection with the following scene. There are about six puppets, but naturally no more than two can appear at the same time. The action is highly dramatic; in one scene a thief enters a man's house and is just making away with his swag when the man's wife wakes up and gives the alarm; the husband then

Bornu Puppet Show Figs. 1–4.

emerges and gives the thief a sound beating. One of the best scenes is that in which a very coy Shuwa Arab girl appears—she wears a long flowing white gown and her hair is adorned with cowries (fig. no. 3). She sings and dances and by her charms captivates a married man, but soon his wife appears, rates him severely for his unfaithful conduct, and gives him a thrashing. A *dogari* then comes along to see what the noise is about, and he and the husband soon come to blows. Then follows a most realistic fight, each party being armed with a long stick. Another amusing scene is that in which a village head informs the *sarikin bariki* that the District Officer is coming to stay at the Rest House; he is a very particular District Officer, and the Rest House must be very well swept and wood and water must be ready. We then see the arrival of the District Officer, who is dressed completely in white and wears a white sun helmet. The village head greets him with the greatest respect, but, alas! all is not perfect in the Rest House and the *sarikin bariki* is severely reproved.

There is only one *dogodogoma* in Yerwa, the big native town near Maiduguri, and his performances take place at the gates of compounds on such festive occasions as weddings, appointments to office, etc. There are said to be only two other *dogodogoma* elsewhere in Bornu, and all three are the pupils of the same teacher.

The Yerwa *dogodogoma* states that the puppet display was originated in Bornu by one Mai Gambo, a native of Dalori district, during the reign of Shehu Umar in the middle of the 19th century. From this man the *dogodogoma* of today all trace their descent through the teacher-pupil line of succession.

It would be interesting to know if the puppet shows given in other Provinces are similar to that described in this account. I have heard of their existence in Katsina, Kano, Zaria and Bida, but I can obtain no exact description of them, while the Yerwa *dogodogoma* knows nothing about their antiquity and is unable to state whether his own show and those given in other Provinces have any common origin.

Reprinted Nigerian Field, IV, April 1935.

'YANKAMANCI—THE CRAFT OF THE HAUSA COMEDIANS

C. G. B. Gidley

One form of Hausa entertainment which has so far not been studied in any detail is *'yankamanci*, that is, the activities of the *'yankama* (sg. *dankama*),[1] Hausa minstrels who traditionally specialize in comedy. A study of the craft of the *'yankama* throws fresh light on words, phrases, and sentences which are deeply embedded in Hausa culture, and on various aspects of Hausa life in general.

For three generations at least *'yankama* have been welcome but the content of their performances, loosely described as *ban dariya* "amusing", is fully known only to Hausa audiences. Some outside observers may have to rely entirely for their knowledge on the sort of tales found in *Magana Jari Ce*,[2] where the minstrels are represented as knaves known for their *shakiyanci* and *ja'irci*, commonly translated "shamelessness" and "disrespectfulness". The notion conveyed by the Hausa name may indeed once have been "villainy", then "brazen effrontery", but in the context of *'yankamanci* today it now corresponds to "satire" as that word is popularly used in the context of an English society—or perhaps "lighthearted disregard for convention".

The word *'yankamanci*, indicating the craft as practised by minstrels throughout the years, is not in any dictionary, nor is another word *kamanci*, meaning a minstrel's craft. This omission is not significant because the ending *-anci* may indicate the craft, status and characteristics, including the language, of a particular category of people, and words with this ending are not always listed as lexical items. There are two relevant glosses: firstly, in 1934, Bargery[3] described *dankama* (pl. *'yankama*) as "a minstrel who catches his reward, thrown from a distance, in his mouth"; secondly, in 1949, Abraham[4] described the same item as "a minstrel who catches in his mouth the largesse thrown from afar", and he added that his epithet is *Jarmai*, "brave man". Today *'yankamanci* needs new description because of the unique range of comical language which it has accumulated in its tradition, not merely because *'yankama* perform in the broadcasting studio.

This study has three aims: firstly to reveal the full content of *'yankamanci* for the first time in perspective; secondly to illustrate it with authentic material; thirdly to prove that local audiences appreciate a brand of "satire" performed according to standards which have become traditional. Today, *'yankama* have a reputation as high—or as low—as comedians anywhere. They have never customarily used *habaici* "hurtful innuendo", *zambo* "provocative speech and song", and *batsa* "indecent remarks" to the extent that some other *maroka* (sg. *maroki*[5] "mendicant minstrel") have done. They have been welcome because their performances are skilful and genuinely designed to amuse men, women and children, and in this they are very successful. Although there may be passers-by who are critical of their frivolity, the local audience does not look at them askance. These circumstances have not attracted the interest of trained observers; perhaps, being frivolous, *'yankamanci* may seem at first to be beneath academic attention. Nevertheless, the craft is worthy of serious study, both in view of the response which the performers' skill calls forth, and also for the special modes of expression which are of interest from a linguistic point of view, and for the way in which they illuminate Hausa life.

The study is arranged in two parts. The first part introduces the *'yankama* and in particular gives a first-hand account of performances by Haji Katsina, a popular entertainer of over forty years ago. The second part describes features of the craft and contains a representation of illustrations; it also includes an account of the themes and practices of the comedians during the last ten years and discusses the standards by which performances are judged by Hausa audiences. The aim is to consider *'yankamanci* as far as possible from a Hausa, rather than from a European stand-point.

PART I—THE COMEDIANS
Haji Katsina

It is appropriate to begin a study of present day *'yankamanci* by looking at an account of performances by Haji Katsina, a comedian who visited Keffi, Lafiya, and Wamba,[6] over forty years ago. No outstanding merit is claimed for him, except that he had the gift of making people laugh. This result was partly due to his skill in expressing himself, and partly due to his skill in pantomime. A Hausa essay, composed in 1928 by the Emir of Abuja, Alhaji Sulaimanu Barau, O.B.E., O.N.N., well illustrates the characteristics of comedians of the period.[7] In this essay Haji Katsina is referred to as practising *roƙo* ("mendicancy", cf. *maroƙi* "mendicant"); the fact that he was a mendicant does not detract from his reputation as an entertainer, and entertainers of this type were often persons of some substance. The Emir's account, given below, vividly portrays him as a *maroƙi* of considerable verbal, musical and dramatic talent.

Zuwan Dankama Haji Katsina

Tun da na ke ganin 'yankama ban taba ganin mai azanci da ba mutane dariya irin Haji Katsina ba. Kome rashin dariyar mutum, in Haji Katsina ya yi wasa a gabansa, ba zai san sa'an da dariya za to kubce masa ba. Yaran makarantar Keffi kullun ba abin da su ke so irin Haji Katsina ya kawo masu wasa.

Ran Juma'a da safe muna zaune, muna tadi, sai muka ji motsin gangarsa a ƙofar gidanmu, nan da nan sai muka fashe zuwa kofar gida don mu gan shi. Kuma kowane yaro da jin gangar sai ya sheƙo a guje, kamar una yi masa kaimi, zuwa ƙofar gida. Aka taru aka yi mar zobe. Da fari muka masa aninai ya cafe kamar yadda gwanin wasan kurket ke cafe ƙwallo, don sauri ma har da baki shi ya ke gamawa. Muka ce muna so ya yi mana rantsuwa da aradu in zai iya cafe dukkan aninai in mun jeho mar. Sai ya ce "Na rantse da abassama, kunkuniya ta faɗa Kaina." Kome dabon da ka yi ba ya yarda ya rantse da aradu.

Da ya gama rantsuwa sai ya dau karatun Alkur'ani, ya jawo wani kundi, na irin littafan nan da Turawa ke yarwa, daga aljifu, ya gyara murya, ya yi ta nasa surkulle.

Da gama wannan sai ya ɗau wa'azi. Ya fara da irin gyaran muryan nan da mahardata ke yi ni baƙi ya shige masu duhu, ya kuwa ƙi cin gaba sai da kowannenmu ya jefa masa aninai. Daga nan sai ya soma da wasu waƙe waƙe masu ban dariya, kana ya ce "Wazantakunna, maigida kar ka ye yawo, zauna a zuba ma taka miyar, mace mai barin kiji ba karya kumallo ta ɓata, ranar cin kasuwa ta rasa cafane, ranar tashin kiyama Walakiri da lawashi zai yi mata duka a ɗuwaiwai, mu tabbata gida biyu, idan dai ba mu tabbata a kasuwa ba mu tabbata gidan buki, duniya gidan daɗi, lahira gidan ƙarfi. Malamai, reniya haramun ce, kyaun mutum abin da aka ba shi kar ya rena. Da kana jin ana faɗan Haji Katsina, ba wani ba ne, ni ne. Don taƙamar tsoron Allah ba ni magana da mata da rana ko rana ta faɗi, sai ko ni hannuna ya yi ɓatan kai ni yi yafuce."

Da ya gama wa'azi sai nan da nan ya sauke ganga ya zame mana alaro, ya ɗauke ta da ƙyar ya aza a ka yana ta kirari. Suka yi tsada da mai daya, bayan ya tantambaye shi irin kayan, ko haja ce, ko goro ko kuwa dwalli. Ya ce a ba shi hujin kuɗin ci ya bar wa matarsa. Da suka shirya da mai kaya, bayan ya yi ta kawo 'yan amaja iri iri dabam dabam, sai ya ɗau ganga da ƙyar sai ka ce wani kaya mai nauyi, ya ce "Ba wani ba ne, ni ne rungume daji, da aka yi sufurina in ɗauko hauren giwa, sai da na kawo hauren akwiya ɗari tara. Aka yi sufuri na Jos in ɗauko gishiri arbaminya, ban ɗauko ba sai na iso da gishiri arbaminya a wanke."

Muka tambaye shi ko ya iya hoto, sai ya ce mana "Ni ba dan hoto ba, amma a kan sake kama". Ya tuɓe rigunansa, ya jajjanye wando, ya ya da 'yar ganga, ya fito da 'yar garma wadda aka yi da sakaina, ya fara taken 'yan hoto. Ya yi ta waƙa amma fa duk abin da ya ke faɗi dabam ne da na 'yan hoton gaske, ya ƙare da cewa "Noma aka fi ni ba shiga rumbu ba. Sai ni ka da gumba, gaba maƙi magani. Sai ni gwani mai-a-ƙara."

Da ya gama waɗannan abubuwa duk sai ya cika mana da kiran salla amma fa waɗancan na haya sun fi ban dariya, don haka sai mu bar kaza cikin gashinta. Amma ga waɗansu labarai nasa nan guda biyu waɗanda suka fi ban mamaki da kuma dariya.

Haji katsina ya ji labarin alkeri da karimci da sarkin Wamba ke yi wa baƙi. Samun sarki mai son mutane da malamai irinsa da wuya cikin sarakunan arna na Binuwai. Shi dai iyayensa da kakaninsa ba su gaji kome ba sai mushrikanci da tsafi. Amma shi Allah ya zaɓe shi, ya shiryad da shi, ya musulunta, kuma ya zama mai son mutane. Ba fatan da ya ke irin garinsa dai ya cika da Musulmi.

Haji Katsina ya yi shiri. Ya rataya gangarsa da takobinsa na ice cikin kube, ya sayi rawani da kandiri, da takalma, ya sa matarsa a gaba, suka tashi daga Keffi suka nufi Wamba. Ran da za su shiga, ya bulbula rawaninsa, ya kima naɗi irin na malamai, ya sa riga da bujen wando, ya kawo sambatsai ya zuba, ya ɗosana malafa a ka, 'yar gangarsa kuwa ya rufe da hannun riga, wanda duk ya gan shi sai ya rantse da Allah wani baddan malami ne. Shi ke nan, ya kama hanya zuwa ƙofar fadar Sarkin Wamba.

Da ya isa sai fadawa suka zaci wani shuhun malami ne, suka shiga maza suka yi mar iso gurin sarki. Sarki nan da nan ya fito, suka gaisa. Ya sa a kai masauki mai kyau, kuma ya ce a kula da shi.

Da azuhur ta yi, sa'an da sarki ya gama salla ya fito, sai ya aika ya zo su gaisa. Sai ɗankama ya sake yin irin shigar malamai ya zo gaban sarki. Sarki ya karama shi, ya karama shi, ya ce ya guso su yi bannu. Nan da nan da sarki ya miƙa masa hannu, sai ya ƙi, ya noƙe ya yi farat ya jawo ganga daga cikin riga ya kaɗa. Shi ke nan sai sarki da jama'arsa suka ƙyalƙyale da dariya kamar za su suƙe. Suka yi ta al'ajabin abin. Sarki ya kawo riga da kuɗi, ya sallame shi.

Ga yadda suka yi da Sarkin Lafiya nada. Sarkin Lafiya mai mutuwa mutum ne mai sarauta, yana da kamewa da hakimcewa da daure fuska. Samun ya yi dariya da wuya. Fadawa da mutanen gari ba su ganin dariyarsa. Da Haji Katsina ya yi labarinsa, sai ya tashi takanas ya tafi gare shi yin roƙo. Ya saukad da shi.

Wata rana da yamma sarki ya fito ƙofar gida, fadanci ya cika sai Haji Katsina ya fito da gangarsa yana kiɗa da wasa mai ban dariya a gaban sarki. Dukkan fadawa sun yi ta dariya sai sarki. Ana nan yana cikin wasa sai ya hangi wani babban basaraken sarki, jarmai, irin mayaƙan nan da sarki ke alfarma da su gun yaƙi, ya doso fada da mutane dii a bayansa, sun daho mar. Da ya tunkaro gaban sarki sonai, sai Haji Katsina ya saro takobinsa na ice, ya ya da gangarsa, ya ko tasam ma basaraken nan da takobin. Basaraken yana zato takobin kirki ne, sai ya banko da gudu da ya ga d'ankama ya gabato shi. Dag nan da sarki ya fara dariya sai da ya yi kamar zai mutu. Ya ga basarakensa, wanda ya ke ta k'ama da shi, wanda ya ke zato ko bindiga ba ta ba shi tsoro, ga shi ya zo ya guji takobin ice. Sai sarki ya kawo kyauta ya ba Haji Katsina.

Translation

The Arrival of the Comedian Haji Katsina

In all my experience of watching comedians, I have never seen one who had so much good sense and who was so entertaining as Haji Katsina. However glum a person might be, when Haji Katsina performed in front of him, he would involuntarily burst out laughing. The boys of Keffi School liked nothing so much as Haji Katsina performing for them.

On Friday morning we were sitting down talking, when we heard the sound of his drum at the gate of our compound. At once we dashed to the gate to see him. All the boys seemed spurred to the entrance at the sound of the drum. People formed a circle around him. At first we threw him coins to catch like an expert fielder catching a cricket ball,[8] and to keep up with us he even caught some in his mouth. We said we wanted him to swear by thunder, to say he could catch all the coins when we threw them to him. "I shall probably swear by the thing above", said he, "soot may fall on my head". No matter how much you pressed him he would not agree to swear by thunder.[9]

After taking the oath, he took up a "Koran", a wad of discarded magazines of the kind which Europeans throw away, which he drew from his pocket. He then started his own kind of nonsense. After this performance he delivered "admonition", beginning with those hums and haws which those learning to recite the Koran by heart habitually resort to when they cannot remember the text, and he refused to go on until we had all thrown him a coin. Presently he began singing comical songs—"And talk of you", he intoned, "Master of the house, do not go for a walk, sit down for your soup to be poured out; a woman leaving her husband without any breakfast will go astray; on market day she will lack ingredients for soup.[10] On the day of resurrection Walnakir[11] will beat her on the behind with an onion top.[12] Let us be well established in two houses;[13] when we are not established in the market,[14] then let us be well established at a feast; the world is a mansion of pleasure, the next world a mansion of strength. My learned friends, despising something is contrary to Mohammedan precepts. A good man does not despise what he is given. When you hear Haji Katsina, it is I and nobody else.[15] Because of my pride in my fear of Allah, I do not speak to women by day, nor after sunset, except perhaps when my hand veers off course and I beckon to them."[16]

After his "admonition" he quickly laid down his drum and became a porter for us.[17] He raised it with difficulty and put it on his head, shouting his own praise. Then he bargained with a customer. He repeatedly asked him what kind of load—cloth, colanuts, or antimony[18]—then he said he required an advance of money to leave for his wife. When a bargain was struck, and after a series of lame excuses for inaction, he lifted the drum as if it were a heavy weight. "It is not just anyone", said he. "It is I who can clutch the whole Bush to my chest. When I was hired to carry elephant tusks, I brought nine hundred goats' teeth. When I was hired as we are at Jos to carry four hundred sacks (literally '400 salt'), I arrived with four hundred empty ones!"

We then asked him if he could imitate the country dancers who entertain and work on the farms. "I am not a dancer", he told us, "but one's appearance can sometimes change." He took off his robes and hitched up his trousers; then he threw down his drum, took out a hoe made of a piece of gourd and started the dancers' rhythm. He sang a song but, mind you, all he sang about was quite different to what real dancers sing about. He ended by proclaiming, "I am only bested when it is a question of farm work, not when it is a matter of going into the corn store. There is no one except myself who can lay low pounded bullrush millet, I am the opposition against which no charm is effective. There is no one in the same class as I am, I am the expert at asking for more!"

He concluded his performance for us with the call to prayer, but the turns which I first described were more amusing, so we had better not let out any more secrets. Meanwhile here are two more amusing and laughable stories.

Haji Katsina heard news of the kindness and generosity which the Chief of Wamba showed to strangers. It would have been hard to find a Chief like him, who had such consideration for ordinary people and learned men, among the pagan Benue chiefs. His fathers and his forefathers had just not inherited anything except the worship of idols and fetishes; however, notwithstanding, he had been chosen by Allah, his feet had been set upon the path,[19] and he had become a Mohammedan—and furthermore he had become a philanthropist. His one wish was to see his town filled with Mohammedans.

Haji Katsina made ready. He slung on his drum and his wooden sword in a scabbard; he bought a turban, a wide-brimmed hat, a staff, and sandals; then, with his wife in front, he set out from Keffi in the direction of Wamba. On the day they were to enter the town, he made his turban bulge from his head, and tied it as large as learned men generally do;[20] then clad in a gown and large baggy trousers, he produced ornamental sandals of rank, slipped them on, and perched his wide hat on the top of his head. His little drum was hidden up his sleeve. Anyone seeing him would have sworn he was learned and distinguished. He made straight for the entrance of the Chief of Wamba's compound.

On his arrival the courtiers thought he was a famous mallam. They quickly retired and announced his arrival to the Chief. The Chief emerged without delay, and formal greetings were exchanged. He instructed that Haji should be conducted to a good place to stay, and that notice should be taken of him.

About two in the afternoon, when the Chief appeared after prayer, he sent a messenger to ask Haji to come and see him. Haji once more clad himself in scholarly attire and appeared before the Chief, who received him in a kindly manner, and invited him to approach and shake hands. Just as the Chief put out his hand, Haji declined it. He hung back, and with a sudden movement produced the drum[21] from inside his gown. Then he beat his drum. That was that. The Chief and his retinue rocked with laughter—it was as if they would become exhausted. They were astonished by what had happened. The Chief brought a gown and money and sent Haji home.

This is what happened with the previous Emir of Lafiya.[22] The deceased Emir was a regally minded individual, reserved, aloof, and stern faced. He hardly ever laughed. Courtiers and townspeople never saw him laughing. When Haji Katsina heard about him he went to him especially to practise mendicancy. The Emir gave him a place to stay.

One day in the evening, the Emir was outside the entrance of the palace, the courtiers were all there, when Haji Katsina brought out his drum and started drumming and performing in front of the Emir. All the courtiers laughed but the Emir was not amused. After a while, in the middle of his performance, Haji caught sight of one of the Emir's noblemen, a valiant man,[23] the kind which the Emir was proud of in battle, making straight for the palace with his retinue streaming close behind him. At the very moment the nobleman arrived, Haji Katsina drew his wooden sword, threw down his drum, and went at him with the sword. The nobleman, thinking it was real, beat a hasty retreat as soon as he saw the comedian confronting him. Presently the Emir started to laugh, and then he laughed as if he would pass away. He had seen his nobleman, whom he was proud of, whom he had assumed not even a gun would alarm, and there he was, on arrival, put to flight by a wooden sword. The Emir gave orders that a present should be brought and given to Haji Katsina."

There is no trace of Haji Katsina today. In November 1965, a search was made in Katsina,[24] Daura, Batsari, Ingawa, Kankara, and Funtua without success. His name was an impossible Hausa name and obviously assumed; and since there is no news of him in Benue either, it seems that he went there on a visit using an assumed name and in disguise.

Summing up the features of Haji Katsina's performances before going on to modern 'yankamanci, the main ingredients of his style of comedy (wasan kwaikwayo mai ban dariya—the translation of comedy given in the Hausa Language Board's dictionary) were waƙe waƙe masu ban dariya "comical songs", wa'azi "admonishment", surkulle "nonsensical patter", which no doubt include addu'a "prayer" as it does today, comical kirari "shouting of personal slogans" and shameless burlesque, parody, and caricature.

Impersonation was also a salient feature. In those days before the spread of even local knowledge, illiterate people were easily taken in by 'yankama on itineration; successful practical jokes were a subject for gossip; the comedians were the bearers and creators of news and their jokes had an educative as well as recreational effect. Nowadays the spread of general education, assisted by modern media such as wireless and television, has spread general knowledge so that opportunities for impersonation on the grand scale are few and far between. Such wireless programmes as *Zaɓi Sonka* "Listeners' Choice" make popular songs well known to a wide listening public, with the result that the parody of popular songs has become the main ingredient in the performances of modern comedians otherwise, except for the constantly changing topical allusions, the main features and themes appear to be still as they were in the past.

Alhaji A. Dama

To turn from Haji Katsina's day to more recent times, it must be remembered that during the second world war the cinematograph enlivened many camps where Nigerian troops were stationed, and travel on active service widened the outlook of many Northerners who, until then, might have been classed as *kifin rijiya* "fish of the well", i.e. an untravelled person, once an epithet for an inhabitant of Zaria. Whereas as late as 1921 even the telephone would have seemed miraculous in Katsina,[25] since the war modern forms of entertainment have tended to distract the attention of ordinary people from 'yankamanci performances. 'Yankamanci has thus suffered a decline. Nevertheless it is happily still in evidence to be studied and enjoyed, ably performed by such modern comedians as Alhaji A. Dama, though no longer with the elaborately prepared practical jokes of former times.

Alhaji A. Dama, whose professional name is a phrase *a dama* meaning "let it be mixed" (sc. *fura* "flourball in sour milk") is the son of a famous *ɗankama* from Gaya in Kano Emirate. He was once a full-time professional comedian but is now a business contractor who gives comical performances (*ban dariya*) from time to time to display his skill and obtain reward. Example from his performances, kindly supplied by correspondents and by the Ministry of Information, are used in the second part of this study to illustrate some of the themes discussed there.

PART II—THE CRAFT

1. Content

Modern 'yankamanci, like Haji Katsina's performances, consists of a mixture of so-called wa'azi "admonition", addu'a prayer together with comical songs, often linked by surkulle[26] "nonsensical patter". Each of these features will be discussed in turn and illustrated by appropriate examples. It may be noted that these performances often contain allusions to religious matters, which might appear scandalous, but which are generally acceptable in the context of these performances as explained in section 3 below.

(i) Wa'azi

Wa'azi is the normal term used for admonition which, in context of 'yankamanci, embraces imitations of gargadi (learning about how to live a good life), which are held in deep respect. 'Yankamanci, however, often includes a humorous imitation of such wa'azi, making play on serious admonition by means of hybrid Hausa Arabic words, for which it is convenient to use the traditional term macaronics. In the same way Haji Katsina prefixed his admonition by intoning wazantakunna, as if the utterance was a learned Arabic invocation. This is in fact a combination of Arabic forms before and after a Hausa word: wazantakunna then consists of wa (Arabic "and"), zanta (Hausa "converse"), and kuna (Arabic "of you" feminine). Examples of such nonsensical macaronic invocations are intoned as a preface to most 'yankama wa'azi in present day 'yankamanci. 'Yankama usually perform as a group of three comedians; in wa'azi one comedian often intones a succession of macaronics in a bleating voice, while a second responds with an interpretation in brusque Hausa. It may be added that they always pose as learned men and dress accordingly, the interpreter appearing to be more important while the other merely recites by rote. All the while both comedians remain solemn and act with complete decorum.

The following, supplied by the Ministry of Information is a typical example of *wa'azi*.

Wa-ya-tuwo-kum	tuwon shinkafa ya damu da romo,
Wa-saka-kum,	a sa mini mara tara ni kaɗai,
Ya-wa-saya-kum,	sayen nama ya wajaba ga maigida,
Wa-ya-manuni-a-manuni,	ya nuna tiɓis ke nan
Et-O-Votre-tuwo	tuwo[27] of rice is mixed with broth,
Et-placing-de vous,	place nine large helpings just for me alone,
O-et-buying-de vous	buying meat is incumbent on the householder.
Et-O-the forefinger,	
Sur the forefinger,	that means it is nicely cooked.

The first macaronic is a mixture of Arabic *wa* 'and', *ya* "Oh", and *kum* "of you" (m) with Hausa *tuwo* "cornmush"; similarly, in the second example, the Hausa verb *saka* "to place" provides the nonsensical middle element. The third line is a mixture of *ya, wa*, and *kum* with the Hausa verb *saya* "to buy", followed by the response of the second comedian. The fourth line is a play upon the Hausa verbs *nuna* "to be well cooked" (with tone pattern low high) and *nuna* "to show" (with tone pattern high low). It is also said to be a play on the Hausa saying *kowane allazi da nasu amanu*, meaning, each person has his own part to play; the tone pattern may also be distorted to suggest further allusions. The reference to the forefinger suggests that it is prodding the joint of meat to feel if it is tender, but the whole is wrapped up in a piece of Arabic persiflage. The original *wa'azi* would perhaps refer to the necessity of laying in *guzuri* "provisions" by good deeds and abstinence in this world, with promise of future enjoyment in the next. The parody continues as follows:

Sai uwargida ta zakuɗa waje ɗaya, aikinta ya ƙare,
Sai maigida ya jawo kujera majlas, ya zauna,
Wa-gauraya-kum,   ya motsa tukunya da kansa,
Wa-tsama-kun,   ya riƙa tsama guda guda har ya yi sau biyar,
Wannan shi ne hamsus salawatu a tukunyar miya,
Ka san salla sau biyar a ke yi kullun,

Watau ka yi maganin mantuwa,
Kowace salla ka raka ta da tsoka guda.
The wife must make way, her work is done,
The master must draw up a chair and sit in state,

Et-mixing-de vous,   the master stirs the pot personally,
Et-extracting-de vous, he keeps on extracting one piece at a time
                   until he has five,

This means five daily prayers in the gravy pot,
You say prayers five times a day,
Therefore this prevents you forgetting,
Accompany each prayer with a piece of meat.

(ii) *Addu'a* with *Surkulle*

Wa'azi as described above is often followed by so-called *addu'a* "prayer" which follows the pattern of serious prayer but introduces a whole array of incongruous subjects. The prayers are usually linked by long streams of patter (*surkulle*). The following example, one of a series sent to me by the Ministry of Information, starts with a short prayer followed by patter.

Allah ya kwaɓe mana fashin girki, Allah ya kwaɓe mana ciwon cikin aljihu, watau gari ya waye mutum ya shafa aljihunsa ya ju babu kome sai hus. Ga shi kuwa yana baƙo a garin da ya je, bai kuma san kowa ba. Ya tsinci kwabo guba, garin karambani sai ya ci ƙosan bebiya na kwabo biyu, ta kuwa riƙe shi, ta tara masa mutane . . . .

Allah ya kwaɓe mana ɗingila, watau ɗingila dingila ita ce a dama fura a ajiye a koma don ɗaukowa sai a tarar kaji sun kifas da ita. Allah dai ya kiyashe mu.

Allah ya kwaɓe mana makuwa, watau a ɗauko kwanon tuwo za a kawo maka sai a yi tuntuɓe tuwon ya kife . . . .

Allah ya kwaɓe mana tsautasyin dare, watau ya zamana gidanka ba a yi tuwo ba sa'an nan ga yara ci-ma-zaune, sa'an nan ɗakinka na yoyon ruwa . . . .

May Allah defend us against failure to put the pot on the fire. May Allah protect us from malaise of the pocket, that is to say someone feels in his pocket in the light of dawn and can only feel fluff, and there he is, a stranger in a strange town, with no friend to go to, he finds a penny, picks it up, and attempting the impossible, eats tuppence worth of cake sold by a deaf mute lady. She captures him and attracts everyone's attention . . . .

May Allah defend us from a second rate situation, and by a second rate situation I mean one in which the flour ball with milk has been prepared,[28] put down, and when one comes back to pick it up, the hen has overturned it. May Allah preserve us.

May Allah defend us from losing our bearings, I mean someone picking up the bowl of *tuwo* and bringing it to you, and then stumbling and upsetting the lot . . . .

May Allah defend us against disaster at night, I mean the position is there is no *tuwo* at home, moreover there are your offspring, and furthermore your roof is leaking . . . etc. etc. etc.

(iii) *Waƙe waƙe masu ban dariya*

The comedians' performances very often also contain parodies of well known serious songs, accompanied on drums in such a way that the rhythm and chant bear a close resemblance to the original. Once again the whole performance is comical but without the vestige of a smile.

The following may be taken as typical examples, though the parody, which depends so much on rhythm and tune, cannot be demonstrated without a much more detailed analysis than is possible here.

(1) *Serious song*
Mala'ikun Alkiyama ba su dad̄in gamo,
Sun jingina manya manyan sanduna sun tsaye.

The Angels of Resurrection are not pleasant to meet
They prop up their huge rods and are adamant.[29]

Parody
Kunun daka ya kori niƙa har waje,
Fate fate sha zamanka ba za mu d̄auke ka ba.

The pounded gruel has driven the gruel from grinding out,
Cakes remain there! We shall not remove you.[30]

(2) *Serious Song*
Lokacin na Aliyyar Duniya
In ya gabato kowa ya sani.

The time set for the present Islamic dispensation to end,
Everybody will know when it approaches.[31]

Parody
Ranar rikicewar kasuwa,
In ta gabato kowa ya sani.

The day the market goes awry,
Everybody will know when it approaches.[32]

The parody continues as follows:

Malamina ba ya cin kwaɗo amma ya kan taɓa ɗan romon
miya,
Kazar gidanmu gwanar tono gwanar ƙwazaba,
Allah ya ba mu tumatir ran nan.

My mallam does not eat cold groundnut gravy,[33]
But he is in the habit of occasionally taking a little
soupbroth,
Our chicken is a clever scratcher and a clever pest.
May Allah give us a tomato on that day.[34]

(3) The next example is a parody of a standard praise song,
sung for the amusement of the late Alhaji Sir Ahmadu
Bello

Maiƙashin arziki da yawa,
Sardauna mai hannuwu dama,
Ruwa suna maganin dauɗa,
Fura tana maganin yunwa,
Sardauna yana maganin ɗari,
Mu kuwa muna maganin ƙosai
Hana kangara ɗan Ibrahim

You are destined for much prosperity,
Sardauna with two right hands,[35]
Water is the remedy for dirt,[36]

Flour balls are the remedy for hunger,
Sardauna is the remedy for cold,[37]
We are the remedy for cakes,
Son of Ibrahim, hold back the headstrong.[38]

(4) The last example consists of a parody of an outstanding song of high quality, concerning the Sokoto lineage of Sarkin Gobir Na Isa,[39] which refers to the deeds of his illustrious ancestors in the Jihad, the holy war of the early nineteenth century. The original song was first sung by its composer Na Rambada who is now dead, though a gramophone record of it by him is still available.[40] The parody, which is given after the translation of the original, was compiled from a tape of a modern performance in 1965. Unfortunately it has not been possible to establish the identity of the singer satisfactorily as the tape contains a number of performances and the '*yankama* concerned are not named. The audience's laughter in response to the parody does not diminish the respect for Na Rambada or their appreciation of his original composition.

THE ORIGINAL SONG
Gwarzon Shamaki Na Malam, Toron Giwa

1. Arna sun san halin Alu mai saje na Isa,
2. Ahmadu, kakanka na mazajen gaban arna,
3. Sun san Bello, ya ci Gawungazagu, ya ci Alkalawa,
4. Atiku, ya darzaza Bauci,
5. Iro na Kontagora ya ci mutanen Gwari
6. To, duk martabarsu na nan gun hannu nai,
7. Garzon Shamaki na Malam, Toron Giwa,
8. Baban Dodo ba a tam mai da batun banza,
9. Moriki, Kaura, da Zurmi duk magana ta zama dai,
10. Bungudu da Gusau sai Kwatarkwashi ga Dandoto,
11. Sun san Garba dan Hassan,
12. Kome ka yi ba a cewa ba daidai ba,
13. Nasabar Shehu ba ta dai da kakan kowa,
14. Baban Shamaki na Malam, Toron Giwa,

15. Ba a tam ma da batun banza,
16. Na tuna wata shekara da anka yi taro Hausa,
17. Kamfun nan ga arbain da bakwai duk sun zo,
18. Ni baya ga Isa ban ji labarin kowa ba,
19. Bana Ahmadu, Hausa ka rinjaye ni na yi,
20. In an ce Isa ba ka jin an ce wani sarki
21. Ni kau duk Hausa ba ka jin wata waƙa bayan tau,
22. Gwarzon Shamaki na Malam, Toron Giwa,
23. Baban Dodo ba a tam ma da batun banza,
24. Ga ma wani turnuku da Argungu ta kawo,
25. Ga wani rincimi da Argungu ta kawo,
26. Ga dokinsu ya tafo, mu ko namu ya tafo,
27. Sai ga Abubakhar cikin mota ya kawo,
28. Ya ce Ahmadu Mohammadu,
29. Sarkin Gobir na Isa, kar ka ji tsoron kowa,
30. Gwarzon Shamaki na Mlam, Toron Giwa,
31. Baban Dod ba tam ma da batun banza,
32. Ahmadu, Sarkin Gabas da Sarkin Rabah,
33. Mun ji daɗi ran nan gamon da munka yi a bakin gulbi, etc.

Translation

1. The pagans know the character of Alu of Isa[41] with the sidewhiskers,
2. Ahmadu, your ancestor was a great fighter of pagans,
3. They know Bello,[42] he conquered at Gawungazangu, he won Alkalawa,[43]
4. Atiku,[44] he forced his way through Bauchi,
5. Ibrahim of Kontagora[45] defeated the Gwari pagan,
6. Yes, all the flower of their nobility was there in his hand,
7. Dauntless patriarch of Shamaki,[46] associate of Mallam Bull Elephant,
8. Father of Dod, one does not provoke you with a trifling matter,
9. Moriki, Kaura, and Zurmi are all one in submission,
10. Bunguda and Gusau obey as well as Kwatarkwashi and Chafe[47]
11. They know Garba,[48] the descendant of Hassan,
12. Whatever you do, no one says you are wrong,

13. The lineage of the Shehu[49] is not like that of anyone,
14. Dauntless patriarch of Shamaki, associate of Mallam, Bull Elephant,
15. One does not provoke you with trifle,
16. I remember a year when there was a great gathering in Hausaland,[50]
17. All the forty-seven districts came,
18. I did not hear any mentioned except Isa,
19. This year, Ahmadu, in Hausa country you are supreme, so am I,
20. If you hear Isa you will not hear any other district head mentioned,
21. And I—my song is the only song heard in Hausaland,
22. Dauntless Patriarch of Shamaki, associate of Mallam, Bull Elephant,
23. One does not provoke you with a trifle,
24. There was an uproar which Argungu caused,[51]
25. There was a fracas due to Argungu,
26. There were their cavalry, and there were ours,
27. There too was Abubakhar in his motor car,
28. "Ahmadu Mohammadu", said he,
29. Sarkin Gobir do not stand in awe of anyone,
30. Dauntless Patriarch of Shamaki, associate of Mallam, Bull Elephant,
31. Father of Dodo, one does not provoke you with a trifling affair,
32. Ahmadu, Lord of the East,[52] District Head of Rabah,
33. We were happy that day we met on the bank of the river, etc.

Parody

1. Baban Shamaki tuwo da miya yai dadi
2. Baban Arai ba a zo maka da batun kosai,
3. Gwarzon Shamaki tuwo da miya yai dadi,
4. Ahmadu, Allah ya ba mu albarkar Dan Fodiyo,
5. Ya yi zaman duniya da imani ya kaura,
6. Gwarzon Shamaki tuwo da miya ya yi dadi,
7. Baban Arai ba a zo maka da batun kosai,
8. Ahmadu, Allah ya ba mu albarkar Nana uwar Daje,

9. Ta yi zaman duniya da imani ya Ƙaura,
10. Gwarzon Shamaki tuwo da miya yai daɗi,
11. Baban Arai ba a zo maka da batun Ƙosai,
12. Ahmadu Allah ya ba mu albarkar 'yan koko,
13. Sun yi zaman duniya da imani sun saisai
14. Gwarzon Shamaki tuwo da miya yai daɗi,
15. Ahmadu, Allah ya ba mu albarkar 'yan Ƙosai,
16. Sun yi zaman duniya su yi suya tai daɗi,
17. Mutanen sun iya Ƙosai wallahi
18. Tai daɗi sun iya Ƙosai wallahi
19. Ahmadu, Allah ya ba mu albarkar Umoru Gero,
20. Ya yi zaman duniya cikin daji ya Ƙaura,
21. Gwarzon Shamaki tuwo da miya yai daɗi,
22. Baban Arai ba a zo maka da batun Ƙosai,
23. Ahmadu, Allah yaba mu albarkar Shinkafa,
24. Tai zaman duniya cikin fadama ta Ƙaura, Alah ya gafarta wa Shinkafa,[53]
25. Gwarzon Shamaki tuwo da miya yai daɗi,
26. Baban Arai, ba a zo maka da batun Ƙosai,
27. Na tuna turnukun da sunka yi bakin gulbi,
28. Yaƙinsu ya tafo mu ko namu ya tafo,
29. Shinkafa tana faɗin ita kam ta tuba,
30. Gero yana faɗin shi kam ya tuba,
31. Maiwa tana afaɗin ita kam ta tuba,
32. Dawa tana faɗin ita kam ta tuba,
33. Waken shina faɗin shi kam ya tuba
34. Sai ka gama lafiya da imani ni ji 'yan fura,
35. Gwarzon Shamki tuwo da miya yai daɗi
      Yai daɗi tuwo
      Yai daɗi wallahi
      Kai tuwo da miya yai daɗi wallahi
36. Baban Arai ba a zo maka da batun banza, etc.

Translation

1. Patriarch of Shamaki, Tuwo with Gravy is good,
2. Father of little Beanflour Cake, one does not bring up the subject of Beanflour Cake to you,
3. Patriarch of Shamaki, Tuwo with Gravy is good,

4. Ahmadu, Allah blessed us with good influence of Dan Fodiyo,
5. He spent his time in the world in the true faith and died,
6. Patriarch of Shamaki, Tuwo with Gravy is good,
7. Father of the little Beanflour Cake, one does not bring up the subject of Beanflour Cake to you,
8. Ahmadu, Allah blessed us with Nana,[54] the mother of Daje,
9. She dwelt in this world in the faith and migrated,
10. Patriarch of Shamaki, Tuwo with Gravy is good,
11. Father of little Beanflour Cake, one does not bring up the subject of Beanflour Cake to you,
12. Ahmadu, Allah blessed us with the sellers of gruel,
13. They dwelt in this world in the faith and traded,
14. Patriarch of Shamaki, Tuwo with Gravy is good,
15. Ahmadu, Allah blessed us with the beanflour cake sellers,
16. They dwelt in this world to fry them up nicely,
17. These people can certainly make beanflour cakes, upon my word,
18. The frying is nice, they can make beanflour cake, you have my word,
19. Ahmadu, Allah blessed us with the good influence of Umoru Millet,
20. He spent his time in the Bush and emigrated,
21. Patriarch of Shamaki, Tuwo with Gravy is good,
22. Father of little Beanflour Cake, one does not bring up the subject of Beanflour Cake to you,
23. Ahmadu, Allah blessed us with the good influence of Rice,
24. She spent her time in the world in the swamp and departed, May Allah pardon Rice,
25. Patriarch of Shamaki, Tuwo with Gravy is good,
26. Father of little Beanflour Cake, one does not bring up the subject of Beanflour Cake to you,
27. I remember the hubbub we made on the riverbank,
28. Their raiders arrived so did ours,
29. Rice was saying she completely submitted,
30. Millet was saying he completely submitted,
31. Another Millet was saying he completely submitted,
32. Guineacorn said she completely submitted,

33. Bean said he completely submitted,
34. You must all end well in the faith said the flourball sellers,
35. Patriarch of Shamaki, Tuwo with Gravy is good,
    Tuwo is nice
    Upon my word it is nice
    My word, Tuwo with Gravy is nice,
36. Father of little Beanflour Cake, one does not bring up a
    foolish subject to you, etc.

As has already been said, detailed analysis of the parody is not possible here, but it is clear that certain lines in it play on certain corresponding lines in the original. Thus lines 1 and 2 in the parody play upon lines 7 and 8 in the original at intervals whenever they occur. Again the phrase *turnukun da sunka yi bakin gulbi* in line 27 of the parody recalls a phrase *gamon da munka yi a bakin gulbi* in line 33 of the original; parody line 4 can be compared with original line 2; parody line 28 resembles original line 26; parody lines 29–33 recall original lines 2–6 and 9–10 relating to the conquest of enemies and the subsequent obedience of districts, instead of the comical surrender of individual crops. Throughout the parody the rhythm and chant closely resemble the original.

2. Themes

The main themes of *'yankamanci*, which are constantly recurring, are the learned pedant, gastronomy, and the domestic scene in all its variety. This has already been exemplified by Haji Katsina's reference to a woman not cooking her husband's breakfast. Comical allusions to women are abundant as in this brief extract from an address delivered by a *dankama* in the *Kasuwar Kuimi*[55] at Kano in 1956.

> "To Jama'a yanzu muna so mu yi ƙoƙari mu karɓi mulkin kanmu daga hannun waɗanda su ke riƙe da mulkin, su ne mata. Ka ga maigida kai ne ka ke shan wahala kullun, kana fita kana memo kayan abinci, sa'an nan kana kawowa gida, idan kuwa ka kawo gida abincin nan ya fi ƙarfinka. Idan an ƙare abinci, ba kai ne za su raba sa'an nan a ba ka."

> "Well, sirs, now we are trying to take over self government from those who hold power over us, I mean the women. Now look here,

sir, you are the one going to all the trouble, you are continually going out to fetch food, and bringing it home, but when you do, it goes outside your control, it is not you who divide it up, it is the women who distribute it, and only then will you get your share."

The above is an imitation of a theme popular with some orators at the time. *Nata* "women" are those in power, *Maigida* "master of the house" is the Hausa man in the street; *abinci* "food" is the country's product: *jama'a* "the people" are the people of the North; *gida* "home" is the North itself. The audience would react with laughter to the comedian's performance which might well be a ridiculous imitation of a political rally held round the corner; yet much can be learned from comedians about the everyday affairs of the past since they often used catchwords of the day that were in everyone's mouth.

Other themes are illustrated by the following extracts from performances by Alhaji A. Dama:

Theme	*Reference*
(i) Against the Race of Women	Duniya ta yi kyau mun karɓi mulki ga matammu.
	. . . the world is good, we have taken over the government from our women.
(ii) A Clear Explanation of Marriage	In za ka yi aure ka tambaya da kyau.
	. . . if you are going to marry make thorough enquiries in advance.
(iii) Advice about Shopping	Idan ka je kasuwa ka sayo nama da ɓargo da tantakwashi.
	. . . when you go to market you will probably bring back meat, a marrow, and the head of a sheep.
(iv) How to deal with a Guilty Chicken	Ka fige fuka fukanta biyu domin kuwa su ne idan kaza ya yi ta 'adi su ke taimakonta wajen hawa sama, watau su ne lauyoyinta guda biyi . . .

Pluck off the two wings which help a chicken to fly up when it has done damage, that is to say her two lawyers.

(v) A Mixed Dish

Tuwon masara taushen kabewa, Dafa duka ta fi su dadi,

Tuwo of maize cob, marrow gravy, Cooking all ingredients at once is best.

(vi) Concentration

Idan ana tuwo a gidanku kar ka je yawo, zauna ka cinye abinka kar ka ba kowa.

When *tuwo* is being made at home, don't go for a walk sit down and eat your own don't give it to anyone.

(vii) How to deal with a Renegade Wife

Idan matarka ta yi yaji kar ka je biko, ka dau dan kilishinka ka aika ka aika ka ga ta dawo.

If your wife runs away in anger, don't go after her to remonstrate, pick up a thin strip of meat from your portion and send it to her, you will probably see her come back.

The favourite topic of food, its production and preparation is well illustrated by a long historical "lecture" by an unknown comedian about the progress of *Gero* "Millet" from seed to spoon, the full text of which was kindly sent by the Ministry of Information in Kaduna in 1965. It describes an imaginary battle in imitation of the Battle of Badr in A.D. 624. It is introduced as follows:

"Wani labari. Karon Badar tsakanin Annabi Gero da Mala'ika Nono. Annabi Gero ya ce was Mala'ika Nono wace rana za mu yi yaki."

"A tale. The Battle of Badr between Prophet Millet and Angel Milk. Prophet Millet asked Angel Milk for the date for the battle."

The plot involves, among others, *Mala'ika Magirbi* "Angel Sickle", *Sarkin Alaro Murhu* "Chief Porter Tripod", *Babbar Bila*[56] *Tukunya* "Trusty Slave Stewpot", and *San Kurmi Igiya* "Market

Comptroller Rope". The narrative describes in ludicrous language the process of sowing and takes *Gero* through life stage by
stage until he succumbs in battle, reaches the pot, and disappears
down the throats of members of the audience who are mentioned
by name. The narrative ends *kafin a yi haka ƙasa suka yi sama
suka yi sanin gaibu sai ciki* "before this could be done the earth
turned upside down (for Prophet Millet and Angel Milk)—they
knew the mystery which only the stomach knows": *sanin gaibu
sai ciki* is a play on phrase common in *wa'azi* and conversation
sanin gaibu sai Allah "only Allah knows what is mysterious to
man".

The audience apparently regards as comical the contrast between real historical narrative and this nonsense. There is usually
play in every line and *dankama* delivers throughout his performance, and perfect timing for Hausa ears. Some of this narrative
is delivered with *kakale*, i.e. alternate rising and falling intona-
tion at a rapid speed, sometimes used by announcers to impress
listeners with an otherwise absent sense of dramatic urgency. The
nonsense is not generally hurtful when performed according to
the tradition (see section 3 below), nor is it detrimental to
authority. The audience is amused by the incongruous contrasts
and absurd juxtapositions which multiply rapidly as the *dankama*
speaks or sings. It may be a porter immediately followed by a
pedant, or absurd words to a serious theme, or perhaps an
invented saying *Allah maganin mutum im bai mutu ba* "Allah is
the remedy for a man when he is not dead".

While learning and religion are themselves never ridiculed,
there is ample evidence of ridicule of the learned pedant such as
one finds in Hausa literature, especially ridicule of the pedant
who is a charlatan and a rogue. There is no intention in
'yankamanci to do more than burlesque an imaginary class of
pedants. Generally mallams are held in the highest respect in
Hausaland. There is no lack of respect implied by the survival of
such sayings as *malamai ba su son junansu, hassada ga malamai,
gaba ga sarakuna gasa ga attajirai* "learned men do not like one
another, jealousy is the hallmark of learned men, enmity the
hallmark of Emirs, competition the hallmark of wealthy merchants". *Malamai suna so su ƙure juna* "learned men like to trip

each other up" is a popular opinion. Storytellers relate tales in which a mallam is made to appear a child when confronted with the simple reality of the world. He is nonplussed when dealing with *Habe*[57] shrewdness and *Bamaguje*[58] forthrightness. The ridicule in such tales is directed sometimes against an imaginary class of comical *duniya* mallams[59] who are fond of the pleasures of life while exhorting others to be abstinent. There is, for instance, a Hausa saying *kada ka yi aiki da aikin malami, ka yi koyi da fadar malami* "don't go by what a mallam does, copy what he says". As a catchphrase the epithet *Malami Sarkin Rikici* is intended to be humorous, and envisages a minor mercenary mallam preparing charms for payment simultaneously by a household and a thief. The mirth which it evokes is only *dariyar keta* "schadenfreude", a precise term meaning, in the context of *'yankamanci* that although slight malice may sometimes be implied, it is only in mild, charming, and somewhat lovable form, such as indicated by the pleasure one feels when one hears that a thief has been robbed of his stolen goods. Hausas love incongruous situations, and at the same time have the greatest respect for *da'a* "etiquette and decorum", *ladabi* "good manners", and *biyayya* "loyalty". It is unnecessary here to prove that mallams are respected. They are highly regarded by all classes of society in Hausaland. This fact will be apparent to anyone who has spent a little time in Hausa society.[60] Nevertheless great amusement is caused by an imaginary character like *Malam Zurke* in *Ruwan Bagaja*[61]; he enters for a competition with another mallam, also a charlatan, carrying an absurd number of Arabic books. He is shown a curved line, the meaning of which defeats him. Any *talaka* "ordinary man in the street" can see it is a representation of the moon drawn in the sand. He departs, disgraced among the jeers of small boys who throw mud. This has no effect on the status of mallams in popular esteem.

The account of the "Battle of Badr" illustrates the way in which millet, other foodstuffs, and common objects are personified. This is a very common feature of the fantasy world of *'yankamanci*, where staple crops and vegetables and farming instruments have life and personality. Sometimes they are depicted as angels and prophets; at other times there appears to be a scale of rank in which *tuwo* "cornmush", the basic item of Hausa diet, naturally has the highest place, whereas *kunu* "gruel" is of a lowlier order:[62] *Maigida* "Master" would not be pleased with it if there was something else which could be provided. All food can be placed in order of merit by the epicures in a Hausa household. In this hierarchy *Tuwo*, like Burns' Haggis, reigns supreme. In the performance of some *'yankama*, traders, pictured as *'yan burodi* "breadsellers", can be allocated stalls in a market where *Tuwo* is eventually acclaimed as Comptroller. This is illustrated by a further example sent by a correspondent in Kano in 1965.

Bayani a kan manya manyan Nijeriya

Guide to Important Nigerian Persons

Na daya	'yan burodi da 'yan tsire su ne wakilan Nijeriya.
Na biyu	'yan fura da 'yan koko da 'yan kunu su ne ministoci.
Na uku	'yan kunun zaki su ne masu jawo hankalin mutane.
Na fudu	'yan naman miya su ne keyateka.

The first	sellers of bread and sellers of meat on skewers, they are the members of the Nigerian House of Assembly.
The second	sellers of flour balls in milk, koko gruel and kunu gruel, they are the Ministers.
The third	sellers of sweet runny gruel, the propaganda experts.
The fourth	sellers of meat and gravy, the caretakers.

Na biyar	ma'anua su ne 'yan komiti.
Na shida	'yan gishiri su ne masu watsa labarai, kowa ya ji da bakinsa ba da kunnuwansa ba.
Na bakwai	'yan tattasai da 'yan tumatir su ne cayamen din Nijeriya.
Na takwas	'yan barkono su ne 'yan zanga zanga.

The fifth	sellers of corn by the measure, they are committee men.
The sixth	sellers of salt, publicity officers, everyone will taste the news with their mouth, not hear it with their ears.
The seventh	sellers of large chillies and tomatoes, they are the chairmen of Nigeria.
The eighth	sellers of hot pepper, they are the demonstrators.

| Na tara | sakaratorin Nijeriya su ne 'yan man ja da man gyada da man shanu. |

Na goma	'yan kwanunnuka da ƙore da 'yan akusa su ne indifen-dodin Nijeriya don kuwa abokan cinikin kowanne.
Na goma sha daya	'yan tukwane su ne shugabannin ƙasa masu kula da abin da kowa zai dafa.
Na goma sha biyu	Shagaban da zai kirawo wannan taro shi ne mai girma, mai martaba, ma naman jiki, duk tsoka, TUWO.
The ninth	sellers of palm oil, groundnut oil, and butter, are the secretaries of Nigeria.
The tenth	sellers of metal basins, calabashes, and bowls, are the independent people of Nigeria, trading companions of everyone.
The eleventh	sellers of pots, the national leaders paying attention to what everybody is cooking.
The twelfth	the leader who will summon this assembly to him no other than the majestic, the honourable the supremely succulent TUWO.

The comedian ends his explanation of Tuwo's place in the hierarchy by addressing the substance personally.

> Tuwo, kowa ya zo duniya kai ya tarar,
> Tuwo, kowa ya zo duniya kai ya tarar,
> Gajere na kwano maj sa manya su sunkuya maka, su ci ka zaune,
> To, jama'a cin tsire halal ne amma tsinken tsire haram ni sai a zare
> a yar. Cin doya da rogo da gwaza balal ne amma ɓawon haram ne,
> said a yar da she waje ɗaya.

> Tuwo, whoever comes into the world is sure to find you,
> The short person of the metal bowl causing the mighty to bow to
> you,[63] in order to eat you seated.
> Well, sir, eating a small piece of skewered meat is permitted,[64] but
> the stick on which the meat is skewered is forbidden, take it out and
> throw it away. Eating yam cassava, and kokoyam is allowed but
> their outer coverings are not permitted to you, they have to be
> thrown on one side.

By this devious comment the comedian indicates that, although there is more to be said, this is the end of his dissertation. It must not be thought that such references to a hierarchical organization are intended to be disrespectful to authority. No flagrant disrespect is intended by performances such as these and no offence is taken. The audience is merely amused by hearing a list of

282

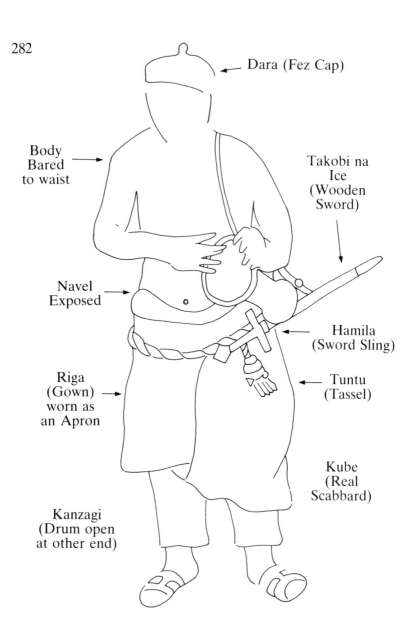

Dara (Fez Cap)

Body Bared to waist

Takobi na Ice (Wooden Sword)

Navel Exposed

Hamila (Sword Sling)

Riga (Gown) worn as an Apron

Tuntu (Tassel)

Kube (Real Scabbard)

Kanzagi (Drum open at other end)

Hausa Comedian, Traditional Dress

Fig. 1.

important titles allocated to market stalls. This is simply a typical instance of one brand of Hausa humour into which too much must not be read. The main thing is for the audience to be amused.

A *dankama* has the following traditional items of equipment, some of which are shown in the illustration.

These are *kanzagi* "drum", *cazbi* "beads", *dara* "fez", *takobi na ice* "wooden sword", *kube* "scabbard", *hamila* "sword sling", *tuntu* "tassel", *wando* "trousers", and *takalmi* "shoes". To show shameless disregard for convention, when appropriate, a comedian does not wear his gown but tucks it into the waist of his trousers so that it hangs down in front as far as the knee, just allowing his navel to show. Islamic instruction about how to dress which itinerant mallams conveyed to pagan villages in the early part of the century, is concerned with the necessity of covering the body from the navel to the knee with clothing. In the old days a bow made of a stalk of Indian hemp (*siya ye*) might also be carried. To this day *garma na mara* "hoe made of calabash" may be carried to imitate *yan hoto* "country entertainers". Sometimes a *dankama* will dress as a wealthy merchant, a nobleman, or a learned mallam, appearing to be a *dattijo* "respectable gentleman". The audience is amused when he suddenly throws off his disguise and starts dancing and beating his drum.

The comedians usually perform in groups of three,[65] standing close to one another in the market and main street; occasionally they make visits, and perform at social occasions at the houses of important people, often on impulse; frequently they go on itineration and their tours include visits to far distant places. In 1965 the Zaria 'yankama were known to go to Kaduna to attend social functions at which the Premier and his Ministers were present; they were sometimes expected to give a special performance for well-known people; they toured in other regions and were occasionally asked to the broadcasting and television studios in Kaduna. The whole tradition of 'yankamanci in the past three generations can be established from Durgundamu (c. 1885) to his son Jan Kosai and, in turn, to his son Alhaji Ahmadu Daɓalo, himself a renowned comedian, now living in Limanci in Zaria town, as his forebears did. It is sufficient to say that it reflects the background of Hausa life during the past three generations. Durgundamu's fame—his name suggests the Short Legged Bother—survives in oral tradition from the last century, handed down from father to son with all the tricks of the craft. A comical pastiche of songs by well-known singers appears to occupy more time in modern performances than it did forty years ago; perhaps this is due to the influence of the gramophone and "Listeners' Choice" on the wireless. The comedians have available in an instant a multitude of metres, some of them their own, from *Alburda* and *Ishiriniya* to *jallaku jalle*, and the traditional stand-by *iye nanaye ayye yaraye manaye dargazazo*, which they use to introduce songs usually sung by girls. Usually, however, metrical devices are not important in producing the general pleasure and interest felt in listening to their absurd performances. The whole effect is *ban dariya* "amusing". It is not an occasion for *tunani* "reflection". The noise is considerable. To take a specific example, Alhaji A. Dama may sing a variety of songs by himself for a considerable period, swamped by the audience, and engage them in a constant flow of repartee. He sings with control and pleasing effect. His Indian music is most popular: his mordants are well performed; his imitation of an Indian drum is excellent, although he is using a *kanzagi*. With his drum he can also imitate a large fiddle by blowing across the open end. Then he sings a mock Yoruba song with accompaniment which burlesques Yoruba singing and drumming perfectly. The audience is laughing, and insists that he should imitate the various nations of the world. He does so, starting with some excellent Sudanese music, although his words are utter nonsense. The audience is delighted with the weird stream of sound which is superimposed on a succession of perfectly executed and familiar drumming patterns (*salon kida* "a pattern of drumming").

Another perennial type of *dankama* is *Jarmai*, a survivor from olden times of whom nothing has so far been said. The *Jarmai* is a buffoon and his entertainment is simple. He wanders about imitating a medieval infantryman, with a wooden sword and bone knife, and, until recently, a bow and arrow made of Indian hemp. He approaches and starts an interrogation which is a traditional part of his performance, perhaps laying his *dankama's* wooden sword on a stranger's neck in a mock threat. "*Ku ne kuka zagi sarki?"* "Was it you people who spoke against the Emir?" The audience laughs and throws him pennies as he looks diabolical and shouts comical *kirari* "challenges" such as *Ƙaƙa tsara ƙaƙa, sai ni Mala'ikan Tuwo Bajinin Danwake"* "Come on then, I'm ready! It is I, Angel Tuwo, The Excellent Dumpling." These *kirari* are ludicrous challenges in imitation of real challenges, for instance, in an ancient battleline. As a species *Jarmai* seems to have lingered longer than other Hausa buffoons, but the progress of modern *'yankama* who have adapted themselves to constantly changing audience demand and competitive forms of entertainment have caused him to be less in evidence than he was. A comic imitation of a warrior may not be so popular now because it is less topical; it may even be regarded as a nuisance, yet it is from the *Jarmai* that modern *'yankama* on television derive, and from whom they take their epithet of *Jarmai*.

The handing down of skill from father to son may now no longer be automatic. Some young men may feel that *'yankamanci* rightly belongs to the past and is out of keeping with the present time: however, if a young man has sufficient *hikima* "wisdom" for the craft he may still learn as an apprentice with a *ɗankama* on itineration, before he starts to train others himself and practice on his own. Usually he will prefer not to practise in his home area, in case he should mistakenly and unintentionally offend a local person, and this might have an adverse effect on his family. It may also be that Hausas like to hear jokes from strangers. The best comedians, performing in the true tradition, are welcome everywhere, and some of them are renowned. Some comedians, on the other hand, relying too much on old situations and old humour, have only a moderate following, and their sons are not eager to take over from them. Generally the craft is well advanced in its decline, well past its peak which was reached in the first quarter of the century when Haji Katsina performed.

3. Standards

The two main terms used in my sources in assessing performances of *'yankama* are *asali* and *azanci*. An attempt is here made to summarize the essential meaning of these two terms in the present context. As will be seen *asali* often involves avoidance of abuses or extremes favoured by other types of minstrels, whereas *azanci* is a much more positive term.

(i) *Asali*

While *asali* "origin and lineage" is important in Hausa society in general, a craft too must have *asali* to be generally accepted. An elderly title holder referring to a comedian, remarked "*Na gani ba shi da kirki, yana taƙama da ministoci, shi ma idan aka bi labarinsa kamancinsa ba shi da asali*" "I think he is no good, he boasts of his contacts with Emirs and Ministers, but if you carefully examine his 'minstrelsy' you will see that it is not performed in traditional fashion." In this tradition comedians avoid giving any offence; committing sin (*zunubi*) against religion. They carefully avoid using the exact words of religious contexts or altering them in any way which would cause offence. As we have seen, one comedian will recite while another interprets his mock Arabic into Hausa seeming always to be on the brink of overstepping the mark, but at the last moment he introduces traditional jargon taken from the conversation of the kitchen,[66] the market, the farm, and family life, an incongruous string of vegetables or a list of staple foods being suddenly substituted for pious warnings.

Haji Katsina may have been in danger of transgression where he used "day of resurrection" *tashin kiyama*. In the traditional jargon of *'yankamanci* this would normally be *ranar rikicewar kasuwa* "the day the market goes away". If the line was accepted by the audience and the *dattijo* in front of whose compound the performance took place, that is the criterion, and our judgement based on western standards is perhaps irrelevant. A typical example of sudden avoidance occurs in the line "on the day of the market she will lack the ingredients for soup". This in serious *wa'azi* might be "on judgement day she will not be rewarded", followed by a reminder of the penalty for an offence and the next line "on the day of resurrection Walnakir will beat her behind with an onion top" in real *wa'azi* would contain the penalty *zai yi mata azaba da sandar wuta* "will chastise her with a rod of fire".

In the true tradition of *'yankamanci* then *zunubi* is to be avoided, but so too are *batsa, zambo*, and *reniya* which as explained below are the stock in trade of less welcome types of *maroƙa*, while *habaici* is used with care.

Batsa means indecent speech and vulgar jokes as purveyed by the *'yan garkuwa*, traditional bands of mendicants who once had a reputation for vulgarity.

Zambo is the term used for insulting abuse such as some Hausa and Yoruba mendicants employ to force donations from unwilling misers, although, since 1957, the Criminal Code has been amended to limit its practice. Their performances typically involve a very rapid style of utterance which, combined with the general accompanying din, makes the insults very hard to follow. One example of *zambo* may be given here by way of illustration:

> Marowaci maye ne,
> Marowaci furan danƙo,
> Sai a shekara ana damu,
> Zumbuli kakan marowata duka.

> The miser is a wizard
> The miser is sticky flour,
> He has to be mixed for a year,
> Skinflint, forefather of all misers.

Zambo is strong stuff, and provokes an angry reaction which eventually, as intended, leads to a final payment to stop the *maroki's* mouth. It is not polite, it may be vulgar, and it is regarded as extremely insulting, the preservation of self respect and dignity being of such importance in Hausa life. While other *maroƙa* may have indulged in *zambo* of this kind, it is avoided in the true tradition of *'yankama* whose aim is to entertain without giving offence to anybody.

Reniya is looking askance at what you are given as a reward, a practice not uncommon with some other *maroƙa*. Rewards given to comedians naturally vary considerably in value, sometimes, in the old days, being as low as one-tenth of a penny or a few cowries. Ordinary *maroƙa* would not uncommonly give vent to their disgust in no uncertain manner. *'Yankama* however, were and are expected to accept any reward however small without any sign of displeasure. This attitude is summed up in the saying *reniya haramun ce* "despising a reward is forbidden" (see the Emir of Abuja's essay, p. 257).

Habaici usually refers to the mockery of an individual by talking with somebody else within hearing using Hausa sayings in such a way that they can be easily overheard by the person concerned who will take them as innuendoes referring to himself. *Habaici* in this sense is a very useful practice in Hausa society at all levels. In *'yankamanci*, where there is no malicious intention to hurt any individual but only to make fun of an imaginary category of people, the kill-joys of the world, *habaici* is used in a modified form, the sting taken from it by skilful touches of humour.

(ii) *Azanci*

Azanci, given in Abraham's dictionary as "meaning and sense", has various uses depending on its context. It is, for instance, the quality which poets possess when finding the appropriate word, metre, or simile. A title of a chapter in *Labaru Na Da* headed *Azancin Waƙa* means "skill in the composition of verse", its principal ingredients being good sense and good judgement. An aspiring *dankama* might be well known for *rashin azanci* "lack of judgement" in the words he uses. But although in the account given of Haji Katsina, *azanci* is translated as "good sense", more than that is implied. There are three everyday contexts relevant to the Emir's use of the word.

(a) Inventive genius (almost inspiration)
Maiwaƙan nan azanci gare shi.
This poet has inventive genius, i.e. his allusions' creative skill.

(b) Idea
Azancina ne ku dawo gobe da safe.
My brilliant idea is for you to come back tomorrow morning.

(c) Plan
Mu kam ba mu da wani azanci.
We have no other stratagem.

To succeed as Haji Katsina did and Alhaji A. Dama does, a *dankama* has to have a retentive memory, well stocked with pieces

of acceptable nonsense, and with facetious comment, interspersed with songs: to employ these materials to good effect he
needs a ready wit and dramatic talent. How essential all these
qualities are will be obvious when it is remembered that a
performance may last for a long time and must appear spontaneous, and at the same time avoid giving offence of any kind in a
public place, where the audience is constantly changing. A
ɗankama must also have a good knowledge of everyday affairs, a
nice sense of humour, and a good temper. Thus all this, combined with his skill in developing his resources, always watchful
for audience reaction and spontaneous in his own, constitutes the
comedian's *azanci*.

Conclusion

'*Yankamanci* remains a comical mode of expression which has
been valued by Hausa audiences. It would as I have suggested, be
unwise to apply western methods of analysis to these Hausa
performances which have survived from the Hausa past. The best
criteria may be in the laughter of the audience and tolerant public
opinion. The practice of the craft clearly includes ridicule of
convention, but Hausa opinion must be taken as to whether any
real offence has been given; on the whole the craft seems widely
accepted as enlivening Hausa life. This study has revealed Hausa
delight in nonsense which, in varying degrees, is universal. In the
case of the '*yankama*, their nonsense is often decked with the
appearance of deep learning, though, paradoxically there is also a
Hausa saying *wasan Bahaushe gaskiyarsa* "What the Hausa says
in jest he really means". It may be unwise to comment on the
relevance of this saying without having been brought up from an
early age in the society, but, on the whole, it appears that
'*yankamanci* has provided an outlet for Hausa fun, comic relief
for the man in the street, and occasional diversion for broad-
minded rulers. There is no harm done to authority, nor is there
any intentional disrespect to any individual—but the humour is at
the expense of an imaginary category of people, who are also
caricatured in Hausa stories. The comedians have usually displayed unusual good judgement, for *maroƙa* of their type in using
their bizarre mode of expression as a vehicle for comical non-

sense. This study also shows the easy relationship which existed between all sections of Hausa society during the first half of this century, and an amiable tolerance by public opinion and traditional authority of a brazen but tempered mode of satire.

Notes

1. The standard orthography is used in this study.
2. Alhaji Abubakhar Imam, *Magana Jari Ce*, Zaria, 1960, Vol. 2, p. 136. For other tales see F. Edgar, *Tatsuniyoyi Na Hausawa*, Lagos, 1913, Vol. i, p. 74, also Alhaji Baba Ahmed, *Ban Dariya*, Zaria, pp. 18–19.
3. Rev. G. P. Bargery, *A Hausa Dictionary*, London, 1934.
4. Major R. C. Abraham and Malam Mai Kano, *The Dictionary of the Hausa Language*, Government of Nigeria, 1949, *dankama* appears under *kama*.
5. Bargery described *maroƙi* as a professional beggar or cadger, often very far from being in a necessitous condition, who gets a living by panegyrising (with or without a musical instrument) patrons and those whom he happens to enlist as such, but vilifying such as refuse to be generous to him.
6. Places situated in the north of Benue Province. They are headquarter towns. For information about the area see S. J. Hogben and A. H. M. Kirke Greene, *The Emirates of Northern Nigeria*, London, 1966.
7. Abuja Emirate is west of Keffi. I am grateful to the Emir for allowing me to use his essay here. He has told me that about 1928 his essay was accepted for his college magazine. The Emir is a learned man, educated at Katsina Training College, with many other eminent leaders of Nigeria and persons of importance in the North. He became 67th Emir of Zazzau and the 6th Emir of Abuja in 1944. I am also grateful to Alhaji Ahmed Joda, Permanent Secretary of the Ministry of Information in Kaduna, for his assurance that my use of the Emir's composition would not cause embarrassment to anyone, and for tapes and documents illustrating *'yankamanci*. I also wish to thank Professor Arnott for his help and kind advice.
8. Cricket was played at Katsina College.
9. Villagers were taught by Mohammedan preachers that swearing by forbidden things, for instance thunder, would result in lightning striking the culprit dead. The instruction is placed in the context of the domestic scene with the danger of soot falling from the roof.
10. A husband always goes to market for these, see Edgar, Vol. 1, Tale 127.
11. The Punishment of the Grave. Two angels, Munkar and Nakir (Walnakir) interrogate the dead man according to Mohammedan belief.
12. The onion top instead of a rod. Guilty Mohammedans are chastised by the angels in their graves.
13. *Duniya* "the world" and *Gidan Gaskiya* "the House of Truth in Heaven". The nonsense here appears to be a rough imitation of *hadisi* "traditions", examples of which are given in Edgar, Vol. 2. It also copies *gargadi* and

wa'azi "warnings" and "admonitions", see p. 259 in *Labaru Na Da Da Na Yanzu*, Zaria, 1931, and especially Cap. 10.

14. Comedians' traditional imagery, the market is the immediate human environment.
15. A challenging proclamation of one's presence (*kirari*), often used to draw one's prowess.
16. No respectable gentleman (*dattijo*) in those times would be seen stopping to talk with a woman in public.
17. For the characteristics of porters in general and especially their preference for light loads, see H. Karl Humn, *The Sudan*, London, 1907, p. 84. In fact there was great *esprit de corps* among porters, some of whom were the salt of the earth.
18. Antimony is the heaviest load.
19. The Hausa text literally refers to him as being tidied up like scattered papers.
20. A practice from Arabia prevailing in Hausaland.
21. The drum's appearance is always accepted as an excuse for the performance provided the *dankama* does not overstep the limit permitted by public opinion.
22. Probably Abdullahi, 1918–1926.
23. *Jarmai*, an ancient warrior title, also the epithet of a *dankama*.
24. By the then Northern Ministry of Information at my request.
25. See Alhaji Mohammadu Bellow Kagara, *Sarkin Katsina Alhaji Mohammadu Dikko*, C.B.E., 1865–1944, Zaria, 1951, p. 30.
26. *Surkulle*, besides referring to patter specifically, also refers to the whole performance of a *dankama* and may be translated as "nonsense". *Surkulle* also means a magic rigmarole and a daft person.
27. *Tuwo*, the staple food of most tribes of the North. It is made from the flour of cereals and eaten with soup or gravy.
28. *Fura*, balls of cooked flour usually mixed up in sour milk.
29. Reference to the interrogation by Walnakir.
30. Reference is for pounded gruel. Cakes are cheap.
31. Reference to the present Islamic dispensation considered to have begun in A.D. 1882 and estimated to last for 100 years.
32. Human environment as the market.
33. The mallam is represented as a connoisseur of food and is placed in incongruous juxtaposition to the family hen.
34. A pardon would be more appropriate.
35. Reference to the generosity of the late Alhaji Sir Ahmadu Bello, Premier of the North at the time.
36. This and subsequent lines are a play on sayings containing the word *magani*.
37. The saying is really *Rana tsaka maganin dari* "the midday sun is the remedy for cold". Reference to generosity displayed by gifts of gowns, remedies for cold, in ridiculous juxtaposition to the comedians' penchant for cakes.
38. *Kangara* does not really mean "rebellion", although often so translated. It means a stubborn attitude to authority bearing a resemblance to dumb insolence, supposed to be an attribute of the headstrong.
39. The District Head of Gobir in the Isa District of Sokoto.

40. Tabansi Records Kano Sarkin Musulmi II Record Number 45 TAN 179.
41. Aliyu Jeddo, a Fulani military leader in the Jihad.
42. Mohammadu Bello, Sultan of Sokoto, 1817–1837.
43. The Gobir Capital, captured 1808.
44. Abubakhar Atiku, Sultan of Sokoto, 1837–1842.
45. Sarkin Sudan, 1880–1901; 1901–1929.
46. Shamaki, Dodo, and Mallam I have not identified. *Gwarzo* and *Bada* imply "Lord" and "Master".
47. All places in East Sokoto. Dandoto District is substituted for Chafe (a place) to suit the metre.
48. Anyone called Abubakhar has a nickname Garba. Poetic licence with "the son of" meaning "descendant of", so that the present Sultan, Alhaji Sir Abubakhar, derives his lineage in the song directly from his uncle, Hassan, who was a Sultan.
49. Shehu Usman Dan Fodiyo, who led the Jihad.
50. Sokoto is pictured as Hausaland. *Kamfun* is a contraction of *Kamfuna* (see the Hausa text), the Sokoto districts, forty-seven at the time.
51. Argungu was never completely subdued by the Fulani. I have not discovered the context of the event nor the remark by the Sultan.
52. All Eastern Districts were combined under one command.
53. Inset lines are sung aside by accompanying comedians.
54. Daughter of Shehu Usman Dan Fodiyo.
55. The Kano Market of ancient renown.
56. *Bila*, an Abyssinian slave, later freed and made a muezzin in the time of the Prophet. Hence *Bila* means a reliable person as in *Audu shi ne Bila* "Audu is a thoroughly reliable individual".
57. *Habe* (singular *Kado*). Fulani words for the indigenous inhabitants of Hausaland, speaking Hausa as their native tongue. The Habe rulers were defeated by Fulani in the Jihad.
58. *Bamaguje* (plural *Maguzawa*) pagan member of the Maguzawa tribe.
59. Worldly mallams.
60. For Hausa society see H. A. S. Johnston, *Hausa Stories*, Oxford University Press, 1966, Library of African Literature, the introduction. For Islam in Northern Nigeria see J. Schacht, *Studia Islamica, Colligerunt R. Brunsching, ex fascicudo VIII*, La Rose, Paris, 1957, p. 123.
61. Alhaji Abubakhar Imam, *Ruwan Bagaja*, Gaskiya, p. 9.
62. For the lowly position of Kunu, see *Magama Jari Ce*. Vol. 2, p. 122.
63. An epithet of "tuwo is sa maza ladab", "you who make the mighty show respect by bowing low before you (to eat)".
64. Permitted (*halak*), not permitted (*haram*), in the Mohammedan Code.
65. Often *Malam, Maigida*, and *Aboki* (Pedent, Master of the House, and Friend).
66. Alhaji A. Dama is popularly known as "Ministan Kicin", "the Minister of Kitchen". The word ministan was sometimes used jokingly, for instance, as a shout by a football crowd delighted by the dribbling skills of a footballer, shouted with vigour 1959–1960 in Kaduna and Jos Football Grounds.

PART IV
MODERN TRADITIONAL THEATRE: YORUBA TRAVELLING THEATRE

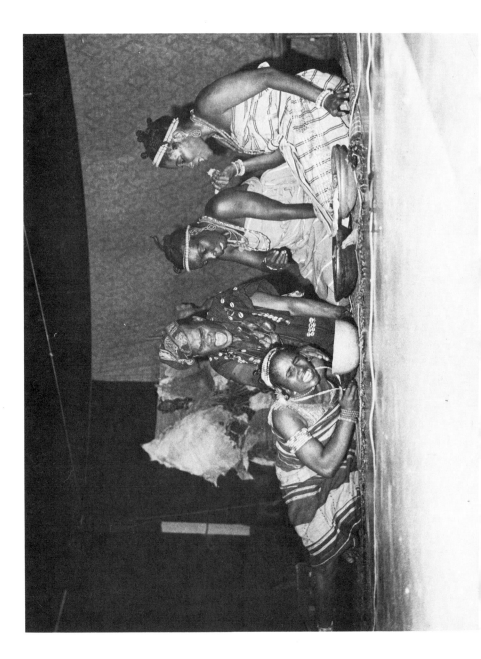

OGUNDE THEATRE:
THE RISE OF CONTEMPORARY PROFESSIONAL THEATRE IN NIGERIA 1946–72
Ebun Clark

The aim of this study of the Ogunde Theatre is to give a historical documentation of the development of the theatre from 1946, the year he formed his professional company, to 1972. Textual analysis is deliberately omitted from this study because the various types of plays he produced were determined by certain historical factors. It is therefore necessary to document fully this historical content in order to facilitate future textual studies.

Hubert Ogunde was born in 1916 in the village of Ososa, four miles from Ijebu Ode in the Western State of Nigeria. He worked first as a teacher before joining the Nigeria Police Force. Like many of his theatre contemporaries, such as A. B. David, P. A. Dawodu, Layeni and G. T. Onimole, his theatre career began under the patronage of the church. In 1944 he produced his first opera, *The Garden of Eden and The Throne of God*, by commission of the Church of the Lord, a Cherubim and Seraphim sect based in Lagos. The performance was in aid of the church building fund.

The huge success of the production spurred Ogunde on to writing more operas until he decided to leave, quite unlike his contemporaries, his amateur status as an artist and turn professional. By this act, Ogunde began the rise of modern professional theatre in Nigeria, a movement in which he remains the supreme artist and father figure.

The Professional Company

Tiger's Empire in which The African Music Research Party presented Hubert Ogunde, Beatrice Oyede and Abike Taiwo was the play that launched Ogunde Theatre, the first contemporary professional company in Nigeria; it was performed on Monday, 4th March, 1946.[1] The advertisement for the play was the result of Ogunde's call for "paid actresses". It marked the first time in Yoruba theatre that women were billed to appear in a play as professional artists in their own right. *Tiger's Empire* was an attack on colonial rule. It was followed by *Darkness and Light*, although Ogunde does not remember writing it. This is the only play that has escaped his memory.[2]

The formation of the company sparked off many articles on the theatre in the press. Two such articles will be quoted from because of the interesting points they make. The first writer, for instance, advocated, amongst other things, the formation of a "copyright law", saying in a letter to the *Daily Service*, inter alia:

> . . . The African has got a potential talent in stage craft, and if given the opportunity could compete with any other race and even outshine them. The last three years, at least, have brought into light Africans with great creative resources who have won admiration of both natives and aliens for their originality, foresight and organizing ability on the stage.[3]

The second writer, confining his patriotism to the immediate social questions of the day observed that "Our progress as a country does not depend solely on the number of so-called enlightened politicians but on the development of as many aspects of our national life as possible. We must advance on all points—in politics, in education, in art and in poetry, if we are to prevent a lopsided development."[4]

This sympathy and support for Ogunde's small beginnings inspired him to launch another successful play on the 6th and 13th of May, 1946 at the Glover Hall.

This was *Mr. Devil's Money* performed by "a set of twenty-four stars all donning costumes of up country designs and dancing to the strain of music supplied by a band of ancient instruments".[5]

An expatriate officer, Major Anthony Syer on seeing a rehearsal of this play was quite overwhelmed by the theatrical competence of the group and expressed his admiration and enthusiasm in a colourful letter to the *Daily Service*.

Since my arrival in this country, I have seen many African plays and operas . . . but I had the greatest surprise of my life when I attended the rehearsal of the African opera entitled *Mr. Devil's Money* by the African Music Research Party, written, composed, and produced by Hubert Ogunde, a young native producer scheduled to be staged at the Glover Hall on Monday, May 6, 1946.

The theme is based on an old African story depicting the "here and after" of a man who signed a pact with an evil spirit in order to be wealthy. To see the cast rehearsing the Opera, dances, to hear the cheap Native drums supplying the music with precision without any mechanical aid, the clapping of hands, and the high standard of discipline maintained throughout is to think one is back at a London Theatre. The singing is excellent. Dance formations, lightings and the stage setting are concrete proofs that the African is no more behind as many people think. The present necessity is public support and encouragement to this gifted young artist.[6]

The rush to see the play was so great that tickets were sold on the black market and some "criminals" even printed "counterfeit tickets", an occasion which caused Ogunde to issue this stern warning:

Some criminals are now in the habit of printing counterfeit tickets for our plays and have succeeded in selling a large number on two occasions and also in our latest play *Mr. Devil's Money* staged at the Glover Hall.

This is to warn all printers against printing such tickets, and our patrons against buying tickets that do not bear the official stamp of my party and my own signature.

Hubert Ogunde
Managing Director
The African Music Research Party
88, Cemetery Street
Ebute Metta.[7]

From 1944, when Ogunde began his theatre career, to 1946, he had not toured with his plays except occasionally to Abeokuta. His lack of capital was the stumbling block. But his fame was such that people in the provinces refused to be left out any longer, and began to petition him to tour with his plays. Ogunde therefore inserted an announcement in the press:

The African Music Research Party, Lagos in response to popular requests by letters, telegrams and personal calls from the provinces, will now tour the Western Yoruba area to stage our famous play by Hubert Ogunde. A. R. Music.[8]

The tour which took the group to Ilaro, Abeokuta, Ibadan, Ijebu-Ode, Ososa and Sagamu, lasted only a week, between August 2 to August 10, 1946. But with it, the Ogunde theatre became, like its masked counterpart, the Alarinjo, a travelling theatre.[9]

At this time in Lagos, a public outcry had been going on for a year over the growth of a "social evil" which was entering into the Lagos society and corroding it. This evil was popularly known as the "Aso Ebi Craze", a craze which required both men and women to buy the most expensive materials for social gatherings. The rule was that "when someone wants to celebrate a marriage or a funeral obsequies (sic) she chooses a piece of cloth to wear on the occasion and approaches relatives and friends to buy the same stuff to wear with her as uniform on the day. The number of people to wear the uniform with her will depend on her popularity and social connections".[10]

This craze, of course, bred intensive competition with celebrants trying to outshine one another. Ogunde decided to make his first social satirical comment by writing a play designed to expose the vulgarity and ostentatiousness of the craze. He called the play *Human Parasites: a tragedy in two acts*, commenting that " 'Aso Ebi' is a social evil . . . Aduke who kissed and keyed (sic) a thousand lovers for the sake of 'Aso Ebi' . . . what happened when boys refused to be keyed is better seen than described."[11]

> The portrayal of this menace will no doubt help in no less degree to show "Aso Ebi" and the psychological effect of such a show cannot fail to prove beneficial. We urge our playwrights to put more shows portraying the social and political problems of our time for the education of the masses.[12]

After the performances of *Human Parasites*, Ogunde again took his company on tour; this time on a month's tour of the Northern Provinces.

He made no mention of the plays he intended to perform during his Northern tour, but we do know that he staged *Strike and Hunger* on his first and only night in Jos, for half an hour. After the show began, "a constable entered the stage in uniform through the dressing room . . . and said 'This is the organizer, I arrest you' pointing to Ogunde . . . about forty other constables entered the hall, scattered the audience, broke down the stage and marched Ogunde and five members of his party to the station. On the way to the station three of the arrested persons were alleged mercilessly beaten by the Police who were alleged to have inflicted wounds".[13] The outcome of the court case which followed was that Ogunde and two other members of the party were found guilty on the charges against them and fined ₦250.00.

Aroused, the *West African Pilot* in an editorial headed, JOS, A EUROPEAN RESERVE?[14] commented that Ogunde had performed in "several towns in Nigeria without let or hindrance". It urged "the Nigerian Government to institute an enquiry into the social conditions prevailing in Jos" stating that "the people of this country cannot tolerate any brand of South Africanism in Nigeria".

The net result of this press coverage was that it pushed Ogunde more into national prominence, and helped to a great extent to popularize his theatre. Instead of being just the darling of the Yoruba people, he became a national hero. He finished a highly eventful year with a tour of the Western area from October 31–November 9.

During 1946, Ogunde made efforts to raise funds for scholarships to send young members of his troupe abroad to learn the various techniques of the theatre. He, however, decided he needed to learn more about the theatre himself, so he made arrangements to travel abroad with his leading lady, Clementina Ogunbule, who later married Ogunde and became Adeshewa Ogunde.[15] To this end, he applied for passports and visas but was summarily refused the passports, and this refusal started a new confrontation with the government. This time Ogunde made use of the *Daily Comet* to put forward his case to the public.

> I shall be doing a great injustice to myself and my country, if I fail to bring to your notice, and for the information of the general public the facts surrounding the refusal by the Police Immigration Authorities to grant passport for me and my partner to travel to

the United Kingdom for the purpose of seeing at first hand, the working of a theatre with its complicated network of various branches.[16]

The article then continued to state the aims of the party and the reasons why he decided to travel to the U.K. "in order to return and improve our present standard of production which is still very poor". He explained that he wrote to the Guildhall School of Music and Drama, and the Central School of Speech and Drama in London for admission. He received a letter from the School which indicated that it was "necessary for all prospective students to have personal interview with the Principal before admission".[17]

Ogunde submitted this letter to the Police Immigration Authorities and completed the necessary forms for the passports. His sponsors for the passports, he said, were "no less than Chief Ladipo Solanke, Barrister-at-Law, W.A.S.U. Missioner, Dr. Doherty and the Rev. E. O. Orekoya of the Methodist Church, Ebute Metta". He had, he stated, been waiting since September 1946 for a reply from the Immigration Office; in the meantime he had changed his plan to study for a year and asked instead to be allowed "six months to visit the many theatres and opera houses in London and in the provinces . . . for the purpose of gaining more experience to be used in the development of our own".[18]

On one of his many visits to the Immigration Officer the interview was reported by Ogunde himself in a release:

Officer: By the way, what are you going to do in England?
Ogunde: I want to gain more knowledge and experience in my business.
Officer: But the *Pilot* and *Comet* say you know everything in Nigeria and if the white man goes away you will build your own ships and fly your own aeroplanes and train your own soldiers.
Ogunde: I have never read such statements in these papers.
Officer: Here, look at this.

(At this stage he showed me an editorial in the *Comet* of that date with the heading "Chains That Call" in which the editor translated a portion of my opera *Worse Than Crime* and used the translation as theme for his editorial.)

Ogunde: No reply.

Officer: Did you stage a play last Monday?

Ogunde: Yes, we staged *Herbert Macaulay*.

Officer: Yes, I was present. You depicted Africans as all good on the stage.

Ogunde: Yes, because we are good!

Officer: Four things you will not show Africans to have on the stage (1) Africans don't take bribes, (2) Africans don't tell lies, (3) Africans don't steal, and (4) Africans have no venereal diseases.

Ogunde: All these vices are present anywhere in the world and, I am afraid, in Heaven. They are not peculiar to African Society.

Ogunde and

Officer: (laughter).

I then left him to return on the next Monday.[19]

Ogunde finally pointed out in his release that other applicants for a passport at the time got them issued quickly.

As far as the *Daily Comet* was concerned,

The case echoes of victimization (which may or may not arise from official aversion to his nationalist bend), it also belies the postulate that Europeans are sincere in training Africans in order to improve their own.

If, on the other hand, the authorities are reluctant to grant him a passport in view of his not receiving a full assurance admittance from the Guildhall School of Speech Training and Dramatic Arts, what can the authorities offer as an excuse, considering his change of mind to spend six months instead of one year visiting the many theatres and opera houses in London only?[20]

The Immigration Office at this stage replied by promptly issuing Ogunde and his partner their passports and visas.

After this obvious victimization by the Immigration Office, the public rallied round Ogunde. They gave his company an overwhelming reception during its next tour of the Western provincial towns. Free accommodation was offered in all the provinces, and "Their Highnesses, the Olowo of Owo, the Deji of Akure, the Alafin of Oyo, the Oshemowe of Ondo, the Oni of Ife, the Ewi of Ado-Ekiti, the Alake of Abeokuta, the Ebumawe of Ago, the Liken of Ibefun were prominent among the supporters of the party".[21]

Other prominent supporters of the Party were the *West African Pilot* and the *Daily Comet* which lauded Ogunde in editorials. The *Daily Comet* paid "tribute to a genius" in the following vein:

> Actor playwright Hubert Ogunde of *Strike and Hunger* fame has grown into what people call a newspaper personality. But in spite of what has been written about him, even in our editorial columns, to pay another tribute to him on the occasion of his final tour to the province before his departure for London, as no undue emphasis of his contributions to the preservation of Yoruba culture . . .. As Ogunde's party rides through the West in one stage of triumph after another in the next few weeks, there will be many wishing they were like him, well they could be! . . .[22]

On his return from his triumphant tour Ogunde once again staged *Human Parasite*, his last play before he left with his partner for the United Kingdom on July 3, 1947. There they were "Scheduled to meet Mr. Rank, Chairman of Odeon Theatres to discuss the possibility of Hubert Ogunde's Party touring Europe and America during the summer of 1948 . . ."[23]

For Ogunde to have financed his trip unaided indicated not only the success and popularity of his party but also his financial achievement in a short space of time. As the *West African Pilot* put it, this was possible by reason of his "determination to court and capture the imagination . . .. He sat down, racked his brains, composed native airs and dramatized them. By 1947, he has become Nigeria's theatre king . . ."[24]

When Ogunde returned in September, he arrived with £2,000 (₦4,000) worth of theatrical equipment. He also gave the public an indication of what it should expect in his forthcoming performance, for example, "an introduction of the tap dance into the African 'Batakoto' and also into the African Rumba". A "special demonstration" he went on, "will show that the people of Nigeria, especially the Yorubas, have the rhythm and the physical steps of the tap dance in their 'Epa' dance, and a routine dance will show the relation between the 'Waltz' and the African Batakoto".[25]

The "forthcoming performance" was the play *Towards Liberty*, in which the "Ogunde Theatre Party" presented "Rosalind and Grace, Abiola and Adeshina" at the Glover Memorial Hall on Monday, November 10, 1947 at 8 p.m. With this production Ogunde made yet another political statement for self-rule. And of even greater interest, we also notice that he changed the name of his company from African Music Research Party to Ogunde Theatre Party.

After the performance of *Towards Liberty*, Ogunde again went on a tour of the West of Nigeria, extending it this time to towns like Warri, Benin City and Sapele, now in the Bendel State of Nigeria.

His constant touring with his company affected the number of operas he wrote. In 1947, for instance, his only opera was *Towards Liberty*, and in 1948, *Yours Forever*. It was in 1948 however that he decided to take his company on a tour outside Nigeria, going to the then Gold Coast with the opera *King Solomon*. The tour was a disaster, mainly because most of the audience did not understand Yoruba, and Ogunde was ignorant about the taste of the theatre audience there. He was later to learn that they preferred variety and old time music hall shows. Ogunde returned to Nigeria penniless and "owed his cast a month's salary, and the lorry-owner the fare".

What is of particular interest in the next phase of Ogunde's development as a professional is his increased involvement in the social and political realities of Nigeria between 1945 and 1966. The dangers of such involvement and often near disaster to his career were played out far too poignantly to be disregarded. Besides, it seems that these same conflicts served ultimately to strengthen Ogunde's reputation and vary the range of subject matter and technique in his plays.

In this section of the study of Ogunde's theatre, greater emphasis has been placed on the political growth of Nigeria from 1945–66 and Ogunde's consistent attitude and response to the vicarious order of events.

In 1949 Ogunde produced a folkloric opera called *Half and Half* on 6 June. According to a preview of the opera which appeared in the *Daily Service* of 4 June, 1949, *Half and Half* is:

> One of the greatest stage miracles in these parts . . .. After writing and composing fifteen operas and plays on Religious, Political and Romantic themes, Mr. Ogunde has now started to produce

ancient Nigerian Folklore the first of which is his new *Half and Half.*[26]

The plot was drawn from the popular folk tale about Odewale, head hunter in a town called Ijaye. While hunting in the forest one day, he saw a deer which miraculously took off her skin and became a beautiful woman. She then changed the nearby leaves into costly female dresses which she wore and went to market. Odewale quickly came out from his hideout, took the skin, returned to his hideout and waited the arrival of this wonderful creature. On her return she found that Odewale had taken her skin, and followed him home to become his wife. Odewale already had two wives, Sangotunde and Borisade.

These two senior wives were suspicious of Adesina, the new wife and did not rest until they had tricked Odewale into revealing that Adesina was half animal and half human. The poor hybrid creature returned to the forest leaving her heartbroken husband behind.

Half and Half, in fact, is the old Owo myth of Igogo, described by J. P. Clark in his *Aspects of Nigerian Drama*, where he says:

> Another beautiful drama . . . associated "with a figure of antiquity and now observed more or less as the vegetation festival is the annual Igogo at Owo in Western Nigeria. The central figure is Orosen, wife of the founder of Owo. A changeling creature from the forest, the story of how her rival spouses eventually encompass her downfall by tricking their man into revealing the true identity of his favourite wife throws vivid light upon the conventional day to day conflicts and complexities obtaining in every house of polygamy.[27]

On November 8, 1949 the coal miners in the Enugu Colliery went on strike demanding higher wages commensurate with the rise in cost of living. Although the strike was not a national one like the General Strike of 1945, the impact of the Enugu Miner's strike was not less felt by the Nigerian public. This was because eighteen miners were shot and killed by the police during one of the miners demonstrations. The shooting incident caused a national sense of outrage and it provided immediate topical material for the Yoruba theatre groups. Ogunde however did not produce his own version of the shooting incident until nearly a year after. He called it *Bread and Bullet*, and its premiere was in October 1950. When he took the play to the Northern cities in 1951, he was banned from showing it in certain areas there. The *Daily Service* notified the nation of the ban with the following report on May 11, 1951:

HUBERT OGUNDE'S PLAY IS SAID TO BE SEDITIOUS.
Kano A.S.P. Bans Staging of *Bread and Bullet*.

The Play was to have been staged last Monday at the Colonial Hotel Hall, Kano, when the Assistant Superintendent of Police, it is understood, invited Mr. Ogunde to the Police Station and after reading out from the criminal code laws relating to sedition, he is reported to have said: 'the words contained in your play *Bread and Bullet* are seditious and I, therefore, ban the play from being staged in Kano. As a result, the play was not staged and those who had filled the hall to watch the play had to return home disappointed. On Tuesday, May 8, the police served a summons paper on Mr. Ogunde ordering him to appear in the Magistrate Court on Wednesday to answer to a charge of posting posters of the said play in the township without permission. Squads of policemen are reported to have gone round the streets tearing off the said posters which had been posted on trees and walls.

After the hearing of the Magistrate Court, the *Daily Service* on May 14, 1951 declared that "Hubert Ogunde" had been "fined six pounds for posting posters . . .. Mr. Dawodu, barrister-at-law", we are told, "defended him". Ogunde was not only banned in Kano, but also in Kaduna and Makurdi. But he was ironically allowed to stage his play in Jos where he was first banned in 1946 for staging *Strike and Hunger*. Other towns such as Zaria, Funtua, Gusau and Minna also permitted the performance of the play.

Before Ogunde produced *Bread and Bullet* in 1950, he had earlier the same year re-staged the *Black Forest*. It will be remembered that this opera had its premiere in 1945. It is necessary to turn our attention once again to this opera. In the Sports, Music and Drama column of the *Daily Service* of January 10, 1950 there appeared a review of this old opera which ran thus:

Hubert Ogunde and his popular Theatrical Play have done it once again. This time, at a repeat performance of their play *The Black Forest* last Friday night at Glover Memorial Hall, Lagos where the audience were thrilled, not only with an excellent native opera, but with refined African music played on foreign and native instruments combined.

The opera itself has been re-arranged to include a dialogue, a dance of the ancient Yorubas and a Grand Finale that drew a great ovation from all corners of the house.

In music, sceneries, lighting, costumes, presentation and make-up, *The Black Forest* is a credit to the composer-playwright, Mr. Ogunde, who is now generally accepted as the saviour of Native music and drama in Nigeria.

It is understood that a series of other plays will be staged at the same hall during this week and next.

These include the popular *King Solomon*, *Yours for Ever*, *Human Parasites*, and *Mr. Devil's Money*.

I have not quoted this review at length in order to show yet again the adulations and interest that Ogunde's theatre always generated. Rather, it is intended to indicate and stress a second important redirection of Yoruba theatre by Ogunde. First, the "refined African music" was "played in foreign and native instruments combined", and secondly, the opera had "been re-arranged to include a dialogue". With this information, we are made aware at once of two new styles appearing in Ogunde's theatre. Previously, his operas were accompanied solely by native musical instruments, and did not include dialogue. Since we are not told in the review in what language the dialogue was rendered, we may well conclude that it must have been all in Yoruba. But the surprise, as we learn from the preview in *Bread and Bullet*, was that the play ran in both Yoruba and English. The injection of English by Ogunde into his operas was again another major significant new style.

Ogunde's inclusion of foreign musical in his orchestra, his introduction of dialogue in both Yoruba and English into his operas in fact marks the style of a well-known phase in Yoruba theatre, that of the Yoruba Concert Party Theatre. The importance of the review on the re-staging of *The Black Forest* therefore is that it affords us the opportunity of noting the year Ogunde began his Concert Party Theatre in Nigeria, by bringing certain features of the Ghanaian Concert Party Theatres into

Nigerian theatre. It is an important point to note for this is the theatre that scholars generally associate Ogunde with. Their concentration on the "horseplay and sex appeal",[28] as the characteristic style of his concert theatre period is quite secondary to the major revolution that occurred in this era, the era in which Ogunde moved Yoruba theatre from a scripted theatre where the actors sang their lines to an improvisational theatre in which the actors eventually spoke their lines. Any meaningful analysis of the Nigerian Concert Party Theatres must therefore take cognizance of this factor.

On reading the above review certain questions immediately arise. Why did an artist who was generally accepted as "the saviour of native music and drama" in Nigeria begin to infuse foreign musical instruments and a foreign language into his theatre? This is the artist who had once disdainfully declared that in

> films and plays, foreigners depict Africans as buffoons and social degenerates who have no culture, music, dance, and way of life, but are mere loyal imitators of their masters. Africans shall be most guilty if they fail to prove to the world by practical demonstrations, that their detractors have been guilty of gross misinterpretations by presenting on our own stage and if possible on theirs too, African culture and way of life and those melodies and graceful dances that are of purely African origin.[29]

Why did he begin in 1950 to imitate the theatre of the foreign detractors, thereby renouncing the guardianship of his cultural heritage? To answer these questions, we have to retrace our steps to 1948 when a new type of professional theatre came into being in Nigeria, that of Bobby and Cassandra Modern Theatre Party, a theatre that concentrated solely on presenting Western variety musical shows.

Bobby Benson and Ogunde were not unknown to each other; they first met at a dancing school in London during Ogunde's trip to the United Kingdom in 1947. And strangely enough, they again met on the boat journeying back to Nigeria the same year. According to Ogunde, Bobby Benson enquired about the commercial viability of a professional theatre in Nigeria, and Ogunde informed him of his own successful venture in the theatre. Their conversation must have encouraged Bobby enough for him to try living off the theatre, and he was well equipped and knowledge- able about the entertainment world to take the risk.

Originally, Bobby left Nigeria for America to study medicine but once there he soon abandoned that desire in favour of music, dance and drama. In both America and London he had the opportunity for many years of studying and observing the various types of theatre in the two countries. It is therefore not surprising that he preferred to launch a professional variety theatre based on the Western theatre rather than emulate the Yoruba theatre and their style which he was neither conversant nor at ease with. At this point a short deviation is needed in order to explain why Bobby Benson's foreign oriented theatre was able to gain a firm foothold in the Nigeria of the forties and early fifties.

Variety or concert theatres were nothing new in Nigeria. As Michael Echeruo shows, entertainments of non-African origin had been in existence since the 19th century.[30] They were sponsored either by the Church or schools. Again Nigerians who were avid filmgoers were familiar with the American and English musical shows, and during the forties a number of amateur theatre groups occasionally produced variety concerts. One "Black and White Variety Concert" produced by a group in July 1945 was extremely popular. So when Bobby Benson and Cassandra launched their theatre on April 5, 1948 with Bobby Jam Session Orchestra, they were not starting something altogether novel. What was new about Bobby's theatre therefore was that it was the first professional variety theatre company of its kind in Nigeria, specializing in comedies in the line of Abbott and Costello.[31] His theatre therefore cannot be classified as being part of the new Yoruba theatre movement. His actors did not perform in Yoruba, and the little dialogue that there was in his sketches was spoken in English. His theatre also did not concern itself with projecting or protecting the indigenous culture. But the eventual popularity of Bobby's new type of professional theatre had an undeniable impact and influence on Yoruba theatre.

But unlike the beginning of Ogunde's theatre career in 1944, we do not get the impression that Bobby's theatre made an immediate impact on the public. In fact his theatre's popularity did not become apparent until a year after its inception. On August 31, 1949 the public were informed of "a big show at 8 p.m." in the "Glover Memorial Hall" which will take place on "Friday 2 September 1949" with "Cassandra and Bobby (Anglo-American Trained Artists) and Zealinjoh, 12 years leading trumpeter in Africa, in a show entitled *Congo-Samba Tojazz* with Benson's Jam Session Orchestra".

The review of the production indicates the beginning of the popularity of Bobby's theatre; it ran thus:

> Cassandra and Bobby's show was a Big Hit. Cassandra and Bobby's *Congo Samba Tojass*, staged on Friday 2nd September at Glover Hall, made such a hit that repeat performances were demanded and staged on the 5 and 7 instant and drew as large an audience each time. Jass (sic) a musical, *Samba*, a Spanish play and *Miss Coatt*, a comedy, were early hot favourite among the various items on show. *Jass* (sic) a "boogie woogie and Kangaroo jitterbug was performed by the whole band and thrilled the audience with perfect timing, rhythmic movements and tuneful harmony.
>
> It is understood that further demand for another repeat has been made in Lagos, Ibadan and other towns".[32]

So by 1949, Bobby Benson's theatre had already established itself; like the Yoruba theatre of Ogunde, it also became a travelling theatre. His tours grew more extensive, embracing parts of the country beyond the West by 1950. In the Sports, Music and Drama column of the *Daily Service* of February 22, 1950, we were told that:

> When Bobby Benson and his Jam Session Orchestra got their new kit kar, they decided to take a joy ride around the Western towns and see how the other half lives.
>
> The other half would not let them go, so they gave them the good old Calypso, then Samba, then Blues and all the titilating stuff that Lagos dance fans had grown to associate Benson with, and their trouble began.
>
> First one town in the Western Province then the next and still the next, until Lagos Jazz fans grew furious and sent Bobby a priority telegram, to come home at once.
>
> That playing tour of the West has given Bobby an idea. Now he is off again in March, not only to the West but because someone gave him the challenge to "go East young man".

His provisional itinerary is as follows but Benson is too wise to take a 50 to one bet that he won't come back on 4 April as scheduled, because both the Easterners and the Westerners will not let him come back so early.

However here it is:

March 1950, Ibadan 4 to 5, Ilesha 6, Oshogbo 7, Benin, Sapele 10 and 11, Warri 13 to 14, Onitsha 16, Enugu 17 and 18, Calabar 24 to 25, Aba 28 and 29, Port Harcourt 30 to 31 and back to Lagos on 4 April, 1950.

From the above, we can deduce that Ogunde now had a highly successful and popular theatre to contend with. In short, he had now a rival competing with him as Nigeria's theatre king. Being a shrewd businessman, he realized that Bobby's theatre was changing the taste of the Nigerian audience towards a Western oriented musical comedy theatre. It is therefore not altogether surprising that Ogunde, in restaging *The Black Forest* in 1950, decided to give the public the new style they now preferred. With his two years experience in the Ghana Concert Party circuit, Ogunde was more than ready to cope with Bobby's challenge. Fortunately, too, for Ogunde, and this is something of an irony, the political atmosphere was now beginning to change from the national political front of the forties, with its direct relationship on cultural nationalism, to one of party politics. Ogunde however did not completely emulate Bobby variety theatre. He gave the public jazz, boogie woogie in his opening and closing glee, and also spoke dialogue. But at the same time he retained the opera or play as the main focus of his programme.

The rivalry that existed between Bobby and Ogunde is no hypothesis but fact; it can be substantiated through a private handbill that once circulated amongst the Lagos theatre fans in 1952. It was an invitation to an Ogunde performance of *Mr. Devil's Money* at the Glover Memorial Hall on Friday October 10, 1952. One immodest paragraph announced that:

Ogunde has promised to thrill you with the latest music in his opening glee; he also promised to beat Bobby Benson with his latest instruments. His orchestras are eager to show you real music and drama.

Whether or not Ogunde beat Bobby is not a point we will dwell on. But in 1952 Bobby disbanded his theatre, mainly because his partner Cassandra had left Nigeria. So from than on Bobby concentrated on night club entertainment, building his own empire as the father of modern popular Nigerian Music. A large percentage of popular dance band leaders such as Roy Chicago, Victor Olaiya, Eddie Okonta and the late Rex Lawson served their apprenticeship under Bobby before forming their own bands. The contrast to be drawn here is that no similar pattern occurred in the Yoruba theatre. None of the leaders of Yoruba theatre today served under Ogunde.

In 1951, Ogunde celebrated the seventh anniversary of his theatre with the production of a new work called *My Darling Fatima*. The piece is of some interest because of its theme. It will be recalled that in 1944 Ogunde began his theatre career with an opera carrying a biblical theme. For his seventh anniversary Ogunde based his new opera on an Islamic theme. As the *Daily Service* review of April 29, 1957 stated:

> This new play titled *My Darling Fatima* is a Muslim morality play which portrays the day of judgement after the demise of all human beings in the world and their reappearance in Heaven before judgement seat. The audience who witnessed it in the Glover Hall also reacted to it as evident by ther quietness when it was staged.

The main characters in the play are Alfa Lemonu, a teacher in an Arabic School, his senior wife Moriamo, his sister Amuda, and a friend called Abdul Yekini. Fatima is the daughter of an Arabic scholar who offers his daughter in marriage to Lemonu in appreciation of his "kindness and devotion to duty" in the Arabic school. For their individual reasons none of the above characters wants Lemonu to marry Fatima. The play deals mainly with the way each tries to forestall the marriage, and the disasters that occurred in the process, but all ends well for all the characters in the play. The information that the audience was silent during the performance is of importance. It supports my own observation that there seems to be an erroneous presumption that the audience in Yoruba theatre are persistently noisy because of the general practice of audience participation. This is not so; as the review shows, there are moments in the theatre for participation and moments for reflection.

A look at the script of *My Darling Fatima* shows that the new use of dialogue within the opera is not apparent. Ogunde himself confirms my observation that there was no dialogue in this opera, stating that for the final time he returned to his old opera form. *Portmanteau Woman*, *Beggar's Love*, both produced in 1952, were followed in 1953 by the production of *Highway Eagle* and *Princess Jaja*, but according to Ogunde, they were all situation comedies, and were performed both in Yoruba and English with the lines sung or spoken. But with *Princess Jaja* he began to experiment with an all dialogue play, leaving out songs.

The production of *Highway Eagle* however did not recieve the usual unanimous praise that always accompanied Ogunde's production. A critic writing in the *Daily Service* of August 15, 1953, dismissed the play, in which the lines are sung as well as spoken, as an unconvincing portrayal of the life of a highway robber, saying inter alia:

> Christopher, who plays the role of Awodi-Oke, has many qualities for the stage . . .. But in the earlier stages of his part, there is certainly nothing suggestive of the highway man in the personality and comportment of Awodi-Oke who has unhappily been assigned for the role. Even his voice lacks the note of authority which it should carry and the impetuousness of his apprentice is so much condoned by Awodi-Oke that the learner's personality almost over shadows that of the boss.
>
> Awero is a born actress, there is no dispute about that. But only a fool, and I do not think Awodi-Oke is one, or expected to be, will reveal the secret behind the success of his roguery, more especially when one or more murders have been committed without any promptings. How unnatural it appears when Awero at the sight of the victim says: "Awodi-Oke, I've no husband, I've been looking for one. Won't you be my husband?" And in the comedy of errors, Awodi-Oke with all high positions and success attributed to him in his underground realm just falls for Awero like that.
>
> The Court scene is not well presented. The Court interpreters who interfere up to the point of contempt of court with the people and the accused persons should be given secondary prominence.
>
> That stage of the last scene where Awodi-Oke has a noose around his neck is offensive and unprecedented either in fiction or on stage.

The unnamed critic of this production missed three important points in his assessment. Firstly, a play like *Highway Eagle* and indeed its similar successor *K'ehin Sokun* are morality plays written for specific reasons. With *Highway Eagle*, Ogunde's message is that crime does not pay; so his apparent offensive or grotesque ending showing of the highway robber with a noose round his neck is used to drive this point sharply home to his audience. Secondly, Yoruba comedy plays abound with court scenes because they give an opportunity for horseplay and slapstick humour. The playwrights make no pretence of representing an actual court procedure. Finally, Ogunde, as a former law enforcing agent, is quite aware that many beautiful female detectives are often used as ploys to capture known criminals who acquire wives as profusely as they acquire their wealth. Obviously the element of time played an important part in the rapid way in which Awodi-Oke fell for Awero and eventually revealed all his criminal activities to her. Here Ogunde surely is right to resort to this dramatic licence.

Except for *Delicate Millionaire* and *Village Hospital*, both produced in 1957 and 1958 respectively, Ogunde wrote no more plays throughout the fifties. By the time these two plays were produced, Ogunde's theatre was definitely no longer operatic in character. Indeed it was around this time, the mid-fifties, that, as we have seen, he changed the name of his company from Ogunde Theatre Party to Ogunde Concert Party. What Ogunde did mainly in the fifties was to subject his theatre to frequent gruelling tours within and without the country, touring with "re-arranged" productions of old plays and the few new ones.

Apart from *Song of Unity* which was specially commissioned for Independence in October 1960, Ogunde wrote no new plays from 1960–63. In 1963 however, he composed a song which he called *Yoruba Ronu* or *Yoruba Think*. The title of the song later became the slogan of the Nigerian National Democratic Party, a splinter political party then ruling the former Western Region of Nigeria in place of the powerful Action Group Party. In 1962 a quarrel had arisen between Chief Awolowo, the leader of the Action Group and his Deputy, the late Chief Akintola. The Action Group, up till the division between the two leaders, had been one of the major political parties in Nigeria, and the one that Yoruba people largely took as their political organization. The division between Awolowo and Akintola caused untold economic as well as political catastrophe in the former Western Region. The Yoruba who formerly had one political organization to refer to and draw patronage from now had two, while their opposite numbers in the other regions enjoyed their old tribal solidarity. A majority of them retained their allegiance to the Action Group, probably because the formerly powerful political party now became the political underdog. But quite a few shifted their allegiance to Akintola's Nigerian National Democratic Party, which won the Western Region elections, when the leaders of the Action Group called on all their supporters to boycott the elections.

Ogunde's aim in composing *Yoruba Ronu* was to ask Yoruba people to unite once again to become one of the most powerful and prosperous groups in Nigeria. Given the political atmosphere of that period, the recording of the song became immensely popular. On February 11, 1964, the Secretary of the Egbe Omo Olofin, the cultural arm of the Nigerian National Democratic Party, wrote a letter to Ogunde. I quote it in full because of its historical importance. The letter ran thus:

> Dear Sir,
> You will remember that Chief H. O. Davies spoke to you about your staging a play at Ibadan on the night of the 29 February, 1964 on the occasion of the inauguration of the EGBE OMO OLOFIN and you agreed to such a performance.
> As time is drawing very close, the organizing committee would like to know from you how far you have gone with your arrangement and what you intend to charge for the occasion.
> Please treat this letter as urgent in order to enable the committee to finalize their arrangements.
>
> Yours faithfully,
> (Sgd.) H. O. Davies
> for Organizing Committee.

Ogunde fulfilled the engagement. He wrote a play for the Egbe Omo Olofin which he called *Yoruba Ronu* or *Yoruba Think*, after the title of the popular song. The title too was appropriate for the occasion, for as I mentioned earlier, it became the slogan of both the Nigerian National Democratic Party and its cultural arm, the Egbe Omo Olofin.

The play is an allegory depicting how a traditional ruler, Oba Fiwajoye, was betrayed to his enemy Yeye-Iloba by his deputy. The King's enemy later found a way of imprisoning him together with two of his senior chiefs. The Deputy then installed himself as the king and subjected his people to a harsh rule. Eventually, the people killed the usurper, and Oba Fiwajoye was released from prison to join his people; and peace and prosperity reigned for ever more in the kingdom. Ogunde included the title song in the play and it became the climax and one of the most moving sections of the play. *Yoruba Ronu* is not only interesting because of its direct attack of Akintola's method of gaining political power for himself and its indictment of his rule. It is also of interest because in it, Ogunde revealed once again his uncanny gift for predicting events. For two years after the play was written, Akintola was killed during the first military coup of January 15, 1966 and so were his powerful allies. Awolowo was later released from prison after the second coup of July 29, 1966 to play a prominent part in General Gowon's salvage operation of the country.

Ogunde, as a matter of fact, was only drawing upon history, using the story of the famous nineteenth century Yoruba Field Marshal, Afonja of Ilorin, who in his revolt against the Alafin of Oyo, allied with Alimi the Fulani. When the Fulani used the opportunity to extend the Muslim Jihad to Yoruba country, they found the people divided. The parallels between the nineteenth century and contemporary Yoruba history this time was close, as indeed Chief Awolowo himself had pointed out during the open breach between him and Akintola. Ogunde could be said, therefore, to have done for the Yoruba in this play, the same service as Jean Anouilh did for the French in his play, *Antigone*, during the German occupation. But the irony was that those who commissioned the play did not know what they had let themselves in for.

The allegory was easy for all to interpret. Oba Fiwajoye was obviously seen as Chief Awolowo, and the Oba's deputy who sold him to his enemy as Akintola, whilst Yeye Iloba seemed to represent the person of the Sardauna, Sir Ahmadu Bello.

Ogunde duly showed the play for the inauguration of the Egbe Omo Olofin on February 28, 1964. In the audience were Chief Akintola and other prominent political figures. Half way through the show Akintola realized that the play was a direct attack on his person as well as his rule, and he walked out of the show, followed by several others in the audience. The play however continued to the end and was greatly enjoyed by those who stayed.

Ogunde later staged *Yoruba Ronu* in Lagos on March 2, 1964 at the Glover Hall as part of the 20th Anniversary celebration of his theatre. He also performed the play on April 10, 11 and 12 at the Glover as originally requested by the Egbe Omo Olofin, and on March 31, he toured with the play to Ilesha. But as the show was about to begin, he was informed by the police that his theatre had been banned by the Western Region Government from performing throughout the whole of Western Nigeria. According to Ogunde, when the people in Ilesha heard of the ban, they rioted, and in order to avoid bloodshed he immediately left for Lagos.

Ogunde however had the last word on his ban. Although he did not make his usual press statements when under controversy, he did retaliate against his ban with a play called *Otito Koro* or *Truth is Bitter*. The biting opening of the play can be considered as his statement of protest to the Government that banned him, and in particular its leader:

> We do not kill a dog because it barks
> And we do not kill a ram because it butts
> What have I done that you withhold my daily bread from me?
> L–I–F–E!
> Help me ask from the worthless elder
> Help me ask from the wicked one
> The evil doer thinks that other people talk about him
> The evil doer runs away, even when no one pursues him
> We have made a promise to our God
> That we shall tell the truth, even if it is bitter
> If you have not done ill, why did you stop the play?
> If you are not treacherous, why are you afraid of my songs?

The world loves a liar
The honest man is tied down like a horse
The world hates truth
Truth is hard, truth is bitter
You have told the people of the world that
I have spoiled the town
I will make a report of you to all the sons and daughters of
   Oduduwa

Oh yes! you that feed on lies
You fraud!
You break down other people's house to build your own
You appear like a gentle ram
If you are bought by some people
You can be bought out by others
Hawk feeds on cursed foods
Feeds on anything
The world loves a liar
The honest man is tied down like a horse
The world hates the truth.

We that are banned
We wait on the Lord
We leave everything to God—the Silent
Judge to fight on our behalf
It is yours, yours, yours
What is more
You cannot walk at noonday
Because of the passion of the world
You have become like the rhino
That walks only in darkness
It is your, yours
What is more
The day of vengeance is coming, we know, it is very near
The day of vengeance is coming, we know, it is very near[33]

The ban lasted two years, and naturally caused Ogunde a great deal of financial loss, as the bulk of the Yoruba speaking people live in the Western Region. It was however quite a comfort that he could still perform in the remaining sections of the country.

Then came the first Military Coup of January 15, 1966. Ogunde immediately wrote to the former Military Governor of Western

Region, the late Lieutenant-Colonel F. A. Fajuyi and to the former Head of State the late Major General J. T. U. Aguiyi Ironsi, asking them to lift the ban imposed on his theatre by the Akintola regime. The Military Governor replied by lifting the ban on February 4, 1966 with a notice in the Western Region Government Gazette. With the lifting of the ban, Ogunde could once more perform to majority of his Yoruba-speaking audience. After the second coup on July 29, 1966, the Commandant of the Battalion stationed in Ibadan requested a command performance of *Yoruba Ronu*. Ogunde performed it on September 20, 1966 at the British Council Hall. Amongst the eminent personalities in the audience was Chief Obafemi Awolowo. This time nobody walked out of the show.

A year later, the Federal Military Government invited him to form a dance troupe for performances in the Nigerian Pavilion at the Expo '67 in Montreal, Canada. Through this invitation, the government gave Ogunde the opportunity of forming another entertainment company called the Ogunde Dance Company. This brought to three, Ogunde's major entertainment companies; these in the order of their formation are: Ogunde Theatre Company, 1946; Ogunde Record Company, 1947; Ogunde Dance Company, 1966.

All the three companies are inter-related, but at the same time have their individual functions. The Theatre Company, the subject of this study, is the oldest, and is solely for play productions. His Record Company is for the recording of his popular songs for social dances, while he uses his Dance Company only for his European tours.

The Dance Company has performed as a guest troupe at several prestigious festivals and places like the Llangollen International, Eisteddfod; Farefield Hall, Croydon, Great Britain; and Apollo Theatre, Harlem, New York. Those who make up his theatre company also constitute his dance company. But oftentimes he augments the dance company with visiting well-known acrobatic or dance groups from all over Nigeria such as the Ilorin Acrobats, the Agbor and the Atilogwu dancers. To all of them, he is a ready patron.

Over the years, Ogunde has become the acknowledged leader and father of contemporary Yoruba theatre, a role which he has played without fanfare and out of the limelight. Besides running his own theatre he has helped others from crises and ruin. After the late Ogunmola's long absence from the theatre due to illness, it was Ogunde who financed his return to the theatre circuit, and sponsored his shows all round the country, urging the public to embrace Ogunmola once again. What is less known is that he has also financially helped Duro Ladipo, when his group went on a tour of Europe in 1973.[34] Considering his pioneering work in the field of professional theatre and extraordinary theatre experience, it is not surprising therefore that he is the President of the Union of Nigerian Dramatists and Playwrights.

Notes

1. *West African Pilot*, 2nd March, 1946.
2. *West African Pilot*, 30th March, 1946.
3. *Daily Service*, 25th April, 1946.
4. "The African in Dramatic Art", *Daily Service* Editorial Comment of 3rd May, 1946.
5. *West African Pilot*, 3rd May, 1946.
6. *Daily Service*, 4th May, 1946.
7. *West African Pilot*, 10th May, 1946.
8. *West African Pilot*, 1st August, 1946, *Daily Service* 1st August, 1946.
9. See Prof. Adedeji's study of the Alarinjo Travelling theatre in this anthology.
10. *Daily Service*, 5th February, 1944.
11. *West African Pilot*, 23rd August, 1946, Editorial Comment.
12. Ibid.
13. Ibid., 3rd October, 1946.
14. Ibid., 23rd October, 1946.
15. She died in an accident in September, 1970 on the way to Ilesha where the company was going to perform a play. A year later, Ogunde wrote a play in her memory called *Ayanmo*. She had three children for Ogunde. The two senior girls Tokunbo and Tope are now leading members of the company.
16. *Daily Comet*, 30th January, 1947.
17. Ibid.
18. Ibid.
19. Ibid.
20. Ibid.
21. *West African Pilot*, 31st March, 1947.
22. *Daily Comet*, 31st March, 1947.
23. *West African Pilot*, 2nd July, 1947.
24. Ibid., 3rd July, 1947.
25. Ibid, 8th September, 1947.

26. The preview is wrong here, *Half and Half* was not the first folkloric opera by Ogunde. Others such as *Journey to Heaven* and *The Black Forest*, both produced in 1945 also dealt with the folkloric content and themes.
27. J. P. Clark, "Aspects of Nigerian Drama", see Ch. 2 of this anthology.
28. Ulli Beier, *Yoruba Theatre*.
29. *Daily Comet*, 12th March, 1947.
30. See Echeruo's, "Concert and Theatre in late 19th Century", reproduced in this anthology.
31. Personal communication by Mr. Bobby Benson to Professor J. P. Clark.
32. *Daily Service*, 4th September, 1949.
33. Opening lines from *Otito Koro* recreated by Hubert Ogunde for the author.
34. Personal communication by Ulli Beier to J. P. Clark and confirmed by Hubert Ogunde to the author.

Reprinted Nigeria Magazine, Nos. 114–116, 1974–75.

E. K. OGUNMOLA: A PERSONAL MEMOIR
Ulli Beier

The first time I came across that delightful art form known as "Yoruba Opera" was in Lagos in 1951. Those were the days before the so-called "slum clearance", when the centre of Lagos was not yet the anonymous conglomeration of office blocks that it has become since. The triangle between Martin Street, Broad Street and Nnamdi Azikiwe Street, for example, consisted of small Brazilian style houses, rather overpopulated, it is true, but teeming with life and vibrant with music. In those days I liked to take walks through the dimly lit streets at night. Architecturally the town was extremely pleasing. It was not just the masterpieces of Brazilian architecture, like No. 10 Elias Street and Olaiya's house in Tinubu Square which have survived until today, but the whole intricate pattern of buildings, the wealth of architectural ideas and the imaginative detail that gave old Lagos its particular flair.

On one such night, I noticed a poster advertising a play called *Adam and Eve*. I went to the old Glover Hall, having no idea at all what it might be. What I found was a fund-raising function of the Seraphim and Cherubim Church. The Hall was crowded, predominantly with women who had come in their best *aso oke* dresses and big headties and many of whom were surrounded by children. I cannot remember the names of any of the actors. In fact, I do not think that there was a programme listing them. They appeared to be members of the congregation who had thought up the play in order to help their Church raise some money.

The experience was totally new to me. I had, in my ignorance, not yet come across Hubert Ogunde and his concert party, even though he had been running a professional troupe for several years.

It was a charming performance. The back-drop representing the Garden of Eden was executed in a schoolboy manner, but nevertheless very attractive. For the first time I experienced the gentle sway and rhythmic shuffle that runs like a nerve through the

321

322   DRAMA AND THEATRE IN NIGERIA

performance. In the Western tradition of theatre, actors who are
not engaged in actual dialogue or action have to occupy themselves with stage "business" in order not to look stiff or artificial. In
Yoruba Opera the problem has been solved simply and beautifully by making such characters unashamedly "onlookers" but
letting them sway gently to the rhythm of highlife-derived music.
What I remember most clearly of this performance is that Adam
and Eve were both dressed in long, black, old-fashioned swim-
suits. Adam was a thin and wiry young man, a vivacious actor and
clearly the clown as well as the hero of the play. Eve was luscious;
the black swimsuit had difficulty in containing her, and Adam,
when he woke up from his sleep to see her for the first time,
broke out into a flourish of appropriately ribald jokes.

I left charmed and intrigued and slightly puzzled, but I had no
idea that Yoruba Opera was to become one of the greatest
pleasures of my life. My real discovery of Yoruba Opera came a
year later when I came across E. K. Ogunmola in Ikere Ekiti. I
think this was my first visit to Ikere. I came to stay there quite
accidentally. I was in fact merely driving through but found
myself intrigued by the splendid entrance gate to the palace that
was surmounted by two very tall cement soldiers. Walking
through the gate I discovered one of the most beautiful palaces of
Yorubaland and I met Adegoriola, the Ogoga of Ikere, who
kindly invited me to spend some days with him in the palace.

On my last night in Ikere, Ogunmola's company appeared
from Ado-Ekiti to perform *Joseph and his Brethren* in one of the
schoolrooms. Stylistically, the performance was not too dissimilar
from the one I had seen a year earlier in Lagos. The music was
derived from highlife, with a certain influence of Church hymns
clearly detectable. There was the same swaying movement of the
actors throughout and also the use of a special kind of *recitative*,
to which Yoruba, being a tonal language, lends itself particularly
well. (To European ears even spoken Yoruba sounds recitative!)
Ogunmola's play, however, was preceded by a number called the
"Opening Glee", in which the audience is told in advance about
the story they are about to see, and in which a suitable moral is
drawn. This was a particularly charming number. The "Opening
Glee" started with a group of shimmying girls, who formed a kind

of chorus. When the pace of their dance had heated up, Ogun-mola suddenly burst out from behind the simple back-drop curtain to take the lead in their midst and to sing the moral of the song. He was dressed in a kind of Pierrot's costume, with a wide red floppy collar.

What made this performance an experience of a different kind, however, was the quality of the acting. There was a sensitivity here, an attention to detail that was totally captivating. Even with virtually no knowledge of Yoruba one could follow any tiny shade of meaning and mood. The acting was selectively realistic. Realism on stage can often be a bore, but Ogunmola always understood what was *typical* in human behaviour and he knew how to isolate it and at times exaggerate it for greater effect. Ogunmola's plays did not present a mirror image of Yoruba life: they gave a sharpened, heightened, concentrated image. He always succeeded in going right to the essence of character. He achieved this not with a complex or philosophical dialogue that would lay bare the souls of the dramatis personae. On the contrary—his dialogue was lifted straight from everyday conver-sation, and his moralizing was simple to the extent of being naive. In fact his plays do not read particularly well. Ogunmola put his characters across not through words, but through gesture, movement and expression. Often the most powerful effects in a play lay in brief moments of silence.

I was so intrigued by this performance that for the next few days I followed Ogunmola around on his tour of Ekiti. I saw several more performances and among them was the play that was to remain my favourite, *Love of Money*.

The plot of this play is deceptively simple. The hero, Adeleke, enjoys moderate prosperity and happiness with his wife Moro-layo and their two children. But already his friends, who form a kind of chorus, warn him of the instability of fate: "Fear the son of man," they say, "because money does not stay in one place for generations." Confusion is soon brought into his life by the shrewd and alluring Mopelola, who appears one day to say that she had decided to marry him. Adeleke is flattered by the beautiful temptress and he walks into her trap immediately. He persuades his wife that she needs a co-wife to help her. The new wife moves in and does not take long to pick quarrels with the senior wife. Infatuated with Mopelola, Adeleke drives his first wife away, and she leaves with her children. Mopelola now finds it easy to get a stronger and stronger hold on him and she is now ready for the final kill. Her accomplice and boyfriend R.S.K. is a "money-doubler". The gullible Adeleke is persuaded to borrow ₦100 so that in twenty-four hours he will see it transformed magically into ₦300. Like a sleepwalker, Adeleke walks into this final trap. Helplessly he finds himself duped by the crooks, and to make his humiliation complete, he sees Mopelola quietly packing her bags. She has no more use for him. "My father who begot me was a rich man; my mother who brought me up was a rich woman; a goat cannot give birth to a kid that grows up a sheep. I am ready to leave—I am going!" Left without wife, without children and with debts, he has to suffer the final humiliation of being blamed for his misfortune by his friends: "A man gets what he deserves; you have been trying to speed the hand of God."

This sounds like an obvious story and one that merely lends itself to very banal moralizing: pride goes before the fall; beware of women ("the girls of nowadays are hard—they shave your head and paint it black"), and the fool gets punished even if he is innocent.

Even in Ogunmola's own translation of the play, we get little sense of the excitement and subtlety of the performance. Here and there the language is colourful or humorous—but the play still sounds much too simple in cold print.

To see a performance of *Love of Money* was quite a different matter. Ogunmola's portrayal of Adeleke was always subtle, moving and humorous. Right from the opening scene, where Adeleke goes through the typical self-congratulatory phases of the successful rich man, Ogunmola was able to suggest his vulnerability. One did not really need the chorus of friends to know that here was a man too vain and too weak to meet any real challenge. All that is not really contained in the text, but it was suggested by Ogunmola's every gesture and movement. Even in that very first performance I saw in Ekiti in 1952 the part of Mopelola was played by the girl who was later to become his wife and who was to perform the part for many years to come, until eventually she switched over to the part of Morolayo, leaving the part of Mopelola to a younger actress. What I witnessed then was the beginning of that mature and subtle teamwork between Ogunmola and his wife that was to delight and astonish us again and again in later years.

The part of Mopelola was acted with beautiful economy. A sense of intrigue and danger was cunningly suggested under the sparkling surface of charm and laughter. A cruder performance would have provoked antipathy in the audience for Mopelola and contempt for the foolish Adeleke who could be corrupted so easily by her deceitful manner. But in fact one felt completely captivated by her. Most men in the audience would have walked knowingly into the trap, just as Adeleke did.

Ogunmola was not only an actor, but also a producer of no mean talent. One scene that is unforgettable from *Love of Money* is the preparation for the wedding of Adeleke and Mopelola. Ogunmola would play this on a completely empty stage, with only himself and Morolayo present. And yet, between the two of them, they managed to convey a busy, bustling, nervous household. This scene became one of the highlights of the play in later years, when Mrs. Ogunmola had taken over the part of Morolayo.

Audiences loved this play because it portrayed Yoruba society knowingly and because they could recognize themselves. Ogunmola knew about every weakness of the human character and he would expose it, but he would expose human beings without harshness. There was no bitter satire in these plays—only understanding. He made us laugh about his stage characters, but it was his particular genius that forced us to include ourselves in the laughter. The moralizing of Ogunmola's text was always mellowed by the performance. He never made us despise people. On the contrary, one loved both the "good" and the "bad" characters, one loved the wise ones and most of all the foolish ones.

I do not know how often I saw *Love of Money* during the following twenty years. I guess about thirty times. I never grew tired of it. Of course, no two performances were ever alike. This was not because Ogunmola had a quick turnover in actors. His leading lady stayed with him to the end of his life and in the photographs of *Love of Money* that appeared in *Nigeria Magazine* No. 44 of 1954 I recognized at least one actor who was with him to the end. Ogunmola inspired great loyalty in his company and kept his troupe together extremely well.

His performances varied because he left much to improvisation on stage. He never wrote down his plays in any detail until he was finally asked by others to do so and even then he never wrote down a very full version. His performances, however well rehearsed, always left room for the inspiration of the moment. Moreover, his performances became more and more subtle and more and more professional as he grew older. His understanding of human nature increased, and so with every performance one felt that one got to know the familiar figures of *Love of Money* a little better.

My first encounter with Ogunmola excited me a great deal. I felt everybody ought to know about this gifted man. I could not understand why he was not famous already and why he had not been given the support to enable him to create a fully professional company. He seemed to be wasting his time teaching in a primary school.

I recorded some of his songs and gave the tape to the Western Nigeria Broadcasting Station who broadcast it. When Ogunmola performed in Oshogbo, for the first time in 1953, I was able to take D. W. McCrow along, the Editor of *Nigeria Magazine*. McCrow enjoyed the performance and we arranged for the company to perform in the open air in Ede the next morning, to enable McCrow to take the pictures which finally appeared in *Nigeria Magazine* No. 44. I also wrote a piece for the *Journal of the African Music Society* (Vol. 1, No. 1, 1954). But for a long time none of this made the slightest difference to his career. The audience in Oshogbo clearly enjoyed his performance, but their approval was guarded ("he is really trying") and they compared him unfavourably with Ogunde, who had been capturing their imagination for years. Perhaps in those years Ogunmola could not match the sheer professionalism of Ogunde, and his more subtle approach did not at first make the same impact as the jazzy glamour of Ogunde's performances. In fact it took some years before local audiences learned to stop comparing the two, before they learned that they were looking at two entirely different things, and that each could be perfect in his own way. There was, by the way, never any rivalry between the actors. They kept cordial relations throughout, and not merely on the surface.

In 1955 Ogunmola moved to Oshogbo, which enabled him to operate from a bigger centre. In the same year we managed for the first time to arrange a performance by Ogunmola at the University of Ibadan—but in those days most of the staff still preferred their annual performance of the Mikado to any African Drama. The real break came for E. K. Ogunmola when Robert July came to Oshogbo and saw him perform. Robert July was then the representative of the Rockefeller Foundation in Nigeria. He was highly impressed by what he saw and negotiated a grant for Ogunmola that gave him a period of six months with the Drama Department at the University of Ibadan, during which he could work on the production of a new play, get acquainted with more complicated stage techniques, experience other productions and demonstrate his skill to the students. At the same time the grant provided money for a lorry, generator, lights, basic costume and a revolving production fund, that would enable Ogunmola to go fully professional at the end of the period.

The result of this stay at the University was the famous production of the *Palm Wine Drinkard*, which was a tremendous success and which Ogunmola finally took to the Algiers Festival. I still find it regrettable that Ogunmola was not given a chance to create his own play out of Tutuola's book, but that he was given someone else's dramatization, that turned the realities of Tutuola's supernatural world into the feeble device of a dream. Even so, the *Palm Wine Drinkard* provided Ogunmola with one of his greatest parts and many people will remember him exactly as Segun Olusola described him in *Nigeria Magazine* No. 77 (1963): "In his 'praise song of the spirit of palm wine' he surpasses anything that has ever come on the local stage. Whether he sings it or leads the chorus to recite it, his pauses, nuances, gestures, word associations or the eloquent mimes when he puts his expressive face to full use . . . you are witnessing a great performer in the act with a relish for the liquor that is easily transferable to the audience."

Demas Nwoko's production had added some tightness and speed, without interfering with Ogunmola's basic style of performance. His costume design and sets were brilliant and spectacular, thus giving the play a very wide appeal. There was a great deal of humour in these designs too that blended well with the tone of much of Tutuola's writing.

At the end of this stay with the Drama School, Ogunmola achieved his ambition of founding a fully professional company. From then on his popularity rose fast and his perfection grew steadily. I missed few opportunities to see his performances, even though at this stage I had become much more closely associated with another Yoruba Theatre company, that of Duro Ladipo. The *Palm Wine Drinkard* remained on Ogunmola's repertoire for years to come, but gradually the costumes and sets became tattered and lost some of their former glamour. The production too moved away gradually from the Arts Theatre discipline to Ogunmola's own more relaxed style of production. In some ways this was a pity, but really it merely proved that Ogunmola was a man with a very strong vision of his own, who would not for long incorporate other people's ideas, however brilliant.

In this respect he differed greatly from Duro Ladipo, who always loved to discuss his productions with others, keenly sought criticism of his performances and was wide open to ideas. His approach was completely different from Ogunmola's and he was interested in different aspects of drama. I never saw his theatre as being in direct competition with Ogunmola, for they developed quite different styles and talents. The excitement of living in Nigeria at that time was this very profusion and variety of talent that sprouted everywhere.

The two composer-actor-producers did not see themselves as competitors either, until the government's selection of a Yoruba opera for the 1965 Commonwealth Festival in Britain brought some serious misunderstandings and temporarily caused a great deal of bitterness among the companies. With Ogunde being at the time based in Lagos and in fact banned by the Western Region Government because of his famous play *Yoruba Ronu*, the selectors literally had to make a choice between plays as different as the *Palm Wine Drinkard* and *Oba Koso*. The humour, the refinement of acting, the brilliant timing, the spectacular costumes and designs of the Drinkard formed a complete contrast with the poetry, the complex drumming, the real sense of tragedy and the monumental presence of Ladipo in *Oba Koso*. Unfortunately, many of the arguments raised for and against the one or the other play had little to do with theatre and a lot with politics. Some comments by adjudicators were indeed trifling and irrelevant. For example, it was said against the *Palm Wine Drinkard* that "Yorubas drink palm wine from calabash, not a horn." If I remember the unpleasant scene correctly, the Western Region Selection Committee selected *Oba Koso*. The Federal Selection Committee ordered a replay and favoured the *Palm Wine Drinkard*. In the end the Federal Minister of Information overruled and decided on *Oba Koso*. Both companies became pawns of political party squabbles during the time and it left some bitterness and tension between them, antagonisms that were not resolved until much later.

During the coming years Ogunmola led a more and more active life. He took his plays all over the country and drew huge crowds wherever he went. One thing that became clear to me during this time was that he was not merely "popular", the audience loved him and developed a personal loyalty to him.

In December 1966 I left Nigeria for Papua New Guinea and for some years I was to live without Yoruba Operas. When I returned on a visit in December 1970 in order to attend the Ife Festival of the Arts, I was told that Ogunmola had fallen seriously ill. Wole Soyinka took me to visit him in the University Hospital at Ibadan. To see him prostrate and partly paralysed was a tremendous shock. I had never known him to be sick, not even mildly. He had always shown incredible stamina; his energy had seemed boundless. I had no idea how old he was: he was one of those alert, ageless people who did not seem to change over the years. Now he looked ravaged, but his courage had not left him. He was a philosopher, who could accept the hardest fate calmly. But it was also clear that he was quietly determined to do the impossible: to get back onto the stage.

Unfortunately Ogunmola was still too ill in December 1971 to witness the first performance of the film *My Brother's Children* at the Fourth Ife Festival of the Arts. This film was made for the International Family Planning Association, and its real purpose was to tell Yoruba people about family planning. The producers, Tony Isaacs and Segun Olusola, had the brilliant idea of asking Ogunmola and his genius as an actor and producer. Tony Isaacs, a well-known BBC film producer, was astonished at the sheer professionalism of the company. There is a brilliant quarrel scene in the film between husband and wife, which was improvised and filmed without rehearsal or retake. Tony Isaacs told me that he finished the shooting in less than half the time allotted. It is a great shame that neither the *Palm Wine Drinkard* nor *Love of Money* have been preserved on film, but in the absence of these, *My Brother's Children* will preserve for posterity the greatness of Ogunmola.

Even during these sad times Ogunmola still had time and thoughts for his friends. When the Mbari Club in Oshogbo gave a party for me to mark my return to Nigeria after several years absence, he sent a friend, who presented me with an album and an illuminated address.

During those hard days his wife kept the company together. They continued to play some of the old favourites. But who could play Adeleke like Ogunmola? Who could play the drinkard? Friends rallied to his help. Ogunmola's fellow playwright Wale Ogunyemi stepped into the role of the drinkard in order to give the company a boost.

When I returned to Nigeria a year later in order to take up a position with the University of Ife, Ogunmola was still ill. He lived quietly in Ibadan. His recovery was very slow, but his determination never left him.

Suddenly in May 1972 we heard the incredible news that Ogunmola had announced his return to the stage. His memorable return to the stage had been sponsored by Hubert Ogunde. Peter Brook happened to be on a visit in Ife then and we took him to see Ogunmola's first reappearance in Oshogbo in the Fakunle Major Hotel. It was an incredible event. The nightclub, which sometimes serves as a theatre for Yoruba Operas, could normally hold perhaps three hundred people, but on this occasion there must have been at least a thousand, tightly packed, standing in the aisles, filling out every square inch of the Fakunle Major Hotel and crowding the street outside. The excitement and the noise were incredible.

An incredible roar of delight went up when Ogunmola at last appeared on the stage. Never before has any actor received such a reception. People were beside themselves with joy. Ogunmola had to wait a long time before the noise had died sufficiently for him to address the crowd. He said that rumours had gone round saying he had died. But thanks to the grace of God he was back there with them and that his greatest wish, to be back on the stage, had been fulfilled. The people laughed and wept and shouted. The noise never died down again and the play had to be acted under this blanket of noise. The actors passed a microphone from one to the other, but even so, we could not hear what they were saying. Nobody cared: Ogunmola was there, alive and back on stage. He was still moving somewhat stiffly, and with difficulty. He was unable to take the lead part and his company had suffered from his long absence. But who cared? Ogunmola was alive and back on stage. We could not hear his words, and it was sad to see him acting a supporting role. But his presence was felt big and strong and warm by everybody. And that incredible, roaring noise was like a kind of ovation. The intense feeling never left the crowd through the long evening.

Peter Brook later said he had never seen such strong communication between an actor and his audience. "That man would have communicated with his audience even if he had been invisible."

Ogunmola's return to the stage did not last very long. He struggled gallantly for a while to lead his company. But then he suddenly died. Some felt that he may have hastened his end by exerting himself too much in his comeback. But then it must have been immensely rewarding to him to experience the love his audience felt for him, to see how much he had been missed. That night at the Fakunle Major Hotel was his greatest triumph.

To anyone who ever saw him on stage he remains unforgettable.

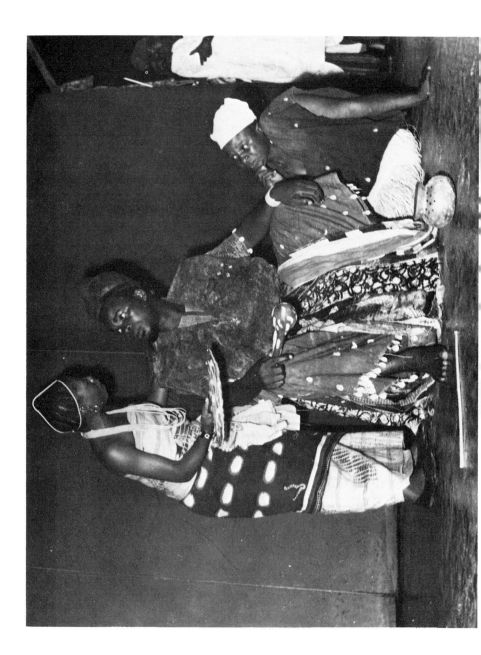

THE POPULAR THEATRE: A TRIBUTE TO DURO LADIPO
Yemi Ogunbiyi

I first personally met with Duro Ladipo in New York in the winter of 1975. Although I had seen him perform several times, both on stage and on television, I had never been privileged to meet him. Then, after the performance of *Oba Koso* at the La Mama Experimental Theatre in New York, I invited him and his celebrated actress wife, Abiodun, over to dinner the next day. And since some other Nigerians were also visiting, Duro Ladipo most readily agreed to come. It was, in many ways, a memorable meeting. Over an improvised substitute meal of pounded yam, we talked about his works, about his vibrantly active career and the tremendous growth of his Company, a growth which was evident from the performance I saw the night before. We talked about the changes *Oba Koso* had undergone since I first saw it eleven years before the 1975 New York performance. We also talked about what I considered to be his own contributions to Nigerian theatre and the need for him to go on working, even against all the odds that the Nigerian theatre artists faced, as at the time we talked. Finally, of course, we talked about the need to ensure that proper records were kept about *who* did *what* in the Nigerian theatre, *when* it was done, and *how* it was done. As it happened, I was at the time studying film-making in New York, having just completed my Drama programme and had become convinced more than ever, of the need to document Duro Ladipo's works on film. We agreed to meet again anytime I got back to Nigeria and to explore possibilities in that direction. I never met him again. He died on the March 11, 1978, shortly after I got back to Nigeria.

Three years after his death, even in a tribute such as this one, dedicated to the real meaning of Duro Ladipo, it is still difficult to fully appreciate the magnitude of his loss to the Nigerian theatre. For one thing, the Duro Ladipo National Theatre still manages to exist, kept alive by Mrs. Abiodun Ladipo, struggling, not unlike a latter day Helen Weigel, to keep the flag flying. But it is the Movement without the expansiveness of Duro Ladipo, without the tremendous and awe-inspiring power of the man himself, without the fire, real and imagined, which "Sango" Ladipo emitted during those eighteen years in which he single-handedly ran and managed the Duro Ladipo theatre. In some respects, there had been no one quite like him in the history of the Nigerian theatre. The two other most important names in the theatrical tradition which he helped to perfect, Hubert Ogunde and Kola Ogunmola, were, though remarkable artists in their own ways, quite different from him. It is generally agreed that he was, in a rather complex way, the most traditional minded. This complex uniqueness of Duro Ladipo explains, in part, why even now, beyond *attempting* a critique of his works against the background of the forces that produced them, the best that can be done is to *record* and *describe* some of his achievements and in so doing, put them in perspective. That is the aim of this short essay.

Born in Oshogbo on December 18, 1931, the late Duro Ladipo was the son of an Anglican catechist who had attempted to raise his children in a very strict Christian atmosphere. But in a town so rich in traditional Yoruba culture as Oshogbo and with a young man so tirelessly inquisitive like Duro, the dream of his father was never to come true. For, as a young man, to the utter dismay of his father, Duro Ladipo was steeped in traditional festivals and ceremonies. Here is how Duro Ladipo recalls those years:

> From my childhood, I showed a keen interest in traditional Yoruba Culture and customs, as amplified by the fact that I followed closely the activities of different masquerades and cultists, often to the dismay of my father. The Egungun and Ose festivals at Ila-Orangun, plus the Obatala, Sango and Otin festivals at Otun-Aiyegbaju were some of the important traditional festivals in which I showed my interests even as a young man.[1]

Obviously, his involvement with traditional festivals and practices, convinced him of the need to introduce, for the first time, talking drums into the Church as part of an Easter Cantata he had composed. Considering the talking drum too incompatible with Christian religion because of its use in traditional festivals and rituals, the Church rebuffed his innovation, thereby forcing him to seek a more secular setting for his compositions.

But it is well to note that even at this stage in his career, negative as the Church was, Duro Ladipo already had a following of some sort. A critic, Mr. Omidiji Aragbabalu, who wrote a review of a Duro Ladipo performance for *The Daily Service* in 1960 paid glowing tribute to his foresight and vision.

> Duro Ladipo, a young composer from Oshogbo recently produced a Yoruba Easter Cantata which was performed at the All Saints Church, Oshogbo. The Cantata, which was composed for soloists, choir and drums, had as its subject, the crucifixion of Christ . . . . The composition of Ladipo was truly Yoruba in character and a welcome change from the usual dreariness of the English hymns . . . . The Church authorities hardly appreciated the importance and significance of his work. They insisted on having conventional English hymns incorporated into the performance, thus ruining the artistic effect of the work . . . . He has certainly taken a step in the right direction. If Christianity is to survive in Nigeria, it must undergo the general process of Nigerianisation.[2]

That was in June of 1960. In December of 1961, the Oshogbo composer was invited to perform, this time a Christmas Cantata at the newly founded Mbari Club in Ibadan, which was barely six months old at the time. Founded by a group of artists and intellectuals, including Wole Soyinka, J. P. Clark, Chris Okigbo, D. O. Fagunwa, even Ezekiel Mphahlele (who was at the time teaching at the Ibadan University), Uche Okeke, Demas Nwoko and *Black Orpheus* editor, Ulli Beier, the Club had quite early earned for itself an international reputation as a Centre for the liveliest artistic minds in the country. Not unexpectedly, Duro Ladipo's piece was well received. Inspired by, and excited about the Ibadan Mbari, Duro Ladipo was determined to create a similar club in Oshogbo. Against the advice of sceptics who argued that Oshogbo was too small and provincial a town to serve any purpose as a Cultural Centre, Duro Ladipo proceeded to convert the downstairs rooms of his Oshogbo home, where he had previously run a bar (The Popular bar) into a base for his activities. The local people themselves renamed it *Mbari-Mbayo* ("when we see it, we shall be happy"). On March 17, 1962, the Centre opened with a performance of his first musical drama, *Oba Moro*. From that point, he went on to compose some twenty full-length plays, that is, not counting some fifty or more other sketches which he composed for Nigerian television.

Looking back now, it is evident that the idea of the Centre as conceived by Duro Ladipo was prudent and most rewarding, that is, in cultural and artistic terms. No meaningful study of the Nigerian theatre can afford to ignore the contributions of this Centre to our theatre. In thinking of a home base, so to speak, of a real physical structure from where to operate, and in seeing it as a matter of utmost priority at a time when the Duro Ladipo theatre was just starting out, Duro Ladipo chalked up for himself a "first" in the annals of our theatre history. Certainly, one of the obstacles in the way of evolving a vibrantly rich theatrical tradition in Nigeria has been the marked absence of theatre structures and buildings owned and managed by individual theatre groups, that is, usable structures where they can quite freely "show" and do their works in their own distinctive ways. Even the very idea of locating the Centre in Oshogbo, bore out the real artist in the man; for while it ensured his closeness to his roots and consequently to the people, he lost out on the seemingly attractive, if perverted material rewards of the urban centres. But then, he understood the dynamics of culture, its revival and propagation in a society like ours. He understood it far more than any other theatre practitioner in his tradition; indeed, far more than the "Festac-approach" of myopic bureaucrats who advocate the establishment of more State Arts' Councils as the most viable way of promoting a rich cultural tradition in Nigeria. He understood, it seems now, that ultimately any meaningful and relevant theatre must draw its strength from the people, while seeking at the same time to inspire them. And by the people, he was not thinking of the few select, privileged groups who could afford to pay for shows at our "National" Theatre in Lagos—but rather, the greater number of the members of the community to which he immediately belonged, the working class persons and peasant folks who thronged town halls, city squares, market-places, even schools to watch him and his group perform. And for such a theatre to thrive, Ladipo believed, and quite rightly too, that it must exist in that community *in situ*. Ladipo understood the nature of the sacrifice dictated by pioneering efforts—he understood that while it ensured his artistic integrity, it did not necessarily ensure material gains.

True, the Duro Ladipo Company made money from its extensive country-wide tours, but that fact does not obviate the point being made here. Rid of all the false elitism that has blighted the vision of otherwise committed young theatre practitioners, the internationally-known Duro Ladipo, whose group had performed in more countries than any other Nigerian group and had been nationally honoured twice, remained at Oshogbo, basically to the end.[3] For instance, every new play of his opened at Oshogbo first because the local Oshogbo audience was the *first* audience. They served as his barometer for testing out his works and like the genuinely popular artist that he was, he was willing to rework details that the local audience found unclear. After he completed work on *Moremi*, the first people who saw the play were the Ife chiefs who had served as his consultants when he was conducting research on the work. Their suggestions were incorporated into the final version of the play. The difference between this approach and that of other Yoruba travelling theatres is obvious. With the possible exception of the late Kola Ogunmola, who worked in Oshogbo before Duro Ladipo and may even have inspired him, a majority of these groups gravitate to the big cities of Ibadan and Lagos, where they inevitably get cut off from the rich sustenance of their backgrounds which inspired them in the first place. Duro Ladipo avoided these pitfalls and was obviously the better for it.

Aided by Ulli Beier and Susan Wanger, he transformed the *Mbari-Mbayo* into a Cultural Centre, an Arts Gallery and a meeting point for young artists seeking to develop their talents. Apart from art exhibitions, which became a dominant feature of the Centre, festivals were arranged, competitions organized and quite a few *Mbari-Mbayo* books were published. For instance, during the 1966 season, "eight young theatre groups around Oshogbo including Boys' and Girls' Clubs" performed fortnightly on the *Mbari-Mbayo* stage.[4] During the same season, well over 1,000 visitors came on "pilgrimage" to this shrine. The series of experimental workshops conducted at the Centre for young artists by Dennis Williams and Georgiana Beier opened up new vistas for such local talents as Twins-Seven-Seven, Jimoh Burai-moh, Muri Oyelami, Adebisi Fabunmi and Asiru Olatunde.

In writing about this period of Duro Ladipo's career, it ought to be stated that some critics have, unjustifiably it seems, questioned his own contributions towards the founding of the theatre named after him and his claims to responsibility for some of the achievements attributed to him. Arguing that Ulli Beier, "a foreigner", was the prime motivator of Ladipo and perhaps, the real founder of the *Mbari-Mbayo* Centre and other activities generally associated with Ladipo, the well-known Nigerian art designer and sculptor, Mr. Demas Nwoko wrote:

> Ulli Beier is not an artist, but he . . . created by suggestion, a theatre troupe basically after the style of the existing Ogunmola and Ogunde vernacular troupes. He suggested a historical theme from the legends . . . Through further suggestions during produc-tion, original indigenous music and appropriate dances (along with poetry) were used. Added to this, for decor, were back-cloths of typical modern art-school colours which were the results of the art workshops he had organized. The result was exhibition of slices of African customs and traditional art forms loosely linked by improvised dramatic movements and speech. *Oba Koso*, as the play was called, was a very exotic presentation and it was sent round Europe as a demonstration of our fine culture.[5]

Mr. Demas Nwoko's position is unfair to Duro Ladipo. Ladipo had been involved in theatre work long before he met Ulli Beier. His early childhood interests in festival dramas and traditional rituals, which I referred to above, substantiates that view. In the mid-fifties, as a pupil teacher at the Holy Trinity School, Omofe, Ilesa, Duro Ladipo organized the end-of-year concert pro-gramme. After he left Ilesa and moved to Northern Nigeria, he founded the U.N.A. School's Dramatic Society at Kaduna. The Dramatic Society had two major productions, *Omonide*, by M. S. Ayodele and Duro Ladipo's own interpretation of Shakespeare's *As You Like It*. They also did a Christmas Cantata, composed by

Ladipo. In each of these productions, Duro Ladipo manifested qualities which were to become the hall-mark of his style—the dexterous use of traditional musical instruments, chants and dance steps. And in each case he was able to justify his different techniques and stylistic preferences. He had not, as yet, met Ulli Beier. In fact, he met Ulli Beier after he left Kaduna in 1959 to settle down at Oshogbo.

And the argument that because Ulli Beier "suggested a historical theme" which may have influenced Ladipo or which he even gladly accepted to work with, Ladipo cannot rightly claim credit for the artistic achievements attributed to him, is also without merit. First, it ought to be stated that Duro Ladipo himself was for ever eager to acknowledge the assistance of Ulli Beier in helping him realize his artistic objectives. For instance, in the 1968 programme notes of the Duro Ladipo Festival week, held at the Obisesan Hall, Ibadan, to commemorate the five years of the Company's existence, Ladipo wrote about the founding of "a small group of drama company from the students of Grade Two Teachers' Training College, Oshogbo, with the advice of Prof. Ulli Beier . . ." But Duro Ladipo was persuasible enough to know that assistance in matters of creativity is a very limited factor, because in the end, the real artist is his own man, on his own, alone.

The whole argument smacks of pedantry, and so hardly useful in our assessment of the artist. How much was suggested? How much was accepted or rejected? All right, so Beier "suggested" historical themes to Ladipo. But then, the question is: so what? Did Ulli Beier actually compose the historical plays for Duro Ladipo? Did Ladipo not write these plays himself, composing the music, while falling back largely on the tradition of Yoruba Theatre, a tradition which goes back to Ogunde, Ogunmola and even the Alarinjo? In the last analysis, is not every artist some kind of a collaborator, borrowing, imitating, picking, selecting, sometimes taking and culling from and occasionally relying (in the words of T. S. Eliot) "on those who have gone before them"? Does any artist ever have his meaning alone? Isn't the artist (being, of course, a social being) constantly being influenced by even the minutest fragments of particular times, places and spaces, all of which filter through and invariably surface in whatever form in such an artist's work—even in spite of the uniqueness of his primary experience? Are these not known facts and accepted conventions of art generally?

To be sure, Duro Ladipo was quite receptive to a number of new and different ideas, not caring whether these ideas came from "foreigners" or his own kinsmen. But eclectic and receptive as he was, his preferences were clear and as I will show, in the end, the indelible mark of his individual and unique talent was dominant. Far from being a man who "did not really understand the philosophy behind the structure" which Beier was supposed to have founded for him, Ladipo advanced his own reasons for turning to Yoruba historical themes

> My plays amply demonstrate the dignity and respect with which the Yorubas treat their Kings. Historical facts are not invented stories as the materials upon which I have based my historical plays demonstrate. I wrote these plays for the following crucial reasons: first, to ensure that Yoruba folklore and traditional stories are never forgotten; secondly, to amply demonstrate the richness and uniqueness of Yoruba culture, a culture which has resisted the assault of white Christian religion; thirdly, to ensure that the dances, the music and the splendour of Yoruba as a language never become things of the past, a splendour so easily discernible in such traditional chants as *ijala, ofo, ewi, oriki* which I have used severally in my works; finally, to proudly enshrine in our hearts the names of great Yoruba kings and mythic heroes, for in the end, they are the real gods![6]

And starting out first, with *Oba Moro*, he went on to write a trilogy on the Oyo Empire, the other plays being *Oba Koso* and *Oba Waja*. And the evidence that these works are not the ghost-written works of an Ulli Beier is compellingly strong. Indeed, they come across as the systematic efforts of Duro Ladipo in active collaboration with the members of his Company.

No sooner did he start the Mbari-Mbayo Centre than he expanded the Choir group which he still ran, into a fully-fledged theatre of its own. That did not seem, on the surface of it, a difficult thing to do. After all, Oshogbo already had a flourishing tradition of Yoruba theatre of its own, actively nurtured by Kola

Ogunmola. And besides, Ogunmola's departure from Oshogbo at this time, to take up a temporary job at the University of Ibadan Theatre Arts Department, may even have created a vacuum which Duro Ladipo felt a need to fill. But to see it in these terms alone is to miss the singular achievement of Duro Ladipo. From the beginning, he sought to cut for himself a distinctly different image from that for which Kola Ogunmola had became popular. Basically a composer, Ladipo sought to liberate Yoruba musical drama from the deadening influence of a combination of Yoruba church music and monotonous highlife tunes, both of them, qualities to be found in both Ogunde and Ogunmola. The opening and closing glees, the slap-stick comedy, the ludicrous humour, the bongo drums, the European musical instruments, the preponderance of morality plays and fairy tales—all these gave room to new, original and free directions. In their places, Duro Ladipo introduced genuinely traditional Yoruba instruments, the *bata*, the *dundun*, the *sekere*, the *igbin*. He recruited traditional drummers, dancers, and singers and proceeded to immerse himself in the serious study of classical Yoruba music, poetry and history. The result? A different kind of Yoruba theatre, self-consciously traditional (in the best sense of the word), invigorating, intense and with a charm of its own. Imbued with a genuine sense of cultural revivalism, Ladipo reached beyond the morality plays characteristic of the forerunners of Yoruba travelling theatre, into the new territory of Yoruba historical drama. And when Mbari-Mbayo was officially opened to the public, it seemed natural therefore, that the occasion was commemorated with the production of *Oba Moro*, a Yoruba historical tragedy.

To be sure, not all his works were based on Yoruba historical and mythico-legendary material. However, his best known works, and certainly his most enduring artistic efforts belonged to this group. They include *Oba Moro, Oba Koso, Oba Waja, Moremi* and *Obatala*.[7] And even where the material was not entirely his own, he tended to historicize his material and adapt it to his own needs such that it ended up seeming like a page of Yoruba mythico-legendary history. *Te'ni begi lo ju, Aaro Meta, Otun Akogun, Ajagunnla, Karunwi*—all these belong to this category. It ought to be noted, in this connection, that a bulk of his works were adaptations. But they are adaptations which bore the firm stamp of his approach to the theatre. In his hands, the materials became entirely his own. Mr. Muraina Oyelami, who worked with Duro Ladipo, confirmed in a taped conversation I held with him that Ladipo beautifully re-worked biblical stories and that unless particular attention was paid, the original source was generally never obvious to the audience. The story of Samson and Delilah became the story of how the "Olori" of powerful Yoruba Oba gave away his secrets to an invading enemy group. He called it *Jaleyemi*. The biblical story of Joseph and the conspiracy against him by his brothers he called *Afolayan*. *Kobidi* was the story of David and Goliath, and so on.

In certain respects, some of his plays were closer to the established tradition of Yoruba theatre started by Ogunde. In fact, contrary to the general view that he did not write morality plays, Duro Ladipo wrote quite a number of them. Either *Suru Baba Iwa* or *Tanimowo* could have easily passed for an Ogunde play. *Iku* was a comical morality piece which was inspired by Ulli Beier's adaptation and translation of Hugo Von Hofmansthal's late 15th century version of *Everyman* which Beier had called *Eda*. *Eda* became a very popular piece in the company's repertory of plays, due partly to the role of Eda as rendered by Mr. Lere Paimo, who was, until 1971 when he founded his own Company, the second top-most member of the Duro Ladipo Company. Lere Paimo is a witty comedian for which he is justly popular with his audiences. As a member of the Duro Ladipo Company which tended to emphasize serious historical themes, based on human intrigues and conspiracies, he stood out distinctly and quickly earned for himself the reputation of a quick-witted comedian. His presence in the Company emphasized a comical dimension which otherwise may have been absent without him. Before Mr. Moses Olaiya (Baba Sala) came into the limelight in 1967, Mr. Lere Paimo had helped create in Duro Ladipo's theatre a comical tradition which was novel in the tradition of Yoruba travelling theatre and which Olaiya then developed into a major form. Duro Ladipo also worked on Frederick Durrenmatt's *The Double* which, with the aid of Ulli Beier, he translated into Yoruba for radio.

The last category of his plays were the short television sketches and pieces, by far his most numerous works, and by no means the least popular. These plays like *Ejagbingbe, Oyelogbawo, Ewe Ayo, Akeju, Gbade-gesin* formed the only bases of acquaintance between Duro Ladipo and a large section of his admirers who never saw him perform on a live stage. In 1975, Duro Ladipo created *Bode Wasinmi* for Nigerian Television, Ibadan, a bi-monthly series which sought to recreate life in a typical Yoruba Village of the 1920's. Although these TV plays were short pieces, they must be seen within the frame-work of his longer works. Thematically, they shared a lot with his other works. Like them, these television pieces were generally concerned with human misfortunes and intrigues in a world peopled with Yoruba rulers, "bales", Kingmakers and their subjects. But above all, historical plays were his real forte.

Although Duro Ladipo's major source of material for his historical plays was Samuel Johnson's *History of the Yorubas*, he was not always loyal to the Johnson versions. At every instance, he reworked the materials, adding new dimensions and some-times sacrificing strict chronological details for dramatic effect. But a second reason for ignoring details of Johnson's interpreta-tion, where he felt the need to do so, is contained in his explanation of his own version of Sango's story in *Oba Koso*. He wrote:

> I ought to refer to Samuel Johnson's *History of the Yorubas* and point out the slight difference between his version of the Gbonka-Timi episode during the reign of Oba Sango and Oba Kori, and my interpretation of it. To be sure, historians are deserving of our praise, since they are hardly ever living witnesses to the details they so accurately describe. However, my interest was specific, namely to show that Sango was a victim of intrigues. I also picked up other details from elders, "babalawos", devotees and worshippers of Sango and particularly, the Obas of Oyo and Ede.[8]

In effect, Samuel Johnson's text was merely a guide. Duro Ladipo relied extremely on the oral tradition.

Oba Moro was the first of these historical plays. *Oba Moro* is important in the framework of understanding Duro Ladipo's works because in it, Ladipo set a pattern which he perfected in the major works that followed. In this first play, beyond deciding on the details of the story line, he alone composed the music of the play. Essentially what he did was to forge from a broad spectrum of traditional Yoruba dance and music, a uniquely strident musical dance, linked together with solo and choral song, highly accentuated by the precision of the dance steps at different stages of the performance. The result was most rewarding. In one stroke, *Oba Moro* is dance-drama, mime, acrobatic display and a demonstration of superb drumming feats. Unlike previous Yoruba traditional drama (Ogunde and Ogunmola) which derived its strength solely from the charm of its lively performance, *Oba Moro*, in addition to this outstanding quality, was invested with a subtlety of text, complete with the intricacies of composition which are the dreams of any composer of music or dance-drama. When in the end, the Alafin triumphs over the intrigues of his chief, the supremacy of his will acknowledged, the procession to return to the ancient Oyo capital gets underway and the Alafin breaks into a chant, it is the finest example of Yoruba poetry, image-laden, moving and dignifying:

> When the eagle flies high into the sky,
> People think he is lost,
> Yet he returns to his nest,
> The leopard may pursue the antelope
> Through forests and across rivers
> But when he finally tears it down,
> He must return to his cave
> Let the horn-bill show us the way,
> Let the cocktail fly ahead of us,
> Let the egret accompany our march:
> However sweet the journey,
> The parrot must return to its nest.[9]

This style was perfected in *Oba Koso*. But then, *Oba Koso* was another story.

By far his best known work, it was, perhaps, too, his most successful. It is perfectly possible that for most of his ardent admirers, his reputation as a renowned artist, rests *only* on that play. Such was the great impact of the play. After it was first performed on the occasion of Mbari-Mbayo's first anniversary in March of 1963, it was said to have been performed some 2,000 other times at home before Duro Ladipo's death. It was performed at University theatres, market-places, schools, traditional Sango festivals, and palaces of Obas, and in particular, before two successive reigning Alafins of Oyo.[10] The play's career took it to some fifteen foreign countries, where, after it won the first place at the Berlin festival in 1964, it went on to win seven other awards at International theatre and cultural festivals. When in 1965, the Federal Government of Nigeria awarded Duro Ladipo the National Honours and the insignia of the Member of the Order of the Niger (M.O.N.) it was in recognition of his contribution to the propagation of Nigerian culture, particularly through the performance of the play. That year, at the Commonwealth Arts Festival in Britain, the play received rave reviews from an appreciative British public.

From the outset, *Oba Koso* was conceived ambitiously. Ladipo thoroughly researched the details of Sango's life not only from Samuel Johnson's text but also from all those who may have vital details about the life of this legendary figure. As if possessed by the spirit of Sango, Ladipo became a Sango priest himself and was eventually led into the secret cults of the deity. So, in fact, in certain respects the preparation and actual performance of the play may have been emotionally and spiritually gratifying for Duro Ladipo. His research work concluded, he extracted the details he needed for maximum dramatic effect from Sango's flamboyant life, keeping all the bare outlines except in one respect, his inclusion of the Gbonka-Timi encounter. It is generally believed that the Gbonka-Timi episode did not occur during the reign of Sango.[11] That did not bother Duro Ladipo, since, as he himself put it, ". . . my interest was specific, namely to show that Sango was a victim of intrigues."[12]

Although the reign of Sango predates the earliest known written records of Yoruba history, he is believed to be the third Alafin of Oyo and may have reigned for seven years. Oba Sango wielded tremendous power and prestige which seemed unmatched in Yoruba history. "He had a habit of emitting fire and smoke out of his mouth by which he greatly increased the dread his subjects had of him", Samuel Johnson tells us.[13] At the period in his life when this drama is set, he was said to have grown over-indulgent and complacent in his power such that two of his war-mongering generals, Gbonka and Timi, to whom he had entrusted much power, now threaten his authority and the peace of the town. Under pressure from the elders of Oyo to do something about his head-strong generals who insist on going to war, even as it is evident that wars had drained the resources of Oyo, Sango turns to Oya, his wife and confidant, for advice. Oya's advice is pragmatic: send Timi away, ostensibly as gate-keeper of the border post at Ede, an action which, while rendering Gbonka jobless and idle, could cost Timi his life. When the play begins, Sango is about to meet with the elders of Oyo for the first time. From that point on, the play follows, for the next seventy-minutes or so, the events that unfold after Oya's advice back-fires.

But this short summary does not do justice to this powerful drama. It says nothing of its texture, nor of its strength as a physical and intellectual experience. These qualities are high-lighted through a unique blend of the drumming, the poetry and the dance rhythms. Two examples will suffice to make the point. The play opens with loud and excited drumming to herald the King's public appearance. Led by Sango's personal bodyguard, a chorus of Sango's wives begin to sing his "Oriki". Totally subsumed in their excitement, they fail to notice, at least momentarily, Sango's appearance. And then suddenly, "with eyes as bitter kolanuts" with a loud bellow, breathing flames from his mouth, he prostrates his subjects before him even as the drums change their rhythm to affirm his presence. Slowly, but stately, he dances in acknowledgement of the praise from his people, demonstrating in his own person, the reassertion of temporal authority and the ordered life of the community. But in his characteristic impatience, he halts his own dance and quickly gets on with the business of receiving his generals at court. Again, that movement is accompanied with a shift in rhythm. These shifting rhythms, produced by strident, stammer-ing sounds of Sango's favourite drums, the *bata* drums, plus the thunderous, fiery entry of a towering fire-spitting Sango, combine to make the opening sequence, perhaps, the most powerful segment in the play.

No less captivating, however, is the closing sequence of the play. Now deserted by his own people whom he set out to protect, Sango senselessly swings his axe, slaughtering his own people. Suddenly realizing what he has done, he laments and declares his reign at an end:

Sango: Save me, O my head!
            O my head, save me
            The head, which one follows into the world,
                treats one as it likes.
            O my head, save me!
            Ah! I have killed my wives!
            I have killed my chiefs!
            If the bata drum is made to sound too high
            It is sure to tear in the end
            The plots in Oyo are becoming too much.
            My end is getting near, I, Sango!
            Ah! It is, it is . . .

Sango and   It is a pity . . .![14]
Towns-
people:

In the end, deserted even by his wife, a remorseful Sango stands alone in an open field, pulls a rope from his clothing and hangs himself.

As a dramatic spectacle, *Oba Koso* is probably unsurpassed amongst Duro Ladipo's works. Much of that power derives from the figure of Sango and Duro Ladipo's adept realization of that role on stage. Although Ladipo was never considered a remarkably great actor, his real strength being, to my mind, in the areas of musical composition and theatre management, however, as Sango, he brought magic to the play. In an uneven review of possibly the first production of the play, the well-known television producer and director, Mr. Segun Olusola praised Duro Ladipo for exhibiting "a studied characteristic prance of the old king" in those remarkable entries and for showing "an amazing concentration and involvement in his role".[15] But he also faulted the play for lacking "stage craft" and for failing to make use of both "stage realism and magical dexterity". But the fact is that traditional Yoruba theatre does not always rely on stage realism. Essentially, it is a theatre which combines illusionism with a rejection of it, depending on what is being depicted, a theatre which is as heavily stylized as it is straight-forwardly realistic, one which is at once intellectual and at the same time anti-syllogistic.

Traditional Yoruba theatre knows its limitations (that is, in the technical sense of lighting effects, stage props, etc.). However, it accepts those limitations and works within them because it does not constitute serious problems, either for its practitioners or its audience. What it lacks technically, it makes up for artistically. Language (in this respect, the cut-and-thrust dialogue of *Oba Koso*), drumming, dance, mime and music adequately create the changing moods in the play. The simple painted back-drops of scenes in *adire* clothes adequately serve to complement music, language and dance in conveying a sense of scenery and even mood required to carry the play. Even the costumes are generally quite expressive and add immensely to the atmospheric totality of the play.

And yet, in the same token, "stage realism" is not totally ignored. The sight of Sango actually spitting fire, prancing about unpredictably on stage in the manner of the legendary king, must be understood within the framework of psychological realism where the performer plays his part convincingly even though the entire production is partially stylized. No one who has seen the play will fail to note the gory scene in which Duro Ladipo as Sango, his face transformed into a terror-bearing mask, swings his deadly axe in a feat of uncontrollable anger, killing some of his wives and subjects. In the Sango legend of old, Sango actually killed thousands in that swing! Faced with the task of realizing this legendary feat on a live stage, Ladipo lets himself be guided by the techniques of stage realism. He reduces the legendary figure of a "thousand" victims of Sango's anger to a more theatrically convincing figure of a few individuals! It can even further be argued in this respect that while not detracting from the stature and awe of Sango, Ladipo may have sought to de-mythologize the legend thereby reminding the audience that, though a good god, Sango was first and foremost a man.

Also, the performers of traditional Yoruba theatre have no illusions of being participants at the event, particularly one in which they see themselves as merely retelling a known story in their own unique way. It is not what happens that really matters, nor indeed (to take an extreme view) is it important what is done. What matters is the intense spiritual experience shared by participants and spectators alike. For instance, the stylized mimed movements of Timi pulling his bow in order to release its arrow on Gbonka, movements employed to enhance artistic rather than natural effects, is in keeping with the theatrical conventions of Yoruba travelling theatre. For the audience, it is assumed, knows the Timi "of the flaming arrow", whose arrow "becomes fire in the body of the person it hits"! The audience knows it because presumably, the Timi's *oriki* is known to all. Similarly, for an audience that knows the Sango story and knows that Sango hanged himself on the branch of an "ayan" tree, it was sufficient to have Sango pull a rope from his clothing, put it round his neck and tighten it at the appropriate time to indicate the hanging. In the finest tradition of stylized theatre, it highlights what is most crucial, meaningful and effective and in this respect, what is the most crucial is the demise of Sango—not so much how he does it, since this is common knowledge, but rather, the intense emotional and spiritual experience which it generates, for only in that context can the apotheosis of Sango be meaningful.

These underlying qualities of the play are its strongest points. And if they are not readily obvious at first contact, the fault may not be that of the play, certainly not in its lack of "stage craft". Neither is the problem contained in the playwright's failure to make use of "stage realism". An awareness of the endearing qualities of the play presumes a familiar knowledge of the theatrical tradition to which the play belongs. The need for such familiar knowledge is even greater when confronted with a piece like *Moremi*, especially as it was Ladipo's most experimental piece and so, in certain respects, his most intellectually demanding.

Like the two other Nigerian playwrights who have in one way or the other adapted the Moremi myth for stage (Oyin Adejobi and Femi Osofisan), Duro Ladipo based his version of the myth on

Samuel Johnson's text. According to Johnson, after Oduduwa founded the city of Ile-Ife, it was constantly harassed by a neighbouring Igbo ethnic group, who repeatedly raided the city with fierce-looking masquerades. And then Moremi, "a woman of great beauty and virtue", and probably the wife of Oranmiyan, decided to discover the secret of the enemy. First, Moremi sought help from the deity, Esinmirin, in her task to overthrow the Igbos, with a promise to offer to the deity, "the costly sacrifice she could afford". Moremi's plan was to have herself taken prisoner by the Igbos. As wife of the king of the Igbos, she learns that the dreaded masquerades are not spirits but ordinary men dressed up in straw. After she escapes and reveals this knowledge to the people of Ife, the Igbo masquerades are met and destroyed with firebrands during their next raid. The Igbos are subjugated and forced to settle in Ife. Meanwhile, Moremi fulfils her promise to Esinmirin by sacrificing her only son, Oluorogbo. Oluorogbo is subsequently deified.

The story seems straightforward enough. But Ladipo gave it, it seems, a stronger and more convincing interpretation, an interpretation which rejects Johnson's facile interpretation of the fear created by the Igbo masks. A short but incisive review of the first performance of the play spells this out clearly. The relevant extract of the review deserves to be quoted in full:

> Ladipo argues that anybody but an imbecile can recognize that there is a man under the mask, be it made of straw or cloth. The point, however, is that the masquerader has acquired some kind of supernatural power by being in close contact with the ancestor whom he personifies. Moremi goes into the enemy camp in order to discover the incantation, the magic spell that will break this supernatural power. Thus the conflict of power in Ladipo's *Moremi* becomes a spiritual conflict. This also helps him to give a sounder motivation for the sacrifice of the child. In Johnson's version, we get the feeling that Esinmirin extracts an exorbitant fee for a rather simple piece of advice. Ladipo sees the relationships between the Ifes, Igbos and the gods as being rather more complex. The reason for the weakness of the Ifes is their failure to placate the local gods. The invaders have brought their own warrior gods with them, but they neglect the spirits of the soil, the rocks and the river . . . Thus the sacrifice of Oluorogbo is a

sacrifice for peace. He is deified because he has become the link between the Ifes and the spirits with whom they have entered a new relationship.[16]

This last reason—the sacrifice—is also advanced to explain why the reigning Oni of Ife, at the time, Alaiyemore does not exploit his victory over the Igbos. To do that, according to Moremi in the context of the play, will invalidate the sacrifice. On the contrary, he accommodated the Igbos, gave their king an Ife chieftaincy title and settled them in a section of the city.

In addition to this subtle interpretation of the myth, Ladipo attempted another experiment with this play. He incorporated into the first production of the play, which opened on March 26, 1966 in Oshogbo, a group of Ibo dancers, the *Otu Osomeze* dancers from Agbor. To be sure, the story of Moremi lends itself to this kind of experiment because of the clash of two different cultures, yet it was not an easy experiment. Here is an intimate account of the effect and result of the experiment:

> By incorporating them (the Agbor dancers) into his play, Ladipo enriched his drama with new dances, new rhythms and new tunes. The producer's task was not an easy one: the Agbor dancers had no experience on stage. They speak little Yoruba. Only a very skilful composer could blend the Agbor calabash horn with *Igbin* drums of Ife. Yet, the first performance of this play on 26th March, 1966 in Oshogbo was carried off with great aplomb.[17]

It is pertinent to note here that Duro Ladipo's unique experiment here preceded by one year, Ogunde's internationally-acclaimed Dance Company in which Agbor dancers, Atilogwu dancers and an Ilorin dance group were brought together in a single company. It will be recalled that the Ogunde Dance Company represented Nigeria at the Expo '67 in Montreal, Canada and that the Company went on a highly-acclaimed tour of the United States after the Montreal trip. It is not unlikely that Ladipo's success with his own experiment in *Moremi*, encouraged Ogunde's elaborate attempts in similar direction.

No study of Duro Ladipo could be complete or definitive—certainly not now. A lot more remains to be known about his working methods both as a director and theatre manager. Since virtually all of his plays were never scripted (that is, before production), there is still more gathering of material to be done. But this much is certain for now and that is, that Ladipo was one of the few true and genuine artists Nigeria ever had. In the brilliance and sweep of his imagination, the boldness of some of his experiments, even against great odds and in his dedication to the craft, he certainly had few equals. His decision to take up a research appointment at the Institute of African Studies, at the University of Ibadan and engage himself in more research work on Yoruba mythologies and history while also exploring avenues to film his works, bore out his singular dedication to the furtherance and promotion of a meaningful cultural tradition in our country. Just before he passed away, he had become convinced of the need to branch into films and had even featured in *Ija Ominira*, a short feature film which was based on Bayo Faleti's novel, *Omo Olokun Esin* and directed by Ola Balogun. His television version of *Oba Koso* which he did for Columbia Broadcasting Station (CBS) during his U.S. tour has remained a quarterly favourite on that network.

In the end, his real legacy is contained in his example, the example of a man who made relatively little money from his works but derived intense joy and contentment from the overwhelming sense of artistic fulfilment which he experienced, the example of a man who firmly believed in a meaningful cultural revivalism as a means towards total liberation and sought fervently to initiate it through his art, a man who knew and appreciated the fact that ultimately, the power to make an impact as an artist resided with the masses (yes, the masses) of the people, those masses who nurtured his art, gave him much-needed support and from whom he drew his strength. There could never be a more meaningful tribute to the memory of this remarkable artist.

Notes

1. Duro Ladipo, *Oba Koso (pelu Itumo ni Ede Geesi)* Lagos, Ibadan, Macmillan and Co, Nigeria Ltd., 1970, pp. xi–xii.
2. Omidiji Aragbabalu, "Cantata at Oshogbo: A review", in *The Daily Service*, Friday, June 17, 1960.
3. Although Duro Ladipo had moved to his Bode Wasinmi residence in Ibadan before he died, Oshogbo remained his base and the Mbari-Mbayo Centre was kept alive by him.

4. See the programme notes of the 5th Anniversary of Mbari-Mbayo held between Friday, March 17, and Saturday, March 18, 1967.
5. Demas Nwoko, "Search for a New African Theatre", in *Presence Africaine*, No. 75, 3rd Quarterly, 1970, p. 68.
6. Duro Ladipo, *Oba Koso*, *op. cit.*, vii (translations by the Editor).
7. It is difficult to provide dates for these plays, especially as there are no proper records as to when they were "composed", as distinct from when they were produced. For the same reason, it is difficult to state exactly the number of plays to be credited to Duro Ladipo. This seems to be a problem with Yoruba Travelling Theatres generally. With Duro Ladipo, the situation is even better since he at least, scripted some of his plays after the first few productions. Mrs. Ebun Clark, who did work on Ogunde reported how the veteran artist had no memory of having put together some of the plays he had actually done earlier in his career!
8. Duro Ladipo, *op. cit.*, viii.
9. Duro Ladipo, *Oba Moro* in *Three Yoruba Plays* (English by Ulli Beier), Ibadan, Mbari Publications, 1964, p. 51.
10. After years of doing this play, his audiences, both at home and abroad (Brazil, for instance) came to see him as the very reincarnation of the legendary Sango and even called him by that name. When Duro Ladipo died, Ibadan-based newspapers (see *Sunday Sketch* of March 12, 1978) reported the lightning which destroyed several homes in Ibadan!—an obvious reference to the legendary feats of the ancient Sango. Duro Ladipo himself did not seem to mind the reputation—in fact, he rather enjoyed the Sango sobriquet. After dinner at my place in New York in 1975, I proceeded to uncork a fresh bottle of brandy, remarking as I did that the occasion was deserving of it, especially as it was a singular privilege to have Sango pay a visit to the house in peace! At the end of the day, as he and his wife stood up to leave, Duro Ladipo grabbed the near-full bottle of brandy. Anticipating my reaction, he cut me off by reminding me: "A'iri a jeku oro!"—"No one ever sees the left over of a god!" I bought myself a fresh bottle of brandy the next day!!
11. See Samuel Johnson's *The History of the Yorubas*, Lagos C.S.S. Bookshops, 1921 (first published), p. 156.
12. Duro Ladipo, *op. cit.*, ix.
13. Samuel Johnson, *op. cit.*, p. 149.
14. Duro Ladipo, *Oba Koso*, *op. cit.*, p. 124.
15. Segun Olusola, "The Age of Kings", in *Nigeria Magazine*, No. 79, December, 1963.
16. "An experiment in Drama" by A Critic in *Nigeria Magazine*, No. 89, 1966, pp. 157/159. I relied extensively on this short review for this section of the essay.
17. Ibid., p. 157.

PART V
THE LITERARY TRADITION

CONCERT AND THEATRE IN LATE NINETEENTH CENTURY LAGOS

Michael J. C. Echeruo

The fact that the concert was very popular in late nineteenth century Lagos would not in itself have been a matter of great importance were it not tied up with cultural and historical considerations. The "pop" concert in Europe was, historically, a lower middle-class affair;[1] and lacked some of the special features of the Lagos concert of the same time. Obviously, though, one cannot consider these Lagos concerts in isolation from the general scheme of the concert and the music-hall in England and the continent, especially as there was a keen desire on the part of the small Lagos *elite* to demonstrate an interest in and an appreciation of music and theatre in so far as these were symbols of status and of culture. Moreover, most of the promoters of concerts in Lagos were people who had had some experience of these musical performances overseas. Hence the several references in the newspapers of the time to standards of production and performance in European theatres. A Lagos critic of 1882[2] spoke for many of these enthusiasts when he argued that

> those who had experience of musical performances in Europe fully understand the reason why ours in this country is always below par. In Europe artists are specially trained for their work. They advanced (sic) from the provinces to the capitals. They are accustomed to act and sing every night of their lives and therefore gain an *ensemble* totally unknown in this country.

This kind of thinking does show how conscious the promoters of the Lagos concert were of their European antecedents.

The missions played an interesting part in determining the development of these concerts in Lagos. There was at all stages, it is true, some amount of Missionary misgiving about (and later, hostility to) native dances and musicals. But since, in most cases, the schools which supported these concerts were mission-owned,

357

the reverend gentlemen in charge of these schools must have given some encouragement to concerts, generally. It was this reason, perhaps, that led some critics to blame the Reverend Supervisors for the fall in the standard of concerts in Lagos.[3]

The Missions continued to support concerts for their own reasons. Soon after the Catholic Mission built St. Gregory's Infant School, they were attacked by the C.M.S. Mission on the grounds that the intention was to attract Protestant converts to the Catholic faith through the regular concerts. The argument was that the regularity of the Catholic concerts was intended to win more converts to Catholicism. This charge caused a great deal of ill-feeling between the Missions[4]; and the newspapers of the period are full of correspondence on the matter. The Acting Superior of the Catholic Mission, Benin, Rev. P. Pellet, in a letter on the subject in the *Lagos Observer* admitted that "once or twice a year it is used as a concert room, say if you like, as a theatre; but is this a reason to say it has been built for concerts?" The quarrel was altogether a poor one, coming as it did from reverend gentlemen. But the incident itself shows how intimate the concert was to the Missions and the Lagos public.

The Missions came into the concert life of Lagos in another way. The Protestant Mission in West Africa, though essentially an English body, tried here and there to include an item or two of West African life in their Christian teaching. They encouraged Africans to enter the Ministry; though to be baptized, one often had to take a Christian (i.e. an English) name.[5] An unexpected development for the Missions (they had no experience of this in Sierra Leone) was the extent of the demand for local themes and a local "approach" in many matters, including concerts. Such an experiment with indigenous material might have realized itself into something of value if its development had been wisely directed. We find, however, that its standards were very low, and that the fact that these plays were in the native language made these shortcomings more noticed. The *Lagos Observer* of January 18, 1883 complained about this situation:

> Some cabalistic attempts must have been made to provoke me into usages of unparliamentary language with respect to the nature and

> characters introduced into some of our entertainments, *a propos* of that which was held at the Breadfruit Schoolroom . . . I can tolerate civilisation in the vernacular but I detest the exhibition of low forms of heathenism in any language.

The same day a contributor complained that "native dances and entertainments have deteriorated from what they used to be many years ago; no wonder then, the contempt that educated Lagosians evince in them". He went on to suggest that the Police law should be made "more stringent and a wee bit moral" to enable it to ban these displays. A week later, another contributor reported the use of the "*tom tom* at the stage, rude expressions in the native language and dancing of a fantastic kind".

This deterioration gave the Missions their opportunity. At the Annual Conference of the Wesleyan Church in 1881, an address was presented which among other things, expressed concern that "some places, chapel and school premises, set apart as they are for the worship and service of God, have been unlawfully abused by the holding therein of entertainments which were not only devoid of religious tendency but seemed to enter into undisguised competition with the music hall and the theatre". This was made the basis of a general appeal a year afterwards for a united stand against the new menace.

> Brethren, we call upon you to stand by us in an uncompromising opposition to this mistaken and dangerous policy. Even if success were to be gained thereby, it is too dearly bought to be worth having. And, in truth, such gain is unreal and must in the end bring damage and loss to the Church that seeks it . . . I would say that not one out of five of the songs in the programme was appropriate for a Methodist School room. I am quite sure that the spirit which these entertainments foster is wholly at variance with the spirit that Methodists ought to cultivate. Sgd: VERITAS.

The fact, however, was that the concert, in whatever form, had come to stay in Lagos, precisely because it satisfied some of the social and cultural needs of the community. And in those circumstances, though most people regretted its shortcomings, they still overlooked them.

Another factor, outside the Missions, favourable to the growth of the concert in Lagos was the presence of a small, well-educated and "cultured" *elite* made up mainly of the expatriate colonial Civil Servants and the Missionaries; the Brazilian Community which increased in number after the Emancipation (1888), Sierra Leoneans who came out as professionals with the Missions, in the Government Service, or on their own; and a number of "educated" Lagosians.[6] Mixed as it was and cultured as it thought itself, this community enabled the Lagos concert to develop something like an "international" character, which in turn gave an impetus to the growth of indigenous participation. There are several records of concerts sponsored or performed by the settler-population. The Brazilian Dramatic Company, under the patronage of the German Consul, Heinrich Bey, performed a "grand theatre" in honour of Queen Victoria's birthday, on May 23, 1882. The stage on the occasion, we are told, "was tastefully decorated"; and the performances consisted of "humorous, dramatic and other pieces, songs and performances on the violin and the guitar". This particular concert was so popular that there were requests for repeats.

Brazilian interest in concerts and theatre appears to have originated from their earlier African experience previous to the slave period in South America. Dr. J. F. Ade Ajayi[7] comments on this quality in the Brazilians who secured their freedom before Emancipation. "In Brazil and Cuba", he says, "slaves had come continuously for centuries from the same regions of West Africa. A tradition had grown up there that slaves worked better when kept together in linguistic groups . . . with chances (sic) to amuse themselves and their masters with their traditional ceremonies, dances and songs". When these Brazilians came back to Lagos, they brought back their great love for song, now sophisticated with some of the refinements of European musical practice. Names like J. J. da Costa, J. A. Campos, L. G. Barboza and P. Z. Silva (for a long time stage manager of the Brazilian Dramatic Company) were well known in Lagos concert circles.

The expatriate Civil Servants did not get involved in the theatre life of Lagos at this time as much as would be expected except in so far as they acted as patrons and chairmen of school performances. One of Mr. Herbert Macaulay's very successful concerts (May 18, 1889) was performed under the patronage of

His Excellency the Governor and Mrs. Denton; and the Bread-fruit School Entertainment Society received steady support from Mr. Charles Foresythe. For all this support and influence, interest in concerts among the Nigerian section of the community can be said to have derived from a traditional love of dance, song and ritual. Whatever handicaps the Nigerian section encountered came as a result of the necessary adjustment to the Western modes of the formal concert. But even then, there was a great deal of effort on the part of expatriate officers to step up standards in indigenous productions by means of criticism. But their attempts were apparently neglected. A critic of the *Lagos Observer* complained that the faults of these productions had "so often been dilated upon the foreigners who, having no encouragement made themselves conspicuous by their absence".

There was, in addition, talk in several circles of the special musical qualities of the African. "We are a musical race", the *Observer* declared on November 9, 1882, "and though it may seem a bold assertion, it is a fact that this beneficial gift of the creator has been acknowledged to fall more largely to our share than any other nation of the world". From the history of the Ibadan Choral Society, we know that after their first concert on December 29, 1886, "it was deemed necessary that in order to create a love for the theatre it should be free". They soon discovered that this was unnecessary because there was, in any case, a spontaneous willingness to participate in these theatrical activities provided they were not too provincially English to make any meaning to ordinary Nigerians. The Ibadan Choral Society, to its surprise, found that the people of Ibadan did not need any coaxing. The support of the "masses" was so complete that in subsequent performances they had difficulty keeping enthusiasts out of the crowded halls. We are told by the Secretary of the Society for 1886 that "several Mohammedans and heathens of importance" attended the concerts. Moreover "the people did not confine themselves to the normal prices asked for seats, as a good many came forward and paid (extra) sums of money". What was required, according to the Secretary, was "to enhance at its proper value the appreciation of the efforts undertaken with the object of introducing habits of civilization gradually into our midst".

This desire to "civilize" the people tended very often to conflict with the nature of the activities of these Choral and Dramatic Societies. There was at this time some anxiety felt and expressed over the importation of European manners along with Christianity, and over the consequent discarding of local material. In retrospect this agitation was for an indigenous inspiration in the theatre and the concert, a feature which, had it worked itself out, would have certainly made a great difference to the cultural and literary history of Nigeria. Attempts were made occasionally to include some Nigerian-inspired items in the concert programme. At Coker's Handel Festival of October, 1882, we hear of a local musical composition which went by the title *Souvenir de Lagos*.[8] There was also at this time a strong demand for Yoruba Literature and for a standard Yoruba orthography, at times for reasons we would today call "Africanist".[9] There were protests over other things. In June 1889 teachers of all denominations in Lagos held a meeting at which they demanded that European dress should no longer be worn in Lagos. They voted for the "adoption of the native costume in furtherance of the cause of Christianity and education". It is important to note, though, that this reaction did not often come from the top of the Lagos *elite*, which did, in fact, oppose such protests. The *Lagos Observer* laughed off the teachers' resolution demanding native dress in Lagos:

> Some people, unfortunately, being more fond of abstract speculations than of practical application of any given remedy for an acknowledged malady, we are not inconsiderately amused to learn that Christianity and education would be better patronised in Lagos by the transformation in question. Change of names was the maddening cry of a few years ago and some hare-brained patriots would need prate of a recurrence to primitive quasi-nudity.[10]

This attitude which would today be regarded as amusing, was then possibly regarded as clever and enlightened. The reply to poses of this kind came in a letter to this Editor in June 1, 1882. After speaking of his belief in the rise of the African and of the confidence which the learned productions of Dr. Blyden and Dr. Horton have given him, the writer went on to review the validity of carrying over values of whatever kind from Europe to impose them on Africans. "That a country should rise with a literature entirely foreign almost assumes to me the form of an impossibility", he asserted

> It only means that all the legends connected with our race, and some of the brilliant exploits of our ancestors as handed to us by tradition, must for ever be consigned to oblivion. The legends of Troy, it must be admitted, for interest, stand pre-eminent; but what can equal for beauty and Poetical embellishments the legends of Ile-Ife, that cradle of mankind as tradition relates. Their oratorical powers have immortalised the names of Demosthenes and Cicero but their orations in many points cannot be said to excel those that have been delivered in the house of Ogboni at Abeokuta or those in the palace of the Alafin of Oyo, or those that have moved the soldiery to deeds of bravery in the camp of field-marshal Ogedengbe of Ilesha? If the world had got only the English translation of the *Iliad* and the Greek of the *Paradise Lost*, or if the English edition of *Divine Comedy* were all that is available, what little lustre would they have shed on the genius of Homer, or Milton and of Dante! It is in their native languages that they have severally gained an immortal wreath for themselves in the world of literature; and it is in those more than any other that they ought. It becomes us then as those seeking the good of their country, to deprecate most vigorously a habit of boasting with borrowed plumes; otherwise the fate of the Jack-daw in the Fables of Phaedrus would soon be ours.

This passage is about the first and most pointed of several comments on the need for an indigenous spirit in Nigerian living and thinking; and some of the "gentlemen" of the 1880's needed to be told that the world had no place for mere imitators.

It was not as though these "reformers" were losing sight of the limitations of the Nigerian literary situation, or minimizing the need for apprenticeship.[11] The critic of the *Lagos Observer* who called himself "Cherubino" did believe in apprenticeship and did not spare any Nigerian who did not distinguish himself in performance. Many readers must have thought his hard-hitting and frank criticisms very unpatriotic, for on May 20, 1882, he found it necessary to defend himself against the possible charge that he was being merely destructive. "It is not", he pleaded, "to hold up to ridicule these our amateur compatriots. It is not that I would have done better myself, far from it. I am conscious of the service that they in their way are rendering to our country: my object is to stimulate them to fresh energies, (since) these failures were not from ignorance but from gross carelessness".

It is not surprising that in these circumstances there was demand in the papers for a national public hall. It was felt that if the Church was, for its own good reasons, opposed to indigenous entertainment in their schools, then the community ought to build its own hall to enable these native performances especially to continue. This demand could only have been made because it was realized that concerts could be a paying concern in Lagos. "That we have nothing of the sort here (that is, professional actors) is in no way proof that we are not a musical nation but simply that our entrepreneurs do not possess the gift of common-sense. Our performances will always pay when we have an average work well supported."[12] One generous Lagosian prom-ised in October 1882 that if the scheme for a public hall was taken up, he would subscribe £50 (₦100) towards it. In an editorial comment the *Observer* pointed out that "a plain com-modious building would not cost much, and can be let out for meetings, concerts, entertainments etc.; the income may be sufficient to pay expenses in part and keep the hall in repair." Government was asked to intervene in the matter, because, as somebody put it then, "this want (of public halls) the Govern-ment, rather than the efforts of private individuals, ought to supply". The Lagos Administration was blamed for not looking into this vital cultural and intellectual side of Lagos life: "Our young men instead of going to dancing rooms and other places of debasing tendencies may spend their evenings in lectures and other pursuits that will increase their intelligence." By December of that year, the *Observer* reported that a large-hearted gentle-man had promised to give up a portion of his premises for the purpose, "which he would not part with otherwise". Two others promised the "munificient donation" of a hundred pounds (₦200).

There was no records after this report of a public hall being built in response to this apparently popular need; the regularity of these concerts and the initial response of the well-to-do section of the Lagos public would in other circumstances have been enough to guarantee that there would be one. All the same, producers continued to use what they could find, schoolrooms, etc. Difficulty arose, naturally, when they attempted to stage elaborate concerts involving large casts. The production of Gilbert and Sullivan's *Trial by Jury* in August 1886, and the earlier "Handel Festival" of 1882 had to face this difficulty. The Handel Festival had the advantage over *Trial by Jury* of having a stage-designer, one Mr. Lawson, the Colonial Engineer, who was able to provide "a gallery specially constructed" for the 140 persons in the choir. This gallery was called "a happy innovation on our stage managements".[13] At the production of *Trial by Jury*, there was an attempt, amateurish it must have been, to suggest "on the one side, the idea of a Court of Justice, the other half that of a well furnished Drawing Room: a screen dividing both". In most other cases, there was a great deal of makeshift, and now and again of bold, if unsuccessful, experimenting. The Lagos Grammar School Concert of May 9, 1882, was adversely criticized on the grounds that the style of decorations was "truly rural—a mixture of the Arabian, Gothic —ancient and modern—and the grotesque, the latter chiefly dominating".

The chief difficulty, however, in the productions of the time was the lighting of the stage and hall. There was as yet no electricity in Lagos, and lighting must have been specially necessary for performances which did not begin before 8 p.m. Two kinds of lamps appear to have been used at these concerts: "suspending" and "Chinese lamps", as they were called; and their use depended on the size and shape of the halls. There was a complaint in June 1889 that though the set was well lighted, "the body of the Hall was only a shade better than Egypt's darkness". The writer went on to wonder that the producer did not realize that "suspending lamps" were the thing to use in a hall like that, "particularly when boothed with dark-green palms". A production at Faji School in April 1882 was also criticized on this account, the critic on this occasion insisting that it was "dingy sombre-looking". It must have been a great relief for "Cherubino" when he found a change at the Handel Festival:

... the stage, my lords, ladies and gentlemen, was for once, brilliantly lit, and the variegated lamps with their lights shewed the decorations to perfection.

The Handel Festival was a special occasion for Lagos music and theatre fans. Conducted and produced by Prof. R. A. Coker,[14] this Festival was quite an elaborate affair, in terms of the demand on the artists and the construction of the stage and set. Correspondents concluded that it would be "extremely difficult to have it often, as the amount of labour and worry involved is enormous". Reviews spoke glowingly of individual performances especially of that of one Miss Hethersett, "a Jenny Lind of the Wild Woods" who "quite surpassed herself in the rendering of Handel's *Angels ever bright and fair*. She sang it with a grace and charm all the more enchanting because natural. The imploring gestures that accompanied the passage *Take oh take me* were worthy of a finished actress".

Professor Coker continued to feature in the Lagos concert world especially as a conductor and organist. He brought with him the experience of several years' stay in England and revitalized Lagos music life, first through his productions. His was about the most outstanding period for music in Lagos, "when music was carried to a pinnacle so high that our progress becomes a problem".[15] Not of course that he was alone in bringing about this rise in Lagos music life, which was in any case considerably influenced by others from the Abeokuta institution. Prof. Coker was, in fact, only one of the four students specially mentioned for showing "encouraging tokens of musical faculties" at Abeokuta.

A name heard more often than Prof. Coker's in connection with Lagos Entertainment was that of Mr. Herbert Macaulay. The first reference to him appeared in the *Lagos Observer* of March 2, 1882.[16] Macaulay played the part of a "swell" in the entertainment and his part was considered "well acted, though a trifle overdone". Macaulay was probably only finding his feet at this time, for the references to him from 1888 speak of an accomplished actor and entertainer. His comic role in *Trial by Jury* was reported "very successful". At the Hope School Entertainment of December, 1888, he was expected to give "just a helping hand" but he became "the champion of the evening". He soon came to be invited to private parties, where, as at the party held by Mr. and Mrs. Schmidt for the Acting Governor, Denton, "Mr. Herbert Macaulay—our youthful enthusiastic performer—delighted the company by his performances. The vibrations of his violin were no less exquisite than his singing." Lagos loved a man like him, and appreciated his "persistent efforts to relieve the dull monotony of Lagos life by his occasional entertainments".

Perhaps Macaulay's concerts filled the same role then as the cinema was to do, later, in Nigerian cities—providing relief from boredom for rich and poor, educated and illiterate alike. At the Handel Festival everybody in Lagos wanted to see the performers, "all the reserved seats being crowded and people pressing upon one another to pass the barriers" to hear one Mr. John "yelling forth his solo in an undaunted manner", or listen to Miss Thomas sing with a "well trained voice of such sweetness". It must have been irritating, as well, on some occasions to find the less literate portion of the audience "interrupting the performance at the middle with meaningless applause". "Managers", one infuriated enthusiast wrote, "might with advantage have friends to suppress the enthusiasm of this portion of the audience". Occasionally, too, a dramatic group—perhaps one which called itself "The Melo-dramatic Society"—would stage a trifle or other, like *Tobacco Whiffs, The Rival Lovers* or *Don't Use Big Words*, and "that portion of the audience would have the time of their lives"—to the annoyance of the sophisticates who wanted serious plays whose object should be to "elevate the moral and intellectual tone of the masses rather than pander to low and vulgar tastes". When St. Gregory's played Molière's *He Would be a Lord*, they said nothing, having themselves been caught along with the masses.[17]

But they never played Shakespeare; and never mentioned him in their papers, though Macaulay, Longfellow and Tennyson, Aristotle, Homer and Milton were often quoted or cited. The Old Grammarians' Society agreed on March 24, 1925, that their next meeting will be "An Evening with Shakespeare"—but it was only to "discuss" him. Perhaps Shakespeare as a dramatist was little known; moreover, the school-certificate cult of Shakespeare had not quite come, for both English literature and Shakespeare were out of the school syllabus. Not till 1950 do we hear of a full-scale production of Shakespeare, a showing of the *Taming of the Shrew*.

It is at first surprising that the tradition of the theatre which has grown during the 1880's should have suddenly died out. It would appear, however, that the enthusiasm of these times, in not being fundamental in concept and organic in its development, depended exclusively on the honest (if in other respects, misguided) endeavour of these "Victorian" Lagosians to improve themselves culturally, through imitation, in order to be accepted. Especially as these concerts depended on the small middle-class elite, they could only survive as long as the intellectuals were willing to continue their support. The concert, in other words, did not develop strong and independent roots in the Nigerian soil. When professional, commercial, and later political interests diverted the attention of this elite, the spirit of these concerts began to fade away. In 1950, one enthusiastic Nigerian made an appeal through the *Daily Times*:

> Unless we are prepared to get down to it, unless we are prepared to put on paper for posterity our traditional hymns and folk-tunes, unless we are prepared to CREATE, then we might as well rule out the word PROGRESS from our dictionary. If some Africans with the initiative will volunteer to back up a *revue* then we the younger men will supply the talent. Off hand I could name at least forty people who could take part in the show; yes, forty!

Nobody answered this call in 1950.

Notes

1. See the *Oxford Companion of Music*, pp. 226–228.
2. *Lagos Observer*, March 2, 1882.
3. "But in justice to the Ministers, we must say, that the programme referred to, was considerably 'weeded' . . . by the Rev. Mr. Baxter on the night of the rehearsal"—Editorial note: *Lagos Observer*, October 26, 1882.
4. Made by Rev. J. Vernal in *Church Missionary Intelligence and Record*, Jan. 1889.
5. Quite often the surname of the officiating priest.
6. "Educated" was a prestige word at this time, e. g. "there are three ladies clubs in Lagos . . . the New Era, the Ladies' Social, and the British West African Educated Girls' Club . . . the last two decided on having a play . . ." *Pioneer*, Jan. 9, 1925.

7. *Christian Missions and the Making of Nigeria*: typescript of Ph.D. thesis at Ibadan University Library, p. 69.
8. The Breadfruit School Society played *The Embassy of the Dahomeans to the Egbaland*, in 1882.
9. "The Arabic language . . . will better satisfy our language; the inducement it would give to scholars here and in Sierra Leone . . .; Mohammedians, . . . as far as the interior and along the Niger would be almost irresistibly stimulated to read all works in Yoruba". *Lagos Observer*, June 1, 1882.
10. "An original Dramatic Play entitled 'Native Dress . . .' written by S. C. Phillips, is now available. It deals at length with the question of our native dress in the most dramatic and interesting manner." *Lagos Musical Journal*, April 1916.
11. "Now as the African has no literature of his own, . . . which could bear the scrutiny of the enlightened world, it is for him to take example from superior nations, . . . thereby providing himself with ideas." *Lagos Observer*, Feb. 1, 1883.
12. *Lagos Observer*, Mar. 2, 1882.
13. *Lagos Observer*, November 9, 1882.
14. Coker studied under Mr. Buhler at Abeokuta before he left for a prolonged stay in England to study music. He returned to the Female Institution in Lagos as a teacher of music. An accomplished organist, Prof. Coker was simply unsurpassed as a teacher on the pianoforte. He was reputed to be the first native organist in Lagos. *Lagos Musical Journal*, December, 1915.
15. *Lagos Musical Journal*, August, 1915.
16. With his name spelt "M'Caulay", the newcomer he was!
17. On December 21, 1882. "The stage was artistically put up and brilliantly lighted."

Reprinted Nigeria Magazine, Vol. 30, No. 74, 1962.

THE ADVENT OF TELEVISION DRAMA IN NIGERIA

Segun Olusola

It is early in February 1980, Lekan Ladele, Television Producer of the Ibadan television series, *Bello's Way*, is poring over
a play script submitted by Funmi Dominu, a playwright. No, this
script is not *Bello's Way*: it is to be the first episode of a series of
sixteen-minute television plays titled *Eclipse*. You will not
remember it from television because Lekan Ladele even though
he was enthusiastic about this unique style of dramatic writing,
could not persuade himself or any one of the "television managers" to produce the play for transmission. Since the playwright
was contemplating a regular engagement with Nigerian Television at that time, Lekan Ladele thought it would be a good idea if
he deferred a decision on *Eclipse* until the writer accepted a
regular job and became part of the system, a prospect that the
playwright had always dreaded.

Why should an experienced television drama producer like
Lekan Ladele be hesitant about producing an obviously highly
innovative dramatic work? And for that matter, why should an
accomplished theatre artist like Funmi Dominu be reluctant to
take a regular job with Nigerian Television? In a way, it can be
said that each was afraid of "death" should their interests merge,
and yet they must come together in order to survive. This essay
will attempt briefly to analyse why the primitive inclinations of
the playwright differ from those of the television producer, a
difference that must be resolved for the future of a virile,
television drama in Nigeria. But first, to the beginnings.

In my younger days as a broadcast programme producer, it
regularly was impressed on me how lucky I had been to get one
out of ten ideas of mine accepted at the monthly programmes
meeting, a veritable ideas factory floor of the fifties dominated by
Cyprian Ekwensi, Deinde George and Yemi Lijadu. My resultant predilection towards a crippling self-censorship was happily

370

halted by the historical jolt of 1959 in the heady atmosphere of the early days of television. The development of creative television programmes, and television drama in particular, was largely inspired by the experience of writers and producers of radio features and dramas of the mid-fifties. But there were other agents at work in the dramatic arts, and it was the coming together of these disparate activities that presaged the advent of television drama in 1960.

Although Hubert Ogunde's theatre company was already well established in the early fifties, it was still very much a family group of popular entertainers with accent on song and dance. Ogunde's presentation style already influenced a large number of schools and teachers' colleges and their end of year "concert" activities reflected much of this influence. One of Ogunde's earliest theatrical associates, Kola Ogunmola, already embarked on a more daring venture, a travelling road show with a strong content of juju music. At the University College, Ibadan, amateur dramatic activities headed in a different direction—the performance of choice classics, with straight plays competing for attention with West European operatic repertoire. Among the small groups of the expatriate population, dramatic activities were organized as sections of the Recreation Clubs in Lagos and Ibadan. Then in 1957, a group of working-class Nigerian drama enthusiasts in Lagos and Ibadan came together and formed what was to become "Players of the Dawn".

By the time television was introduced in 1959, the educated elites in the city centres of Lagos and Ibadan were already used to the once-a-month amateur dramatic presentation either at the British Council or the University College, while the less educated working class urban dwellers looked forward to a quarterly season of Ogunde Theatre presentation or Ogunmola's Travelling Shows. Since these two sectors of the Ibadan Community constituted the bulk of the television audiences of 1959 to 1960, it was natural for the earliest television producers to conclude that audience expectations would include some measure of dramatic presentation. The first attempts to meet those expectations were not particularly imaginative—an occasional invitation to Hubert Ogunde to bring a half-hour "song and dance" into the less than adequate studio space at the then Western Nigerian Television, Ibadan, and some scenes from the classics featuring local amateur groups. When in 1960, Wole Soyinka returned to the country ready to launch the first ever professional theatre group, his colleagues in radio, television and the local amateur scene rallied round him and it was not long before they all saw a natural outlet in television. After an uneasy false start, the first drama presentation on Nigeria Television was broadcast in August 1960.

Before the production, the managers of television were genuinely worried and took steps to prevent the production. The publicly declared reason was the "very high cost of the production"! But more forbidding must have been their fear that once launched, a television programme of ideas in dramatic form, created by a singularly imaginative writer like Wole Soyinka would cause ruptures to established, if questionable, models of a developing colonial society. Their consternation and resultant threatening stances were suitably conveyed to the producer, their own employee. On the other hand, the playwright had his own fevers of doubts and second thoughts. A director of some experience himself, the reality of a play commissioned of him and the production of which he would have very little control over was sub-consciously objectionable. Neither the novelty of the medium nor his own mutually friendly disposition towards the television producer totally overcame his doubts.

A remarkable feature of the 1960 affair, one which differentiates it from the 1980 incident which I referred to in my introduction above, was that the play, *My Father's Burden*, a very incisive criticism of the emerging Nigerian bourgeoisie bribing and corrupting its way through, was televised. The affronted emerging ruling class ignored the message. The producer did not lose his job but the seeds of the disenchantment between Nigerian television and the artist were sown. Wole Soyinka never wrote for television again. By 1980, the souring of the relationship between the television producer and the independent artist has developed a forest of fungi you can smell at distance. What went wrong?

There was no shortage of noble objectives by the originators of Nigerian Television, that is, theoretically. And the most publically eloquent of those objectives came from the founding father himself, Chief Obafemi Awolowo, at the gala opening of Africa's first television station in 1959 at the Parliament grounds. Said Chief Awolowo: "Television will serve as a teacher and entertainer and as a stimulus to us all to transform Nigeria into a modern and prosperous nation." But in order for television to be a reality, the Western Nigerian government had to enter into a partnership agreement with some foreign "specialists" and it was soon discovered that the foreign partners had other objectives which, although not patently contradictory, were not mutually compatible. The first contradictions became apparent in the choice of programming. The local patrons planned to "teach and entertain" through the use of Nigerian teachers and entertainers. But the foreign partners were quick to point out that they could "teach and entertain" by importing films of foreign teachers and entertainers at a much reduced cost (actually one tenth) to the joint venture. In 1960, we transmitted *Cisco Kid* and *Hopalong Cassidy* for less than £10! (₦20). Since both partners had agreed to operate television as a joint business venture, winning such an argument was easy. And so, the Nigerians lost the initiative which was never really regained until recently, in spite of the fact that the business partnership broke up in 1962.

And the pattern of soliciting for foreign partners was repeated in all television regions in Nigeria with the same set of hidden conflicts in objectives. Television which should have flowered a formidable linkage between the Nigerian theatre artist and the television producer served from its inception to split them. It was a typical imperialist ploy with all its attendant economic motivations. In the process of proving a point, as early as 1960, Wole Soyinka was commissioned to write a play for television which was subsequently produced and broadcast at a cost the television managers found objectionable for any playwright. Evidently, the contract had called for the payment of "£200 (₦400) to such persons in respect of the alleged local programme". Operators of Nigerian Television had no notion of the material *value* that should be put on *television drama*. If a half-hour of *Highway Patrol* was shown on Nigerian Television for as little as ₦10, why should Hubert Ogunde ask for ₦50 to bring a half-hour play which did not even include screaming sirens and shoot-outs?

In the absence of a comparable professional organization in the performing arts, there were no rates to compare performing fees with. Talent fees for radio served most inappropriately as the base. The writers on the other hand knew how much their works could fetch at foreign television and films markets and behaved as if they expected the Nigerian television market to pay the same rates. Television drama production in such circumstances became possible from considerations other than financial. Caught in the middle, the television drama producer coined the phrase "to prove a point"—to prove a point that Nigeria has enough material for television drama, that the Nigerian television producer can produce television drama, that the Nigerian television drama is infinitely more acceptable to the Nigerian audience than the imported foreign television plays. It has been a rather lengthy period "to prove a point" these past twenty years and relationships have been strained sometimes beyond redemption. But the operation of an unfair material value system was even less pernicious by the television producer–theatre artist relationship than the much more deep-seated contradiction inherent in work environment.

The system that a theatre artist, or more specifically, a television playwright, devises, can be as different and unique as there are playwrights. Since these artists are not generally given to explaining their work, observers of the creative television scene can only construct the scheme and motivations of the playwrights' works from results achieved through television productions of such works. Some of the results that I can easily recall include a very personal account of an event of common knowledge, making the viewers doubt their own knowledge of such an event; an indictment of commonly held values and heritages including corruption and respect for elders; an unsettling succession of violent images which leave the viewers perplexed; the story of the next door neighbour or school or town where every day human problems are created and solved leaving the viewer with the feeling of belonging to other people. As can be seen from these examples, whatever motivations the playwright has in designing a play for television, the television viewer cannot be completely ignored. For the playwright, the television audiences are always a consideration—who sometimes may be frightened, confused, pleased, shocked, even bored, but never completely ignored. For the television producer, the audience, of course, is paramount and as if to maintain a constant reminder of this indispensable client, the managers of television operations have devised pervasive systems of reporting, interdependence and cross-checking, such that the television producer does not remember anything else but the audience and his own pay packet. This process commences the moment a cadet television producer signs on and continues all through junior, intermediate and senior grades. We can therefore point to a similarity in the custom that the theatre artist and the television producer must cultivate in order to achieve a satisfactory television play broadcast.

In the Nigerian experience of the past twenty-one years, the television audience would seem to be a common interest to the theatre artist and the television producer only to a point. The theatre artist, for instance, has always had other commitments, other interests and avenues that would engage his varying talent. A few living examples will suffice. Hubert Ogunde had cultivated countrywide theatre audiences for over ten years before the advent of television—and he reached them through live performances, phonograph recordings and publications. He survived without television audiences. Wole Soyinka never really needed television either to make a living, or a name. In the last twenty years, he was either teaching or writing, each of which had made him famous and kept him above the bread-line. If he was neither famous nor well-to-do in 1959 when television was introduced in this country, he was confident enough in his talent to know that he could turn his back on television and achieve both. Television might have promoted the development and popularity of the works of the late Duro Ladipo (that is, in the last few years of his life) even though it was obvious that television needed him more than he depended on television. The founding writers of *The Village Headmaster*, Fela Davies, Nelson Olawaiye, Alex Akinyele and Demola James, severally earned their living and fame in

DRAMA AND THEATRE IN NIGERIA

fine art teaching, government service, public relations and occasional theatre work. Moses Olaiya is at present capable of
thrilling audiences in faraway Gombe, while Ola Rotimi is
teaching and writing at the University of Port Harcourt. Wale
Ogunyemi is earning a living at the Institute of African Sudies in
Ibadan. There is no theatre artist or playwright in the last twenty
years who has owed his living or fame exclusively to television.

However, for the television producer, the experience has been
of a different kind. Partly because of the public service monopoly
inherent in the organization of Nigerian television, and partly
because of the structure of television organization, the television
producer is invariably embraced totally by the medium. After
he has been hooked, he may achieve a measure of reputation
and comfortable living in the process. Television does not admit
the worship of any other god but Television. Since the development of television drama depends on the inevitable cooperation
between the theatre artist or playwright and the television
producer, the state of television drama at any given time reflects
the nature of this relationship. Furthermore, the television producer does not enter the relationship with the same confidence
and control of the creative resources available to the playwright.
Within the television organization, he is constantly reminded of
his dependence on the interrelationship with other interest
groups—camera operators, technicians, accountants, supervisors, designers, administrators and television producers of
other programme forms.

Whatever system of work is devised for such a multiformat
workshop, producing musicals, documentary, discussions and
drama cannot be wholly ideal for the television drama producer
and even much less suitable in the opinion of the television
playwright. The television playwright devises his own system,
while the television producer operates within a system and
structures devised by other people. Since television drama must
go through the system and structure of television, the playwright's concepts tend to be absorbed into the television system
and structures to the consternation of the playwright. The result
is, at best, a distrust for the television producer by the theatre
artist and scorn for the theatre artist by the television producer.

Very few human relationships can last that exchange of honestly rationalized antagonisms. It is a matter for debate, the extent these feelings affected the development of television drama in the early days, and how other relationships tempered the antagonisms.

Among the first generation of television producers with some claim to competence in the dramatic arts were John Ekwere, Patrick Itioghe, and Christopher Kolade, two of whom have, for some time, abandoned active television production. Advent stories are told invariably by participants or historians and since my only qualification is being present at the advent, what is missing in the objectivity of the historian may now be supplied from the recollection of the participant, a kind of historical pegging of television drama-scape from one viewpoint.

Wole Soyinka's *My Father's Burden* scored a number of firsts when it was televised in August, 1960. It was the first television drama in English language on Nigerian Television. It was also the first ever commissioned play on Nigerian Television. The live transmission with all its attendant difficulties resulted in the first published review of a television play captioned "WNTV's Burden" in the *Television Times and Radio News* of August 18, 1960. As a long-standing member of Actors' Equity of Great Britain, Orlando Martins became at the age of 60, the first Nigerian professional actor to perform in a television drama in English. And mid-way in the hour-long transmission, with "actors tripping over a web of cables" and the resultant power failure, the old man lost his lines—but the show continued!

The late Duro Ladipo's experience was different. One of his earliest backers was a retired Anglican bishop in whose backyard most of the playwright's television plays were rehearsed. At one such rehearsal, the bishop was shocked by scenes of the biblical last supper for which the television producer had procured a large keg of palm-wine and akara. Most of Duro Ladipo's earliest plays for television were dramatized bible stories, including the famous Crucifixion. Much later, when the troupe moved to the Mbari Mbayo base at Oshogbo, the histories gained prominence and Mbari Mbayo became the regular rehearsal grounds for such plays as *Oba Koso* and *Oba Waja*. *Oba Waja* was later on translated into English by Ulli Beier and produced for television in 1964 the first such experimental television play.

The demands of the Independence Commemorative production of the "1960 Masks" "*A Dance of the Forests*" by Wole Soyinka prevented the group from launching its production on television until late 1961. Earlier in 1961, a television play titled *Night of the Hunted*, adapted from an unpublished trilogy, *House of Banigeji* by Wole Soyinka was produced and transmitted live. In the years 1961 to 1964, most of the major dramatic activities of WNTV stemmed from the close collaboration between the station and the "1960 Masks". And one of the most important results of that collaboration was the play *Dear Parent and Ogre* by Dr. Sarif Easmon which was televised live after a successful stage presentation in Lagos and Ibadan. That was the production during which a leading actor was called to the telephone just before air-time and informed of the death of his baby boy. He returned to the studio and as if nothing had happened, proceeded to play his role without a sign of distress. He informed members of the cast and the producer of his bereavement after the late night transmission and drove back to Lagos to console his wife.

But those years also had their lighter moments. For instance, in 1974 a Board reprimand was considered against the director of the television play, *The Avenger*, by C. Olude for allowing a scene in which a woman in bed-slips was dragged into a bedroom by a man. Action was suspended when it was discovered that the role of the woman in the television drama was played by the wife of the television drama director! In 1965, Hubert Ogunde broke a studio rehearsal of one of his regular television plays and walked into the office of the Director of Programmes to demand a rise in artistes fees or . . .. When his ultimatum was not met, he promptly loaded his cast into a waiting lorry and drove out of the studio premises and did not return to television for another ten years. Three live goats were slaughtered for the video-recording of J. P. Clark's *Song of a Goat* in 1965, in order to get as near perfect a ritual beheading as possible. And although the director had regretted before the rehearsal that he had no allowance to offer lunch to the members of the cast, members were more than satisfied with the barbecued goat feasting after the recording!

Television drama received quite a boost in 1965, with the week-long African Festival of TV Drama, scheduled to mark Nigeria's Independence celebrations in that year. Among the productions featured during the Festival were *Song of a Goat* and *Masquerade* by J. P. Clark, *The Trials of Brother Jero* by Wole Soyinka and *Oba Koso* by the late Duro Ladipo. But perhaps the high point of Nigeria's television drama development occurred in 1968 with the inception of a regular drama series, *The Village Headmaster*. The only attempt ever to film *The Village Headmaster* occurred in 1969 with the original cast including Ted Mukoro as Headmaster and Roseline Birch as Fatia, his daughter. Well past mid-way in the shooting schedule, everything came to a standstill because a very important person in Roseline's life felt that television was obstructing her studies and she was "abducted". Although the television series went on to survive a twelve year run, the abandoned film-stock of the original *Village Headmaster* is still lying in the archives of the Federal Film Unit.

And suddenly it is 1980! Certain events of the last three years would seem to presage an end to the uncertainties, inadequacies and tentative experiments associated with television drama in its development period. The coverage of FESTAC demanded of television producers additional training in skills required for the production of art programmes like plays, dance and musicals. Since the festival, the rising quality of television drama production would seem to suggest a more sharpened appreciation on the part of television production personnel. The staging of the first Nigerian Television Authority (NTA) Festival of Drama in 1978 revealed the importance that the new country-wide television organization attached to television drama as a programme genre. The general quality of the hour-long entries from twelve television stations was quite high and even more remarkable was the number of winning drama productions from the relatively newer television stations. There is a growing interest in the development of the television drama series in every television station and at the time of writing, an NTA sponsored series is being produced on location in the Jos highlands.

Opportunities now exist in the NTA for playwrights, actors and other theatre artists to accept full time staff appointments to enable them to write and perform plays regularly to the exclusion of other assignments. There is now a distinctive shift of resources in favour of local programming arising from the policy enunciated by NTA ensuring that 80% of all programming should be locally produced. In the end however, it is the audience who calls the tune for the future of television drama as they have done unmistakably, by reacting most favourably to such dramatic productions as *The Village Headmaster, Winds Against My Soul, For Better for Worse, Case File, Masquerade, Hotel De Jordan* and the growing number of single play specials on Nigerian Television.

THE NIGERIAN THEATRE AND THE PLAYWRIGHT
Femi Euba

Ultimately, the question of commitment must arise, wittingly or unwittingly for the playwright. In other words, he must ultimately come to decisions about the overall meaning, social and political he wishes his plays to express and how best he could effectively convey it, indeed, about his role. The entire question in itself presupposes a lot of assumptions. For instance, it also assumes a ready availability of dedicated collaborators, such as actors, critics, and even a responsive audience. And then there is also the playwright's own ability and experience.

It seems, at this stage of Nigeria's development, that in looking at the Nigerian theatre through the eyes of the playwright, these are pertinent issues to consider. For instance, is there, in fact, a Nigerian theatre, and if so, how functional is it to the playwright, or how does he use it as his medium of effectiveness?

The main concern of this essay will be with the playwright's using the English language as his medium of expression, although this deliberation is not in any way synonymous with a desire to simply ignore the folk and popular dramatist writing in the vernacular as incapable of good theatre. On the contrary, the popular folk dramatist is quite capable. However, it is the fact that the English language playwright by his very existence, has posed most of the problems under discussion here, and it is through him that they are seen more glaringly. For instance, without denying that the neo-traditionalist of the popular theatres has his own basic problems like making the profits, for he has a professional company, he is less bothered by the problem of technical sophistication (he can set up and stage his plays almost anywhere); by the problem of actors (a large number of his company often consist of members of his family); the problem of audience (he more often, has his audience wherever he goes); and of language (he often uses the vernacular).

Sometime ago in a lecture given on a similar subject in the U.S.,[1] I likened, with some naivety then, the somewhat clutching feelings I often experienced when confronted with the question of a Nigerian theatre, to an automobile that suddenly had a flat tyre and jerked to a stop. In retrospect, and now with a background of more direct experience, I find the deflating imagery very appropriate and still expressive of my feelings about the Nigerian theatre. A concrete explanation of this observation is the idea of having a National Theatre. Such a grand idea should normally be soul-stirring with the joy and pride of artistic achievement. For it implies a certain climax in the development of a nation's theatre, an attempt to justify a national collective effort and performance in the theatre arts within a suitable and workable theatre-complex, where its actors, directors, playwrights and even personnel are all a spokesman and showcase for that nation's artistic accomplishment. The realization of such an idea is indeed usually a victorious breakthrough of the arts in the bureaucratic and political world of the System, and as such every effort is made to take advantage of it.

While our National Theatre in Lagos can boast of such realization in name, the joy of achievement seems to hold only for as long as the illusion of the facade remains in focus. For the puncturing reality is that there is no National Theatre in the full implication of the idea. Rather, what we have is the structure that once acquired its name through FESTAC, the Second World Black and African Festival of Arts and Culture, in 1977. And apart from its present status as the major "residence" of the Ministry of Culture, Youth and Sports, all its achievements so far have been, regrettably, the occasional production of a play (which usually is not by any means a product of a resident National company), the constant feature film shows, and the occasional art exhibitions. And all these need not be bad as an effort to utilize the building, only nobody should be mistaken about it,[2] there is no National theatre, in the true sense of the implication.

But this idea of a National theatre is in a way a culmination of other equally deflating circumstances in the development of the Nigerian Theatre. It is now about two decades since our leading playwright, Wole Soyinka, founded the short-lived "1960 Masks", which was then hailed as "the nucleus of our National Theatre". Quite right, it opened up a new theatrical era for playwrights and actors alike, considering the upsurge of activities in, and around the then University College of Ibadan. The budding playwrights were more or less turning out imitations of Soyinka, and the young student-actors, some of whom were in the "Masks", constituted the Travelling Theatre group of the University College of Ibadan.[3] It need not be a surprise to note that none of the potential playwrights[4] of that beginning stood the test of years of development and therefore did not come up to much, if at all. Rather, one should think of the moment as important in terms of the kindled interest[5] which later on was to foster the imagination of new, more serious writers, very few of whom, like Femi Osofisan (but again to be expected), have, in fact managed to weather the setbacks that have since dampened the "national" theatrical interests of those nascent years two decades ago.

Actually, two decades, it must be emphasized, is not a long time in a nation's theatrical development, and allowing for the many handicaps the playwright has to work himself through, the time-span seems just adequate for him to shed the fancies of former illusion, assimilate and "imitate" present realities, from which he finds his own voice and vision, and then develop.[6] 'But alongside the playwright's artistic problems were hitched other demanding problems, recurrently buttressed to frustrate his development. Let us consider these problems against the playwright in terms of everything that constitutes what we mean by Theatre, that is, structure, acting, directing, the audience, and the material of the playwright itself.

Structure

The representation above of the National Theatre as a culmination of setbacks obviously includes a structural implication. It is quite baffling that the voice of reason which has been crying for some time now[7] has not quite affected our sensibilities in the right direction to building a theatre to our own imaginative specifications—a true Nigerian theatre that would liberate our playwrights, and therefore our plays, finally from the structures of the proscenium setting. Rather, even with a more workable theatre like the Oduduwa Hall at the University of Ife,[8] the obverse seems to be the choice—the ambitious, pathetic bent to perfect the "Box" stage—from the Arts Theatres through the J. K. Randle Halls to the National Theatre, and, alas, for crying out loud, beyond![9]

Of course, one is not saying that to imitate is necessarily a bad thing. But when either the imitation of the model is not a true one as with most of our proscenium stages, or nothing original grows out of imitating, then perhaps there is something basically wrong somewhere.

However, this is probably not the place to go into the causal factors which have resulted in the almost deliberate repetitive sameness of our Nigerian theatre structures. Suffice it to say that these factors are generally what affects many misconceived projects of our times, from the contracting of new roads or the telephone system, to the "manufacturing" of our own goods. Rather, one should attempt to show the likely dangers of such theatre-structural malpractice to the playwright's inventiveness.

A good director will, of course, always create ways and means of adapting to or wriggling his actors and set out of the trappings of our Box theatres, even though there is a limit to his resourcefulness. This was the situation with Akin Isola's *Madam Tinubu*, when it was taken out of the reasonably adaptable semi-thrust stage at the University of Ife, on to the limited entrances and exits of the red-plush tabs of the National Theatre main stage, or the constricting picture-frame of the University of Lagos auditorium.[10] In either case, there was very little the director could do regarding inventiveness since the theatres offered no incentive to experimentation. At any rate, theatre in Nigeria has not quite reached a stage of development that could generate the probably much-needed director's theatre—for the very fact that there are not enough creative directors. Consequently, the playwright, especially the more established one often finds himself directing his own play either because he does not trust the handling of the work with somebody else, or he fancies himself as the true "artist of the theatre", and therefore the only one capable of directing his own play.

Artist of the Theatre

There has been a long-standing personality conflict since the emergence of the artistic director in the European Theatre at the turn of the century, between the director and the playwright. The playwright is usually not quite happy with the director's interpretation which appears to falsify his own artistic vision. On the other hand, some directors have been known to prefer weak scripts in order to be able to unleash their full imaginative forces[11] and bring them to bear on the script in an effort to make it a better one, but again sometimes much to the displeasure of the playwright who feels somehow unfulfilled as the artist of the theatre.

And yet, much as the playwright would like to have it, it does not mean they could be good directors or are capable of realizing their own plays on the stage. In fact, in my own experience, very few playwrights could do the latter successfully. For what often happens in effect is that the playwright subjects himself to the continuation of his already or near exhausted vision, but very rarely would he go beyond the limits of the vision. Often, and this is quite normal, the playwright cannot translate this creative vision into verbal explanations, let alone his capacity to transpose it on to the stage. Therefore, it is often necessary for another person to do the interpreting for him, and in doing so liberates for him the hitherto stifling limits of that vision. Thus he sees new avenues and insights that either confirm his conception or heighten and complete it. In other words, the playwright who finds himself doing his own thing is often limited, and the more he does this, the more he is in danger of slowing down the development of his vision. And while there may be one or two Nigerian playwrights that get away with successfully mounting their own plays, it is quite obvious that the majority, including the budding ones in the universities, do not have the ability or technical know-how to direct in the first place, let alone their own plays. And it is with these we should concern ourselves.

For, with the scarcity of good directors, the option often open to the promising, budding playwright is to either copy the more established and experienced playwright-director, or settle for an inadequate director. In either case, he is faced with the legacy of a box-stage. And even where he is lucky to appreciate and attempt to imitate an experimental production outside the "box", he is still more or less writing with the proscenium in mind.

It must be emphasized that the director or the playwright-director does not have to use the proscenium, but he invariably is stuck with it because he knows no better. A case in point is the series of hastily written plays by young playwrights I have watched rehearse and perform at the Pit Theatre in the University of Ife. This little theatre is quite adaptable for both theatre-in-the-round and proscenium staging. But it is interesting to note that the excitement and enthusiasm with which these productions are rehearsed and performed never goes out of the proscenium to experiment with the pit itself. But then these directors have rarely experienced plays done any other way. A similar case, although not as obvious, is the ridiculous and easily avoidable theatre-influenced box-set staging, which our television productions often display with impunity.

Little wonder then that a lot of these "young" plays, and by extension, the playwrights themselves, never get started or develop from the level at which they begin. Whereas, if they had been compelled by force of circumstances to work in an open space, theatre space being essentially an open empty space, or at worst, and as a last resort, in a more adaptable theatre, we might have a more exciting and developing theatrical tradition than is the present case. The only other alternative is to abandon the four-wall enclosure and take to the streets. But then the limitations of this approach to any serious theatre are too glaring to be considered here.

Playwright and the Actor

In the foregoing, I have tried to single out the theatre structure and to project it in the light of the problems of the Nigerian playwright. But as we can see, the structure is really inseparable from the material and all that goes to form theatre. And just as directing, or the director presents a problem to the playwright, so is the actor and the audience.

"Crude" as the folk and popular dramatist's way of doing things might sometime appear to the technically conscious theatre enthusiast, to him must go the attribute of setting the pace in the rise of the professional theatre in Nigeria, starting with Hubert Ogunde's theatre in the 1940's, that is, some fifteen years before the conscious rise of the Nigerian playwright in the English language. In this regard, he has come some way to establish some rapport with his audience. He has also taken advantage of his actors, who, as stated earlier, are mainly members of his family, sustain and protect his professional status from crumbling through lack of funds, possible mismanagement or actors' agitation and opportunism. And even though some of the newer companies encounter problems of management, actors and audience, it can be generally stated that professionalism still holds for the folk and popular dramatist and his company.

Not so the playwright writing in the English language who has hardly been able to establish his company professionally or himself with a fully professional company. Neither Soyinka's "1960 Masks" nor its offspring, the "Orisun Theatre" and others that followed survived more than five years of inception, before the tidal wave of problems struck their death-knell. And at any rate, most of these companies never got beyond semi-professionalism.[12]

The pattern of deadlock in these companies becomes more apparent when one considers one of the operative forces, namely, dedication to the theatre. The general misconception, surprisingly, also held within the universities, seems to be that a playwright's only desire to gather a group of people together is a wish to do his own plays. And so he attracts them from different walks of life, including some from already existing companies, especially if there is some promise of money involved. And so we have a situation where only a handful or less are seriously committed to the theatre. There is as yet no record of an all-round devoted group, dedicated beyond monetary gains, beyond the easy fun and games or the vagabond-life usually attributed to theatre-life, beyond the selfish ends of narcissistic fame and popularity, at least not that I know of.

Lest it appears like an exaggeration, widely reported events of mismanagement occasioned as recently as FESTAC should epitomize this constant breakdown of superficially well-meaning intentions in the development of the Nigerian theatre. That it should be an epitome is, however, hardly ironical as in reality it was the culmination of all the previous mistakes. In this regard, not much appears to have come out of that festival—except perhaps the reminiscences of the fluidity of money that attracted many people, together and individually, towards cheapening and maligning the otherwise demanding artistic values of the theatre.

It must be emphasized, however, that it is not always the fact that the right ideas and fundamental procedures are lacking. For there are quite a few people who know that in order to consolidate a true Nigerian theatre, the groundwork should include an honestly funded, honestly managed company of devoted actors, playwrights, directors, technicians and personnel. And for any development to take place at all, it would be wise for the company to spend a good deal of time in preparatory work of intense training and in exploration of values and talent at the expense of making profit, which should not be the first objective. But as is often the case in Nigeria, there are political and social affiliations and interests which "contract" responsibilities not to the most deserving qualified but to a mediocre favourite. The result is that art is put at the mercy of politics. Even in the universities, a few of which like the University of Ife, favour the development of the creative arts, and experiment with a resident fully-paid company of actors, there is still a misconception of what theatre is and what, in fact, goes to make it. As such, the activities of the company, how it should function as well as its staffing are often grossly measured against the academic curricula background of the university.

What then have all these done to the serious playwright? A look at some of the individual activities of the playwrights would at this stage be valuable. But before embarking on this, it should be noted that playwrights, like all creative artists, are known to be very individual, private and sensitive people. Perhaps, playwrights are more so than any other artist because they deal with "felt-life" experiences which surface in their consciousness, and which they heighten to such intense moments for their audience to see, feel, recognize and identify with or objectify critically. Fortunately, or unfortunately as the case may be, they like to feel that such intense moments, which have brought to life the characters in their plays, have been lived only by them at a particular moment of writing, that they alone have seen it that way.[13] To a certain extent, this is true. But ironically, they invite the audience to share and live through those intense moments with them, to support and justify their perception, and concede that they in fact are right. But of course, opinions differ from one audience to the next and even within a particular audience. However, any moment adverse to the playwright's conception is bound to touch his prideful individualist position to the quick.

The playwright therefore seems at once to like and dislike the situation he finds himself in—that is, however much he feels a sense of achievement with what he has expressed, he being the fundamental force in the theatre, he is at the judicial mercy of actors, directors and critics. Clearly one can see why a playwright might wish to direct his own play. And if, as established above, the playwright in the Nigerian theatre finds himself inevitably the director of his work, what then are the problems he faces with interpreting his conception to actors and the audience?

To start with a Nigerian company of actors is often a mixture of untrained and trained, amateur, semi-professional, and few professional. On the surface, there need not be any serious problem with such a composition. And in a country where there is an established standard of stagecraft and discipline, such a mixture of professionals and amateurs could be valuable, for then, the untrained could have a direct on-the-job opportunity to measure against those standards and discipline of the trained and experienced members of the company. But in a Nigerian theatre, where such standards have yet to be set up, the duty of establishing often mainly devolves on the playwright-director, who attempts the best he could to visualize and create the standards for his company.[14] Usually, his personality and previous experience and knowledge of such standards are very important here in the success or failure of the task.

We can temporarily ignore the way he handles problems of finance, lateness at rehearsals and training the company towards an adequate ensemble organization. Assuming that the task is successful, we might observe that such a company is likely to hold together for as long as the playwright-director is the force. Transfer the company to another director or playwright to manage, and we might observe a different set of standards according to the new person's conception of theatre and the stylistic demands of his play. This of course is not saying that such a situation cannot occur in an established theatre; on the contrary it is conceivable. But the problem here is on the one hand with the playwright who is the director of his own plays and therefore trains his company according to the stylistic demands of his plays; and on the other hand with the company which is used to its director's form and style of play. When the company changes hands, it is quite likely that there will occur the problem of breaking the company from the old to the new, especially if the new playwright-director's conception of theatre, according to his plays and experience, is very different from the old already absorbed one.[15]

Again, the point being emphasized here is not the fact that the company is exposed to different styles and conceptions, for such exposition is necessary and advantageous if only to promote the flexibility of the actor. But a company needs a full-time director, not committed also to playwrighting, backed by adequate staff, who is able to integrate from the onset all the existing styles into the training of the company.

The Audience

While it is true that a good audience-reception is always encouraging for the playwright and may affirm his confidence in playwrighting, it is equally true that an audience can make the playwright become either over-confident to the point that he does not feel challenged to critically explore his vision; or be lazy, with the result that he offers his audience the same old play or set of plays. Both realities cannot hold the playwright and his work to a long-term quality of achievement. But then what is the situation with audiences in the Nigerian theatre, with regard to English-language playwrights?

A 1979 Unife Theatre production of Akin Isola's *Madam Tinubu* had a very poor audience at the National Theatre in Lagos, that is, after it had played to full houses at Ile-Ife. A reason immediately posed for this was the general nonchalant attitude of the Lagos audience towards plays written in English. Similarly in 1979, Ola Rotimi's popular play *If. . .* played to empty houses in Lagos. The poor showings at the plays are in sharp contrast to the successful receptions that would normally greet an Ogunde play or a Moses Olaiya (Baba Sala) comedy in Lagos. While it can rightly be argued that the productions of both *Madam Tinubu* and *If. . .* suffered from poor publicity, it is still correct that most Nigerian playwrights writing in English find it difficult to hold a substantial Nigerian audience or fill a theatre. A look at the situation of things with reference to the works of two of the leading Nigerian playwrights should be helpful. And to make it less complicated, we can confine ourselves simply to a locality where these playwrights are most likely to have their warmest receptions—the university campus.

Ola Rotimi, for instance, has over the years acquired a prominent reputation among Nigerian audiences, especially on university campuses. Campus audiences literally need only a moment's notice before flocking to the theatre to watch a play by him. They understand his language, and bubble with excitement in anticipation of the next action or theatrical effect. Many of them who have seen any play of his several times would see it again come another production. The constant revival of Ola Rotimi's *The Gods Are Not to Blame*, played each time to full houses, will prove the point.

Wole Soyinka, on the other hand, an equally distinguished and more established playwright, does not evoke the same kind of response. Although some of his works, especially the earlier ones, could be said to have made and can still make popular appeals, notably *The Trials of Brother Jero* and *The Lion and the Jewel*.[16] However, most of his plays will not fill the theatre quite as much. And if they do, only a small percentage are his real audience, in the sense that they understand and acknowledge his theatre. The greater percentage would watch out of curiosity, and though they are often held by something they are unable to make out, they usually come to the same conclusion—that he is too intellectual.

Implicit in the different attitudes of the Nigerian audience to the two distinguished playwrights is a critical judgement of some sort. But what sort of judgement? On the surface, one tends to deduce that the problem lies more with style than what the play is actually saying. And perhaps this is true to a certain extent. For instance, it can be argued that Soyinka may be better understood and have far greater audience appeal with a simpler and more straightforward style as *The Lion and the Jewel*, than with the more complex style of say *The Road*. Similarly, Rotimi became less understood when he decided to explore the more complex style of *If . . .*, even though his audience was still very much with him.

However, it might be more profitable to approach the problem from the audience point of view. A study of theatre-audiences in general will show that in its reactions there is a tendency at first towards a sort of lethargy, a dominant characteristic in what John Fernald[17] calls audience "persona" which is only "very slightly related to the qualities of the single persons who compose it", and which "reacts in the theatre at the mental and emotional pace of its slowest member and not the agility of any of its quicker-witted components". If so indulged, an audience would preferably like to sit back in its seat and ride along with the entertainment (for which after all it has paid) without having to task its head to unravel the unexplained, the ambiguous and all other subtleties that keep the brain active and exercised.[18] And yet, here lies the rub. The audience has paid to be entertained by an art-work, which is expected to be something more than what they would ordinarily see in the streets, in other words, some-thing dramatic. And the kind of relaxation which its "persona" literally would indulge itself upon, or so it appears, would eventually get the audience to doze off, because there is nothing interesting to keep it awake. Hence in effect, it expects some sort of "magic" to excite and sweep its lethargy away.

Now, there are of course several ways of exciting an audience, and perhaps the most basic is the one achieved through the story-line by its age-old technique of raising tension and resolu-tion through suspense, adventure, etc. This technique in its various forms is still the crowd puller of many films and commer-cial theatres. On the other hand, the excitement could come through theatrical values, speech-delivery, dramatic ironies and conflicts, language, etc.

A close look at the playwright–audience relationship in the Nigerian theatre will reveal, in its short history, that it is generally based on the surface story-line excitement, whether it is the highly moralistic or the nationalistic productions of Ogunde's theatre, or the historical music-dramas of Duro Ladipo's theatre, or the love-potioned plays of say Ene Henshaw. Actually, this is not necessarily a bad thing, since as has been noted it is basically a crowd-puller in many commercial theatres. Therefore, for the emerging playwright, the option is either to exploit this apparently commercial factor, or break out adventurously with non-profit experimentations to finding a new audience for a supposedly new theatre experience. How then do these two options apply to the playwrights under consideration?

Without suggesting in any way that Ola Rotimi's plays are surface-material with no intellectual depth, it seems that there is a deliberate effort and tendency on his part to win the audience over in his productions with actions, language and theatricality, which could readily be absorbed into the story-line. And for the same effect his actors are constantly expressing values, mannerisms, and speaking in the "dialect"[19] very familiar to the audience. And why should he not do this, since in a way one could argue that a playwright must consider his audience, for after all, without an audience there is no theatre.

With Soyinka on the other hand, there is no such apparent joy for the audience. He also expresses traditional values, but in the process puts the audience to task both visually and mentally. He knows what they want, but either deliberately does not give them, or gives them so unfamiliarly, asking them to reach out, stretch themselves enough to absorb the ideas he explores. The result is that a Soyinka production commands less audience than one of Rotimi. But is it true that Rotimi is more committed to a Nigerian audience than Soyinka has been? Let us seek a clue from some of the ideas in their plays. For instance, on the question of values, how committed are both playwrights to expressing the values of the Nigerian audience?

Kurunmi by Rotimi and Soyinka's *Death and the King's Horseman* for example, are both based on historical facts. Both are concerned with a certain idea of death. Kurunmi as the

Are-Onakakanfo, who, as the Yoruba field-marshal, constantly meets face to face with violent death on the battle-ground and must now once again put himself to the deadly task, this time in firm support of tradition. So must Elesin-Oba put his traditional conviction to the task of death, as the dead King's companion to the world of the ancestors. How then has each playwright orchestrated this idea in terms of traditional honour?

Rotimi, in *Kurunmi*, takes a sort of naturalistic concept, proverb-packed, action-packed although with dramatic economy, especially in Acts 3 and 4, the rather episodic events leading up to Kurunmi's defeat and death. There is no sustained dramatic action to gravitate the central idea towards this tragic end, except one that comes up all of a sudden at a late stage—the ominous implications of crossing the Ose River. But then, in an omen-conscious, supernatural-minded society, this action is perfectly gripping, even though it is weakened by the fact that the audience are ahead of the disaster. In this, as in other actions, the play, to sustain the audience's interest, relies heavily on the cunning of a traditional story-teller, by juxtapositioning action and the familiar language of proverbs, to draw response in sympathy or laughter. There is also what Mr. Dapo Adelugba calls "stage icons" or pictures, Ola Rotimi's forte, used for the same effect of exciting the audience.

Soyinka, on the other hand, relies heavily on the evocative power of the language. The "icons", if one may call them that, are embedded in the imagery which forms an integral part of and explores the dramatic action. In *Death and the King's Horseman*, Soyinka uses Elesin-Oba's traditional commitment to death to explore the Yoruba metaphysical world-view of death in relation to the world of the living which Elesin is in the process of leaving traditionally, and the world of the unborn, which anticipates a continuity of tradition by future Elesins. This artistic problem, concretized by a conflict between Elesin's duty and honour, and the British hermetic logic and civilized judgement, is orchestrated by a single dramatic action—Elesin's gradual, intricate and systematic "dance" into the world of the ancestors, which is in sharp ironic contrast to the frivolous off-the-key, colonial mentality and decadence which manipulates and halts the process of tradition. All the play's mythopoeic imagery relates one way or the other to this dramatic action. And with this, Soyinka gives the Nigerian audience no joy of their accustomed relaxation and easy unravelling. He does not appear to believe in the need to win the audience. Or if he does, it is with the creative processes of culture, presented with vibrant freshness and ironic, poetic nakedness, asking them (the audience) to perceive, reflect, assimilate and get transported by the mythopoeic experience of his theatre. The cathartic effect can be gripping, but, perhaps unfortunately, only to trained ears and eyes. For he is not saying anything out of the context of culture (in fact he is very much with culture, probably more than any other Nigerian dramatist). It is only the way he puts it that makes it seemingly far-fetched. Does this make him indulgent and extravagant?[20]

This brief analysis, exemplifying the two playwrights' conception of theatre should suffice, since the present exercise is not a critical analysis of their works but simply to highlight the problems in the relationship of the playwright and the Nigerian audience.

Language

However, the problem of language, the medium of communication is so crucial to the emergence of the Nigerian playwright and theatre that it deserves some comment here, although I have no wish at this time to resolve the all-imposing problem.

The disadvantages of the playwright using the English language as his medium of expression are obvious and have been dealt with variously and at some length.[21] And yet, since the writer is free to choose his own medium and his choice happens to be the English language, it seems more profitable to dwell on ways and means of using it to the fullest or help further its achievements as part of the playwright's creative process of development. One way is to follow a kind of Rotimi's "Yorubanglish" dialogue, which tries to translate the Yoruba nuances of expression into literal English. Another is to attempt transposing these nuances into rich, poetic expression in English language.

Elsewhere, I have tried to make a case for a type of theatre in which the rich resources of ritual drama can be utilized to the full, a theatre where the communicant (votive-worshipper-spectator) at the height of participation is intoxicated with the communicative mystification of the ritualist (priest-dramatist) that he beholds and is held by his god (the drama-content, the mythopoeic element) with both awe and joy. To make a concrete example of this, we shall have to go back to Soyinka's *Death and the King's Horseman*—to the scene that ritually dramatizes the central action, where, through the ritual of Elesin's passage-dance (feet in dialogue with the drumming), the Praise-Singer is at once the communicant beholding his "god", and the "god" himself (the dead Alafin, waiting at the gate of the passage to the ancestral world). Through him and the evocative dialogue that ensues with Elesin, we the audience are held by a sort of "epidemic", cathartic process and we perceive the traditional demands and implications of Elesin's ritual calling.

This is the language and response of ritual drama, and it is only possible in a theatre where the resources of culture are so entrenched in and controlled by the medium of communication. Such a medium therefore becomes enriched with new vigour and spontaneous freshness and originality.

While I do not advocate that every playwright should necessarily aspire to write this way, it seems to me pertinent to say that the playwright using the English language must continue to explore within his medium and Nigerian background, with the view to finding a true Nigerian theatre.

Notes

1. *African Theatre and the Playwright*—lecture given at African Studies Centre, University of Indiana, Bloomington, 1973.
2. Visitors to Nigeria often have grand expectations of it, no doubt from what they know of the normal functioning of other National Theatres.
3. 1960–61 session—the Travelling Theatre Company toured with their first production, *Suberu*, a Nigerian adaptation of Molière's *That Scoundrel Scapin*.
4. J. P. Clark, whose first play, *Song of a Goat* was done by the "1960 Masks" in 1962, does not belong to this group.
5. In retrospect, a similar interest was kindled for the folk and popular dramatist by Hubert Ogunde about two decades before, during the nationalist-consciousness of the 1940s.
6. Perhaps a fine example of this development is Femi Osofisan who has been very much influenced by Soyinka, but now has come into his own.

7. Soyinka's essay, *Towards a True Theatre*, which appears in this anthology, is the first I know on the subject.
8. That Oduduwa Hall is workable is accidental. Originally it was not conceived as a performing theatre.
9. The Cultural Centres like the recent completed one in Ibadan continue to emphasize the facade more than grapple with the realities of a Nigerian theatre.
10. The play was the 1979 Convocation production of the University of Ife, directed by the present writer.
11. Reinhardt of Germany, one of the pioneers of the modern director was known to have relished the idea of incomplete or imperfect plays, for they gave him the opportunity to subject them to his theatrical flights of fancy.
12. Mainly because of no fund-support, it has been difficult for these companies to exist professionally from the start. However, conscious attempts have been made in the Universities like Ife and Ibadan which have fully-paid resident companies.
13. But the advice of Henrik Ibsen to the Norwegian students in 1874 would seem to apply here: "All that I have written these last few years, I have lived through spiritually. But no poet lives through anything in isolation. What he lives through all of his countrymen live through with him. If it were not so, what would bridge the gap between the producing and the receiving minds?" (*Task of a Poet*, Ibid., p. 3.)
14. Normally, a lot of these problems would be tackled by good professional training schools. To date there is only one such professional programme which I know of which attempts to de-emphasize the academic and pay particular attention to standards, and attitude to theatre, and that is the Ife University Dramatic Arts Programme. But even that programme is still very young and undergoing a period of experimentation.
15. This was the situation when the University of Ife company changed directors, from Ola Rotimi to Wole Soyinka. Both of them, renowned playwrights in their own rights, but with extremely distinct styles of writing and directing. For instance, whereas Rotimi encouraged and worked with the raw material more suited to his plays, Soyinka needed a more flexible, potentially polished material for the poetic language and the intellectuality of his plays. (For further explanation, see the section where the two playwrights are discussed.) In the process, some members of the company became redundant.
16. Both plays are the most frequently done, probably because of their simplicity in style, and the sparkle and wit in language.
17. A reputable British director and teacher, formerly principal of the Royal Academy of Dramatic Art in London.
18. "Mental activity does of course occur in appreciation of theatre, if the play is intellectually demanding enough. But intellectuality of a play is most savoured after seeing its performance: if mental effort, beyond certain limits, is expected of an audience during performance, its concentration will not be equal to the task." Ibid., pp. 30–31.

19. Mr. Adelugba writes of the "Yorubanglish" language characteristic of Rotimi's plays. See "Three Dramatists in Search of a Language", in *Theatre in Africa*, ed. by Oyin Ogunba and Abiola Irele.
20. Barry Reckord, a Caribbean playwright once called Soyinka's *A Dance of the Forests*, "an example of Africana Exotica" (TRANSLATION Vol. 3, No. 11, 1963—Section, "Polemics"). Be that as it may, it should be noted that from that play to say, *Death and the King's Horseman*, is a gradual and significant growth of a playwright whose forte is in the power of unifying action with language.
21. For example, J. P. Clark's "The Legacy of Caliban", in *Black Orpheus*, Vol. 2, No. 1, 1968.

MODERN YORUBA DRAMA[1]

Akinwumi Isola

I

Before the (new) era of Western education, ritual drama and the alarinjo (travelling masquerades) were all that was known in form of drama among the Yoruba. The various religious and secular festivals had, and still have their dramatic aspects in the form of specific gestures, dances with strict movements and songs with special tunes and well-chosen words. The festivals, which occur at regular intervals, provided the communities with occasions for merry-making and for spectacular shows. But they did not come often enough.

The alarinjo theatre[2] provided some variation with its own flexibility. Apart from the annual festival performances, the alarinjo masquerades went about, performing from town to town for the greater part of the year. The alarinjo masquerades delightfully blended the religious with the secular. It was a popular theatre with the village square as stage and no fees charged.

The Modern travelling theatre, is, however, a new breed. It arose from Christian inspired operas and service of songs until Ogunde[3] changed the orientation and moved it to a play form. The Yoruba travelling theatre companies, of which there are now about a hundred, take their plays round the country. Most of these plays are not scripted. The plays that are scripted are yet unpublished and therefore are not available either for critical studies or other interested groups for staging. Mention must be made of the effort by the Institute of African Studies, Ibadan University to reduce a few of the plays to writing. Duro Ladipo's *Oba Koso*, Kola Ogunmola's *Omuti* are examples.

Modern Yoruba plays, on the other hand, first had their existence as written scripts. In fact some of them have never been staged. The texts are available for critical studies and for use by theatre companies. In general modern Yoruba plays are longer

399

and have more complicated plots than those of the travelling theatre companies. They are the properly published literary plays that belong to the list from which examination set books are selected.

Modern Yoruba plays have something in common with other genres of Yoruba written literature: they too borrow a lot from oral literature, especially from oral poetry. So that in spite of some evidence of foreign formal influence, modern Yoruba plays still have a strong structural link with ritual drama and travelling theatre plays. In many contemporary modern Yoruba plays one comes across references to ritual drama either in the form of deities being worshipped or in the form of traditional ceremonies being performed. The inclusion of these features lend colour and movement to the action in some of the plays. There is also a generous use of social songs, drumming and dancing, largely borrowed from the practice of travelling theatre groups. It is the contact with Western literature, for example, that led some Yoruba playwrights to divide their plays into acts and scenes, inventing ingenious translations like "Idan" (Magic) for "act". Another set of writers have, however, preferred to present actions in their plays in scenes throughout, rather than divide them into acts or parts. Whatever form a writer has adopted, the borrowings from oral literature can hardly be missed in most of them.

The story in Odunjo's *Agbalowomeri* is largely that of magic-objects and of fabulous treasures in secret places in a thick forest. That idea is borrowed from Yoruba folktales. The theme in another folktale is used to explain action in Okediji's popular play *Rere Run*. The play opens with song from the tale: "Ero ti n rojeeje . . ." The folktale is about a travelling mother who asked a co-wife to take care of a daughter she was leaving behind. The travelling mother left eggs among other items of food for her daughter. The co-wife maltreated the daughter of the travelling mother and gave her stale yam to eat instead of the hard boiled eggs. The daughter complained and cried her heart out and finally disappeared into the bowels of the earth to register her protest.

The story illustrates what happens in contemporary life when, for instance, "caretakers" in the form of governments refuse to give the people what is due them. In *Rere Run*, workers organize themselves into a union in order to fight for their rights. The union leader, Lawuwo, is uncompromising in his negotiations. The employers, led by Onimogun, feel a threat to their business and profits. They get rid of Lawuwo, break the workers' resistance and instal a stooge as union leader.

Of greater importance is the use made by writers of materials from oral poetry. Oral poetry is very important in the life of the Yoruba. Many important occasions call for the chanting of oral poetry. Whenever such occasions arise in the plays, writers most enthusiastically incorporate materials from oral poetry. Oral poetry, with its cultural associations becomes very handy for a writer who wants to create particular moods and atmosphere.

A good example is to be found in Ogunniran's *Aare Ago Arikuyeri.* Aje has just returned from a successful military expedition. He now wants to offer sacrifice to his "head" to thank it for bringing him so much luck. It is a religious and festive occasion. Religious poetry in the form of Ifa corpus remind the audience of the important role of the human head in the affairs of men. Other verses enjoin men to take good care of their heads and advise them to put their heads even before the deities. After the offerings, *Rara*, a form of social poetry is used to create a festive mood. *Rara* poems here emphasize the duties of wives to their husbands in addition to recounting the various, gallant military achievements of Aje.

The use of *Rara*, a social poem makes it easier for Ogunniran to create the right atmosphere for showing the traditional rivalry among Aje's three wives. When one of the three wives, Fatola, excels the other in performance, and Aje shows greater love to her, seed of discontent is sown. Later on in the same play *Rara* is used to show the various moods of Basorun Ogunmola while talking to his chiefs, while conducting the investigations and delivering judgement.

In Owolabi's *Lisabi Agbongbo Akala, ege* poetry is used to further define the character of Lisabi, the Egba leader. Each time he attends a meeting or leads a group, he chants *ege*. And the picture is that of an intelligent, affable leader. On the other hand, the use of *Rara* in the palace of the Alaafin, in the same play, sharpens, in our minds, the picture of a stern, authoritative and ruthless ruler ready to tolerate no insurrection in any part of his empire.

Whenever there is serious confrontation of powerful men, writers use *ofo* (incantations) to emphasize the seriousness of the clash of power. In traditional Yoruba society, incantations are used on very serious occasions usually when other things have failed to resolve the issue. So it is in the confrontation between Efunsetan and Latoosa in my own play, *Efunsetan Aniwura*. So it is in the fight between Timi and Gbonkaa in Ladipo's *Oba Koso* and also between the two opposing war generals in Owolabi's *Lisabi Agbongbo Akala*.

The use of incantations is linked with the popular use of magic and of other supernatural powers in modern Yoruba plays. For some reason the display of supernatural power never fails to attract the applause of the audience in any performance. It is a nostalgic admiration of a kind of power people have heard so much about, but which today, unfortunately, is hardly come by in reality. So, each time these powers are illustrated in modern Yoruba plays, the most familiar reminders of such powers, the enthusiastic wish of the audience for a realistic revival of supernatural powers cannot be missed. Theatre goers or readers of Yoruba plays will easily remember the following popular examples: Bayo Faleti's *Basorun Gaa*, Akinkunmi, the young fiance of Agbonyin hits Gaa with a magic belt and the powerful old man is instantly paralysed. In *Efunsetan Aniwura*, Itawuyi lifts up his cutlass to cut Efunsetan. She says some words and Itawuyi cannot complete the action. Efunsetan takes the cutlass from him as he becomes dazed and powerless. Examples can be multiplied.

II

A critical look at the scene shows three major trends in modern Yoruba play-writing: the historical, the didactic and protest plays.

The Historical

Some historical Yoruba plays have been very successful with the audience despite the fact that some playwrights of historical drama are not loyal to strict historical details. The Yoruba historical playwright, like his counterparts in other literatures, is not a historian. He is an interpreter of history. His interpretation of history may be subjective and the reasons of the subjective stand varies from writer to writer. Although we have no time here for detailed examination of each historical play, a few illustrative remarks will clarify the point we are trying to make.

Duro Ladipo's *Oba Koso*, is based virtually on Hetherset's story about Sango in *Iwe Kika Ekerin Li Ede Yoruba*.[4] Hetherset's story itself is a subjective Christian edition of the real story of Sango as known by traditional historians and Sango devotees. Johnson, the famous Yoruba historian, remarked that the tragic quarrel between the two war generals, Gbonkaa and Timi, did not happen during the reign of Alaafin Sango. In history, Sango was not as pitiable as is portrayed in *Oba Koso*. The name Oba Koso does not mean "the king did not hang" it means "the king of Koso". Sango is also called *Oluoso*, i.e. Olu of Koso. This is the real meaning among Sango devotees and the poetry chanters who are custodians of oral history. Hetherset may have edited the story of Sango to suit his Christian interests. Ladipo, however, must have had additional reasons. If Sango in this play is to be a tragic hero, then the audience has reasons to pity him somehow. Perhaps that was why Duro Ladipo preferred Hetherset's story in the first place. So, it appears that ordinary history was not good enough for Ladipo's play.

Adebayo Faleti had to "tamper" a little with history to get out his *Basorun Gaa* in its play form. As we said earlier, a playwright interprets history and, therefore has to find plausible reasons for the actions of his characters. In the play, *Basorun Gaa*, Oba Abiodun has only one child, Agbonyin and so he wants to ensure that she succeeds him in order to keep family line in power. This decision angers Gaa and provides a good reason for his wanting to kill Agbonyin. In real history Oba Abiodun had more than one child. In fact, his first child was a boy named Adegbile. So, Abiodun could not have wanted Agbonyin to reign after him. Also in the play, Gaa uses the pretext that he is looking for the animal agbonyin to sacrifice to his Ifa oracle, and cannot find one easily, so Agbonyin is used instead of agbonyin. In real history, there was no reason at all for killing Agbonyin. Gaa was simply callous. He was not even looking for an animal to sacrifice to his Ifa oracle. It was just an irredeemably wicked act. There are other minor points like the fact that Majeogbe's head was not cut off in real history. So, Faleti has decided to interpret history this way in order to give it the dramatic veracity of literature.

Another interesting example is my play, *Efunsetan Aniwura*, where historical facts have been sifted to suit the author's intentions. For example, in history, Efunsetan had an only daughter who herself died in labour. The psychological effect of that would have partly explained Efunsetan's actions. Also, the Efunsetan of history did not commit suicide, but was murdered by two of her slaves who were in turn executed. The politico-economic rivalry between Latosa and Efunsetan has also been suppressed in order to give no room for pitying Efunsetan, partly because the author believes that no extenuating circumstances should be provided for someone who was so wicked that she really was killing expectant mothers among her slaves.

There are other historical plays which perhaps could have benefited from a little authorical interpretation in order to drive the points home more convincingly. One of such plays is Owolabi's *Lisabi Agbongbo Akala*. The main point of the story seems to be to commend solidarity and self determination to the Egba by showing the examples of their forefathers. The last part of the story, the betrayal of the great leader, Lisabi, by his own people, however, defeats that purpose. A suppression of that part of history or a totally different interpretation would have given a better literary satisfaction. A too close fidelity to history also robs Lawuyi Ogunniran's *Aare Ago Arikuyeri* of a greater literary impact. The turbulent military life of Aare Ago Aje does not deserve that kind of cowardly ending. A more rewarding attention could have been paid to the life and philosophy of Basorun Ogunmola himself.

One other play, Olabimtan's *Olaore Afotejoye* deserves mention here. The play discusses a topical current affairs problem, the political crisis in the old Western Region. Because some of the actual participants in the drama of that history are still yet very much alive, awarded the use of the actual names of historical

figures. He, however, used substitute names that are obviously
suggestive of the original. Some physical descriptions of characters are so clear that the knowledgeable reader cannot fail to
identify the real personality to whom it refers.

The Didactic

The greater number of Yoruba plays are written on simple
stories designed just to entertain and to teach morals. There are
at present almost twenty titles in this category alone. The general
pattern seems to be that vice is punished and virtue rewarded.
Although the general aim is to instruct, the specific subjects may
vary widely. In *Won Ro Pe Were Ni*, Bayo Faleti examines the
remote causes of crime in the society while Babatunde Olatunji's
Asiri Tu focuses attention on jealousy between co-wives in a
family. While it is true that most of these plays comment
somehow on matters that affect the society in general, one fails to
see much of deep, insightful presentation and discussion of the
problems created by the prevailing socio-political system in the
country. Does it mean then that Yoruba dramatists are apathetic
to the terrible economic exploitation and the heartless political
deprivation of the people by the ruling elite? Happily, the
emergence of what we, for convenience, call protest plays has
provided the much needed revitalization of the genre.

Protest Plays

By protest plays we mean those plays that attempt to decry the
poor economic condition and the political powerlessness of the
working class. Some of the plays also discuss aspects of corruption, exposing it for condemnation.

Rere Run by Oladejo Okediji is perhaps the most popular in
this category. It has been translated into English as *The Shattered
Bridge* by Bode Osanyin. The University of Ife theatre also has a
pidgin version for stage.

Rere Run is the story of the struggle of workers for better
conditions of service and of how employers cleverly infiltrated
their ranks, broke their solidarity, and shattered their dreams.
Lawuwo, the union leader and a committed activist, does not
believe in any compromise. But Onimogun and his Chiefs

cleverly portray Lawuwo as a traitor in order to discredit him among his fellow workers. Using divide-and-rule tactics, the employers sponsor Idowu as a rival union leader. Idowu's aim is to destroy Lawuwo, the popular leader, in order to consolidate his own position. Idowu specially commissions money doublers to steal union money from Lawuwo's wife, Morenike. Weak-minded Morenike, fearing Lawuwo's angry reaction, commits suicide by drug overdose. The shock created by this incident shatters Lawuwo's sanity. His mental disturbance disqualifies him as union leader. The union is disorganized and Idowu is named new leader. Workers are forced back to work and the struggle fails.

When the play is well produced, the sympathy of the audience lies with Lawuwo. At one performance I saw a lady break down, crying as Lawuwo went mad when he discovered that Morenike was dead. The usual feeling at the end of performance is anger against Onimogun and the Chiefs and bitterness towards cruel employers in general. Some people have argued that the ending of the play is reactionary. They say that the defeat of the workers could discourage positive action. They would prefer an ending where the workers are victorious. Here lies the problem with ending protest plays. A positive ending that ensures victory for the oppressed has a way of creating false relief. The audience goes home, satisfied, thinking that the problems have been solved and therefore thinks less about it. A negative ending, on the other hand, if well handled, leaves the audience dissatisfied and embittered. There may be a wish to do something to prevent such suffering by workers. The important thing, therefore, is not just the ending, it depends more on the effect of the whole story and the way the conclusion is reached. *Rere Run* is essentially a positive play.

In *Koseegbe*, I attempt to discuss the problem of endemic corruption. The play is about a senior customs officer who sets out to stamp out corruption in the establishment. Reactionary elements in the society have peculiar ways of protecting their interests. So, they plan to frustrate the efforts of revolutionaries by sabotage and blackmail. When Mako, the senior customs officer catches some big men red-handed and decides to expose them publicly, he steps on the sore toes of powerful people. The machinery to destroy Mako is set in motion. First, his close assistant is bought over. Then, he himself is cleverly implicated in a love-affair scandal. A hemp-smoking offence is framed for his undergraduate son.

With imprisonment hanging over the head of his son and the possibilities of the sack for him too, the reactionary elements who have planned his fall ask for compromise. In the first performance of the play, Mako was scared and he agreed to negotiate. So, the evil men won. In the final version, however, police detectives who have been following the activities of the big rogues, arrest all of them at the meeting where the negotiations are being discussed.

The latest play in this category is my latest work, *Aye Ye Won Tan*, recently performed by the University of Ife theatre. It is the story of a king who promised a lot of good things for the workers before ascending the throne. Once on the throne, he starts moving in new circles and cultivates greedy bourgeois habits. He becomes corrupt and refuses to keep his promises. The people rise up and demand that the king should swear before the traditional city deity. His attempt to rig the ceremony fails and he is arrested. It is an illustration of what the people themselves could do to save themselves.

III

The Yoruba people are great theatre goers. That is why about a hundred professional theatre groups can thrive among them today. Very recently a record audience was recorded at a performance of *Efunsetan Aniwura* at Liberty Stadium in Ibadan when over fourteen thousand people watched a single performance. The performance was arranged by Radio O-Y-O as part of the activities to mark the third anniversary of its establishment. This great response to drama has great potentialities. Artists that have valuable messages for the people can count on a ready audience. It is a very accommodating audience that is ready to appreciate great works and also to sympathize with second rate performances in order to encourage artists.

To the Yoruba audience the beauty of the language is as important as (if not more important than) the action itself. The Yoruba playwright who is careless about his language cannot retain his audience for long. Most Yoruba playwrights pay great attention to the beauty of the language they use. So it is that these plays that have been greatly acclaimed are those where serious attention to language is pre-eminent.

Apart from the beauty of language borrowed from traditional literature as discussed earlier, a playwright's ingenuity also shows in the way he brings in his own creations. Let us look at *Rere Run* for example. Okediji knows the importance of proverbs in Yoruba rhetorics and he uses proverbs ever so often without boring the reader. He pleasantly surprises the reader by introducing twists to proverbs; he turns normal proverbs to questions; he explains proverbs; he piles up proverbs; he modifies proverbs. Okediji loves proverbs. The overall effect of this makes *Rere Run* a captivating blending of content and form.

Faleti in his plays, exploits, successfully, exotic poetic devices in order to retain the attention of the reader. The poet in Faleti seems to be at his best in his *Basorun Gaa*. Apart from the appropriate selection of traditional poetry, Faleti composes his own poems, putting this in the mouth of important characters, especially Gaa himself. Gaa uses poetry purposefully. One of the most poetic speeches in Yoruba drama is made by Gaa when he tries to defend his actions in front of Oyo chiefs after he has killed Majeogbe, the then Alaafin. Although the Chiefs thoroughly hate him, each time he speaks the Chiefs are carried away by his powerful speeches. There are very few Yoruba plays that do not take matters of language very seriously.

It is rather surprising that in spite of the popularity of the theatre among the Yoruba, relatively very few plays have been written and published. While we have at least sixty published novels in the Yoruba language, we have just about thirty published plays. There is a general problem about publishing books in local languages in Nigeria. Publishers are always very reluctant to invest their money on books with limited circulation. Scripts submitted and accepted for publication since 1974 in some cases, are still in press. It is a sorry situation. The theatre holds immense possibilities among the Yoruba. They could be used to create the much needed awareness about the political and economic situation of the country. They could also be used to encourage unity and uphold culture. One would like to see more plays than novels written. Plays, at present, have instant impact. Until the film industry expands, the theatre will be the more potent medium.

Unfortunately, most unscripted plays produced by travelling theatres are not very carefully prepared. Most of them are still sketchy and only manage to draw laughter. Published plays provide better material for stage. One would therefore want the government to come to the aid of writers by subsidizing the publication of books in Nigerian languages in general.

Writers also need assistance to improve their skills and ensure the relevance of material. Workshops should be organized for this purpose. The recent inauguration of the Yoruba Writers Association is a welcome move. It is hoped that this association will be able to make moves to improve the quality and quantity of Yoruba literature.

MODERN YORUBA PLAYS

A Reading List

1942: Adeboye Babalola, *Pasan Sina*
1958: J. F. Odunjo, *Agbalowomeri Baale Jontolo*, Longman
1965: Adebayo Faleti, *Won Ro Pe Were Ni*, Oxford University Press
1971: Adebayo Faleti, *Basorun Gaa*, Onibonoje
1973: Adebayo Faleti, *Idaamu Paadi Minkailu*, Onibonoje
   * Adebayo Faleti, *Fere Bi Ekun*, Onibonoje
1965: Olanipekun Esan, *Orekelewa*, Oxford University Press
1965: Duro Ladipo, *Eda*, Mbari Mbayo
1971: Duro Ladipo, *Moremi*, Macmillan
1972: Duro Ladipo, *Oba Koso*, Institute of African Studies, Ibadan
1968: Afolabi Olabimtan, *Oluwa Lo Mejo Da*, Macmillan
1970: Afolabi Olabimtan, *Olaore Afotejoye*, Macmillan
1973: Babatunde Olatunji, *Asiri Tu*, Nelson
1978: Babatunde Olatunji, *Egbinrin Ote*, Oxford University Press
1970: Akinwumi Isola, *Efunsetan Aniwura*, Oxford University Press
1981: Akinwumi Isola, *Koseegbe*, Oxford University Press
   * Akinwumi Isola, *Aye Ye Won Tan*, Aim Publishers

* To be on sale in 1981.

410 DRAMA AND THEATRE IN NIGERIA

* Akinwumi Isola, *Omo Olumo*, Onibonoje
* Akinwumi Isola, *Were Lesin*, Onibonoje
1971: Adegoke Durojaiye, *Gbekude ati Ise Abe*, Oxford University Press
1973: Oladejo Okediji, *Rere Run*, Onibonoje
* Oladejo Okediji, *Sango*, Aim Publishers
1973: Olanrewaju Adepoju, *Sagba Di Were*, Onibonoje
1974: Olanrewaju Adepoju, *Ladepo Omo Adanwo*, Onibonoje
1977: Lawuyi Ogunniran, *Aare Ago Arikuyeri*, Macmillan
1980: Olusesan Ajewole, *Eni Bimo Oran*, Evans
1978: Olu Owolabi, *Lisabi Agbongbo Akala*, Oxford University Press
T. A. Ladele, *Igba Lo De*, Longman
1978: Aderinkomi, *Gbe Wiri*, Macmillan

Notes

1. "Modern Yoruba Drama" here refers to plays written in the Yoruba language. Authors that are Yoruba and who portray the Yoruba world in their works, but who write in English or in other languages than Yoruba are not included in our discussion. Yoruba literature in general embraces only works written in the Yoruba language.
2. See Adedeji J. A. "Alarinjo: The Traditional Yoruba Travelling Theatre" from *Theatre in Africa*, edited by Ogunba & Irele, Ibadan University Press.
3. See Ebun Clark: *Ogunde: The Rise of the Nigerian Theatre*, University Press Limited, 1980
4. *Iwe Kika Ekerin Li Ede Yoruba*, Church Missionary Society of Nigeria.

* To be on sale in 1981.

LITERARY DRAMA AND THE SEARCH FOR A POPULAR THEATRE IN NIGERIA
Biodun Jeyifo

I. The Literary and the Popular: A Necessary Divergence?

The theatre is a lie; the thing to do is to bring it as close as possible to the greatest truthfulness. The theatre is a painting; the thing to do is to make this painting useful, that is to say, to make it accessible to the greatest possible number of people so that the picture which it presents will serve to link men together . . . .

Sebastian Mercier

Most books of theatre history assume, and, in fact, elevate to the level of a categorical critical norm, the notion that the course of drama runs in two broad, divergent streams: a *popular* tradition and a *literary* tradition.[1] This premise very often runs into a subtle qualitative differentiation: the popular tradition, the tradition of strolling, itinerant players, mountebanks, jugglers, acrobats and mummers, is ephemeral and evanescent, even if it is often robust, vital and professionally disciplined; and the literary tradition, the tradition of great writers, of texts inspired by and inspiring other texts, this tradition is more intellectually prestigious, more assured of the gratitude of posterity. The most obvious illustration of this divergence is the respective fates seemingly assigned by both critical posterity and contemporary wisdom to the *text* and the *performance*: the text will outlast the performance, and even at the very moment when the two share contemporaneous existence, the performance lasts for a few hours every night for a few weeks, while the text is virtually available all the time.

The most cursory look at contemporary Nigerian theatre would seem to further confirm the presumed separation between the popular and the literary. Our most talented, accomplished literary dramatists do not remotely begin to approach the vast popularity of the professional theatre groups, who, in the main,

411

are not writers or producers of lasting dramatic writing. This situation can in fact be more graphically stated: the now established "classics" of Nigerian literary drama, say Clark's *The Raft* and *Ozidi* and Soyinka's *A Dance of the Forests*, *The Road* and *Madmen and Specialists*, are the least performed plays of published Nigerian literary drama. Indeed, both *Ozidi* and *The Road*, perhaps the two outstanding literary masterpieces, have never to date been performed by the non-amateur leading repertory companies in Nigeria. Apparently—and superficially, as I shall presently demonstrate—there would seem to exist a divergence between the *literary* and the *popular* in contemporary Nigerian drama.

At a fundamental level of critical investigation into the inner movement and high points of theatre history, the notion of a permanent divergence, a given schism, between the literary and the popular is really a partial truth verifiable only at the apparent surface of theatrical reality. There is always a mutual borrowing and interaction between the literary and the popular. And some of the world's greatest literary playwrights have also been immensely popular and directly accessible to the most humble and lowly of the theatre-going audiences of their day. The outstanding illustration of this is always the example of that great trio of classical Greek Antiquity, Aeschylus, Sophocles and Euripides and their successor who diverged to the comic art, Aristophanes. If we may judge by the direct contents of Aristophanes' *The Frogs*,[2] it seems that the ordinary theatre-goer of his day was very familiar with the works of the great literary playwrights and could, in fact, recall the famous lines and memorable personages of their dramas. The example of Elizabethan drama is perhaps even more relevant to the present discussion. The contemporary records tell of "university wits", or learned playwrights educated at the universities of Oxford and Cambridge (among whom were Marlowe, Greene, Peele and Nashe) who were highly contemptuous of such "uneducated" popular writers like Shakespeare and Ben Jonson. As anyone familiar with British theatre history knows, of the learned "university wits" only Marlowe shares a place, a decidedly lesser place at that, with Shakespeare and Jonson in the development of English drama.

A schism between the literary and the popular traditions in drama is thus not mandatory. If there seems to be a divergence between them in any period or national-social context, critical intelligence and theatrical practice must probe the historical, cultural and ideological roots of the schism and seek to transcend it. The encouragement for this kind of enterprise is in fact given by a closer look at other equally apparent areas of our contemporary literary drama. Soyinka is "difficult", "obscure" and "inaccessible" only if one is thinking of plays like *A Dance of the Forests, Madmen and Specialists*, and perhaps *The Road*. The popularity and wide appeal of his other works such as *The Lion and the Jewel, The Trials of Brother Jero, The Strong Breed* and the revues and sketches in the collection titled *Before the Blackout* are uncontestable. The directness, wit, satire and ebullient spirit of some of these plays which capture the eccentricities, absurdities, prejudices and follies of much of our contemporary social life make them ready, accessible fares if the institutional base for their popular projection can be found and sustained. So also are some of Clark's plays, like *The Song of a Goat* and *The Masquerade*, and above all others, the works of Ola Rotimi and Wale Ogunyemi. If these works are not now playing to the huge audiences regaled by the popular companies of Moses Olaiya, Hubert Ogunde and the late Duro Ladipo (whose outfit has remained largely intact), this is due, not so much to any inherent default in the plays, but to the abiding problem of building durable repertory companies for the literary drama in Nigeria. Ola Rotimi's work with the Ife University Theatre indeed provides a persuasive illustration of this point. Rotimi's Ife days[3] saw the creation of our only true repertory company to date and through it, the widest, most popular projection of our literary drama. This projection reached almost the same scale as that encompassed by the popular Yoruba professional troupes. Such literary dramas as *Rere Run* (a Yoruba play by Dejo Okediji, which is one of the most powerful and richest literary creations in our contemporary drama), *The Gods Are Not to Blame, Our Husband Has Gone Mad Again* and *Kurunmi* have become landmarks in the *unacknowledged* movement towards the convergence of the literary and the popular in our contemporary drama, thanks to the vibrant producing outfit created in the Ife University Theatre. The emphasis here is on the word "unacknowledged", for as we shall see, the aspiration of a *popular* expression, a popular appeal by our literary dramatists has been a largely haphazard, unconscious affair.

For always, one returns to the intolerable fact that the best works, the most profound creations of our literary drama, are not accessible to even a large part of the very limited audience which problemmatic linguistic and sociological factors make inevitable for literary drama in English at this stage of our national history. If the case is not yet as desperate as that with much of contemporary Nigerian poetry in English,[4] it is serious enough for a playwright, J. P. Clark, to have remarked once:

> Very likely, the so-called literary theatre in Nigeria is beginning to miss this complete identity of purpose and response enjoyed increasingly by the folk theatre in Yoruba.[5]

The problem is not merely that our masterpieces of the contemporary literary drama are either not performed enough or performed at all but, more crucially, when they are performed they evoke a considerable degree of ambivalence and even hostility as to their "relevance" or communication. And from the experience of the present writer, the problem goes even further than this, for sometimes private discussion with relatively competent and experienced actors and actresses who have performed some of our literary dramas has shown that they have not really "understood" a play, not performed in the spirit of the play's inner truths.

It must, of course, be recognized that a gifted literary playwright will not always achieve a "complete identity of purpose and response" with his audience. But still it remains true that befuddlement or plain incomprehension as a fairly general response reveals that the best of our literary dramas must be re-examined and critiqued from the perspective of a necessary convergence of the literary and the popular. Let us examine some reasons why, after a more or less entertaining evening of a performance of some of Soyinka's or Osofisan's plays, the audience often asks: "What is he saying?"; "What does he propose as a way out of this mess?"

II. Literary Drama, Popular Theatre and Culture as Ideology

> A given culture is the ideological reflection of the economics and politics of a given society.
>
> Mao Tse-tung

About two decades ago, it used to be generally held as a persuasive critical argument that the obstacles in the way of a popular appreciation of our then emergent literary drama were the issues of language and the lack of experienced theatre companies to produce the new complex, sophisticated literary dramas. As to language, one Nigerian critic, speaking of the new African literature in general, pronounced that writing in the borrowed, "elitist" language of the colonials was a dead-end for African literature.[6] Others were more equivocal. In an influential essay titled "The Legacy of Caliban", J. P. Clark advanced the thesis that authentic literary works could be created, were, in fact being created, by the artist capable of utilizing

> . . . a reliance upon the inner resources of language. These are images, figures of meaning and speech, which with expert hand-ling can achieve for its art a kind of blood transfusion, reviving the English language by the living adaptable properties of some African language.[7]

The question of the English language as a *possible* medium for an authentic Nigerian literary drama, a drama which can reach vast audiences is no longer a serious problem. Both dramatic practice, on which we shall presently have more to say, and the rapid expansion of those literate or fluent in the use of English, standard, colloquial or "pidgin", have negated the seriousness of the "problem". And Nigerian literary drama now embraces other languages besides English.

As to the "problem" of experienced producing groups capable of theatrically realizing plays like Clark's *Ozidi*, Osofisan's *The Chattering and the Song*[8] and *Once Upon Four Robbers*[9] and Soyinka's *The Road, A Dance of the Forests, Madmen and Specialists*, and others, this also is no longer applicable to the contemporary Nigerian theatrical scene. Geoffrey Axworthy, the first director of the old School of Drama at Ibadan, reminisces on the early days of the Nigerian literary drama, and his words may be a good indication of what we are advancing here:

> A wave of indigenous playwriting followed, and a widespread assumption, all too understandable in the euphoric days just before Independence, that the Nigerian theatre had arrived, whereas it had a long road to travel before acting and production matched the quality of the best writing. *A Dance of the Forests*, which Soyinka wrote and produced for the Independence celebrations of 1960, confirmed the range of his writing—and the need for companies and technical resources to match it.[10]

If the "strength, range and vitality" of Nigerian theatre companies were once in doubt, the works of such producer-directors as Soyinka himself, Dexter Lyndersay, Ola Rotimi, Kalu Uka, Dapo Adelugba, Bayo Oduneye, Wale Ogunyemi and now Femi Osofisan and Bode Sowande, have dispelled such doubts.[11]

If the reasons for the ambivalent reception of the best of our literary dramas and their distance from a popular projection are not really to be found in the linguistic medium or appropriate producing outfits, the explanation has to be sought elsewhere. And the only other possible source is that most basic to the reality of drama as the most *social* of the literary arts: the audience-playwright relationship. To my mind, the literary playwrights have not sufficiently clarified the issue of their audience, or the *publics* for which they write.[12] Stated plainly and directly, a *popular* literary drama will emerge only if, and when, there is a conscious wish for its emergence. But as we have remarked earlier, this aspiration exists in contemporary Nigerian literary drama only as an instinctive, unconscious and haphazard effort.

The feeling that our literary dramatists are only unconsciously and instinctively groping towards a *popular* expression, as accessible theatrical practice which will remain literarily sophisticated and profound, is strengthened by the realization that even the more complex plays like *Dance of the Forests* and *Madmen and Specialists* are not just bookish, unstageable plays. They are not intellectual exercises meant to gather dust and mould on the shelves of libraries and private studies in the manner of some of

T. S. Eliot's failed efforts at realizing a poetic drama for early twentieth century British drama. These plays—Clark's *Ozidi* and *The Raft* and Osofisan's new plays—are theatrically stageable, rich creations fusing the new textual dramaturgical modes with our indigenous theatrical penchant for ritual, ceremony, festivity, dance, song and mime. Although speaking only of Soyinka in the following quote, Martin Banham may be deemed to refer to our other literary dramatists when he says:

> I think that Soyinka has always written with a popular audience well in mind in that instinctive way that measures and assesses reponse and "feels" its way to an audience, that is a gift of the natural communicator through words and actions. He uses to great effect the unspoken comment, hinted at by a word or two, yet left to the audience to develop to the full through reference to their folklore, myths, and proverbs.[13]

The real significance of this important critical perception is that the union of Western-oriented textual dramaturgical modes with our own still vital indigenous theatrical techniques must become a *conscious* attempt to achieve greater directness, greater clarity, greater popularity. J. P. Clark has expressed rather strongly the controversy on this matter and I quote him here at some length:

> So much for the various kinds of traditional drama. Now how many are there of the type we have called modern? Two, if our count is correct. One is the folk theatre of Hubert Ogunde, Kola Ogunmola, Duro Ladipo and their several imitators, and the second is what some have called literary drama. *Some would say the latter has its heart right at home here in Nigeria and its head deep in the wings of American and European theatre! The works of Mr. Wole Soyinka, Dr. Ene Henshaw, and my own plays, I am told, clearly bear this badge, but whether of merit or infamy it is a matter still in some obscurity.*[14] (Emphasis mine)

The question of the relevance and accessibility of our best literary dramas will leave the closet of "obscurity" only to the extent that these dramas become more than mere *formalistic*, if often brilliant, experiments in the fusion of conventionally disparate theatrical traditions. So far indeterminacy, contortions of form and convolutions of masks and dramatic poetry mark the

union of the non-verbal, extra-literary techniques with the verbal, dramaturgical modes, in many of our finest literary dramas.
Often it is indeed at the very point of dramatic climax and
thematic significance that intelligible communication breaks
down and the dramatic poet lapses into obscurity and indirection,
even if these scenes are metaphorically, visually and theatrically
stunning. The most famous, or notorious examples of this pattern
is the central, emblematic scene in the heart of the forest in
Soyinka's *A Dance of the Forests*. The same is true of the
shattering climaxes of *The Road* and *Madmen and Specialists* as it
is of some crucial scenes in *Ozidi* and Osofisan's *The Chattering
and the Song* and *Once Upon Four Robbers*.

If a way is to be found out of the present dilemma of a literary
drama which is eminently stageable and theatrical yet often
obscure and inaccessible, unconscious, instinctive formalistic
experiments must become conscious, determined. And such
determination and conscious aspiration can come only from an
attention to the socio-historical roots of our present cultural
dilemmas. To quote Mao once more: "a given culture is the
ideological reflection of the economics and politics of a given
society". To the extent that the politics and economics of the
present Nigerian society reflect indeterminacy and confusion
about genuine economic and political autonomy and self-
direction from foreign domination, and furthermore, to the
extent that "the people" is conceived as a vague category by the
national ruling class in a populist political rhetoric which leaves
most of the people abused, exploited and violated, to that extent
will our present culture, art, literature and drama reflect indeterminacy, confusion. For so long will the best of our literary drama
reflect, often, violent, bitter, despairing disillusionment. I quote
unabashedly and with some approval, the caustic words of the
radical English playwright, John Arden, on Wole Soyinka, with
the qualification that his words apply not only to Soyinka but to
many of our Nigerian (and African) literary dramatists:

> I suspect that in Wole Soyinka we may be seeing a kind of
> indeterminate prodigy. His work is not exactly rootless—but it has
> an awkward double root—one half in Europe and one half in
> Nigeria. It may be that one half-root is set in dry sand and the

other in fertile soil. Western official culture—as taught in our universities and at the Royal Court Theatre—has nothing of lasting benefit to say to Africans or Indians or anyone else in the Third World. The most that can be learned, I suspect, is some degree of *technique*. Wole Soyinka has learnt this—and learnt it very well. But it is becoming more and more evident every year that the ultimate end of such technique is going to be the improvement of revolution in the Third World, and nothing else. The revolution will be both national and international and directed against continued Western exploitation, both economic and *cultural*. Wole Soyinka is a very skillful dramatist: but historically he is a half-way house. It is the plays from West Africa of the next generation which will make his position clear to us. But if he survives, he may well be writing them himself.[15]

The wager, then—a historical wager—is that the brilliant "modernist" techniques of our contemporary literary drama will take root in popular subsoil, will be disciplined by a compulsion to place the truths of the times in the hands of the decisive popular masses. One thinks here of Brecht's unforgettable dictum on the need, not only for an acute intelligence to perceive truth, but also for the cunning to know in whose hands it will be useful and practical. This means that our best creations in literary drama, the works attaining to profound levels of social, cultural and historical truth, will speak directly to wide, popular audiences, without engendering befuddlement, confusion or even hostility from them. Many creations of contemporary Nigerian literary drama, such as *Kongi's Harvest, The Road, Madmen and Specialists* and *Opera Wonyosi* by Wole Soyinka, *The Raft* by J. P. Clark, *The Road to Ibadan* by Elechi Amadi, *Afamako* and *The Night Before* by Bode Sowande, Femi Osofisan's *The Chattering and the Song, Once Upon Four Robbers*, and *Who's Afraid of Tai Solarin*? do not retreat from the social convulsions and crises which have wracked the Nigerian state and society. And even those plays that use the ritualistic and mythological inspiration of folk and oral traditions like *Ozidi, Dance of the Forests* and *The Gods are Not to Blame* do also show an acute concern with urgent contemporary issues. But precisely because they have not been consciously written for and about the popular urban and rural masses, these crucial groups and classes play a passive, almost invisible role in these plays. And these plays have all, more or less, been heavily imbued with a mood and spirit of despair, disillusionment, and even sometimes with a savage, cynical, misanthropic vision. The literary drama will become popular theatre only if and when the popular audiences see themselves, their concerns and aspirations sharply and movingly reflected in this drama.

The practical note on which I want to end this short essay is that the literary drama, to really become popular, must literally move out of the universities in which it is still largely confined. The recently formed "Guerilla Unit" of the Dramatic Arts Department of the University of Ife is one step in this direction.[16] If this move really takes place in a more decisive way, we shall soon be talking of a very different literary drama in Nigeria.

Postscript, 1980

Going over this essay again, I find that certain issues of its political perspectives need to be made more explicit. In precise terms, I want to emphasize the dimension of class consciousness behind the surface populist perspective of the essay. It is one thing to call for a popular literary drama, a drama which deals with the great popular, democratic issues of our society, and which plays to the popular urban and rural masses; it is another thing entirely to say that such a drama can only emerge from, and be strengthened by a conscious class analysis of our society. This second point is not clearly expressed in the essay. And it is a point that increasingly needs to be stated and re-stated, given the present direction of our society, and the tendency of many of our writers (and critics) to scoff at a mention of their class perspectives or outlook.

We must rid our present literary, theatrical and critical culture of its wilful, opportunistic political innocence. The post-Civil War Nigerian society is a society of sharpening class cleavages; and the grains of sand are running out quickly in its social and historical hour-glass. One must now go beyond the call for plays, poems, novels and critical writings which embrace popular causes or reveal a democratic spirit. At the present moment the organized urban working class in Nigeria stands at about four million, the largest in black Africa. The rural peasantry is not as well-organized, but it is not invisible either. And every day the national press highlights, even if only inadvertently, the increasing restiveness of the vast, seething urban unemployed subproletariat. A popular drama in Nigeria at the present time cannot but emerge from a conscious, critical and creative class analysis of such phenomena as these.

Notes

1. See, for instance, Vera Mowry Roberts' *On Stage*, New York, Harper & Row, 1962, or Richard Southern's *The Seven Ages of The Theatre*, New York, Hill & Wang, 1961.
2. *The Frogs*, edited by Gilbert Murray, London, George Allen & Unwin, 1908.
3. For an account of Rotimi's work and an interview with him, see *New Theatre Magazine*, Third World Theatre issue, Vol. XII, No. 2.
4. For a controversial debate on the "elitist", "privatist" direction of much of contemporary Nigerian poetry in English see the exchange between Soyinka and Chinweizu *et al.* in *Transition* 48, Vol. 9, pp. 29–44.
5. In "Aspects of Nigerian Drama", published in the collection by the author titled *The Example of Shakespeare*, London, Longman, 1970, p. 86.
6. In "The Dead-end of African Literature" by Obi Wali, *Transition*, 10, 1963.
7. In *The Example of Shakespeare*, p. 37.
8. *The Chattering and the Song*, Ibadan University Press, 1978.
9. This play is yet unpublished but was given a lively production directed by the playwright himself in a Department of Theatre Arts, University of Ibadan production in mid-1978.
10. *New Theatre Magazine*, Third World Issue, p. 17.
11. There are useful accounts of contemporary Nigerian theatre in both the already cited *New Theatre Magazine* issue and the revised edition of Gerald Moore's *Wole Soyinka*, Evans Brothers Ltd., 1978.
12. Soyinka has some interesting and revealing things to say on this issue in *In Person: Achebe Awoonor and Soyinka*, ed. Karen L. Morell, Institute for Comparative and Foreign Area Studies, University of Washington, Seattle, pp. 94–107.
13. *New Theatre Magazine*, *op. cit.*, p. 11.
14. *The Example of Shakespeae*, p. 85.
15. *New Theatre Magazine*, *op. cit.*, pp. 25–26.
16. This "unit" has been touring Ife town and environs with sketches from Soyinka's latest short pieces collectively titled, *Before the Blow-up*.

Reprinted Nigeria Magazine, Nos. 127/8, 1979.

PART VI
THEATRE MANAGEMENT, ORGANIZATION & PRODUCTION

THEATRE MANAGEMENT IN NIGERIA: APPRAISAL AND CHALLENGES

Olu Akomolafe

This essay is based on a managerial examination of theatre business in Nigeria, particularly in the last two decades. It will examine the scope of expansion in terms of organization and management within the various types of theatre forms functioning in the country. It will also examine the operational methods of the Nigerian professional theatre in relation to the problems involved. The essay will not include a critique of plays, but artistic comments will be made where necessary. The role of a theatre manager in the promotion of Nigerian theatre will be extensively discussed.

There has been distinct developments in the emergence of the theatre business in Nigeria. It survived the hazards of the Nigerian Civil War and, by the close of the seventies, it had attained a remarkable growth. The movement of theatre for the business entrepreneur started with Hubert Ogunde in 1944.[1] He was commissioned in that year to produce a play as a fund-raising activity for the Church of the Lord in Lagos. It marked the beginning of the organized commercial theatre in Nigeria by a Nigerian on a fairly large scale.[2]

The director-manager system, therefore, started with Hubert Ogunde. He was the artistic director, composer, and manager of his theatre. This organizational approach was adapted by the succeeding founders of theatres like the late Duro Ladipo and late Kola Ogunmola. In spite of pioneering difficulties, they made successes of their executive posts. One of the results of their successes was the theatrical upsurge of the sixties and the seventies, an upsurge which led to the founding of several Yoruba travelling companies in the country. As at the time of writing this, there are some eighty or so theatre groups in the Southwest of Nigeria alone! Some of these groups, such as the

Duro Ladipo Theatre and Isola Ogunsola Theatre specialize in historical plays, while others such as the Ogunde Theatre built their reputation on social drama. The comedians amongst them include Moses Olaiya and his Alawada Group, The Awada Group, Papi Lolo, etc.[3]

Three features are common to all these groups. First, they all operate on commercial bases and are absolutely independent. This means, in effect, that they do not enjoy any financial assistance from the government or any funding agency. Secondly, the groups are itinerant in nature. Initially, the convention was to go on tour with two to three plays but later they finally changed to travelling with only one play. Thirdly, the companies have similar organizational set-ups. The director-manager is usually the founder of the company and is consequently the chief artistic and administrative executive. In the last few years, however, Moses Olaiya employed a full-time manager to handle the business of booking, touring arrangements, and publicity. In certain respects, this constitutes an advance in the professional theatre scene.

In 1974, an association of Nigerian theatre practitioners was formed as the first Theatrical Syndicate in Nigeria with Hubert Ogunde as the President. The purpose of this association is to meet and deliberate on theatrical professional issues in the country, and also to share ideas of common interest which will help to promote theatre in the country.

The second aspect of theatre management in Nigeria is to be found in institutions. For instance, the Department of English at the University of Ibadan, in 1962, mounted productions in its 300-seat Arts theatre as part of its practical activities. Following the success achieved with the productions, the University established a School of Drama in the 1963–64 session.[4] The purpose was to provide a training ground for future theatre artists and to organize workshops for professionals in the theatre to gain skill and experience. The late Kola Ogunmola was the guest artist at the School of Drama during the 1963–64 session and he was assisted to produce the play *The Palmwine Drinkard*, an adaptation of Amos Tutuola's novel of the same title. In 1980, the University of Ibadan finally founded a resident company.

Meanwhile, the University of Ife which was founded in 1962, started drama productions in 1966 in its Institute of African Studies.[5] The theatre company was formed in 1972 with an endowment of ₦34,000 from the University. That grant may well have been the first ever to be given by an arm of government in Nigeria towards the founding of a theatre company. The impact which the University of Ife theatre has made in and outside Nigeria is generally considered tremendous.[6] Partly as a result of this achievement, the universities of Lagos and Ibadan have founded their own resident companies in 1975 and 1980 respectively. Other institutional companies that have emerged since then are those of the Television House at Ibadan and the Arts Council in Benin City.

The problem of administrative coordination within and among these theatres demands great attention. The need has surfaced for properly trained theatre administrative executives who will relieve artistic directors of routine administrative duties. Bernard Shaw was believed to have said that it is essential for hard-minded businessmen to go around with the artistic-directors whose main duty would be to cut the production budgets by half. This was exactly what the managers of theatres did in America between 1850 and 1950. They created "a villainous, penny-squeezing, scrooge-like image of theatre managers and producers which retains a certain validity to this day".[7] Although economy remains important, a theatre manager must have other functions to perform, if live theatre is to survive and prosper according to the needs of society. In 1965, The Rockefeller Panel Report published a paper "The Performing Art: Problems and Prospects" in which it recognized these new responsibilities by defining a good arts manager as:

> "a person who is knowledgeable in the art with which he is concerned, an impresario, labor negotiator, diplomat, educator, publicity and public relations expert, politician, skilled business-man, a social sophisticate, a servant of the community, a tireless leader—becoming humble before authority—a teacher, a tyrant and a continuing student of arts."[8]

The Nigerian theatre manager, like his counterparts the world over, should be a great planner. All other management functions:

organizing, staffing, directing, and controlling are all dependent on planning. The theatre manager within the professional company or in the institutions must familiarize himself with the decision-making process and tools so that he can identify the objective of the institution, state the philosophy, define the goals and objective, outline policies and procedures, analyse, evaluate and design jobs; prepare budget to implement his plans; and, manage his time and that of the organization. The manager-director in the professional companies, like Ogunde, Moses Olaiya and Ogunsola attempt to combine all of these demands with the artistic strain of directing plays and managing the actors. The Universities of Ife and Ibadan have started to turn out trained theatre administrators who need to be employed into theatre companies.[9]

Nigerian Theatre today is confronted with problems which could be divided into two management areas. The first problem is within the companies and the second are the problems within the societies and communities. Among the internal problems of the companies are maintenance of the stability of staff; poverty; unskilled personnel, etc. The external problems are those of language differences among the peoples of Nigeria; bad roads; lack of communication links, particularly by telephone; slow mailing/postal system; very few playhouses, and lack of financial assistance.

A theatre manager confronted with the above problems would almost be frustrated. The professional manager-director today employs members of his close or distant family in his company to ensure loyalty and support. Some are known to have had as many as five wives in order to maintain a regular number of actresses to perform in the productions! One advantage of this however is that such relations would be able to endure hardships when funds run low in the company as a result of poor returns from the box office. Most actors receive their acting training in the various companies. It is hoped that in the future, there would be an appreciable number of free-lance artists who would be contracted into productions. When that happens, managers would evolve a new management approach through contracts and actors' unions, and would then design a national salary scale structure for Nigerian professional actors.

The language problem is a great barrier to the progress of theatre in Nigeria. It is, to say the least, one of the greatest inhibiting factors. There is not a single Nigerian language that cuts across the tribal borders. For instance, Yoruba, with upwards of 5,000,000 speakers is one of the major vernaculars of West Africa, but although about two-thirds of the population of the western region of Nigeria are Yoruba, and although the language has the status of being an official language, it is not used as a *lingua franca*. Somehow, English remains the more widely spoken language.

All the professional theatre groups in the Western towns perform in Yoruba, the dominant local language. They perform in such other places where there is a sizeable amount of Yoruba speaking people. This same problem goes for the Ibo and Hausa speaking areas. Because of wide distances between the available urban towns in the North and East of Nigeria theatre business is yet less prominent as compared with the situation in the West. Theatre needs a ready audience with as much proximity to the playhouse as possible. The university theatres have the college community for its audience. The University of Ife, for instance, has an indoor theatre with a capacity of 1,200 seats to cater for the teeming population of about 20,000. Within a radius of 3 kilometres, there is a potential audience of about 12,000 which represents about 60 per cent of the population. For all members of this potential audience to see a play at an average of a thousand people a night, the play would have to run for 12 days. Productions mounted on these campuses are mostly for elite audiences.

There is also the problem of communication network. Easy communication network—telephone, postal system, good roads, etc. are extremely vital to any business person. It is even more vital to a theatre manager. Patrons have to be informed of oncoming productions or changes in the programme. Patrons themselves may want to contact the box office to find out about productions and performance rates and times. Travelling theatres need good roads that are safe to travel on for their performances. Letters need to travel safe and fast from one town to the other. The situation today in Nigeria is not encouraging. The roads are unquestionably death traps and letters take about two to three weeks between distances of about sixty kilometres apart. Budgets on travel as a cost unit item are usually high because one has to travel out on the bad roads to pass on simple information on matters that could quite easily be disposed of in two seconds on the telephone.

Subscription sales system as a way of theatre promotion technique cannot be practised because of the above problems. At the Oduduwa Hall in Ife, we introduced a subscription sales system on the campus for film shows. The great advantage of the subscription system is that it helps to retain patrons to the particular theatre. To the subscriber, he/she is entitled to reduced ticket package sales and becomes a regular invitee to major events in the theatre. Familiarity is built between the theatre and the patron whose contact address is registered on the mailing list of the theatre for regular news. The system as practised at Oduduwa Hall is that a patron purchases a booklet containing ten coupons for eight Naira (₦8.00) instead of ten Naira (₦10.00). Each coupon is brought to the box office to be exchanged for the evening's valid ticket. The Patron therefore attends ten film shows for the price of eight. It has been a success and has greatly improved attendance.

Theatrical visual effects in terms of grandiose sets are uncommon in Nigerian professional theatres simply because most theatre companies are more often on the road. Instead, they use painted back cloths which today are rarely used in other parts of the world. University theatres continue to experiment on various stage sets, but they too are already adopting an open stage system.

About the greatest shortcoming in Nigerian theatre scene today is the unavailability of adequate playhouses. Theatre managers need playhouses to put up their companies and the plays. School halls, hotel lobbies and a few community centres continue to be used for productions and these are far from adequate. There will be active theatre work if there are playhouses adequately equipped for the purpose. Since the universities of Ife and Lagos completed their ultra-modern theatre buildings, recreational life on campus has improved simultaneously. There is at least a programme of either music, drama, dance or film show going on at Oduduwa Hall each evening.

It would be observed from the above that management needs are of great importance in Nigerian theatre today. The future of the Nigerian theatre has to be planned on the basis of the records of existing situations. Businessmen must be encouraged to invest in theatres by building playhouses in the major cities. There is also a need for government agencies and institutions to build more theatres. It would be possible, then, to have more non-profit theatres and a greater growth of the arts will be achieved. Companies, industries, and corporations must be prepared to give financial support to the theatre.

It is evident that most performing organizations in the world operate under constant financial strain, that their operating cost almost always exceeds their income. But anyone who is familiar with the financial records of the performing arts organizations will agree that the gap between box-office receipts and operating costs has increased in the last few years. The situation in Nigeria is one of great challenge to theatre managers to enable them to combat the existing social hazards. The problems of rising inflation, of a poor communication system, of lack of playhouses and of little or no public financial assistance, all combine to make the challenge a difficult one. In spite of these, however, the last twenty years have witnessed a remarkable development and it is certain that the situation will improve in the future if the infrastructural facilities are also improved.

Notes

1. Ebun Clark, "Ogunde Theatre: The Rise of Contemporary Professional Theatre in Nigeria 1946–72", *Nigeria Magazine*, No. 114, 1974, p. 3.
2. I am aware of Prof. Echeruo's study (which also appears in this anthology) which clearly demonstrates the presence of theatre activities in Lagos during the last half of the 19th century. But virtually all these activities were organized by what was known as the "settler population"—expatriate colonial civil servants, missionaries, several dramatic groups such as the Brazilian Dramatic Company. But even more germane to my point is the fact that these 19th century theatre groups were hardly organized on large scale commercial bases.
3. The comic groups, known largely as the "Alawada Group" were initially restricted to their Yoruba language areas. Some of them later introduced

432   DRAMA AND THEATRE IN NIGERIA

"pidgin" English which enables them to communicate beyond the Yoruba speaking areas.

4. School of Drama: Directors of School of Drama include G. J. Axworthy now of Sherman Theatre, Cardiff University; Wole Soyinka, now head of Department of Dramatic Arts, University of Ife and Joel Adedeji now head of the Department of Theatre Arts, University of Ibadan. Each of them combined the duties of artistic and administrative directors.

5. The University of Ife moved from Ibadan (its temporary site) to Ife in 1967. That year marked the beginning of real active theatre in the Institute of African Studies. The historian, Michael Crowder, was its first administrative Director, followed by Ulli Beier and Banji Akintoye. Ola Rotimi, Akin Euba and Peggy Harper were responsible for the artistic aspects of drama, music, and dance respectively. The present writer was the Institute's business manager.

6. University of Ife Theatre performed at the Cultural Olympics in Munich, Germany in 1972 and at the Senegalese National Congress in Dakar in 1972. It attended an international Black Theatre Festival in New York, in May of 1980.

7. Langley, Stephen, *Theatre Management in America*, Drama Book Specialists, New York, 1980, p. 22.

8. *The Performing Arts: Problems and Prospects*, The Rockefeller Panel Report, New York, 1965.

9. Universities of Ife and Ibadan have Certificate, Diploma and Degree programmes in Theatre Management.

MUSIC, DANCE, DRAMA AND THE STAGE IN NIGERIA

Meki Nzewi

If one ever dares to observe that drama unincorporated with music and dance is alien to the theatrical sensibilities of the unalienated Nigerian of any ethnic background, the chances are that he would be hounded, branded and written off as a heretic by our core of Euro-American-oriented literary dramatists and stage critics. But the truth remains that stage presentations not structured to, sequenced by, vected through, or tippled with music and dance or stylized movement is alien to the inherent Nigerian theatre sensibilities. And this writer is not a heretic. On the modern stage in Nigeria one notices that even the vendors of "dry" theatre do, intentionally or by instinct, implicate elements, if not "chunks", of music and dance into productions of play scripts modelled slavishly on Euro-American literary drama.

The argument is, therefore, that the idea of "dry theatre", that is, drama of un-relieved dialogue and stage movement has been adopted from the Euro-American literary stage practice. And this writer's experience in over ten years as a theatre practitioner, is that a major cross-section of the modern theatre audience in Nigeria expects modern drama for Nigerian stage to be lacquered with some degree of music and dance. What is at issue is the role and nature of such music and dance in Nigerian drama.

The music under consideration here is that found in a dramatic presentation. It must, however, be stressed immediately that music for the projection and continuity of dramatic intention has different implications from music merely inserted into a dramatic proceeding.

Dance is stylized and structured movement in time-space. In the context of Nigeria's artistic conceptions, dance involves, or at the marginal, implies music. Dance in the Nigerian traditional context, and in the context of this discussion, also includes mime,

433

gymnastics and acrobatics structured to, or orchestrated by, music.

There has been a misconception fostered by the Euro-American's inhibited evaluation of the music and dance traditions in Nigeria, and, also, of the traditional attitudes to music and dance in Africa generally. This misconception which seems to have been accepted without challenge by most Nigerian academics is that traditional music and dance as a corpus are conceptually utilitarian and only peripherally entertainment-based. At the other extreme is the average modern-educated Nigerian who, in ignorance, assesses Nigeria's traditional musics and dances by the imported Euro-American practices and thereby presumes that traditional music and dance in Nigeria are solely entertainment-based. It is important for our purposes here to point out that in most of the creative and performing arts traditions of Nigeria, there is a distinction between utilitarian dance and entertainment or "pure" dance conceptions. What has been said for dance automatically goes for music, including dance-based music types.

Begho is probably unaware of this when he observes that "Music-concert traditionally, is not encouraged as an entertainment form to delight the mind through the ears".[1] However, we are here dealing with semiotic dancing with particular reference to the stage; that is, with dance as a significant or figurative mode of communicating or promoting dramatic intention. This has been ably discussed by Begho although, the exclusively Yoruba theatre scene which informed his experiences and limited his sampling was misleadingly purported to represent Nigeria, as if modern theatre in Nigeria is exclusively a Yoruba phenomenon! Straight drama as a literary genre has obviously come to stay in our educational system. As a fledgling live-art exhibition presented primarily for its entertainment-educational value, it is, perhaps, too early to assess its acceptability beyond the pretensions of the Westernized audience-type found mainly in the universities. The term drama, and its implications, has academic distinctions for, perhaps, only the Nigerian theatre academics who seek to compartmentalize the creative dimensions of the performing arts in order to model them on Euro-American practices. The term, drama, shall be used in this essay to mean "straight" plays as well as the story-line implication of a theatre scenario. The term theatre, will be used as a gestalt, for stage works which conceptually integrate drama, music and dance. This usage will only be in distinction from drama and without excluding other definitions of the term.

The stage as a physical environment for presenting an artistic display is nothing new to the theatre sensibilities of any human society; although a people's realization of theatre is informed by their operative world view as well as social-political systems. The variations in the form and physical appurtenances of the stage, with respect to the psychological and physical rapport between the performers and the audience, are modelled by the rationalization of theatre. Where theatre goes much beyond make-believe, and is transacted as a super-ordinary coming to terms, by a community or group, with their world view and socio-political systems, the physical and psycho-spiritual rapport between performer and audience are tenuous. Where, on the other hand, theatre is conceived as a recreational celebration of life and the art of living, there is greater psycho-spiritual and physical distance between the performer and the audience. Thus, theatre as a specialized creative-interpretative process is no longer primarily a specialized mode of fraternizing with the forces and effects of the cosmos. Rather, it becomes an affected system for complimenting life. The stage, traditional and modern, in Nigeria is still in a process of shifting from the effective-affective to the impressive since most, if not all, of the traditional roles of theatre have been appropriated by the modern state and religious systems.

The implication of "Nigerian stage" remains ambiguous in the traditional sense when stage implies not only the physical venue but equally the concept, style and content of what goes on in it. On the other hand, one can cautiously talk about modern *Nigerian* stage as a feature of our modern-literary acculturation as long as it is understood that the expression is misleading if it is intended to define a uniquely *Nigerian* stage. A modern *Nigerian* stage is still a nebulous proposition. However, the only distinction necessary to this discussion is that of "traditional stage" for the corpus of ethnic diversities, and "modern stage". The discussion that follows will approach the modern stage from the perspective of the traditional practices which are still available even if only in the artistic and aesthetic dimensions.

The above definitions serve to streamline the key terms in the topic to a given context—the Nigerian contemporary scene (traditional and modern). Next, it is necessary to examine, briefly, that major malaise, the dilemma of transition, which plagues the modern Nigerian stage today. An appreciation of its nature and stresses would, perhaps, assist in focusing our thoughts and energies towards a meaningful future particularly in the modern literary genre.

A dilemma of transition has identifiable syndromes. And it could be caused by self-perpetuating conflicts: the artistic state at a given moment in a cultural history is bound to undergo a process of revision and redefinition. This occurs when theatre practitioners revamp or revolt against the status quo and evolve new trends on the quondam practices. This could be self-contained process circumscribed within a cultural homogeny; or it could be informed by consciously adopted and integrated influences from other cultures. A dilemma of transition, on the other hand, could result from a case of calculated cultural brain-washing whereby the natural cultural-artistic sensibilities of a person or a group are systematically undermined and supplanted by foreign cultural perceptions. A resurgence of the suppressed cultural-artistic sensibilities at any historical moment is inevitable if the original cultural environment is not correspondingly annihilated. Such a resurgence could result in a crises of identity.

If Nigeria's modern socio-cultural systems along with Nigerian literary theatre practices had been achieved through a process of self-generated evolution, considerations could have centred around quality and relevance. However, because modern stage practices in Nigeria, in conjunction with Nigeria's modern social, political, economic, and cultural thoughts are a menticide case, our current dilemma of transition is fraught with issues of typology, authenticity, pioneer-mania, guidepost and audience-management, along with the more pertinent considerations about relevance and quality.

The modern physical stage in Nigeria is an unimaginative transfer of the Euro-American stage but devoid of the facilities and sophistications of the latter. The need is to evolve a modern stage informed by Nigeria's traditional models and which will be central to the formulation of modern theatre types and forms that will be uniquely Nigerian. The now defunct experiment of the Ori Olokun theatre at Ife was about the one remarkable attempt to design a modern stage loyal to an authentically traditional Nigerian situation.[2] The current imported concept of theatre (both the physical stage and the dramatic literature), which is propagated with arrogance by Nigeria's literary and particularly, academic dramatists discourages culturally meaningful creative emancipation. The modern Nigerian dramatist is under constraints to fit his creative vision and perspective into learned and entrenched Euro-American models of dramatic literature and presentation. A play is not necessarily Nigerian if it discusses Nigeria's cultural milieu within the formal and typological frameworks of Euro-American plays. A play would start becoming uniquely Nigerian when the conceptual and creative approaches cast off the mental constraints imposed by acquired Euro-American standards. The result would be works resulting from the unique creative integrity of the individual and informed by the peculiar sensibilities of Nigeria's indigenous cultural-artistic practices. Such theatre works could be modelled on traditional types fashioned to keep track of Nigeria's modernizing socio-cultural environment. The problem of suitable modern venues is probably beyond the control of the dramatist since he might not be in an economic or advisory position to design and build what he needs.

The issue of authenticity has been the most distorted and contradictory in Nigeria's modern theatre scene. A lot has been written on the issue by inchoate stage critics as well as self-arrogating and, quite often, unresourceful academics who do not seem capable of discussing Nigerian creative writing, music and dance without exhibiting erudite reliance on some Euro-American writers, authors, practitioners and ideational referents. Considerations of space will not make it possible for us to rake the written and spoken forage about authenticity and Nigeria's modern stage. But it must be observed that most of the self-appointed "authorities" on authenticity have not overcome the very fundamental disabilities of subjective and ethnocentric biases, whereby what is approvable by them as authentic is primarily informed by "who did it".

It is perhaps necessary to call some attention to how others approve our authenticity. Writing about his "Reflections on Third Ife Festival", Berger does not seem to have been impressed that musical works by Akpabot and Akin Euba really did reflect Nigerian character.[3] (It must be stated emphatically in passing that there is really nothing like Nigerian musical or dance character. There are stylistic traditions and characteristics demarcated by as many homogeneous ethnic traditions as there are in Nigeria). Berger makes a pertinent observation that "the use of African drums alone does not yet make African (modern) music". Both Nigerian musicians, according to him, have made ineffective attempts at a synthesis of African and Western musical ideas. Any perceptive Nigerian who has listened to compositions by these two pioneer Nigerian literary musicians will tend to endorse Berger's observations. But then these two pioneer Nigerian literary musicians spent many formative and stabilizing years of their modern musical career being indoctrinated in the Euro-American musical traditions. Berger's observation does call greater attention to the argument about what identity we propose for modern African and Nigerian music, dance, drama, visual arts. Such arguments should explore the ramifications of material resources, media, stylistic intention, idiomatic range, form, literacy and creative integrity. Theoretical prescriptions and skirmishes are bound to issue forth. But the resolutions can only be meaningfully achieved through the availability of practical samples.

Unfortunately, and typical of an average Western patron of the African artistic and creative milieu, Berger used Europe and European cultural artistic history as his paradigm for determining and judging Nigeria's artistic trends.[4] Thus he thinks that what Europe has rejected, rightly or at periods of creative morbidity, should automatically be rejected in Nigeria as proof of our cultural loyalty and intellectual dependence on Europe and America.

A more subtle question that arises from Berger's observations is: Can the creative personality effectively exorcise himself of "any trace of foreign influence"? The creative personality in any place and period of human history has always been enriched by experiences external to his native creative-cultural heritage. When Berger laments that "the real victim" of star-artist culture is "the future African music deprived of its original flavour and its vital potency", he betrays his ignorance of the sociological realities of traditional artistry in Nigeria's ethnic societies. Practically all Nigerian ethnic societies recognize the star cult in the performing arts. What varies is the social regard accorded to such star performers. If we have our perspectives right, "future African music" would not be a victim of what is inherent in its system. There will be a continuum of its "original flavour". This implies that its creative and presentational sensibilities will be in tune with its operative cultural context; while its "vital potency" is a measure of its meaning within its contingent human environment and social-artistic aspirations.

Berger also discusses the enigma of authenticity with particular attention to dance. He gave a critical appraisal of the works and attitudes of some theatre practitioners and patrons in West Africa at the time. From his account, we find the notion of the "authentic" quite elastic. Ulli Beier's stand is that "everything is authentic which has not been influenced by Europe or the West". This definition presumes that Nigeria and, indeed, Africa has a monolithic cultural-artistic tradition. Peggy Harper, for her own part, is of the view that "the foreign dance techniques inhibits rather than develops the artist's potentiality". She thus seems to deny that exposure broadens the artist's vision and enriches his resources. Her viewpoint also tends to deny that there is a large measure of parallelism in the fundamental elements of dance movements the world over. What distinguishes dance cultures is the semiotic resources of dance gestures and styles which affect the choreographic vision. If one were to agree with Peggy Harper she would have been long out of a job in Nigeria for her integrity as a choreographer on the modern stage in Nigeria would be assessed as negative and, in fact, pernicious to the potentialities of Nigerian dancers whose development she has been inhibiting.[5]

Keita Fodeba's theoretical premise that "a spectacle is authentic when it recreates faithfully the most characteristic aspects of life which it wants to show on stage" is progressive and realistic. Some others, according to Berger, express the view that "African dances are no longer authentic as soon as they are put on stage". African dances have always been put on stage and the concept of the stage is as African as it has been any other people's. One wonders why African dances, traditional or modern, are the only ones that should lose authenticity as soon as they are put on stage. However, since modern stage is presumably implied, the view serves to stretch the argument beyond merely the artistry of dance to consider utility as an inalienable factor in dance conceptions and creativity. The argument starts losing ground when it is considered that there are two major ideo-artistic categories of traditional dances in most Nigerian ethnic societies: the Free (compositional) Medley dances of utilitarian and mass psychological formulations; and the Stylized Formation dances of primary kinematics and entertainment conceptions. In the former, psychological responses basic to the idea informing the dance, also the actor-audience and actor-actor interactions generated by the traditional stage environment, enhance individual compositions on a given theme. In the Stylized Formation dances, such responses merely affect individual dance-aesthetics. On the modern imported stage, none of the two categories would lose authenticity with respect to dance as an artistic exhibition. But a Free Medley dance would lose in interpretative and qualitative dimensions if it is staged outside the real life situation that motivates the dancers. And, anyway, the artist-audience relationship in traditional Stylized Formation dances is fairly the same as we find on the modern stage.

A creator, as different from an imitator is an authentic personality. And the audience reserves the freedom to sanction his legitimacy and relevance. Corollary to this is the recognition of phases of authenticity in a creative situation. Each phase is legitimate in its own right and its environment, given the integrity of the creative genius. These phases are: Conservative authenticity which implies conservation (static treatment) of world view in creative vision; progressive authenticity, which defines a continuum of world view in creative vision; and pragmatic authenticity which rationalizes creative philosophy according to available resources and demands. If it is possible to simulate a traditional situation for a traditional dance of any category on a modern stage, the exercise will be a retention of the conservative practice in a modern setting.

If it is possible to capture the ideational and theatrical objectives of a traditional festival drama in a modern theatre work in which the traditional characters, venues and effects are portrayed in their modern equivalents, it would be discovered that there is a continuum of the traditional dramatic aspirations in a modern dramatic situation.

And if a literary music composer effectively transfers the spirit and stylistic characteristics of traditional music into a modern composition written for Western musical instruments, it is a pragmatic achievement demanding mastery of the traditional and conventional creative ingenuities. He has rationalized the plight of the traditional musical system in the face of modern compositional aspirations and learning processes.

What has been hypothesized for one artistic discipline goes for the others. There is no doubt that there is need for the three aspects of authenticity for a richer variety and cross fertilization of ideas considering the inevitability of Nigeria's contemporary socio-cultural milieu.

Pioneer-mania could be defined as the wilful tendency for those older and more strategically entrenched in the artistic professions to undermine and suppress the genius of their younger enterprising contemporaries as a strategy to protect their unviable positions at the top of the modern bureaucratically manipulated creative and performing arts environment. Pioneer-mania, with its allied ego-cult syndrome, is an inhibitory factor in the realization of true and dynamic modern Nigerian theatre (drama, music, dance) and the plastic and decorative arts. Consumer-approved artistic leadership and viable schools of creative ideology/style is achieved in an atmosphere of free, open, competitive, creative and theatrical enterprise. Instead, the modern Nigerian creative and performing arts scene is rife with destructive dimensions of personal as well as group insecurity;

and is being subverted, particularly, by a growth-deterrent doctrine of "the first on the scene should remain the best and
only"—in a creative environment that is starved of competent
manpower!

There is also the issue of guide-post, of a sense of direction;
this will not be resolved until there is sufficient productivity to
enable a perceptive audience to pick the gems from the trumpery
in a true traditional style. One of the most unhealthy trends in
Nigeria's modern stage practice is the wholesale importation of
the practice of the professional critic who wedges himself between the audience and the artist/creator. But the common
instances of our audience directly signalling their approval or
disapproval of an on-going stage presentation through spontaneous verbal and other behavioural responses are most encouraging. As long as the audience remains the focus and the consumer
of modern theatre creations, it should, as in traditional practice,
retain the right and clout to guide creators and artists towards a
relevant sense of direction in our search for modern theatre
suitable for a modern Nigeria.

The next logical dilemma is audience-management. This is an
aspect of theatre development which is relatively unstudied and
generally neglected in practice. Audience-management is taking
cognizance of the behavioural tendencies and trends of a given
audience type in designing and building presentation venues; as
well as in creating and producing stage works. The search for the
ideal modern theatre should be informed by the traditional
audience sensibilities which have survived, encouragingly, in our
modern, albeit inadequate, stage situation. The ideal Nigerian
audience has the tendency to function as a structural and integrated feature of a presentation.

The current aspirations of Nigeria's literary dramatists to create
an audience behaviour modelled on the Western reserved and
detached audience type is a testimony to our mental slavery to
Euro-American cultural ideals which, thank God, in the case of
theatre audience type, is beginning to crumble. Our ideal model
should be an audience that is emphatically and spontaneously
involved to the extent of contributing effectively and structurally to
a presentation and to the healthy growth of the arts.

Drama with integrated music and dance is not a novel concept in theatre. The concept has a number of typological names depending on the degree of integration, and the social/historical/thematic setting, hence opera, musical, music-drama, dance-drama, opera-drama, etc. In line with the approach adopted so far (the appraisal of the modern stage in Nigeria from the perspective of the traditional theatrical heritage) the following analyses and proposals will derive from traditional models. Our concern will not be a survey of the effectiveness and shortcomings of the attempts so far made to involve music and dance of some sort in drama productions on the modern stage in Nigeria. Rather, two theatre models, one traditional, the other modern, will be analysed to furnish the framework for proposing the unique modern Nigerian ideal. The two theatre works selected for this exercise are *Ikaki—The Tortoise Masquerade* as the traditional model, and *The Lost Finger* as the modern literary model.

The theme of *Ikaki* is a socio-spiritual communion—a drama of mythical conflict based on the Kalabari world view about the tortoise. *Ikaki* is a reduction to life-plane dimensions of a mythical confrontation between Ikaki, the tortoise, and the Kalabari people of Oloma. The idea furnishing this theatre type is concerned with coping with calamitous elements/forces/experience through humouring and harmonizing their effective/affective nature. Thus, a serious, in fact, tragedic theme, has, in the case of *Ikaki* been given a most light-hearted, almost burlesque, treatment as theatre presentation. In Horton's own words "the play tames the disturbing experiences that inspire it by a subtle distortion of their content".[6] This is not always the pattern for we do find that other festive-drama ideas of similar scope like the New Year festival drama receive serious psychological treatments for reasons of different audience (community)—commitments to the resolution of the drama, a resolution which could be catastrophic in actual day-to-day-life proportions.[7]

Having been reduced to tangible interactional proportions the *Ikaki* scenario provides massed communal entertainment through sequences of comic anecdotes, character sketches, music and dance sketches all unified by the consistency of characters and the idea that furnished the theatre. Although every feature and sequence of this integrated theatre may be sketchy or symbolic, it succeeds in teleprompting the associated story and values. There is no elaboration of plot as such because the story line and messages are popular knowledge among the citizenry by virtue or acculturation.

The presentation involves three uni-axial planes of participants (see diagram 1). Central to the presentation is the core spirit-actors who are masked characters. These principal role-actors, five in number, have *Ikaki*, the star, portrayed ambivalently as the hero and the villain.

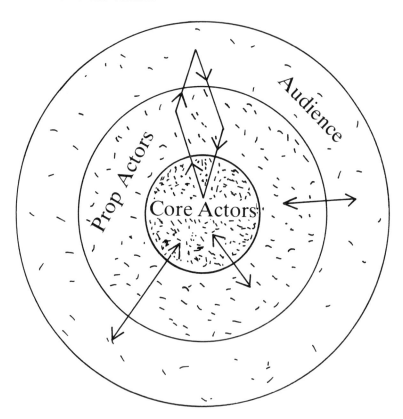

Fig. 1: Ikaki Festival Drama: Uni-axial plans of participation.

On the middle plane are the "prop"-actors or "chorus". They are members of the Ekine society which sponsors and stages the drama. They are fully integrated audience-actors who act as the psycho-dramatic link between the core spirit-actors and the community that patronizes the myth.

On the peripheral plane of participation is the empathic audience—the community present whose vocal interaction and other behavioural participation help to determine the super-structural elaborations of the scenario. The details of this elaboration would be different on every occasion of presentation but the substance would be the same. Their main contribution to the enaction is to spur the artistic-aesthetic spectrum of the acting.

The locations for the various episodes shift to natural venues some of which could be symbolized or simulated. The two days festival drama has the following timing, locations and scenario in its programmes:

Programme	Location	Scenario
Announcement the Night Before	1.	Publicity through music and final preparations for role actors
PRELUDE		
1st Day—Morning	2. Community Common Ground (C.C.G.)	Rallying to the Venue: Coded communication through music
	3. Club House (Dressing Room) to C.C.G.	Dance parade: Character portrayal through dance and costume
PART I	4. Waterside	1st Episode: sketched through mime and music
1st Day—Midday	5. C.C.G.	Theme-dancing (symbolic dance patterns to teleprompt the mythical background) with supporting slapstick anecdotes
	6. C.C.G.	Multiscene: 2nd Episode through musicalized dialogue with slapstick anecdotes as side scenes

Programme	Location	Scenario
AFTERNOON INTERMISSION (REST)		
PART 2	7. C.C.G.	Slapstick anecdotes to music background
	8. Simulated forest in C.C.G.	3rd Episode sketched through mime
1st Day—Evening	9. C.C.G.	Slapstick anecdotes, dance and coded musical messages
	10. C.C.G. to Club House	Recession
BREAK—NIGHT THROUGH 2ND DAY MORNING		
PART 3	11. C.C.G.	Dance sketches and musicalized dialogue
	12. Symbolized palm tree in C.C.G.	4th Episode sketched through mime and song
2nd Day—Evening	13. C.C.G.	Comic strip through dance-mime
	14. C.C.G.	5th Drama sketch through mime and music
	15. C.C.G. to Club House	Valediction—Recession and Song

The dramatic intentions which inform the artistic conceptions, and by implication the perceivable utilization of music and dance as specialized modes of dramatization in theatre, result in features of music and dance fundamental to the structural continuity of the story line. In the *Ikaki* drama we find various features of music integral to the scenario or significant in the development of the plot: A special slit-down orchestra plays specific melorhythmic patterns recognized as *ikaki* melorhythms to publicize the event . . . "There is another symbolic melorhythmic pattern termed *ikaki ada* to which the spirit-actors do symbolic and character-portraying dances . . ." Ekine members present Ikaki with a drum which he plays at the climax of the first episode at the waterside "apparently attempting to urge his crew on after the fashion of a war-canoe orchestra".

There is a dirge, "half-whistled and half sung in high falsetto" which *Ikaki* uses to enact "one of the many tricks for which he is famous in Kalabari stories". There are drummer–*Ikaki* confrontations (musically encoded vs. verbal language) which propel the plot: "the Drum Master blends into his (melorhythm) a mixture of admiring and abusive epithets". "Ikaki alternately tries to hoodwink the towns-people and takes to his bosom or hurls back the epithets of the drummer". There is also another figurative melorhythmic pattern, *Egepu*, which "alludes to the fact that Ikaki is not only a hunch back, but also suffers from elephantiasis of the scrotum".[8] The Drum Master's role, by the special nature of its centrality to the dramatic process, is conceived as that of a principal protagonist. He is the only human principal who belongs to the same plane as the core spirit-actors. And his role is not only confrontational but is equally vital to the timing and explanation of the sequences: "the Drum Master gives gentle hints" to end an act; "the Drum Master beats the head-hunting rhythm" to explain and orchestrate one of *Ikaki's* mime sketches. But for his role to be an effective factor in the unfolding of the story/theme, the audience must be able to comprehend his drum-language. Given a community/audience that cannot understand his drum language, his role would no longer be effective, perhaps affective. And the scenes in which music is featured as a vector of dramatic action—a "speaking" propellant of the story sequence—will be incomprehensible.

As with music we also find dance fundamental to the ideational formulation as well as the thematic development of the *Ikaki* drama. The theatre itself originated from the consequences of a mytho-mystical dance. Many people died as a result of a special dance pattern executed by *Ikaki* during his last appearance in Oloma. And "after a while, a few people who were left thought they would like to imitate Ikaki's wonderful dancing". After consulting "the great oracle of Chuku . . . they began to put on the Ikaki play".

Dance and movement motifs are used for character delineation: Ikaki "comes out with a canny, mincing step", Nimiaa Poku "gambols and tumbles", Kalagidi dances "with a more elegant, less mincing step than his father (Ikaki)". Dance patterns are employed as symbolic elements to sketch the theme of the drama: the pattern of a specific dance sequence "commemorates Ikaki's death-dealing dance before the people of Oloma". There are dance features used for developing the relationship between actors: "He joins her in the suggestive pelvic dance known as *egepu*, whilst the Drum Master hurls out a torrent of admiring and abusive epithets"; and for direct actor-audience confrontation: Ikaki responds (to the drummer's prompting) "with a bawdy pelvic dance, taking out his enormous testicles . . . (represented by a wooden slit-gong) and shaking them at the women (in the audience). The latter retreat with shrieks of mock horror, followed by requests to see more". There are mood dances: "Poku rejoices at his escape and dances happily". There is also processional dancing to introduce or remove the actors from the stage.

The audience has already been identified as active-participants at their own level in the design and plotting of the scenario, its locations and dramatic interaction. A few instances of their structural relevance to both the development of the drama and the extempore elaboration of the artistic spectrum of the sequences will be illuminating. The audience is elastic and mobile, thus encouraging change of natural venues: "The crowd follows (the core actors) in high spirits" to the waterside. The audience participates as "chorus" to cue the core actors as well as enjoy themselves—enjoyment and relaxation being very important ideational considerations in the conception and design of the theatre: "The onlookers, crowded at the water's edge abuse (Nimiaa Poku) joyously" and that alerts him to take remedial action; "the boat is soon in danger of . . . drifting away toward the sea. The onlookers start to shout warnings". The audience engages in spontaneous verbal confrontation with the core-actors: as Ikaki moves round the square trying to convince everyone about the genuineness of his "put-on", the onlookers "tell him laughingly that the king's children are out of town". The audience determines, by their vocal and other non-verbal behavioural participation, how known sequences are elaborated at the artistic-aesthetic level: "Egged on by the audience (members of the ekine society) flirt and pinch (Aboita's) tender parts"; "the ekine people mill around beneath (Ikaki who is on top of a 'palm tree') and encourage him with their cheers". Ikaki announces that he is going to kill an elephant and "the crowd makes various incredulous noises".

In the *Ikaki* theatre we find drama, music, dance and mime structurally unified in the ideational and artistic realization of a theatre presentation; and the audience behave not only as consumers (entertained patrons), but also as contingent, even if structurally peripheral, factors needed for the unfolding of the drama at both the ideational and enaction levels.

The production brochure for *The Lost Finger* announces it as a "folk mythological opera cinema-drama" which "investigates the vitality of the interaction between the (traditional) society and the supernatural. Also the unrecorded but dynamic role of the fraternity of itinerant warriors".

It is an opera-drama conceived and designed for a modern stage and recommends the following locations: Chief's court, a maiden's room, forest environment, bush path, community common ground and battle camps. It is a literary drama in English lasting about three hours at a stretch, and has the following programme of locations and scenario.

Programme	*Location*	*Scenario*
Announcement		Mood music, orchestral, to establish the atmosphere
PROLOGUE	1. Picnic Grounds	Statement of the myth, the supernatural theme, through vocal-orchestral recitative, mime sketches and song (aria).
	2. Battle Camp	Establishment of the sub theme, the social-political theme of love and war, through music and dance.
ACT I	Scene 1 Chief's Court	Statement of the theme-plot[1] through dialogue
	Scene 2 Maiden's room	Statement of the major plot[2] through song and dialogue
	Scene 3 Forest	Development of the major plot through dialogue

Programme	Location	Scenario
ACT II	Scene 1 Maiden's room	Development of the major plot through dialogue and song
	Scene 2 Forest/Bush path	Development of the major plot through dialogue
	Scene 3 Maiden's room	Development of the major plot through song and dialogue
	Scene 4 Forest	Development of the major plot through dialogue
ACT III	Scene 1 Chief's Court	Development of the theme-plot through dialogue
	Scene 2 C.C.G.	Development of the theme-plot through song and dance
	Scene 3 Battle Camp	Development of the theme-plot through dialogue, song, dance and mime
	Scene 4 Battle Camp	Concurrent climax of the theme-plot and major plot through dialogue, music, movement, and valediction through song and dance
EPILOGUE	1. Chief's Court	Conclusion through dialogue
	2. Forest	Recapitulation of the myth through orchestrated recitative and song (aria)

1. The theme-plot investigates the rationalization of the supernatural factors as they bear on human fortunes.
2. The major plot investigates the fairly mundane human intrigues in a love and marriage situation.

Conceived as a literary theatre, the story is carried primarily in a written dialogue and written song texts. But the music and dance which are integrated with drama in the overall conception and elaboration of the scenario are structural, and also significant elements in the unfolding of the story line.

The musical features and role in the dramatic enaction have been written into the dialogue as song texts or otherwise stipulated in the scripted directives. The actual music recommended for stage productions of the script has been written and scored for an orchestra of Western and traditional musical instruments. In the stage productions of *The Lost Finger* we find that specific musical sketches (music motifs) in the written music score have been used to depict and announce the dominating character— Wentu the Fortune Teller; to establish environments like the court; as effects to enhance psychological situation: "crashes and clashes of weird music". Musical ideas embodied in the dialogue give additional emotive and motive projection to dramatic intentions as when Wentu sings: "Close your ears to my music/For its melodies excite madness"; or when Chief Ebube calls for action and orders: "Shout the war cries/Sound the horns!/Beat the war drums/. . . Let the war drummers tune their drums/And clean their flutes/And let the minstrels sing the praises of our ancestors"; and then he goes on to sing: "Resound the battle drums . . . This is the brave men's song/It is the patriot's song."[9] Symbolic musical sketches are used to marshal events. An example is "Action music" for wrestling sequences. In other instances, special musical characteristics or songs are contrived to carry psychological tension or to anticipate the nature of dramatic activity in scenes or sequences.

In the recitative sections, there are music-verbal dialogues although not exactly in the sense we find the technique used in the *Ikaki* theatre. Here the human voice carries all the textual lines of the dialogue while the orchestrated musical idioms prompts the actor in the manner of questions, answers and interjections.

The music score is written original composition informed by traditional compositional techniques, musical characteristics, and idiomatic and dramatic communications through music. In order to achieve the precise structural intentions prescribed in the script, the artistic conception and the production-vision for the music have recommended the transfer of traditional musical characteristics to Western orchestral instruments—a combination of progressive and pragmatic phases of authenticity. Thus, the performance of the music and the opera-drama, in keeping with modern stage practices, will not be limited to localized audience as is the case with the *Ikaki* theatre (for reasons of incomprehensible features of location-specific elements in the style and technique). Total time of musical presence in the three-hours production is over ninety minutes.

Figurative dance sequences have been structured into the opera-drama, although no specific dance scores have been written. The choreographic patterns used in the production of the performances were designed to capture the moods and character-traits of the different groups of combatants as stipulated in the script: "Obaladike and his warriors *erupt* on stage and *dominate* the stage and audience with demonstrative battle actions, chanting"; "Jarawa arrives on stage with his warriors *looking as fierce and dangerous* as his REPUTATION . . . He *darts* up and down the stage with *precise* and organized *checks*", etc.

Whereas in the *Ikaki* theatre everybody present is expected to be an involved participant of some sort—everybody contributes to the enaction at various levels of dramatic activity, in the performance of *The Lost Finger* the audience was constrained by the physical environment of the available, manageable halls as well as the tight form of the written script to be a passive audience.

We are not concerned here with the success or failure of the two models analysed above, that is, as theatre presentation. The exercise illustrates the fundamental consonances and distinctions in scope, design and form between a typical integrated traditional theatre and a typical, tradition-informed, integrated modern theatre. By "integrated", we imply a synthesis of dramatic dialogue, music, dance and mime as theatre. Some questions do arise, the answers to which will be points to the role music and dance should be expected to play in the modern *Nigerian* stage. Three of these questions are: 1. Could the theatre models have been presented effectively without the involved music and dance? Or, could the dramatic intentions—the story line and supporting actions—in the plots have been effectively communicated without the agencies of music and dance? 2. Would the ideational formulation and the dramatic intentions and messages remain unaltered if the specified music and dance are dropped or replaced with totally different music and dance types or creations? 3. To what degree would audience-interests be sustained in the absence of music and dance in the two theatre presentations? The answer to the first question is definitely "NO" with respect to the *Ikaki* theatre. For in that mythological festive drama we find specific ideas, messages, formulae, and dialogue-sequences encoded in, signified or symbolized through, music and dance. Furthermore, practically all action-sequences are structured on, and propelled by, music and dance. In *The Lost Finger* the answer is equally "NO" because the conceptual approach to the designing of the drama has musical basis. Although there are sections that are carried in straight dialogue, there are other scenes and sequences that can only be effectively transacted through music and dance. The dramatic intention will not be interest-sustaining if the music and dance elements are eliminated unless there is a major rescripting or adaptation of the entire script.

The second question deals with the communication of dramatic intentions or ideas which in the case of *Ikaki* theatre are uncompromisable musical and choreographic processes. Different musical and dance compositions would signal different ideational intentions and dramatic meaning. Thus, although the same theatre proceeding could transpire, the story would be different, in fact incomprehensible without complete audience re-education. Even then, the essence and relevance of the presentation to the community-audience would be incomplete. A new drama involving the same cast would automatically evolve. The stipulated music and dance are thus concept-exclusive. With respect to *The Lost Finger* in which the plot is carried primarily in the dialogue and song texts, absence of the music and dance essence would merely result in a sensually impoverished presentation. Change of the original music and dance scores would not necessarily affect the message or the effectiveness of a production if the new compositions retain the spirit of the dramatic intentions prescribed for music in the script. This would be the case in any theatre productions in which the music and/or dance is personalized (original written creations by an individual or a group), and therefore not popular knowledge/heritage of communal significance. Thus, whereas the dramatic essence of the prescribed music and dance sequences are concept-exclusive, the actual artistic-aesthetic derivation of such music and dance are optional.

The third question deals with the consumer-appeal, that is, the audience-commitment to the implications of music and dance being fundamental to audience approval of a presentation. In the *Ikaki* drama, the music and dance act as the ideational-artistic focus of interest as well as the vectors of dramatic intention; in other words, as the soul and body of the presentation. The emphasis is not necessarily on the soul, the artistic-aesthetic merits of the music and dance, but on their utilitarian and emotional effectiveness (the body). In the absence of the music and dance there will be very minimal consumer-aesthetic focus (the soul) for the audience at the rarefied level of comprehension and entertainment. Music and dance also act as vehicles for promoting dramatic intention at the fundamental level (the body) of comprehension and entertainment. Thus, music and dance give soul to, while propping the body of, the production. A lot of attention would therefore need to be paid to the qualitative merits of the music and dance in their own rights as artistic accomplishments within the overriding context of the production. For slightly different reasons, absence of an action-effective as well as qualitative music and dance will greatly reduce consumer-interest.

It would seem from the foregoing considerations that a typical traditional dramatic theatre differs from an average literary drama with integrated music and dance (be it a music-drama, an opera, a dance-drama, a musical, a play with explanatory music and dance in any modern stage anywhere in the world) in two significant factors: elaboration of plot, which is dictated by the audience-background and the audience-projection that informed the creation. (The plot of a literary theatre type is personal to the author and is aimed at a heterogeneous audience background; the plot of a traditional drama type is popular knowledge within a closed community-audience which sponsors and patronizes it). The other factor is the fundamental utilitarian-commitment which binds the community-audience, almost compulsively to its traditional theatre. They are psychologically and, often existentially affected by its fulfilment. This type of tenuous commitment to the implications and resolution (simulated or real-life) of a theatre presentation is absent in modern theatre.

If we are then to approve that *The Lost Finger* as a modern Nigerian drama satisfied the distinctions of being ideationally modelled on traditional drama as an artistically integrated theatre of dramatic dialogue, music and dance, and almost accept that the artistic merits as well as the semiotic intentions aspired after in the music and dance have fulfilled essential dramatic intentions (again as found in traditional drama), then, perhaps we are now in a position to furnish the following propositions on our topic.

Music and dance as featured in some of the drama presented on Nigeria's modern stage are merely atmospheric intermezzo which interrupt rather than propel the process of dramatic intention. As an example a traditional dance exhibition inserted in a court scene which is irrelevant to the story-line, is inessential; whereas figurative music establishing a court scene is a structural-essential.

At a more relevant level (that is, to the plot and dramatic action), music and dance can be featured as dramatic extension. An instance is an insertion of a choir of dance maidens escorting a bride home without any structured incident to make the music and dance sequence essential to the plot.

The ideal role for music and dance in drama, based on our traditional models, should be that of ideational and structural relevance to the dramatic intention. Music and dance should be synthesized and symbiotic factors conceived for projecting and propelling the plot, or used to sustain dramatic action, or to enhance the dramatic presence of an actor, location, or to evoke a psychological moment.

These recommendations are pertinent as theoretical propositions. For effective application any music or dance used (whether original compositions or adaptations) must of relevance convey the artistic-aesthetic characteristics of music and dance of the human environment and the socio-cultural sensibilities pre-scribed by the theme, plot and script (if available). This proposition is viable for any modern *Nigerian* dramatic theatre work without prejudice to its world view which could be based on traditional, modern or universal theme/s. Finally, the creative personality must assert his integrity; and the audience will approve his genius.

Notes

1. F. O. Begho, "The Dance in Contemporary Nigerian Theatre: A Critical Appraisal", in *Nigerian Journal of Humanities*, No. 2, 1978, pp. 18–33.
2. The Ori-Olokun was a performing arts group started in 1968 at the University of Ife, Institute of African Studies. The idea of the Ori-Olokun, under the direction of Ola Rotimi, was to provide opportunity for the intermingling of practising, so-called "unlettered", performers with university-trained performers in a creative atmosphere, far removed from the secluded atmosphere of the university set-up. To this end, a former hotel/court-yard building, situated in the heart of Ife town, was appropriately converted into a theatre-in-the-round and renamed Ori-Olokun Centre. It remained for over five years a vibrant cultural centre, successfully bringing together town folks and the university community in what was definitely a unique example of theatrical experimentation. With the dissolution of the University's Institute of African Studies in 1975 and the upgrading of some of the players in the Ori-Olokun group to permanent membership of the University staff, the centre went defunct in 1976 and the newly formed Unife theatre took over the functions of the Ori-Olokun players (Editor).
3. R. Berger, "Reflections on Third Ife Festival", *Nigeria Magazine*, No. 106, 1970, pp. 186–198.
4. R. Berger, "African and European Music", in *Nigeria Magazine*, No. 92, 1967, pp. 87–92.
5. In fact, Ms. Peggy Harper left Nigeria, for good, in June of 1978! (Editor).
6. Robin Horton, "Ikaki, The Tortoise masquerade", *Nigeria Magazine*, No. 94, 1967, pp. 226–239. All reference to *Ikaki* in the essay refers to this piece by R. Horton.
7. Robin Horton, "Changing the year—A traditional Festival", *Nigeria Magazine*, No. 67, 1960, pp. 258–274. See also the following essays: O. Nzekwu, "Carnival at Opobo", *Nigeria Magazine*, No. 63, 1959, pp. 302–319. Meki Nzewi, "African Traditional Theatre", *Nigeria Magazine*, Nos. 127–128, 1979.
8. Horton, *op. cit.*, pp. 228–231.
9. Meki Nzewi, *The Lost Finger*, Enugu, Nwamife Publishers (in print), 1980.

TOWARDS A TRUE THEATRE
Wole Soyinka

There were strange theatrical sights in Kampala. Two marvels essentially—a theatre (the structure), and a performance. That I elect to call attention to these two excruciating events is not because I wish to denigrate the efforts of an obviously prestige conscious community, but to indicate the dangers of resigning the initial impetus for a creative institution to the death kiss of passionate amateurs. The building itself is an embodiment of the general misconception of the word "theatre". Theatre, and especially, a "National Theatre", is never the lump of wood and mortar which architects splash on the landscape. We heard of the existence of a National Theatre and ran to it full of joy and anticipation. We discovered that there was no theatre, there was nothing beyond a precious, attractive building in the town centre. But even within that narrow definition of the word, we had expected an architectural adventurousness—Kampala is after all, a cosmopolis—so we felt justified in expecting from the theatre, not only a sense of local, but of international developments in the theatrical field. What we found was a doll's house, twin-brother to our own National Museum. There were cushioned spring-back seats—I approved this, having nothing against comfort—but it was disconcerting to find a miniature replica of a British provincial theatre, fully closed in—another advantage this, extraneous noise at least was eliminated; there were vast corridors round the auditorium (for gin and the attendant small talk), the total corridor space was more than the auditorium; the toilets were sumptuous—there were good reasons for this we soon found, understanding for the first time the meaning of a wet performance. The stage? Well, no one could complain of the efficiency. And there were large rehearsal rooms located in the theatre whose constant utilization appeared to be classed in Ball-room Dancing, led by Indians in 22-inch bottom trousers.

There was one more sample of "atmospherics". Lining the walls of the foyer were posters (from *Look Back in Anger* and earlier) which made you think that the New Shakespeare Theatre Company was touring East Africa. A closer look reveals however that these posters are three years older than the completed theatre. And photographs of Richardson, Olivier and others of the Old Brigade—tarnished slightly from a long stand in the agents' shop-windows of Piccadilly, provided the last word in imitativeness without the substance.

We were, however, fairly honest, and we soon fell to minding the beam in our own eyes. There is the Arts Theatre of our University College, Ibadan which possesses not even the outward deception of the Kampala structure, and cannot boast practicalities such as ventilation or sound-proofing. As if the original crime was not enough, a grant of some thousand of pounds was expended, as recently as a year ago (1961) on new curtains and a few symbols of theatrical "arrival". Interference from student radiograms and cross-balcony yells did not activate the financial imagination into worthier ways of spending this money. Motorcars, indifferent to inadequate barriers, continue to punctuate the actor's lines with roar. It did not matter that audience enjoyment was, and still is, constantly punctured by arid saxophone blasts from a competing highlife ball. No, not all these considerations could persuade the controlling committee to spend the grant on erecting a barn somewhere beyond the depredations of college neighbourliness, disembowelling the present hulk entirely and transferring the gadgets to the new, adaptable space where actor and audience may liberate their imagination.

For it still astonishes me that those who planned the University had the sense to isolate the chapels from the distractions of the ungodly, but not the foresight to place the theatre beyond the raucousness of student lungs.

And yet, there is the irony. There is a larger sense of theatre here, even of a National Theatre, than we found in Kampala. Of the two shows which we saw there, the less said the better. In Ibadan at least, the students, in spite of frequent misguidedness, have at last taken the theatre to the people. This has been due to the dedication of one or two staff members especially. Conscious, one hopes, of the static imposition of the Arts Theatre, they developed sufficient enthusiasm among the student dramatic team to undertake two highly successful tours of folk theatre. It is irrelevant that the plays from which the plays were adapted came from European theatre, the success of transformation could be judged from each performance through Ilesha to Enugu and Port Harcourt. This was some compensation for the long tradition of formalism in university theatre.

Every event in the theatre, every genuine effort at creative communication, entertainment, escapism, is for me, entirely valid. It is very easy to sniff for instance at the efforts of the Operatic Groups.[1] What one must regret is the atmosphere of sterility and truly pathetic preciosity that it seems to breed. For it must never be forgotten that the opera was written for a certain society; recreating that society in Ibadan, causing an "opera expectation" in attitudes is sheer retardation. I am not of course trying to create a morality for theatrical selectiveness. *The Merry Widow* has its place even in the Nigerian scene as a piece of exoticism; the crime is that it is the forces of *The Merry Widow* which have upheld what we may call the Arts Theatre mentality. In the triumph of the Anouilh puff-ball tradition lies the perpetuation of the atrocity, lies the constriction of venturesome rarities like the musical *Lysistrata*—that show would, I contend, have been even more imaginative but for the symbolized tradition of the Arts Theatre. The medium of the Arts proscribed true experiment—the result was a cheap English musical all over again, rescued however by genuine effort.

By all means, let us be accommodating—and I say this genuinely—there is room anywhere, and at any stage of development, for every sort of theatre. But when Anouilh and (for God's sake!) Christopher Fry—and Drew in true fusion of the Monolithic World—possess audience mentality and budding student talent in traps from which the British theatre is only slowly extricating itself, then it is probably time for a little intolerance against the octopine symbol of the Arts Theatre. If there appears to be some exaggeration in this, let me merely point out the theatrical age of the local critic, who, on seeing an example of simple space exploitation exclaims in disgust that it is very amateurish for actors to run in and out of the audience! This notice went on to say, ". . . admittedly the Museum grounds are not very suitable for a dramatic performance, in that case it would have been simpler for this group to find a hall in Lagos where their plays can be staged more conveniently."

When the leading university proudly exhibits and reinforces the Perpendicular theatre, it is hardly surprising that the faithful twice-a-term weekend-pilgrim will resent any invasion of his audience privacy!

There is the future, of course, which is what we are really talking about all the time. The only answer to the Perpendicularians was obvious to me from the start—construct an opposition plane. This has always proved more effective than bickering, and this of course still remains the only aim of tentative theatrical movements in the country. But it has become necessary to resort to words because, while the material facilities appear to elude the opposition, they practically beg to be abused at the hands of the in-breeders. One hears rumours of ambitious schemes for propagating—again that dirty word—culture! And the prestige symbol is again, as always, a "National Theatre". Since I saw the foundations, I have not dared to move near the completed theatre at Nsukka. Before the "theatre" of the Nigerian College of Arts, Science and Technology, was built, the designers pilgrimaged to the then University College, Ibadan, to seek inspiration from the Arts Theatre. In vain did a few harrowed producers plead with them to avoid repetition of existing crime—a replica was built and the "Arts" was superseded in drabness and tawdry. J. K. Randle Hall now—the latest boil—would some imagination have cost it more? And these abortions will continue to rise all over the country, offensive to the eye and repressive of the imagination. It is surely because the structure controls even manipulates the artist that it is more sensible to assist first of all the creative theatre, or at least—and since we are as in all other things, in a terrible rush and all steps must be taken together—at least look for architectural inspiration among countries with approximate traditions and a longer professional history—or simply use that common ordinary gift of sense and refrain from employing mud-mixers and carpenters to design media which must eventually control or influence the creative intellect.

This is no exaggeration. It has been proved for four years by an amateur group in Ibadan, *The Players of the Dawn*, who, in spite of the intelligence of the leaders, have consistently succumbed to the dictates of the British Council pre-historic structures and are incapable of seeing theatre as an activity which did not petrify with Galsworthy at the start of the century.

No one who is seriously interested in the theatre demands a playground for pushing buttons and operating gaily coloured panels. A university especially should refrain from such expensive pastimes. For this is not America where—to take one example, the Loeb Theatre in Cambridge, Massachusetts—a university theatre is built for five to six million dollars, a stupid amoral example of affluent patronage. Where, pray, is the university sense? But the tinny poor-cousins of this which, to judge from Kampala, Ibadan and Nsukka, will soon exert their calcifying influence over the continent should be stopped now, before Zaria and Ife, and even the National Five-Yearly Never-never Plans follow their example. For, as I have stressed from the beginning, we are not merely talking about the structure now, but of the dubious art to which it must give birth.

Note

1. "Operatic groups" in this context refer to groups of predominantly expatriate, though considerably committed university teachers (who worked together at the University of Ibadan up till the late 1960's when their numbers dwindled) with other middle-class Nigerians for the purposes of presenting operas in the tradition of Western classical style. This reference is not to be confused with popular Yoruba "operatic" theatre. (Editor).

Reprinted Nigeria Magazine, No. 75, 1962.

SEARCH FOR A NEW AFRICAN THEATRE
Demas Nwoko

In our bid to evolve an African identity in the theatre we have had a poor start, trapped as it were in the brackets laid down by Western culture. Generally speaking, the young African's first intimation of theatre was at the mission school where simple Christian religious stories were dramatized and European folk-songs and nursery rhymes recited in what were called "concerts". For a long time, the missions fought against the African's desire to dance. But they lost the fight as our Christian parents could not stop our joining secret masquerade cults. Moreover, we soon were able to dance during Christian festivals such as harvest, saints' days, Christmas and Easter. Sometimes, we even danced in churches. In secondary grammar schools, we staged plays from European classics which were set-books for language and litera-ture studies. The African child almost never had an opportunity to study his own language in school and when it became a subject for the School Certificate Examination, it was optional, and one was never encouraged to take such an option. It should be noted that at this stage the African child knew nothing of current trends in Western theatre, so his idea of the theatre was that of Medieval and Elizabethan Europe.

An aspiring dramatist enters university either in his country or in Europe or America. If he chooses to study English or French in his own country, he continues the grammar school pattern. He studies more European classics and watches them performed by the local European community whose taste for art hardly ever goes beyond European classics. So, when he writes his first play, he models it after Sophocles and Euripides and other Greek dramatists or after Molière or Shakespeare. For this show of promise, he is sent to Europe or America for advanced studies in Drama. He gets the first shock of his life when he discovers that the people there have been doing things for two thousand years

462

(or at least four hundred years) ahead of what he knew to be theatre. Before he settles down to the task of catching up with lost time, he is told by everybody that he should become African. This is not only a shock, but is also confusing. He is allowed to stay the year, studying his craft between persistent demands to show his Africanness. At the end of the year he is sent home to research into his own culture, occupies a post in the local university and forms his own generation of artists.

The second type of student goes overseas straight from grammar school to study Drama and receives the same formation as the artists of his host country. At first, not much notice is taken of the fact that he has a different cultural background, as he is required to fulfil similar examination requirements as every other student. At a later stage of his studies, he is encouraged to apply his new knowledge to his own culture but he is not shocked because the preservation of cultural identity is one of the principles inculcated in young people in these overseas institutions, and he has absorbed this in the course of his first play which turns out to be a scientific application of modern Western theatrical techniques. He too comes back to join the home university where he meets the first type still digging deep into the past. He joins the search with his interest for compiling native customs which he quickly reduces to scientific terms to fit into the idioms of the Western culture he has acquired. With these varied types of background, the work of these modern African dramatists differs in that the results of the first group are heavily coloured with African life, with a lot of what is called "African tradition" such as religious rituals and translations from vernacular poetry. The results of the second group are not as prodigious as those of the first because they lack fluency and show an anxiety to explain and justify scientifically the material taken from African life. In spite of this difference, these artists have one objective—to build a modern African Theatre.

(a) The School of Drama at the University of Ibadan

This school was not initially planned to develop an African Theatre as its founder, Mr. Geoffrey Axworthy, was only a lecturer in English and his only qualification as a theatre director was his production of European plays with amateur groups in the University.

Its aim was to run a one-year course for teachers to improve their teaching of English Language and Literature. Axworthy wished to introduce local troupes playing in the vernacular, and some technical aids like modern lighting and the use of the stage and its facilities. When he was joined by some Nigerians (including myself), a two-year course was introduced which aimed at producing professional theatre artists and craftsmen. We started offering courses to students in other academic departments as part of their degree subjects. We hoped in this manner to develop new playwrights as well as theatre critics. Many of our students are now employed in radio and television, and many more are teaching in grammar schools but I regret to say that it seems we have not made African artists out of them. As I said earlier, the very system we used (which is an amalgamation of the European and American university systems) added to the situation where available teaching materials was based almost entirely on Western theatre forms and the students stepped out of our school as if they had trained in any drama school in London. There is very little one can do to change the orientation of the school since our University is international in character and our staff recruited from all over the world.

I had hoped, anyway, that this wrong emphasis would be corrected when these artists started to work but I have since discovered many more deformities in the system which are responsible for the failure of our students to find the live theatre attractive. To begin with, the students loathed practical work because fellow-students from other departments taunted them, branding them as non-academic. So, to prove that their course was academic, they preferred to show off with books by spending their time in the libraries. This psychological problem was not the affliction of the students alone, as it also affected members of the staff. They too discovered that they could not progress in a university without showing that they were academic, so practically all of them abandoned the search for an African Theatre and settled down to establishing themselves as reputable academics. By this mutual shift of emphasis, the School has now become a purely academic department of the University. The students having satisfied themselves that they were as academic as everyone else, acquired the appropriate social status which meant that when they left the University with their Diploma or Bachelor's Degree in Drama they wanted jobs that would bring the same salaries as graduates of other professions. They were automatically lost to the theatre as no young theatre troupe could afford to pay such salaries to beginner-actors. Moreover, they demanded cars, which is the visible manifestation of the young executive and budding intellectual. The best they did for the theatre was to join or found amateur groups which, apart from not being good enough, constituted potential dangers to the growth of good theatre. While the amateur cannot become a substitute for the professional, he is a danger to the artist in the new urban societies such as we have in Africa, because he readily gains official support by virtue of his government connections. The amateur also performs for charity, an act of philanthropy which the struggling artist cannot afford. So it turns out that we have been producing problems for the future theatre instead of training artists for it.

While we have found it difficult to drop the title of "pioneers of modern African Theatre" in the School of Drama, the content of the course is not the one that makes artists of people. Academic discipline is in every way the antithesis of creative discipline. *While the prerequisite of an academic statement is foreknowledge, an artistic statement is intuitively produced and only after birth does an artistic expression become an experience and can therefore become a subject for academic study.*

(b) Playwriting

As opposed to a playwright who creates new plays, the academic playwright adapts works of master playwrights of the world. Academic adaptations are hardly valid works of art as the emphasis is often on technical, rather than artistic, accomplishment. The play is transferred to another culture or time by being translated into another language, costumes are changed, as well as the style of production. The adapter also cuts off parts to save time or adds bits of foreign culture at will for local colour and so just stops short of rewriting the whole play. In spite of this, he keeps the name of the master (sacred as it is) ever-eager to give credit to his source. This reverence turns out to be intentionally or unintentionally artistically dishonest because the adapter points persistently to the similarity of text structure with the original, and insists on keeping the title and name of the author as sub-titles. This ensures mention for his work which then basks in reflected glory. This type of practice is a valid academic exercise, being a sort of study of the original author, and rightly merits attention.

When a writer is inspired by the work of another author and produces a new play, it is a valid work of art. It should contain artistic values that are true expressions of his own personality and exhibit new theatrical values that make it a worthy extension of the work that inspired it. Thus it can bear and support proudly its own title.

(c) Play Production

The principle adopted in a play production exercise in an academic setting is also one that ensures that a truly artistic effect is never achieved. Everything that happens on the stage has to be lifted, in the main, from the pages of books or from an *authentic* source. This is the approach of the director, actors, choreographer, designer and even the stage manager. Having carefully documented his evidence from the tested practices of renowned masters, each applies them to one play in order to produce a technically sound theatre. Technically and academically sound because they can quote their respectable sources as evidence to justify every aspect of their endeavour, the result is usually a riot of incompatible components found in the direction, acting and design as well as in the production as a whole. During the training of artists, equal emphasis is laid on the original individual styles and aesthetic formulations of the masters of the young artist against any of the masters so he can be exposed to all, and left to choose his influences later. The school production naturally became a platform to try out this stylistic knowledge for both teachers and students. It is an impossible feat to achieve an integrated artistic statement with such materials and on such a stage. At best these productions achieve purely didactic ends.

Despite these basic differences in approach, there is a world-wide delusion that artistic works can be academically produced, but no know masterpiece has been so produced. On the contrary the currency of such practice outside the classroom has always marked the decadence of a school of thought and signals its imminent end.

Finally, I have learnt from experience that an academic institution like ours does not produce in the students the personal discipline of mind required of artists in the theatre. In a university, the ideal aim is to develop an enquiring mind and habit to ask questions and find logical and scientific answers to them. This engenders a lot of discourse and debate that often degenerates into argument and outward manifestations that have a disrupting effect on the theatre. Though the ultimate goal of both academic and artist is in "truth", each has a different conception of it: for one, it is scientific while for the other, it is aesthetic which is less tangible, more spiritual and is hardly ever explainable in logical terms. The artist should also acquire the habit of enquiry as well as logical and scientific argument but the resolution takes place within him and not in an exchange with another person. He then delivers the evidence of the resolution intuitively in the form of his artistic expression. Once manifested in the form of concrete existence, the expression can never be scientifically justified in its entirety. In addition to this type of discipline, the artist is expected to possess a dogged desire to achieve perfection through acquiring the painstaking habits of a true craftsman. With this profound difference in personal discipline, most of our graduates have proved quite unmanageable in production and have not shown any willingness to learn.

(d) Our Search for an African Theatre

In Nigeria, many spirited attempts have been made, and are being made today, to evolve an African Theatre idiom and, as I said earlier, this has involved Nigerians as well as foreigners. Though no formal philosophy has been formulated, we will agree that a truly African identity in art is imperative. It is also commonly held that this new art should not ape European art and should not be a mere copy of traditional African art. While the word "synthesis" is usually bandied about to resolve the bicultural situation in modern Africa, individual approach to the problem has differed and, as will be expected, results have been equally uneven. In mentioning some sample projects, I will endeavour to describe the way in which some individuals work and evaluate their results in the light of my own philosophy.

In general, I look upon the involvement of any foreigner in this task as rather unfortunate. Unfortunate because it is a thankless job and it has always been so through man's history when two races of distinctively different cultures are involved. They can validly work with us if their mission is to sell their own culture to us, as cultural exchange is a very fashionable diploma-tic means of showing friendship between nations today, just as it was by marriage yesterday. It is cultural exchange that sustains most young African artists who are selling African Culture all over the world. But as these foreigners insist that they are searching for an African art, let us examine their work.

A dance choreographer, Peggy Harper, a white South African who was trained in the European classical ballet and the modern dance company of Martha Graham, joined the staff of the School of Drama at the University of Ibadan in 1963. Contrary to what I had expected of a person with her formation, she started trying to create an African theatrical expression. Since she knew very little or nothing of African dance, I thought she would have had to learn before creating new forms of African dance. She was obviously in a hurry and started what she called "creative dance" which has since become "modern African ballet". Her idiom is that of modern dance as developed in the United States but the subject is usually African while the music is mostly improvised of African musical instruments. The dance movements are created by breaking down a tribal dance movement sketched by one of her students to a very basic simple pattern, thus transforming it into stiff geometrical forms that appear mechanical when compared with African dance. While her type of dance left a lot of unfilled space when performed to the pulsating rhythmic music of one of our vigorous dances, it has worked out with the modern music of Akin Euba, a modern Nigerian musician.

Undoubtedly, she has created a type of dance which is unmistakably in the modern Western style and therefore cannot be the modern African dance we are searching for. That she has used African subjects and instruments and drawn inspiration from African dance movements is not enough to make the dance African. After all, Martha Graham and her disciples were inspired in part by these dances because modern Western art has drawn a lot of inspiration from the exotic arts and instruments of Africa, Asia and the Far East, but it has remained Western. Peggy Harper's dance cannot become African, despite the preponderance of surface African evidences around it, because it does not respect the basic aesthetic taste of the African in dance: his love of rhythm, and the roused emotional sympathy through persistent repetition of form and sound. These seem to me two major qualities that differentiate African dance from modern Western dances which insist on endless variety. Dance is an aesthetic language with which the people already speak and we should not deny them our talent by trying to impose strange cultures on them because we happen to be conversant with it. Finally, with time and a deeper knowledge of the African dance and, I will say, with a very long period of acculturation, when she is able to speak Ibo as I can speak English, she may be able to produce an African dance.

In drama apart from sporadic academic ventures which fail even before they have begun (because they are very academic and never go further in their Africanization than the costume, music and vernacular songs), there has been an involvement of a foreigner which has left a semblance of a truly indigenous theatre. The result is so real that my repudiation of it will sound like a prophecy of doom which will come when we have all passed away and therefore will be of little interest to us. I am convinced it is very dangerous as it creates a problem that cannot be easily identified with its complete outward appearance of validity. I am referring to the Ulli Beier School (from which has emerged the Duro Ladipo theatre troupe), a good example of such schools which exist in many parts of Africa covering all forms of artistic activity.

Ulli Beier is not an artist, but he developed very clear ideas of what should constitute African art and theatre and went on to produce them. To realize this theatre, he created by suggestion a theatre troupe basically after the style of the existing Ogunmola and Ogunde vernacular troupes. He suggested a historical theme from the legends, a subject that gave ample opportunity for the exhibition of "tradition and African culture". Through further suggestions during production, original indigenous music and appropriate dances (along with poetry) were used. Added to this, for decor, were back-cloths of typical modern art school colours which were the result of the art workshops he had organised. The result was an exhibition of slices of African customs and traditional art forms, loosely linked by improvised dramatic movements and speech. *Oba Koso*, as the play was called, was a very exotic presentation and it was sent round Europe as a demonstration of our fine culture.

The salient danger in this type of art is that the artist cannot claim honest responsibility for what has come to be known as his. He finds he cannot develop the style because he does not really understand the philosophy behind the structure. For this reason, Duro Ladipo is far from being able to write more plays that can repeat the *Oba Koso* form in a more mature way. He has tried superficial copies of it but falls back on the former. With Ulli Beier, he produced another play called *Eda* which was an adaptation of *Everyman*, with the adaptation usually underlined. Since then, Ulli Beier has emerged as a playwright for his Oshogbo School (as it is now called) even though most of these plays have not yet been performed. Can we call plays with African subjects, written by a German, African? In my opinion, he was only doing what the German expressionists did with African art. Ulli never became an African and has since left for a much similar adventure in New Guinea.

The result of Ulli's school is the existence of half-baked young artists who are completely ignorant of what they are doing but continue to reproduce suggested results because they find a ready market in Europe and America. The irony of Ulli Beier's escapade is that, in opposing what he calls "airport art" (meaning tourist art) he has inadvertently produced a brand new genera-tion of artists fulfilling the new tourist attraction of culture hunting. The Germans are still the best sponsors of Duro Ladipo's theatre today and I cannot see this type of art winning any permanent place in Africa, as it virtually dies with the departure of its creator.

Having thus far discussed how difficult, if not impossible it is for a foreigner to create the new African theatre for us, I can conveniently insist that it is only the "son of the soil" who can validly realize this. It is his life and whatever he makes of his life that is valid either negatively or positively. Art is best created intuitively, so a good African artist will eventually create African art intuitively as long as he lives and works for an African society. Achievements brighten the way when they are successful African expressions, but show the artist what should not be done when they are failures. With our experience in Nigeria so far, I will mention some obvious false steps that some of us have made as well as some results that seem to have been more sympathetically received.

As for the writers, the majority of them have lacked a definite direction and sense of purpose, but it seems this cannot be helped as it is difficult to write for a non-existent theatre. They write mostly with the Western stage in mind. While these plays find a market in schools as literature with an African colour and in Europe and America as new African literature and sources of studying African culture, they are hardly of any value to the African theatre director in search of an African identity. Their forms are rigidly fixed and only their subjects show their African source. The only solution to the problem will be to have the writers and poets directly involved in the creation of a living theatre, creating and developing forms and structures with other theatrical artists. In this manner the structure of the play will fit the poetry which will fit the music and dance and all these will come to fit the stage architecture. In this manner, a style will emerge. This was, to a great extent, how the play *The Palmwine Drinkard* was created in 1962–63. This was originally a novel by Amos Tutuola from which, on the suggestion of Dr. Collis and

Mr. G. Axworthy (the first Director of the University of Ibadan School of Drama) the author made a play. The play was handed to Mr. Ogunmola (the owner and director of a vernacular theatrical troupe) who translated it into a Yoruba opera. He transformed the structure of the original simple play to suit his own style by writing in songs in place of some of the dialogue. I took up the direction of the play at this point and started designing its visual images. During rehearsals, we found that the text was still too slight to support the images I had created, so Ogunmola wrote in more songs and dramatic poems where needed. In this way, both the text, structure and design grew together into what we have now. For the Algiers Commonwealth Arts Festival, we still altered parts and fitted in the story-teller, which meant that our idea of the ultimate structure of such an African play continued to grow with time and experience.

Our best known modern dramatist, Wole Soyinka, has succeeded in using the English language as an African medium of self-expression in his plays. He is also involved in the search for a theatre as he also directs a troupe. His style of play production is very much that of the modern European theatre and the texts of his plays are often original in form. This tendency towards originality is very likely the same as that underlining modern Western plays but this can automatically become modern African (because the author is African) when Soyinka settles down to writing consciously for an African society.

There are also the academically oriented dramatists who are often graduates of American universities. They are actively involved in research into African culture, past and present, and therefore have a tendency to exhibit this in their artistic endeavours. Their approach is coldly academic and the problems of language and customs are studied and reproduced as faithfully as possible on stage. They are also satisfied when they have demonstrated their compliance with any existing formulated philosophy on African theatre. For example, African theatre must have ritual, music, dance and poetry because these rule the everyday life of Africans and are always present in all artistic manifestations. So they work these into a play by all means, forgetting that the sum total of these items does not necessarily make a successful African work of art. After all, they are also present in the Western theatre. They find it difficult to understand that a true work of art is born and not constructed or assembled and that when a child is born, it is there and validly so, and does not need any explanation to justify the logic of its existence. If it is an African child it will be black, and if it is European, an African dress will not make it black.

Conclusion

(a) New Art for a New Society

When we talk of a modern African theatre, I would like us to think of a culture that belongs to the new African society concentrated mostly in the cities and towns. Artistically, traditional African society works almost in tribal enclaves, obviously due to difficulties in communication that existed formerly. Over a long period of time, tribes developed theatrical expressions unique to them, to the extent that scholars tended to accept these differences as cultural distinctions between tribes. Even Africans are generally surprised to see a person of a different tribe perform one of their own dances fairly well when taught the dance. There is almost a belief that tribal artistic expressions have their origin in the customs and philosophy of the tribe. Spiritual sources are not ruled out as these purely artistic manifestations become involved in religious activities and often acquire religious colouring in the process. Once this process is completed the art is seen as theirs alone and any outsider (meaning anyone immediately outside the clan) is not expected to understand it easily. Today, the new society is detribalized: it is now nationalistic and will eventually become pan-African as political unity is achieved. The artistic expression of one tribe cannot fulfil the aesthetic needs of this multi-tribal new society. There has to be a marriage of artistic habits and this is being accomplished naturally as the societies share the same religions, artistic works and plays. The duty of the artists of this new society will be to create an art that will express the life and aspirations of this new super-tribe.

I am not advocating an entirely new art. On the contrary, I advocate a perpetuation of our artistic traditions. I find it the most valid alternative, both for the good health of the new African and for our effective contribution to world civilization. If the new African did not drop down from somewhere but has roots in a highly developed culture, you can only communicate effectively with him (as with men everywhere) through the language he already knows and understands best. Therefore aesthetics must be communicated through the artistic idioms he can identify himself with. It is still true that even when the form to be communicated is entirely new, it has to be introduced through the known older forms.

By virtue of the structure of the new African society (which is made up basically of classless social habits) it holds great promise for the growth of a people's theatre. To achieve this most desirable end, dramatists should work with the people in mind at all times. Any attitude that tends to emphasize distinction in status or creates exclusive tastes in theatrical entertainment should be avoided. With our present society any expression of the people's soul will be successfully African and can become very popular. It is always erroneously generalized that an art that is popular is vulgar and that art is always exclusive. Traditional African arts have shown that every human being is capable of appreciating and enjoying art—King or slave, master or servant. To preserve this heritage, any artist who purposely condemns his talent to only a section of our society should not be encouraged with public patronage as there is a possible trace of class prejudice in him. Everybody might not be able to buy the highest priced seats in theatre, but all should be able to enjoy a play, deriving the same aesthetic satisfaction based on the same philosophy of life.

(b) Cultural Synthesis

As for the very annoying question of the synthesis of African and Western culture as found in our lives, we must accept that a lot of Western values have come to stay. We will always have much more of the European in us, especially with our mass education programmes, than the Europeans will ever have of our culture. Their technical and commercial values form the basis of our modernization plans for improved standards of living. Though these may seem superficial, they order our daily lives into a pattern that is often beyond our full control. This automatically affects our habits in spiritual as well as cultural matters, which, in turn, results in a generally chaotic urban cultural life that lacks conviction and borders on the ugly. In most of our cities, the only cultural diversion regularly is the night club where we dance our souls in and drink our health out. Then there is the cinema and the television which can, at present, mainly show foreign life and culture because we make few of our own films. With such a preponderant presence of values that are still very new and foreign to him, the modern African is at the moment in a most uncomfortable situation as these values are often at variance with the philosophy of the society he grew up in.

A few of us might appear quite at ease in both cultures but one should not be deceived, because we are only very good actors and mimics, and it works well for surface fun. Under this apparently easy adaptability, lies only one personality—that of the African. Most of our foreign friends know it by now, as well as I have always known that however much the foreigner wants to become one of us, or demonstrates his Africanness, he has refused to forsake his own dear culture. He insists on that dreadful winter holiday in Europe in spite of our loving sunshine.

The new African must be saved from his cultural ordeal. While African religions failed in the face of Christianity and Islam, art is more fortunate and has become Africa's pride in the world today. So it seems that it is the artist whose duty it is to restore the new African into a wholesome personality, by making his culture dominate his material life. African culture is not incompatible with the material, technical and economic aspects of Western civilization, African culture can effectively make use of modern technology for its realization and dissemination on the scale demanded by the world today, without dehumanizing its values. Western art today is not only completely dehumanized, but is fashioned for the glorification of man-made things, indicating man's sell-out to the machine. We have no machines yet to sell our souls to, and I think it will be a little bit undignified for the African to enslave himself to another's. Let us build our own modern human civilization first, and decay in our own good time.

(c) The Theatre Director

In all the theatres of the world, the director has always been a controversial figure and still remains so as his functions vary with theatrical styles. In Africa, we have inherited the Western conception of the director which, luckily, is anything but clear and so gives us the opportunity to make ours suit our purpose. Traditionally, in dance performances and, more recently, in our vernacular troupes, the director (or manager) is a super-artist who is often writer, actor, musician, dancer and designer as well as an effective co-ordinator of the whole production. Of course, he is all these in varying degrees but has enough knowledge of each to enable him to take a clear decision on the final result.

In the new African theatre, my chosen director would be a good dancer and choreographer, and along with these accomplishments he should have developed an ear for good music. He should have become so conversant with shape and the use of space that he can decide on the most practical use of costumes and props. While he should not necessarily write his scripts, he should choose only poems or writings that fit into his style of production since the visual form comes before the text in importance. The theatre is first and foremost a visual expression using music, sound (sung or spoken), movement (walked or danced), design, colour, two- or three-dimensional shapes and a text to build up an association with the world of nature. There can validly exist a theatre without text while text without visual expression can only become literature and never theatre. This makes it difficult for me to accept writers who have published plays without any experience of working in, or for, the theatre, as really useful. The true African dramatist will grow with the theatre, working directly for a director of a style when one has been successfully established.

The new theatre should not fight shy of establishing a style with definitively formulated aesthetic philosophies within which artists should work. This will encourage the development of a pure art that will help the artist and his existence. The most important thing on the stage should be man, and not the events he is enacting; neither should objects nor the technological trappings of the modern stage distract attention from him. We should not seek to achieve mathematical precision and speed to the detriment of the full development and exposition of the detriment of the actor. In this way subjects and particular production styles can be repeated with fresh appeal to the same audience when played by different actors and with renewed satisfaction when played by their favourites. It is such repetitions that engender cultural stability which in turn creates tradition; tradition which makes a people, a people who make a civilization which is their valid contribution to the world. There is a mass-produced type of repetition in the culture of the industrialized world which has failed to create stability because the ultimate peak is reached too soon. For cultural stability, we also need the passage of time but mechanized industry has beaten time. What the world needs in art today is good time-honoured repetition to stabilize and rehabilitate man's spiritual and cultural existence.

Realism as we know it in the Western theatre is vulgar to the Africans' aesthetic sensibility, hence they react to it with laughter. Not the laughter of an amused person but the chuckle of an adult at the ineffectiveness of a childish prank. They might well be asking: why cry on stage when we know you are not grieved or hurt? Why stab someone to death when we know his life is not in danger? Why kiss and caress on stage when you are not lovers? It even becomes hilariously ridiculous to the audience when the sex act that might follow is then performed off-stage and is usually greeted with an uproar of protest. The spectators cannot stop laughing when the dead man rises after the final curtain. While the European is prepared to allow himself to believe that he is seeing reality on stage, the African prefers to see a performance as an artistic display. Even theatrical tricks in magic and masquerading are made to impress the immature minds of children and the simple and sentimental minds of young women. In order to achieve this purity in art, aesthetically ugly manifestations such as quarrels which create abusive language and physical confrontation, cruelty which results in killing, and other types of death, are enacted in a highly stylized manner. With part of a production realized, it becomes necessary to maintain stylistic unity and consistency by avoiding the re-enactment of life without artistic formalization or stylization.

What is true for acting also holds for design; the African does not expect to see a house or stages nor does he expect to see a real car, a king's crown or even a real policeman's uniform. A theatrical representation of these things is all he expects. Artistry should be supreme and the aim of the actor should be the expression of aesthetic beauty which should run through all facets of the production.

(d) Training of Artists

Having already talked about the dangers and disadvantages of the modern art-school system, I will advocate the re-establishment of the old apprenticeship system. Actors as well as all other theatre artists, should learn their craft in studios run by theatre directors. These students may have different educational backgrounds but, irrespective of this, should go through similar discipline of mind and body in the service of the theatre.

A studio should offer training for all the components that make up the theatre: music, acting, dance and design. There should be no separate training for a director who should emerge naturally in a person who shows good qualities of leadership and an ability to judge artistic quality. To become a successful director, he should also be a talented creator and innovator.

As I said at the beginning of this article, I do not believe in learned talks; I am an artist and believe in achieving results. For me, the search for a new African culture is a crusade and I wish that all talented African artists would join hands and work together. In Ibadan, I have started building the nucleus of the type of studio I am advocating. I will name the centre "The New Culture Studio" where I will try to develop my ideas on African art with any African artist who has a philosophy identical with mine. With a will and hard work I am confident we will succeed. We have to.

Reprinted Presence Africaine, No. 95, 32 Quarter, 1970.

PART VII
APPENDIX

IKAKI—THE TORTOISE MASQUERADE
Robin Horton

One of the favourite protagonists of Kalabari stories is Ikaki—Tortoise. Often referred to as "Old Man of the Forest", Ikaki is a memorable character. On the one hand, he has an insatiable appetite for food, money and women, and seeks to gratify it without any regard for the limits set by established morality. On the other hand, he operates with a vast deviousness and elaborate cunning. Fortunately for the rest of the characters in his stories, however, he often pushes his schemes too far, and so fails to achieve his outrageous aims.

At some time in the development of Kalabari culture, the story-image of Ikaki was taken up as the theme of a masquerade.[1] Quite how, when and where this happened, we shall probably never know for certain. Kalabari, it is true, give a clear-cut account of the matter; but their account smacks more of myth than of history. Mythical though it may be, however, the Kalabari account is of considerable importance for anyone who wants to discover the deeper meaning of the Ikaki play.

Kalabari believe that the Ikaki play was first produced in the long-defunct village of Oloma, in the creeks west of the mouth of the San Bartolomeo River. Ikaki, they say, was a spirit living in the forest at the back of the village—a kind of supernatural supertortoise.[2] Every now and again, Ikaki used to come out of the forest to dance; and whenever he did so, the villagers gathered round to watch him. They found his dancing splendid, and they always pestered him to come back some time and dance again. But each time he came, Ikaki warned them in song:

Ee, omini i ke kuruma, omini i ke kurumaye.
Al' Ikaki, Al' Ibulu.
O bara k'i lamama, o bara k'i lamamaye.
Al' Ikaki, Al' Ibulu.

("Remember my words, all of you; remember my words,
    all of you.
Chief Tortoise, Chief Grey-Hair.
Don't any of you touch me; don't any of you touch me.
Chief Tortoise, Chief Grey-Hair.")

But the Oloma people persisted in calling him back, until one day
he came out with a finer dance than ever before. As he danced,
he sang:

A nwe simeari piriogbo, a nwe simeari buogbo,
A Kula tubo sinyaa.
Kwe kwe kwe ikirioro, kiri kiri tominoruye.
Agemage.
Tomina nama krim, krim.
Agemage.
Tomina ingbe krim, krim.

("In the forest where I live, in the swamp where I live,
I don't call any child of Kula.
Kwe kwe kwe, etc.[3]
Agemage.
Human meat, yum, yum.
Agemage.
Human bones, yum, yum.")

As he danced, he lifted one leg, and all the people living in that
direction died. He lifted the other leg, and all the people living
that way died too. Then Ikaki vanished into the forest and was
never seen again.

After a while, the few people who were left thought they would
like to imitate Ikaki's wonderful dancing. But all were fearful
when it came to the lifting of the masquerader's leg, for they
thought that this would surely bring more deaths. So they went to
ask the great oracle of Chuku what they should do. The oracle
instructed them to make certain changes and to take certain
precautions, and said that if they did these things, all would be
well. Keeping carefully to the oracle's instructions, they began to
put on the Ikaki play, and continued with it until their town was
sacked in one of the many wars of the times. Before Oloma
disappeared, the Kula people came to see the play and were

much impressed. Having performed the appropriate rites, they took the play over for their own *ekine* society.[4] From Kula, Ikaki spread to other towns including New Calabar.

Of the three daughter settlements of New Calabar, it is Buguma that still keeps up its *ekine* society according to the ancient forms; and it is here that the Ikaki play is still to be seen when its turn comes round. Formally speaking, Ikaki is one of the plays owned corporately by the *ekine* society. But *de facto* responsibility for bringing it out has landed for the time being upon the heirs of the late Dokubo Cottrell Horsfall—a noted Ikaki dancer who is said to have learned how to play the main part in Kula.[5]

The Ikaki performance which I describe here took place at Buguma early in July 1966. For convenience, I couch my description in the present tense.

Ikaki begins in the usual manner of *ekine* plays. Society members assemble in the club-house on the night before the performance. The Master of the Drums beats out some of the Ikaki rhythms, and members have a desultory hour or two of practice. (Those actually due to don masquerades have in fact been practising for the past few nights.) Meanwhile, two or three people specially concerned with the play are at work putting the finishing touches to headpieces and costumes. Some time after midnight, most of the *ekine* members form up in procession and go round the town, singing the society's drinking songs, to give notice of the morrow's play. Those working on the headpieces stay behind to finish their job. When it is done, they offer a fowl to the spirit of the masquerade, with the usual invocation for the success of the play. In the small hours, everyone retires for a brief sleep.

Next morning, the Master of the Drums starts to play the characteristic rhythm known as Ikaki Ada. A crowd quickly gathers in the town square. Before long, Ikaki emerges from the society's club-house, flanked by two of his children: Nimite Poku—"Know All", and Nimiaa Poku—"Know Nothing". Ikaki himself, though fairly simply dressed, is readily recognizable by his hunchback and by the schematized tortoise body which is his headpiece. He comes out with a canny, mincing step. Nimite

Poku, dressed mainly in a soiled blue-and-white sheet topped with an old felt hat, follows his step with a paddle sloped over his shoulder. Nimiaa Poku, dressed if anything more shabbily than his brother, carries a paddle and an ancient, leaky basket. He gambols and tumbles round the other two, to their considerable annoyance.

Almost at once, Ikaki leads his children out of the town square and down to *owusera*, the main water-side. The crowd follows in high spirits. Ikaki is looking for a boat. There is no sign of one at *owusera*, so he doubles back to *oru poku*—"the beach of the gods", and there finds what he is looking for. *Ekine* members present Ikaki with a drum, and help him and his children into a boat. With Ikaki at the stern and Nimite Poku amidship, the boat quickly reaches deep water. But no sooner is it well out into the river than Nimiaa Poku plunges the crew into confusion. Paddling almost as briskly backward as the others are paddling forward, he brings the boat to a shuddering standstill. The onlookers, crowded at the water's edge, abuse him joyously. Realizing something is wrong, he takes remedial action by bailing with his basket. Unfortunately, he bails water from the river into the boat. The leakiness of the basket averts the worst; but a considerable amount of water comes aboard nonetheless, and the boat starts to look a little low in the water. Nimite Poku jumps angrily on his brother, and both fall into the bottom of the boat. The audience roars ecstatically. Then Ikaki intervenes to pull the two brothers apart, and gives Nimiaa Poku a sharp cuff. Almost immediately, upset at having hurt his son, he starts to pet him. Eventually, everyone gets back into place. Nimiaa Poku continues to paddle in reverse. Nimite Poku paddles hopefully on in the right direction. Ikaki sits in the stern playing his drum, apparently attempting to urge his crew on after the fashion of a war-canoe orchestra. Caught in a strong ebb-tide, the boat is soon in danger of passing the last waterside and drifting away toward the sea. The onlookers start to shout warnings. Ikaki, dropping his drum, joins Nimite Poku with his paddle, and after a brief but valiant exertion, the two of them manage to bring the boat in to the very end of the last beach.

As soon as Ikaki and his children alight, *ekine* members surround them and lead them back up to the town square, where the more senior, older and less energetic spectators are waiting to greet them. The Master of the Drums has already started to beat Ikaki Ada. Ikaki and his children begin to dance round the square, whilst the *ekine* people form up in procession behind them. In the basic dance-sequence for Ikaki Ada, the dancer first takes four shuffling steps forward. Then he pivots on his left foot, raises the right, and hops four times in a quarter-circle to the left. He takes four more steps forward, then pivots on his right foot, raises the left, and hops four times in a quarter-circle to the right. This sequence commemorates Ikaki's death-dealing dance before the people of Oloma. Ikaki himself frequently breaks off from the basic step into a canny, mincing gait; whilst Nimiaa Poku tries to filch from his bag, then rolls over helplessly in his desire to get away. Nimite Poku comes up and puts him on his feet again.

Soon, Ikaki strikes up a dirge, half-whistled and half-sung in a high falsetto:

Ye, ee-ee, ee-ee.
Ye, Ogo ye Benibo fite-oo
Ye, ee-ee ee-ee.
Ye, Ogo ye Benibo fite, o nayee.

("Ye, ee-ee ee-ee.
Ye, Ogo's son Benibo is dead-oo.
Ye, ee-ee ee-ee.
Ye, Ogo's son Benibo is dead, hear me-ee".)

With the dirge, Ikaki is up to one of the many tricks for which he is famous in Kalabari stories. Ogo's son Benibo is no less a person than the late *amanyanabo* of New Calabar.[6] Ikaki has heard news of his death and has come to town to do some noisy and conspicuous mourning. Posing as a great friend of the dead king, he claims that whilst the latter was alive, he lent him a great quantity of palm-oil for trading with the merchants. With one breath he mourns the death of the king. With another, he mourns the loss of his capital. With a third, he asks for the king's children—obviously with an eye to claiming his debt, which of course is non-existent. Ikaki relies on the bitterness of his dirge to convince anyone that the debt is real. But the onlookers are wise to him; and as he comes round the square, they tell him laughingly that the king's children are out of town.

As Ikaki goes round "trying it on" with the townspeople, the Drum Master blends into his rhythm a mixture of admiring and abusive epithets, which the masker accepts or rejects in his high falsetto. Thus:

Drummer: *Ploploma boi si.*
           ("Ploploma bad-inside.")[7]
Ikaki: *Ee! Iyeri-ee!*
           ("Ee! It is me!")
Drummer: *Epelle sueye epelle tre finji.*
           ("Tricks thirty and three.")
Ikaki: *Ee! Iyeri-ee!*
           ("Ee! It is me!")
Drummer: *Kiri sokua minji paka.*
           ("Digs into the ground and comes up in the water.")
Ikaki: *Ee! Iyeri-ee!*
           ("Ee! It is me!")
Drummer: *Ere furubo, tanda bio, tanda bio.*
           ("Raper of women, hides in the corner, in the corner.")
Ikaki: *Oriaa-ee!*
           ("It is not him.")
Drummer: *Yingi mono, tubo mono.*
           ("Sleeps with his mother, sleeps with his daughter.")
Ikaki: *Atabila-ee! furo pele!*
           ("Atabila! May your belly burst!")[8]

While Ikaki alternately tries to hoodwink the townspeople and takes to his bosom or hurls back the epithets of the drummer, Nimiaa Poku delights the audience at the other end of the arena, by his fatuous gambollings and helpless falls. After about an hour of this, the sun begins to get hot; the Drum Master gives gentle hints; the maskers retire to the club-house; and the onlookers go home for a meal and a siesta.

Toward the cool of the evening, the Drum Master sounds Ikaki Ada once again. Ikaki comes out, escorted by Nimite Poku and Nimiaa Poku. Nimiaa Poku tries pilfering from his father again and falls very seriously in trying to escape. The long-suffering Ikaki revives him.

Later, Ikaki is seen questing for various leaves. Then, after a little while, he is seen putting his head under various bushes in the arena. Here again, he is at one of the tricks familiar to onlookers from the world of story. As Old Man of the Forest, he is expected to take a solicitous interest in the other animals who dwell in his domain. Characteristically, however, he takes advantage of his position. He goes to the dwellings of animals whom he knows have stores of nuts or meat, and warns them that he sees impending misfortune in their households. A little later, he comes back with a native doctor; and while the doctor is attending to the alleged troubles hinted at by Ikaki, the latter loots the food store. All we actually see in the play is the masker delving under bushes and backing out again furtively with a knapsack fuller than it was when he went in. But the onlookers, familiar with the story, "fill in" the details they do not see and are highly amused.

After a while, the cast is swelled by two more characters— Ikaki's well dressed favourite son Kalagidi, and his wife Aboita. Kalagidi joins the other men, dancing with a more elegant, less mincing step than his father, but suffering the same indignities from the moronic Nimiaa Poku. Aboita dances with an escort of four elderly women. A loose, silly thing, she soon has a number of *ekine* members around her. Egged on by the audience, they flirt and pinch her tender parts. Eventually, Ikaki comes to claim her. He joins her in the suggestive pelvic dance know as *egepu*, whilst the Drum Master hurls out a torrent of admiring and abusive epithets. After a little of this, the whole family forms up at the head of the *ekine* people, and passes round the square in procession. It is now sundown and play closes for the day.

On the second day, as is usual with Kalabari masquerades, play does not begin till the cool of the afternoon. Ikaki, Nimite Poku, Nimiaa Poku, Kalagidi and Aboita all come out together. The dance continues to the best of Ikaki Ada, with Ikaki still dirging hopefully for the dead king, and breaking off from time to time for an exchange of pleasantries and abuses with the Drum Master. Whilst Ikaki holds the attention of one section of the audience, Nimiaa Poku entertains another section with his witless frolics, and Aboita titillates yet another section with her equally witless flirtation.

The play closes with two *egberi* or dramatic episodes. First of these is *koro kpole egberi*—"Palm-tree climbing *egberi*". For this, *ekine* members have erected a large, conical scaffold beside the drum house, with a bundle of fresh palm-leaves lashed to the top. Ikaki climbs up this stage palm-tree with a matchet, a small knife called *akpo*, and a large wine calabash. The *ekine* people mill around beneath him and encourage him with their cheers. The Drum Master steps up his mixture of praise and abuse. When Ikaki gets to the top of the tree, he settles himself down, nods with self-satisfaction and breaks into one of his falsetto songs:

> *Ye, na na pu, na na pu.*
> *Ye, koro kpolebo fite-oo.*
> *Ye, na na pu, na na pu.*
> *Ye, koro kpolebo fite-oo nayee!*

> ("Ye, all who can hear, all who can hear.
> The palm-tree climber used to die-o.
> Ye, all who can hear, all who can hear.
> The palm-tree climber used to die, hear me-ee!")

The Drum Master praises him:

Drummer: *Jejekwu!*
("Big Chief!")
Ikaki: *Ori!*
("It is him!")
Drummer: *Or'inaa kini inaa.*
("What he cannot do, no-one can do")
Ikaki: *Ori!*
("It is him!")

Ikaki, it seems, is the only one of the forest animals who has discovered how to climb the palm-tree; and he has no inhibitions about letting everyone know it.

As he sings, he sets to work not only cutting palm-fruit, but also tapping wine. He starts to suck the palm-fruit, and the sweetness of it moves him to another song:

> *Ya bele bele youruba.*[9]
> *Bele bele, ye belebeleye.*
> *Bele bele youruba.*
> *Bele bele nwe beleye.*
> *Uguoguo!*

("Ya, lovely, lovely palm-fruits.
Lovely, lovely, yum.
Lovely, lovely palm-fruits.
Lovely, lovely, yum.
Uguoguo!'')

But whilst Ikaki is at the top of the tree, blissfully praising himself and extolling the virtues of palm-fruits, trouble is coming below. The witless Nimiaa Poku has got hold of an axe, and is amusing himself by trying to cut the tree down. Aboita, silly as ever, is flirting with the *ekine* people, and so doesn't see what her son is up to. Kalagidi makes one or two attempts to stop Nimiaa Poku but without effect. At last Ikaki looks down and sees what is happening. With an alarmed shriek, he throws his palm-cutting instrument at Nimiaa Poku. But it misses Nimiaa Poku and knocks out his beloved Kaligidi. Ikaki is beside himself. He says he will never come down again. He will hang himself in the tree. Then he starts to wail for his favourite son:

Ye, ee-ee ee-ee.
Ye, Kalagidi ofite oona!
Ye, ee-ee ee-ee ee-ee.
Ye, Kalagidi ofite oona-ee!

("Ye, ee-ee ee-ee.
Ye, Kalagidi is dead, hear me-o!
Ye, ee-ee ee-ee ee-ee.
Ye, Kalagidi is dead, hear me-ee!'')

While Ikaki wails at the top of the tree, Nimiaa Poku rejoices at his escape and dances happily about below. The feckless Aboita, delighted that her own favourite has escaped the blow aimed at him, joins him in the dance. Ikaki looks down, sees both his son and his wife rejoicing in the midst of his misfortune, and redoubles his threats to hang himself. Meanwhile, *ekine* members have gathered about the fallen Kalagidi and are making strenuous efforts to bring him to life. After some time, they succeed. Kalagidi gets up and starts to dance once more. Ikaki, seeing this, unties the rope with which he has started to hang himself, and comes slowly down the tree, grumbling about having a wife who could allow such things to happen:

Ye, ee-ee ee-ee.
Ye, ee-ee ee-ee.
Ye, si erebo keni bam, si erebo keni bam.
A fate-oo, Kalagidi.

("Ye, ee-ee ee-ee.
Ye, ee-ee ee-ee.
Ye, a bad wife kills a man, a bad wife kills a man.
I am finished-o, Kalagidi.")

When Ikaki reaches the ground, the *ekine* people cheer vigorously. The episode comes to an end with Ikaki and the *ekine* members dancing round the square in procession.

In the interlude between the first and second dramatic episodes, the Drum Master changes his beat from Ikaki Ada to Egepu:

Obuogbo kuogbo, gidipu; obuogbo kuogbo, gidipu.

("Lump behind, lump between the legs, gidipu;
lump behind, lump between the legs, gidipu.")

This beat alludes to the fact that Ikaki is not only a hunchback, but also suffers from elephantiasis of the scrotum—a disease usually regarded as the mark of an evil life. Pleased at the revival of his son, however, Ikaki takes the drummer's call as more of a salutation than an insult. He responds with a bawdy pelvic dance, taking out his enormous testicles (represented by a wooden slit-gong) and shaking them at the women. The latter retreat with shrieks of mock horror, followed by request to see more.

After some minutes of this, the drum rhythm changes again, and the scene is set for the last episode. Looking for some way to celebrate his son's escape, Ikaki hits on the idea of taking the *peri* title by killing an elephant. To represent the elephant, *ekine* people put down a large section of banana stem with a cord attached to it. Ikaki takes out his matchet and brandishes it in front of the crowd. He is going to kill an elephant, he says. The crowd makes various incredulous noises. As he circles the field, the Drum Master beats the head-hunting rhythm:

Ikpalaga, ikpalaga; ikpalaga bara bara; ikpalaga peri.

("A body, a body; a body with the strong arm,
with the strong arm; a body for peri!")

Then Ikaki closes on the elephant. He circles it with elaborate guile, feints at it from behind, retreats hastily. He circles, feints, and falls on his back. He minces about wondering whether to go on or call the whole thing off. He brandishes his matchet to the crowd to show his determination. He circles and feints again. Then finally he closes in and finishes off the elephant with a tremendous blow on its neck. Roars from the men and delighted shrieks from the women. Ikaki picks up the severed head of the elephant and dances up to where the *amanyanabo* is sitting. The drummer showers praises on him: *Jejekwu! Orinaa, kini inaa! Kiri sokua minji paka!* He nods and pats his chest. As he parades before the king and his chiefs, his weapon shakes as befits a *peri* title holder—his arm moved by the spirits of departed *peri* men.

After a while, the Drum Master switches his beat once more to Ikaki Ada. Ikaki and his family form up at the head of the *ekine* members and make a final procession round the arena. As he goes round, Ikaki sings a triumphant falsetto:

Ye, ee-ee ee-ee.
Ye, Al'Ikaki o bila bat' oona.
Ye, na na pu na na pu.
Ye, Al'Ikaki o bila bat'oona-ee!

("Ye, ee-ee ee-ee.
Ye, Chief Tortoise has killed an elephant, hear-o!
Ye, all who can hear, all who can hear,
Ye, Chief Tortoise has killed an elephant, hear-eee!")

When the procession reaches the *ekine* house, the players go inside to undress and drink, and the spectators disperse to their homes. The play is over.

The Ikaki play is definitely one of the lighter items in the *ekine* society's repertoire. As one of the performers told me: "We put it on after the Igbo play to cool people down".[10] At the same time, it is clearly a major attraction, for which fishermen in remote camps and salaried employees in Port Harcourt, Aba and Enugu make every effort to return. What is its special allure?

First, it is magnificent ballet—a wonderfully concentrated distillation, in the gestures of the dance, of a character whose portrayal is normally spread through a vast corpus of story. The distillation is made specially piquant by the presence of contrasting foils in the shapes of the silly Aboita and the moronic Nimiaa Poku.

But I think Kalabari enthusiasm for this play has deeper roots. For some clue as to what these roots are, we must return to Kalabari ideas about the play's origin—ideas which I sketched at the beginning of this article. Kalabari, as you will recall, say they first encountered Ikaki as a fascinating but deadly spiritual being. Despite, or perhaps because of, his deadliness, they were determined to make their own imitation of him. Finally, as the result of precautions and modifications made at the instance of Suku they managed to produce an imitation devoid of the deadly properties of the original. In this sense, their playing of Ikaki was at the same time a taming of him.

This account of origins raises several intriguing questions. First, why should Kalabari believe that the prototype of this comic play is an essentially deadly force? The answer, I suggest, is not far to seek. For Ikaki is not only an animal or a nature spirit. In Kalabari metaphor, he is also a certain type of personality amply represented in present-day society. This is the amoral, psychopathic confidence trickster—the type who accepts society only in order to prey upon it. Kalabari have a very real fear of the human tortoise; so much so that they are reluctant to contract marriage alliances with certain Houses in which he is believed to abound. In the intelligent, plausible psychopath, that universal threat to the fabric of the community, we can surely see the source of the idea of Ikaki as the fascinating yet deadly Old Man of the Forest.

Given that the plausible psychopath provides the ultimate inspiration for the Ikaki play, in what sense can the play be said to tame him? Well, as an artistic performance, it puts him in a frame and imposes form on him. Again, by portraying him in animal guise, it "distances" the audience from the particular human psychopaths that arouse their anxieties, and allows them to contemplate the type in tranquillity.[11] Finally, the play tames the disturbing experiences that inspires it by a subtle distortion of their content. The Ikaki of the play is as evil and as amoral as his real-life counterpart. The hopping dance which accompanies the Ada beat reminds us of his deadliness, and several of his drum-epithets remind us of his total lack of scruple. But his deviousness and his cunning are modified. For one thing, they are exaggerated and caricatured to the point of absurdity.

For another thing, they are portrayed as having limits that all too seldom restrict the human tortoises of everyday life. Clever and unscrupulous as he is, Ikaki of the play falls in love with a silly woman and marries her, then begets and adores a witless child. Between them, wife and child undo many of his bestlaid schemes. In the play, indeed, the "undoing" of Aboita and Nimiaa Poku is as much in evidence as the "doing" of Ikaki. In these various ways, then, the disturbing real-life experience of plausible psychopaths is controlled, confined, and cut down to size. People laugh from out of their depths at the ravening forest beast, because for once they have got him behind bars.

Notes

1. For a general description of the Kalabari masquerade and its institutional setting, see my "Kalabari Ekine Society"; *Africa*, April, 1963.
2. It is a little puzzling to find that in the context of story-telling Ikaki is regarded as a purely fictional character, whilst in the context of masquerade dancing he is regarded as a nature spirit (*owuamabo*). The explanation seems to be that the *ekine* masquerade society focused from the beginning on plays representing the *owuamapu*. Hence any new play brought into the society, no matter what its actual inspiration, tended to acquire a mythical charter which brought it into line with the general scheme of inspiration by contact with this class of spirits.
3. My informants were unable to translate this, and treated it as water-spirit language unintelligible to men.
4. Readers will have noticed that in Ikaki's second warning song, it is Kula and not Oloma that is mentioned. I suspect this is because Kula fits the tune better than Oloma.
5. Although *ekine* society taboos debar me from mentioning the present Ikaki dancer by name, I should like to record my gratitude to him and his brother for their very helpful commentary on the play.
6. In any particular performance of the Ikaki play, the name called in the dirge is that of the most recently deceased *amanyanabo*.
7. This is Ikaki's actual drum-name.
8. The Atabila fish (*Tilapia nigra*) is said to be the drummer of the water-spirits.

9. *Youruba*: An unusual word for palm-fruit which I have not heard used outside this context.
10. For an account of the Igbo play, see my "Igbo: An Ordeal for Aristocrats"; *Nigeria Magazine*, Vol 90, September, 1966.
11. For a discussion of spirit and animal figures as devices for attaining "distance" in Kalabari art, see my "Kalabari Ekine Society"; *Africa*, April, 1963.

Reprinted Nigeria Magazine, No. 94, 1967.

EZEIGBOEZUE: AN IGBO MASQUERADE PLAY
Nnabuenyi Ugonna

My main purpose is to present the text of a tape-recorded *mmonwu* poetic drama. The text which is an edited transcript translated free style into English was recorded during an arena performance at Ihitenansa on January 27, 1973, in honour of Dr. H. S. Corran who was then visiting the town. One hopes thereby to draw critical attention to the subject of *mmonwu* drama, a form that is rightly regarded as perhaps the most important genre of Igbo oral literature, and provide some, if limited, material for critical study and appreciation of oral Igbo dramatic literature. Furthermore, this should stimulate interest in more researches into similar or related aspects of Igbo oral literature which may, in time, result in the systematic documentation of several literary texts that would serve as useful contribution to material for further studies in Igbo literature. To expose to the academic, as well as the *mmonwu* community, part of the material already gathered in *mmonwu* literature would surely stimulate discussion at all levels related to the subject.

The term, *mmonwu*, is generally used in two different senses either as a general concept for all forms of plays involving masking or as sacred mask drama, in which traditionally conceived masked spirits perform various dramatic activities with speeches and dialogue, on an open air arena or stage. The *mmonwu* play presented here belongs to the latter category.

In the light of our present research this tradition of *mmonwu* was first originated in Egbema Ozubulu in the nineteenth century by an Arochukwu immigrant whose home can still be traced and whose descendants are alive. The name of this Aro man was Okonkwo Ogbuchi who in about 1840 got together some re-nowned *dibia* (medicine men) in Egbema Ozubulu and initiated them into the secret knowledge of *mmonwu* which was reputedly revealed to him in a dream. Thus he formed the first *ekwuru*

Participants in an Igbo Masquerade Play.

(house of wisdom). From this *ekwuru* emerged the first *mmonwu* called Igbokwe who is reputed to be the Father of all *mmonwu*. Igbokwe from the start was said to be very powerful and the early members of his *ekwuru* were famous medicine men who performed rather miraculous feats. In his *obom* (arena) he had *oda*, an earthen platform, from where he spoke prophetically and with authority. Whatever he said must come to pass. There was a little element of *dibia afa* in it. He could tell about the future and the past.

From Ozubulu and *mmonwu* tradition under investigation spread all over what I have designated "the nwaezenogwu area" which stretches between the basins of the Urasi and Njaba Rivers to the north and south and between the towns of Orlu in Imo State and Aboh in Bendel State to the east and west. From the 1880's to the early decades of the twentieth century *mmonwu* theatres were established all over such towns as Ukpo, Lilu, Ihembosi, Ihiala, Ihitenansa, Ugwuta, Akuma, and others. Groups acquired their theatres either from the original Ikwuru Igbokwe in Egbema Ozubulu or from any other *ekwuru* derived from it. In this way all the *ekwuru* in the nwaezenogwu theatrical zone have formed a genealogical link.

The play which text is given below was performed by Ezeigboezue's playhouse. As in all *mmonwu* plays there were three categories of performers: the masked figures, the male chorus and orchestra often collectively called *Okuigba*, and the female chorus known as *mmarigo* or *ereere*. In accordance with the African central staging technique the audience stood round the field though seats were provided for the important guests. The spectators were seated or standing before the appearance of the masked figures in the open-air stage. The *okuigba* and the *mmarigo* entertained the audience before the *mmonwu* characters "answered" in a temporary *ekwuru* near the school. They came into the arena, led by the *akakpo*, the diminutive masquerade who maintains order by causing panic. As they arrived, the *mmarigo* intoned the welcome song. Then *Eze mmuo*, that is *Ezeigboezue*, took charge of the dramatic activities. Apart from the chief masquerade and the diminutive *akakpo* also called *"ukwu"* (foot) *"mmuo"* (spirit) two other categories namely, *dimkpa mmuo* and *agbogho mmuo* participated. The *dimkpa mmuo* is generally almost as tall as the *Eze mmuo* who may be over three metres in height. *Agboho mmuo* or the maiden spirit is conceived as the goddess of beauty.

Translated Text of Play

Masks on the Stage:

Ezeigboezue	— king mask
Esibeagugo	— his first son
Ugerumba	— dwarf mask
Egobude	— maiden mask

Performing Initiates:

Akatakpo	— director of play
Akiriaki (clerk)	— the linguist or interpreter
Opiaomu	— wielder of the yellow palm leaves
Okwaopi	— horn-blower
Okwaekwe	— wooden drummer
Ndi okuigba	— male chorus and dancers
Umu mmarigo	— female chorus and dancers
Ndi oleanya	— spectators

The character traits of the masked figures are implied in their names. *Ezeigboezue* means "king all Igbo people have assembled". It refers to the all embracing and almighty character of the chief mask. *Esibeagugo* "if there is doubt", a warning that all who doubt the power of the masquerade would have themselves to blame for the consequences.

Ugerumba (uge-eru-mba), means magical display has no effect in a foreign land. This implies that no charm from any alien *mmonwu* can touch members of this dramatic group known as Ekwuru Ezeigboezue. *Egobude*, the maiden mask, has a name signifying wealth, fame and beauty—*ego-bu-ude*, that is, money carries fame or money brings about fame. It could also be interpreted as *ego-buude*, which is, money is fame.

I

Spectators surround the arena. Horn and wooden drum players praise *mmonwu* with their instrumentation. The male players perform on the central stage and the maidens begin to chant.

Mmarigo: Maidens, hasten steps
                    Hasten steps for we will go to Oru
                    Maidens, hasten steps
                    Hasten steps for we will go to Oru
                    Where Oru weaves cloth
                    And tailors together
                    Maidens, hasten steps
                    for the non-initiate knows it not.
                    Even if the non-initiate knows the cloth
                    He knows not the material with
                          which the cloth is made Ugerumba, king
                    Whose father legislates and implants
                        the iron staff
                    In the *mmonwu* arena

II

The initiates enter the inner *ekwuru* to raise *mmonwu*. *Mmonwu* answer in the *ekwuru*. As they come into the central stage the *mmarigo* lead-singer intones the welcome song and all the maidens respond.

Okwaaguruagu: Welcome King, welcome;
Mmarigo: Oh King.
Okwaaguruagu: Welcome King, welcome;
Mmarigo: If a king is seen he is greeted.
Okwaaguruagu: Igboezue welcome;
Mmarigo: Igboezue implants the staff in the centre.
Okwaaguruagu: Esibeagugo welcome;
Mmarigo: Esibeagugo dances in the centre.
Okwaaguruagu: Egobude welcome;
Mmarigo: Egobude displays grace in the arena.
Okwaaguruagu: Ugerumba welcome;
Mmarigo: Ugerumba chases ogbodi around
                       Father of females
                       Mask desires a walk and so arises

Father of maidens
Knowledgeable Ezengo, the learned
Father of maidens
Esibeagugo I met on the arena
Boa-egg came out
And called me lead-singer of mmonwu
He called me lead-singer
And asked me to chant mmonwu chants
Then I exclaimed okokooko
Igboezue's maidens sing:

Mmarigo: King, welcome
Ezeigboezue implants the staff in the centre
Esibeagugo dances in the centre
Egobude displays grace in the arena
Ugerumba chases ogbodi around
Spectacles seen on modern roads
Let beholders come and behold he-who-
  emerges-with-wealth
He-who-emerges-with-wealth
Oh! King

III

Enter masks on the stage. They move around and perform acts.

Ezeigboezue: Muoma
Son of Ugonnia, are you present?
Osimiri is more precious than coins

Osimiri: Lion!
Knife used to kill a lion
Spear
Cassava and thorns
  (unsifted cassava).

Ezeigboezue: Ezeosimiri, welcome, my son.
I am a lion
And also he who acts and knows
Osimiri my son . . .
Muoma offspring of Ugonnia!

Muoma: Okeke!
Ezeigboezue: Muoma!

Osimiri:	He who offends gets into trouble
Ezeigboezue:	Wonderful happening that occurs in human land
	It has happened?
	A man after weaving a chieftain's cap
	Put the cap on his head.
	A bachelor with one wife should take care.
	For if something happens to her, all is lost.
Osimiri:	My father (my lord) I am not indeed
	throwing to you ten naira, or is it
	said twenty naira.
	(*There was laughter. What he wanted to say was one naira*).
Ezeigboezue:	(*Starts chanting*)
	Kee kee kee ke nu
	Child uninitiated be not anxious
	Young child you are on a journey
	Ezenwaka
	Child of Ezenwakaibeya, who is learned.
Ezenwaka:	He who destroys and restores!
Ezeigboezue:	All humans, welcome
	It happens that if a man goes to
	Onicha and accumulates wealth
	When he returns to his father land
	He begins to speak the Onicha dialect;
	But when he has exhausted the money he made,
	he remembers to speak the tongue of his native land.
	When a retired government official
	Starts wearing bed sheet
	Or starts wrapping himself in a blanket
	Let it be known that the money he earned is exhausted.
One initiated member:	Epim
Initiated Members:	Aa oo.
Ezeigboezue:	Ekwueme!
Ekwueme:	Obeke,
	He who with knife cut down wealth.
Ezeigboezue:	Child more knowledgeable than his comrades;
	Who is lettered
	Ekwueme!

Ekwueme:	Seven, eight!
Ezeigboezue:	The unlucky one is brother to the prodigal
	For a man not to have money is bad
Spectators:	Not to have money is bad
Ezeigboezue:	(*Jubilating*) Ko ko ko
Osimiri:	(*praising*) Okeke
Ezeigboezue:	Osimiri . . .
Osimiri:	Knife with which lion is killed
Ezeigboezue:	It happens that if a deity becomes very strong he is appeased with a ram;
	If he is lenient, then it is with a cock that he would be mollified
	Osimiri
	Instead of a man to be inconsequential
	Let him like the uga grow fast and depart
	To have no money is bad for a man.
Osimiri:	It is indeed very bad
Ezeigboezue:	Holders of money please pardon me
	Ezeihedinobi, Ihedi
	To beget an idiot is the same thing as to lose a child
	It happens that when humans assemble for a meeting
	It is agreed that it would hold at cock crow
	Humans, some have cocks, some have none
Diizugbe:	Head like drum
Ezeigbokwe:	Yes,
	Diizugbe
Diizugbe:	Spirit you are
Ezeigboezue:	Wonderful events that happen in human society has happened.
Diizugbe:	It has happened
Ezeigboezue:	Osimiri
	If a man gets money, let him spend some and save some
	On the destined day the brave departs
	If the kindred meet and find the means, funeral rites would be performed.
	But if they meet and find nothing, the rites are deferred.
	Three weeks after death
	Human and spiritual advisers would meet.

> Those killed by small-pox who mourned them
> Those who accumulate wealth without enjoying it
> who mourned them
> Man dissolves.

The audience would start clamouring. The uninitiated and the women would exclaim in wonder, the initiated would be applauding *mmonwu*. The mmarigo would be singing and clapping hands; *mmonwu* dances while the hornblower displays his artistry. *Mmonwu* play is at its peak.

Reprinted Nigeria Magazine, No. 114, 1974.

DRAMATIC PRESENTATION IN UDJE DANCE PERFORMANCE OF THE URHOBO

G. G. Darah

This essay attempts a descriptive review of Udje festival dance performance. Udje is a dance form practised by Urhobo national-ity in Bendel State. Believed to have originated in remote antiquity, Udje is, for those who perform it, a classic of dance and poetry against which is measured most of the dance and poetic forms that have flourished in this part of Nigeria. Like most indigenous artistic traditions in rural Nigeria, Udje is now in decline, although a few communities still organize annual dis-plays largely reduced in duration and magnitude. The account presented here is a highly condensed form of an elaborate programme spanning a period of three months—from the engen-dering of the songs to the moment of presenting them in the public arena. It is a programme that taxes the intellectual and organizational skills of the practitioners. Although our emphasis in this paper is on the act of presentation before a crowded arena, the whole activity should be seen as an organic process which culminates in the public performance.

The material is presented in four parts. The first describes the social climate in which the dance is staged, a climate which determines the aesthetic pursuit of the Udje enterprise. In the second part, we outline how individuals and the group prepare for an impending festival. The third section details the presenta-tion procedure on the arena, while the fourth and final section attempts a brief analysis of a sample segment from an Udje song which can be produced in a dramatized form.

I

The aesthetic end of most Urhobo dance-songs is to entertain an audience in a public arena. This goal is expressed in the

504

Urhobo popular saying that a new song is like a bride whose qualities are best appreciated during a bridal procession. The songs are composed and memorized and the accompanying choreographic movements rehearsed in advance of the annual dance-song carnivals. Since the entertainment of an immediate audience is the primary objective of the musical practice, the song texts, dance movements, and costumes of the performers are synchronized to suit a public performance conducted in the manner of an opera. In the course of the performance, emphasis is placed on spectacle and visual representation.

Besides the need to thrill the spectators, the dramatic procedure in every performance is dictated by the factor of inter-community rivalry which informs most of Urhobo song-poetry practice. For Udje on which our analysis is focused, all the participating communities and groups are ranged in permanent rivalry pairs of opposition. This pairing phenomenon is known as *omẹsuọ*. The yearly carnivals serve as "battle grounds" where, as the practitioners put it, each group strives "to sing its rival to a fall". This objective demands that each performance attains the level of theatrical intensity capable of keeping the audience enthralled. For the presentation of a song to achieve this effect it must be done with a creative combination of both verbal and non-verbal elements. The non-verbal aspects include ostentatious costume (*osẹvbẹ*), dexterity of footwork (*owotọ-ọna*), and masterly management of the entire performance.

In the case of a narrative song (*ule ẹshan*), the text must be structured to enhance dramatic presentation on the arena. Such a piece contains three parts—*okparọ* (introduction), *ọogregrẹn* (main body) and *ifuen* (conclusion)—each of which may again consist of sub-sections or performance units. While creating new songs the song-makers (*irorile*) (singular: *ororile*) must ensure that the piece in question satisfies these technical demands. The lead singers (*ẹbuole*) (singular: *ọbuole*) are expected to handle the song with the required degree of technical assurance in order to bring out its full dramatic potential. During the presentation the performance units in the narrative song are led by the *ẹbuole* in attendance in an alternate sequence. In addition, certain sections are either wholly or partly mimed in order to enhance the visual transmission of the intended message. Sometimes, a song may be prologued or climaxed by the bearing into the dance ring of the effigy of the character after whom the song is made. Whenever the above-mentioned technical requirements are satisfied, the resultant performance is described as *muuririn* or *muowan*, that is spectacular or aesthetically profound.

II

Preparations before the Carnival

Intensive preparations for the festival begin several weeks previously; but the few days preceding the first day of performance are devoted to night rehearsals known as *igbe asǫn*. The rehearsals are intended to ensure that all participants are sufficiently disciplined in their actions before appearing in public. There are other preparations which every performer must make before considering himself fit to appear in the arena. These include magical fortification and elegant costume. As already pointed out, the dance arena is seen by the participant as a battleground from which he must return triumphant. Thus he must be accoutred in the manner of a warrior.

A performer insures himself against stage-fright (*omavovbę*) with an appropriate charm. While administering it he may be heard saying: 'E gbe t'uwovbin oma ke rh'ohwo", that is, "a dancer knows fatigue only after a performance". Anyone practised in gymnastic feats wears an amulet known as *etanmu* ("magnetism"). The ingredients for this charm include parts of a monkey's tail, the monkey being reputed for agility and steadfast grip. The following chant accompanies the preparation:

Damukelegbe	Perch on summits
Izagede ewerin yan gan	The monkey is master of giddy heights
Ophopho ghwei egbri-ii	No wind can uproot the *egbri* grass
Ǫyęn ęgha!	It is not possible!

Lead singers don parrot's feathers on the head. The feather symbolizes the chirping power of the parrot. A dancer's outfit includes stringed bells (*igogo*) tied round the waist. The bells serve as metal rattles which produce their own melody whenever the dancer responds to the rhythmic throb of the drums. A long cock's feather (*alele*) is also steadied on the head; and this makes rhythmical movements while the wearer is dancing. Every performer holds in one hand a bright-coloured, woollen fan (*odjudju*) and in the other a handkerchief.

III

During the festival, performances are held twice daily for a maximum of eight days. The last day of the festival is set aside for the presentation of cash gifts (*oghwa*) to the participants by their relatives and well-wishers. The day's performance is appropriately referred to as *igbe oghwa* ("presentation performance"). Each performance session is conducted in regulated scenes or sequences. There are a total of eight such scenes. Sequences V–VII may be repeated several times during the course of the performance. Below, we give the significance for each sequence, followed by a brief description of the action that takes place therein. (The organizational arrangement described here is the same for most Urhobo secular dance displays.)

Sequence I: Igbe eseho (summoning the participants)

The summoning of the participants to the arena is begun by a signal group of drummers (*ekwa*). The group drums and sings through the community or ward. The group may call at the residence of notable members of the troupe to urge them to quicken their preparations. Each participant that is ready joins the signal group. As it goes its rounds, eager spectators also join the group. Once a large enough crowd is formed, it moves in a processional dance to the house of *Uhanghwa*. (Uhanghwa is the muse of Urhobo secular song-poetry.) Its emblem is kept in the custody of someone chosen by the community.

Sequence II: Uhanghwa eyeren: (paying homage to Uhanghwa)

When the troupe gets to the compound of the Uhanghwa keeper, it forms a ring round the emblem which is stood on a stool before the troupe arrives. The *Uhanghwa* priest offers prayers for a successful show. He sprinkles the *Uhanghwa* medicinal water on the participants as he utters incantations such as:

E gbe t' uwovbin oma ke rh' ohwo
Igbe ben ohori hi
Ijije a mr'opha

A dancer knows fatigue only after a performance
The caterpillar never tires of dancing
Compliment greets the bride wherever she goes

The prayers are followed with the singing of three *Uhanghwa* ritual songs to which the troupe dances. Like martial music, the songs instil in the participants the mood of combat-readiness and also express the wish for a triumphant display on the arena. The following is one of such songs:

1st Solo:	Oruimwomwo kenoma
	Uhanghwa ji vbe ni mi gbe
	Oyen igbe na
2nd Solo:	Edjedje a mr'oletu
Group:	Oruimwomwo kenoma
	Uhanghwa ji vbe ni mi gbe
	Oyen igbe na
2nd Solo:	Ughe r'opha ukopha hren
Group:	Oruimwomwo kenoma
	Uhanghwa ji vbe ni mi gbe
	Oyen igbe na
1st Solo:	Let the mischief-maker beware
	Uhanghwa has authorized me to perform
	Behold the dance
2nd Solo:	The sight of a commander causes a stampede
Group:	Let the mischief-maker beware
	Uhanghwa has authorized me to perform
	Behold the dance
2nd Solo:	The bride is the cynosure of the brides-maid's eyes
Group:	Let the mischief maker beware
	Uhanghwa has authorized me to perform
	Here comes the dance.

Sequence III: Igbe vbo kp'ada (procession to the arena)

After the ritual observances the troupe heads for the arena. The procession is led by a maiden who bears the *Uhanghwa* emblem on her head. A short and rousing song is sung and danced to. The singing, drumming, and clapping combine to produce a flourish reminiscent of troops marching to the battle field. This is especially so where several groups are heading towards the arena simultaneously. The resultant pageantry is capable of rousing even those who are reluctant to leave their homes. The following processional song anticipates such an effect:

1st Solo:	Udje r'Aladja* ru'ovborho
	Ọ ro nyo v'uwovbin guenronma
	Udje r'Aladja mi re hrin
	Ọyẹn Udje na
2nd Solo:	Ọvẹrenȶ ru'ada re yo
	Ughe na
Group:	Udje r'Aladja ru'ovborho
	O ro nyo vb'uwovbin guenronma
	Udje r'Aladja mi re hrin
	Ọyẹn udje na
1st Solo:	An Aladja dance troupe is in procession
	Let excitement grip those who hear in their homes
	It is Aladja dance I am going to watch
	Behold the dance
2nd Solo:	The Ọvẹrẹn (*Uhanghwa*) muse is now abroad
	What a spectacle!
Group:	An Aladja dance troupe is in procession
	Let excitement grip those who hear in their homes
	It is Aladja dance I am going to watch
	Here comes the dance.

Sequence IV: Igbe ẹrhuẹrẹhọ (positioning the participants)

As soon as the procession reaches the arena the spectators who accompany it separate themselves from it to join others who arrive early enough to occupy vantage points for viewing. The *Uhanghwa* emblem is lowered on to a stool while the performers dance round it. After a while, the dancing stops. This enables the participants to take up positions. Three rings emerge at this point. The innermost one is formed by the principal partici-

---

* The name of the performing community or quarter is inserted here.
ȶ Another name for *Uhanghwa*.

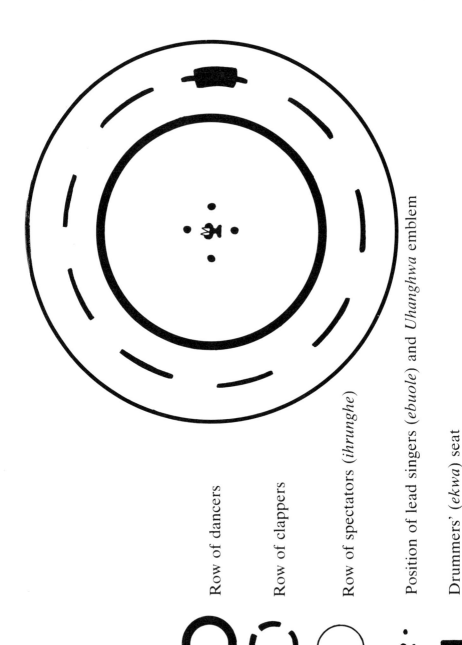

Row of dancers

Row of clappers

Row of spectators (*ihrunghe*)

Position of lead singers (*ebuole*) and *Uhanghwa* emblem

Drummers' (*ekwa*) seat

Fig. 1: *Diagram showing The Theatre in Udje Dance Presentation.*

pants—dancers, lead singers, and drummers. (The drummers—three in number—sit throughout the performance.) The middle ring is occupied by clappers (women), while the outermost one is made up of spectators. As soon as the rings are formed, masters of ceremony locate star dancers (*emusi*) at strategic points along the innermost ring. Throughout the session, lead singers (*ẹbuole*) are free to move within the innermost ring. (See Fig. 1 for a diagramatic representation of the arrangements in this Sequence.)

Sequence V: Warming up Dance

With the above arrangements over, the dance sessions commence. A few short numbers are sung in rapid succession, each with drum and dance accompaniment. The purpose is to warm up the participants as well as to stimulate enthusiasm in the spectators. Each song may be repeated several times. At a point, singing gives way to drumming and dancing only. After a while, the drummers increase the tempo of the drum beats to draw the dancers into an ecstatic mood. This may go on for several minutes. The entire sequence is brought to a close with a tumultuous ovation of ii-i-i-i, ije-e-e-e, meaning—hip, hip, hurrah!

Sequence VI: Ilẹshan (performing narrative songs)

This sequence is given to the performance of long, narrative songs (*ile ẹshan*). The main actors at this stage are the lead singers, although other members of the troupe who know the particular song well enough may join them in the centre of the ring. Ideally, each of the three constituent parts of an *ule ẹshan*, namely, *okparọ* (introduction), the main body, and *ifuen* (conclusion) is led by an *ọbuole* during the delivery. Limited drumming is allowed in the *ifuen* section. The restriction on drumming is to enable the listeners to follow the full story in the song. Usually the narrative song is rendered in a recitative manner. This procedure permits the lead singers to embellish the song text with appropriate extempore phrases and other performance nuances such as gestures, voice inflexion, and mimetic movements. It is the dexterous handling of these performance techniques that combines with the metrical flourish of the song itself to produce the theatrical gaiety expected of this sequence.

Further theatricality is achieved through spectators' spontaneous appreciative ovations (*ekunvbien*) which punctuate the performance of a narrative song. Occasioned by a good turn of phrase, a pithy metaphor, or topical allusion, these ovations catalyse the audience into an ecstatic mood, under the spell of which some spectators may "invade" the dance ring to congratulate the lead singer(s) with a hug or cash gift (*oghwa*). At such moments the dimensions of the theatre are temporarily dislocated as spectators and performers become one huge mass of possessed beings. These climatic junctures interrupt the performance proceedings but they also provide psychological fuel for the participants to perform more spiritedly. When several dance groups are performing simultaneously, the number and frequency of such audience interruptions can attract spectators from other dance rings where the action is less dramatic.

Sequence VII: Udje edjuo (Interlude)

Literally, *Udje edjuo* means "fanning the performance". It is an interlude scene brought in to allow the performers a brief rest after an exacting session. *Udje edjuo* is performed by a woman referred to as *Aje Udje* ("The Lady of the Dance") and this is the only occasion in which a woman plays a major role in the Udje outfit. The *Aje Udje* must be above average in physique and feminine qualities. She is expected to appear in an ostentatious attire. Holding a colourful, woollen fan in one hand, she is ushered into the dance ring by a master of ceremonies. An assistant, another female similarly dressed, walks behind her as she moves gracefully in the ring. She swings her fan in vertical movements purporting to cool the heat from the bodies of the dancers. The assistant also fans her from behind while declaiming her ladylike qualities thus:

Ironron	You are a jewel of a woman!
Tota, wo j'udu bru we-e	Talk on, don't be afraid!
Wo f'avbaren hron	You are our choicest representative

Simultaneously, the *Aje Udje* addresses the performers who respond enthusiastically thus:

Aję Udje:	Udje ishaka mi ni wado
	(Young dancers, I say well done)
Performers:	Iya!
	(Thank you)
Aję Udje:	Udje Esaba* mi ni wado
	(Dancers from Esaba, I say well done)
Performers:	Iya!
	(Thank you)
Aję Udje:	(ii-i-i-i) thrice
	(Hip, hip)
Performers:	(Ije-e-e-!) thrice
	(Hurrah!)

At the end of the loud cheer, the two women remain in the centre of the ring. The drummers begin a fast beat to which both ladies and performers respond. The dancing is brought to a stop with another rousing cheer of ii-i-i-i, ije-e-e-e! As the ovation reaches a crescendo, a star dancer (*ǫmusi*) embraces the *Aję Udje* and makes a mock attempt to lift her up in the manner that a champion would be carried up after a brilliant performance. As the two ladies leave the ring, the drummers again pick up the fast note while all performers join in a vigorous dance sequence concluded with another declamatory shout of ii-i-i-i, ije-e-e-e!

Sequence VIII: Udje ęghwię (closing scene)

This scene begins with either an *Uhanghwa* song or any number suitable for a processional dance. As soon as the song is begun the drummers rise from their seats and join dancers and clappers. At this point the dimensions of the stage collapse, giving way to a single mass. The carrier takes up the *Uhanghwa* emblem and leads a procession back to the *Uhanghwa* house. Thenceforth we have, save for minor changes, a repeat of Sequences II and III in reverse order. When the procession reaches its destination the *Uhanghwa* emblem is stood in the open yard. Three *Uhanghwa* numbers are sung and danced to, after which everyone retires home.

---

* The name of the performing community or quarter is inserted here.

IV

Below we represent a brief analysis of two scenes from the action in Sequence VI, namely, how the lead singers prepare themselves to perform a narrative piece, and a paragraph-by-paragraph commentary of an operatic segment of a typical narrative song.

Before starting the *ule eshan* the *ebuole* prime themselves for the event and also build up excitement in the audience. One or two of them may prance through the dance ring, stamping their feet in the process. The lead singers then test their voice levels by singing through twice or thrice the last few lines of the concluding section of the song. This may be accompanied by drumming and some choreographic movements. These preambles help to solicit concentrated attention from the spectators. In fact, while the lead singers are priming themselves for action some members of the audience may be heard saying "*A doo!*" ("Silence please!") or "*A vb'erho ghwa ayen*" (lit., "receive the songs through the ears"). Once a quiet enough atmosphere is created, the presentation of the song begins.

The other aspect we wish to highlight concerns the manner in which the *ebuole* attempt to produce operatic grandeur in the presentation of the song. As already mentioned, some of the long pieces are structured in such a way as to be easily amenable to dramatic presentation. A song may begin in a leisurely, recitatory manner, gradually increasing in "metrical velocity" and intensity to culminate at a climactic point. This is often the case when the plot of the song involves opposed forces or characters. Domestic strifes furnish song-makers with ideal material for such plotting. In the really successful constructions the tensed moods and episodes are rendered in their proper dramatic pitch through a masterly arrangement of figures of speech and syllabic movements. During the presentation, the lead singers attempt to vivify the dramatic scenes through gestures, mimicry and feet-stamping.

The paragraphs analysed below illustrate some of the features just mentioned. The paragraphs are excerpts from a piece entitled *Logbo* by the Egbo-Ide community. The brawl described is between Logbo and his second wife, Sati. Of Logbo's two wives, Sati is childless. An Ijọ masseur is consulted, who after diagnosis, discovers that Logbo has lost his procreative powers. As soon as the masseur leaves, Sati, long suspected of being barren, tries to take revenge on the husband. Rather than accept responsibility, Logbo resorts to a face-saving tactic by accusing Sati of witchcraft. The encounter proceeds in the form of a tensed dialogue and climaxes in Sati throwing household wares at the husband. The whole episode is rendered in four paragraphs, each introduced by appropriate commentary by the poets. For emphasis, most of the lines are sung twice.

The first paragraph pictures Sati in her initial fits of anger:

> Soon after the masseur departed Sati started fuming
> She paced the room *gbrọgbrọgbrọ* (thunderously)
> She stepped on a drinking cup and smashed it
> An earthenware she stepped on too
> Stepped on earthenware and crushed it
> Logbo unable to bear it all queried:
> Is this the witchcraft you inherited from your mother
> That is possessing you in day time?

Throughout her marital life Sati, according to the verdict of the masseur, has been wrongly suspected of barrenness. And in a society where children are a measure of successful life, to be childless is cause enough for misery. But to add to this the stigma of witchcraft as Logbo does, is one provocation too many. Predictably, Sati's bile bursts:

> Sati already boiling over with rage
> Let loose a torrent of unspeakable invectives:
> May animals devour you, devour you piecemeal
> With filthy teeth like spots excreted on
> A balloon-shaped nose like a thatch-roofed boat
> You knew I ended my menstrual period recently
> Yet you brought a useless penis into my bedroom
> Ever since my bridal days I have had no womb complications
> Even the masseur you invited confirmed it all
> My womb is open and fertile.

To Sati's claim of fertility Logbo replies, again in a provocative manner:

Is your womb open for child-bearing? asked Logbo
I spend fortunes to engage the services of Ijo masseurs
But they succeed only in repairing your alimentary canal
You who ate hot starch to block your foetus
Tell me what weight you lost makes you eat so heavily

Sati by now thinks she has had enough. Choked by anger, she abandons the verbal exchange and hurls missiles at Logbo:

Says Sati: These insults hurt me more than blows can
She took an iron tripod and flung at him
Grabbed a ladle and also hurled at him
A glowing faggot she aimed at his groins
And forced a scared Logbo to flee the room
Don't run away, let me fry you
Don't run away, let me roast you alive!

Much of the theatrical vividness and hilarity which these passages are capable of evoking are inevitably lost in the translation. Seen in context, the enactment of the encounter comes across to the audience with exhilarating immediacy. The lead singers endeavour to impersonate the pugnacious mien as well as mimic the utterances of husband and wife. The rendition of expressions like *gbrogbrogbro* (first paragraph) is accompanied with appropriate corporal movements to bring out their onomatopoeic forcefulness. Similarly, the last two lines in the fourth paragraph are delivered with exaggerated tonal inflexion to emphasize the combative mood they are intended to convey. In fact, the word "fry" appears in the Urhobo version. It adds lexical variety to the passage and also provides epigrammatic finish to the stormy encounter.

CONTRIBUTORS

J. A. ADEDEJI, Professor and former Head of Theatre Arts Department, University of Ibadan; still on the staff of the Department.

Dapo ADELUGBA is the Artistic Director of the Department of Theatre Arts, University of Ibadan.

Olu AKOMOLAFE is on the staff of the Department of Dramatic Arts, University of Ife, Ile-Ife.

James AMANKULOR, director, critic, is Senior Lecturer in Drama at the University of Nigeria, Nsukka.

Ulli BEIER who once lived and worked for a long time in Nigeria and now settled in West Germany, has written extensively on Nigerian culture and art.

Ebun CLARK, is on the staff of the Department of English at the University of Lagos.

J. P. CLARK, playwright, poet and critic now retired from the headship of the English Department at the University of Lagos.

G. G. DARAH teaches Oral Literature in the Department of Literature in English at the University of Ife.

M. J. C. ECHERUO, poet, Professor of English, is on the staff of the Department of English at the University of Ibadan.

R. T. E. ELLISON, a British citizen who served as the Chairman of the Public Service Commission in the former Northern Nigeria.

Ossie ENEKWE, poet, novelist, assistant editor of *Okike*, teaches Literature in the English Department of the University of Nigeria, Nsukka.

Edith ENEM is Principal Cultural Officer in the Federal Ministry of Social Development, Youth, Sports and Culture.

Femi EUBA, playwright, teaches drama and literature in the Department of Dramatic Arts, University of Ife.

C. G. B. GIDLEY is a British citizen who has written on Nigerian art and culture.

517

Andrew HORN is a lecturer in the Department of English, National University of Lesotho.

Robin HORTON who is on the staff of the Philosophy Department at the University of Port Harcourt, has written extensively on Kalabari religion and art.

Akin ISOLA, playwright, teaches Yoruba language and literature in the Department of African languages and literatures, University of Ife.

Biodun JEYIFO, radical critic, founding editor of *Positive Review*. Teaches literature in the Department of Literature in English, University of Ife.

E. O. KOFOWOROLA is at the centre for Nigerian Cultural Studies, Ahmadu Bello University, Zaria.

Demas NWOKO, sculptor, painter, Art Consultant and Managing Director of the New Culture Studios, Ibadan.

Onuora NZEKWU, novelist and former Editor of *Nigeria Magazine*.

Meki NZEWI, director, playwright, musicologist, is on the staff of the Institute of African Studies, University of Nigeria, Nsukka.

Yemi OGUNBIYI, a founding editor of *Positive Review*, teaches drama and literature at the University of Ife.

Segun OLUSOLA is a director on the Board of Nigerian Television Authority.

Ola ROTIMI, playwright, director, now Head of the Drama Unit at the University of Port Harcourt.

Wole SOYINKA, playwright, poet, novelist is also Professor and Head of Department of Dramatic Arts, University of Ife.

Nnabuenyi UGONNA teaches Oral Literature in the Department of African Languages and Literature, University of Lagos.

SELECTED BIBLIOGRAPHY

I. Books and Other Sources

A. *Dissertations and Theses*

Adedeji, J. A., *The Alarinjo Theatre: The Study of a Yoruba Theatrical Art from its Earliest Beginnings to the Present Time*. Ph.D. dissertation, University of Ibadan, 1969.

Adelugba, Dapo, *Nationalism and the awakening National Theatre of Nigeria*, M.A. Thesis, UCLA, 1964.

Adeniyi, Tole, *The Yoruba Travelling Theatre; its origin, organization and structure*, M.A. Thesis, University of Lancaster, 1978.

Amankulor, James N., *The functions of traditional festivals among the Ngwa-Igbo of South-east Nigeria*, M.A. Thesis, UCLA, 1964.

—— *The Concept and Practice of the Traditional African Festival Theatre*, Ph.D. dissertation, UCLA, 1977.

Badejo, P. A., *Bori Spirit Possession Religion as a Dance Event: A Pre-Islamic Hausa Phenomenon*, M.A. Thesis, UCLA, 1980.

Besmer, Fremont E., *Hausa Court Music in Kano, Nigeria*, Ph.D. dissertation, Columbia University, 1971/72.

Ezeokoli, V. C., *African Theatre: A Nigerian Prototype*, D.F.A. dissertation, Yale University, 1972.

Gacheche, G. R., *Wole Soyinka, dramatist and his Yoruba heritage*, M.Phil. thesis, University of Leeds, 1974.

Gibbs, James, *Aspects of Nigerian dramatic tradition*, M.A. Thesis, American University, Washington, 1967.

Graham-White, Anthony, *West African drama: folk, popular and literary*, Ph.D. dissertation, Standford University, 1969.

La Pin, D. A., *The festival plays of Wole Soyinka*, M.A. Thesis, University of Wisconsin, 1971.

Lane, B. D., *Theatre for the unborn: analysis of the plays of Wole Soyinka, 1957–1974*, M.A. Thesis, Kansas University, 1974.

Leonard, Lynn, *The growth of entertainment of non-African origin in Lagos from 1866–1920 (with special emphasis on concert drama and the cinema)*, M.A. Thesis, Ibadan University, 1967.

Mbugbubi, Louis A., *Tragedies of Wole Soyinka: the African Content*, M.A. Thesis, Indiana University, 1973.

Ogunba, O., *Ritual drama of the Ijebu people: a study of indigenous festival*, Ph.D. dissertation, Ibadan University, 1968.

519

Okwesa, F. U., *Traditional Theatre in the Eastern Niger Delta of Nigeria as depicted in the Owu Masked plays*, M.A. Thesis, UCLA, 1972.

Owomeyela, Oyekan, *Folklore and the rise of theatre among the Yoruba*, Ph.D. dissertation, UCLA.

Smith, Judith, *Yoruba theatre in Ibadan: performance and urban social process*, Ph.D. dissertation, MC dissertation, McGill University, 1974.

Sofola, Zulu, *A study of theatrical elements in two festivals of the Umu Eze Chuma People in Nigeria*, M.A. Thesis, Catholic University, 1965.

B. *Books*

John Beattie and John Middleton (eds.), *Spirit Mediumship and Society in Africa*, London, 1969.

Saburi Biobaku (ed.), *The living culture of Nigeria*, Lagos, Nelson, 1970.

Ebun Clark, Hubert Ogunde, *The making of Nigerian Theatre*, Oxford, Oxford University Press in association with University Press Limited, 1979.

Anthony Graham-White, *The Drama of Black Africa*, New York, Samuel French Inc., 1974.

Abiola Irele and Oyin Ogunba (eds.), *Black African Theatre*, Ibadan, Ibadan University Press, 1978.

Bruce King (ed.), *Introduction to Nigerian Literature*, Lagos and London, University of Lagos and Evans, 1971.

Oyin Ogunba, *The Movement of Transition: a study of the plays of Wole Soyinka*, Ibadan, University Press, 1975.

Simon Ottenberg, *Masked Rituals of Afikpo*, Seattle, London, University of Washington Press, 1975.

P. A. Talbot, *Life in Southern Nigeria*.

—— *Tribes of the Niger Delta*, London, Sheldon Press, 1932.

II. Critical Material

A. *Essays and Articles*

J. A. Adedeji, "The art of the traditional Yoruba theatre", *African Arts*, Vol. 3, No. 1, 1969, pp. 60–63.

—— "The Church and the emergence of the Nigerian theatre, 1866–1914", *Journal of the Historical Society of Nigeria*, Vol. 6, No. 4, 1973, pp. 387–396.

—— "Folklore and Yoruba drama: Obatala as a case study", in Dorson, Richard M. (ed.), *African Folklore*, Garden City, New York, Doubleday & Co., 1972, pp. 321–339.

—— "Form and function of satire in Yoruba drama", *Odu*, Vol. IV, No. 1, 1967, pp. 61–72.

—— "The Nigerian Theatre and its audience", *Paper presented at the Conference of Professors of Theatre Research* in Venice, 4th–6th September, 1975.

—— "Oral tradition and the contemporary theatre in Nigeria", *Research in African Literatures*, Vol. 2, No. 2, 1971.

—— "The Origin and form of the Yoruba Masque theatre", *Cahiers d'Etudes Africaines*, Vol. 12, No. 40, 1972, pp. 254–276.

—— "The place of drama in Yoruba religious observance", *Odu*, Vol. 3, No. 1, 1968, pp. 88–94.

—— "A profile of Nigerian theatre, 1960–1970", *Nigeria Magazine*, Nos. 107/109, pp. 3–14, 1971.

—— "Trends in the content and form of the opening glee in Yoruba drama", *Research in African Literatures*, Vol. 4, No. 1, 1973, pp. 32–47.

—— "A Yoruba pantomime: an appraisal of Capt. Clapperton's account of a Yoruba theatrical performance", *Ibadan*, Vol. 29, 63/63, 1971.

Dapo Adelugba, "The need for a performing arts company", *Nigerian Opinion*, Vol. 4, Nos. 10/11, 1968.

—— "School of Drama anals Nine months agrowing", *Ibadan*, Vol. 29, 48/49, 1969.

—— "Virtuosity and sophistication in Nigerian theatrical art; a case study of Kola Ogunmola, *Nigerian Opinion*, Vol. 5, 1/2, 1969, pp. 399–401.

E. J. Alagoa, "Delta Masquerades", *Nigeria Magazine*, No. 93, 1967, pp. 145–155.

James Amankulor, "Dance as an element of Artistic Synthesis in traditional Igbo festival theatre, "*Okike*", No. 17, February, 1980, pp. 84–95.

Edwin Ardener, "Bakwere Elephant Dance", *Nigeria Magazine*, No. 60, 1959, pp. 30–38.

Martin Bahmam, "Nigerian dramatists and the traditional theatre", *Insight*, Vol. 20, 29/37, pp. 29–30.

—— "Notes on Nigerian theatre", *Bulletin of the Association for African Literature in English*, Vol. 4, 1966, pp 31–36.

—— "Theatre on Wheels", *African Forum*, Vol. 1, No. 1, 1965, pp. 108–109.

Ulli Beier, "The Agegijo Masquerades", *Nigeria Magazine*, No. 82, 1964, pp. 189–199.

—— "Yoruba Folk Operas", *African Music*, Vol. 1 (1), 1954, pp. 32–43.

—— "Traditional Yoruba Theatre", *African Arts/Arts d'Afrique*, IV, Autumn, 1969.

J. S. Boston, "Some Northern Ibo Masquerades", *Journal of the Royal Anthropological Institute*, XC, Jan/June, 1960, pp. 54–65.

J. P. Clark, "Poetry of the Urhobo dance Udje", *Nigeria Magazine*, No. 87, 1965, pp. 282–287.

Ernest Ekom, "The development of theatre in Nigeria, 1960–1967", *Journal of the New African Literature and the Arts*, 11th & 12th, 1971, pp, 36–49.

Akin Euba, "New idioms of Music-drama among the Yoruba", *Yearbook of the International Folk music Council*, Vol. 2, 1970, pp. 92–107.

E. Freeman, "The case for a National Theatre Company", *Nigerian Opinion*, Vol. 5, 1969, pp. 401–405.

A. Graham-White, "Yoruba Opera: Developing a new drama for the Nigerian People", *Theatre Quarterly*, Vol. 14, 1974, pp. 33–41.

Peggy Harper, "Dance in a changing Society", *African Arts/Arts d'Afrique*, 1, 10/13, 1967, pp. 76–80.

—— "Dance and drama in the North", *Nigeria Magazine*, No. 94, Sept. 1967.

—— "Traditional dance and new theatre", *African Notes*, Vol. 2, (1) 1964, pp. 15–16.

Harold Hobson, "Nigerian Drama in Premiere", *Christian Science Monitor*, Sept. 22, 1965.

Robin Horton, "The Kalabari Ekine Society: A Borderline of Religion and Art", *Africa*, Vol. 33, April 1963, pp. 94–144.

M. D. W. Jeffreys, "The Ekong players", *Eastern Anthropologist*, Vol. V, Sept./Nov. 1951, pp. 41–47.

G. I. Jones, "Masked plays of Southern-Eastern Nigeria", *Geographical Magazine*, XVIII, No. 5, 1945, pp. 190–199.

—— "Okorosia", *Nigerian Field*, III, Oct. 1934, p. 174.

—— "Ogbukere Ihuuba", *Nigerian Field*, VIII, 1939, pp. 81–83.

E. T. Kirby, "Indigenous African Theatre", *The Drama Review*, Vol. XVIII, No. 4, Dec. 1974.

N. Lvov, "The Musical Theatre of Nigeria", *New World*, Vol. 5, No. 10, 1971.

Molly Mohood, "Drama in New born States", *Presence Africaine*, English ed., No. 60, 1966, pp. 23–29.

P. Morton-Williams, "The Egungun Society in South-Western Yoruba Kingdoms", *Proceedings of the Third Annual Conference of the West African Institute of Social and Economic Research*, March, 1954 (Ibadan, 1956).

J. C. Messenger, "Annang art, drama and social control", *African Studies Bulletin*, Vol. 5, 1962, pp. 29–34.

Onuora Nzekwu, "Carnival at Opobo", *Nigerian Magazine*, No. 63, 1959.

Oyin Ogunba, "Theatre in Nigeria", *Presence Africaine*, English ed., No. 30, (58), 1966, pp. 65–88.

Michael Onwuejeogwu, "The Cult of the Bori Spirits among the Hausa", in *Spirit Mediumship and Society in Africa*, edited by John Beattie and John Middleton, London, 1969.

Soni Oti, "Tragedy's Vocal audience in Nigeria", *Journal of Commonwealth Literature*, Vol. 9, No. 3, 1975, pp. 53–62.

Ola Rotimi, "Traditional Nigerian drama", in *Introduction to Nigerian Literature*, ed. by Bruce Kin, Lagos and London, University of Lagos and Evans, 1971.

Donald Summons, "An Efik Judas Play; The Metamorphosis of Ancient Efik ceremony into a New Year's Eve Celebration and a Judas Play", *Nigerian Field*, XXVI, 1961, pp. 101–110.

Kalu Uka, "Drama in Nigeria Society", *The Muse*, Vol. 5, 1973, pp. 11, 13–15, 36–38.